The
Right
Wine

ALSO BY TOM MARESCA

Mastering Wine

La Tavola Italiana
(with Diane Darrow)

The Right Wine

TOM MARESCA

GROVE WEIDENFELD

New York

Published by Grove Weidenfeld
A division of Grove Press, Inc.
841 Broadway
New York, NY 10003-4793

Published in Canada by General Publishing Company, Ltd.

Library of Congress Cataloging-in-Publication Data

Maresca, Tom.
   The right wine / Tom Maresca. — 1st ed.
   ISBN 0-8021-1270-6   p.   cm.
   1. Wine and wine making.   I. Title.
 TP548.M334   1990
   641.2′2—dc20   90-43459
                                             CIP

Manufactured in the United States of America

Printed on acid-free paper

Designed by Irving Perkins Associates

First Edition 1990

10   9   8   7   6   5   4   3   2   1

*This book is gratefully dedicated
to the hardworking, imaginative, and generous
chefs and winemakers who made it possible,
gave it point, and kept it fun.*

ACKNOWLEDGMENTS

A larger number of unsung heroes and heroines are encompassed in my dedication than I could ever begin to name here. I can't omit, however, explicit acknowledgment of the proprietors of the four restaurants whose cooperation contributed so greatly to the completion of this book: Paul Kovi and Tom Margittai of The Four Seasons, Richard Lavin of Sofi, the late Leslee Reis of Café Provençal, and Piero Selvaggio of Valentino.

During the long writing of this book, I have been aided and refreshed by a great many individuals and organizations. Among the organizations, Food and Wine from France and the Italian Wine Center earn the lion's share of my thanks, and among the friends and colleagues Shirley Alpert, Louis Bonaccolta, Al Cirillo, Fiona Conover, Philip di Belardino, Barbara Edelman, Alisa Hixson, Michelle Jones, Mary Lyons, Mary Mulligan, Domenic Nocerino, Doreen Schmid, Patrick Séré, Niki Singer, Jan Stuebing, and Tom Verdillo. They provided me with everything from data to digestives to criticism as I needed each, and this project required a lot of all three.

Cooks and winemakers, like poets, present their creations in pleasurable forms only to have the enjoyment of them spoiled by analysts like me. If in the pages that follow I've rendered their poetry into passable prose, it's because from the start of this project I had the advantage of good readers. Chief among them I must here thank my wife, Diane Darrow, who midwifed the whole manuscript, and Dan Green, who first saw the possibility of this book and the impossibility of its first draft: For both perceptions I am extremely grateful.

Contents

Germany and Austria
The East Is Not Red Wine Country

PART III
Wines for Special Uses

Stylish and Personal: The Short, Selected Wine List
The Character of the Cooking
The Character of the Wines
Priority to the Wine
Priority to the Food
In Sum

American Classic: The Eclectic, Balanced Wine List
The Character of the Cooking
The Character of the Wines
What's for Dinner?
One Wine Throughout
One Wine per Course
One Wine per Diner
In Sum

Heart of the Country: The Specialized Wine List
The Character of the Cooking
The Character of the Wines
Guess Who's Coming to Dinner
How Many Wines?
Priority to the Wine
In Sum

Westward Ho!: The Overwhelming Wine List
The Character of the Cooking

INTRODUCTION

What This Book Is About

CHOOSING WINE is what this book is about. It's an attempt to answer the "What is the right wine for . . ." question that, at one time or another, every single one of us has asked about foods from fish sticks to venison and occasions from wienie roasts to wedding suppers.

To accomplish this, and to do it right, you've got to play your part. This book and I need an active reader, someone who's going to think along with us, and maybe even argue with us, but, most important of all, taste along with us. You're going to have to use your memory and your imagination to put together and to take apart combinations of flavors and components of occasions. We're going to explore why some wines "work" with some foods and not with others, why some wines go better with one kind of food than another, which wines serve well at casual moments and which are best for formal functions, which wines to drink young and fresh and which wines to bequeath to your descendants. To do all this, you've got to be open-minded and attentive, flexible and patient, and above all willing to experiment.

First Principles

The first and most important thing to know about wine is this: There is no such animal as *the* right wine to drink with a particular dish or to serve on a specific occasion. For any individual recipe there are probably half a dozen to a dozen kinds of wines—and who knows how many brands, châteaux, vineyards?—that would taste wonderful with it, a dozen more that would taste fine, two dozen that would be acceptable, and yet others that most people might not like with that particular dish but you just might.

Taste in wines is as idiosyncratic as taste in anything else, and you are the final, indisputable authority on your own palate. Everybody else may agree that Domaine Romanée-Conti's Grands-Echézeaux is the greatest wine in the world (they don't and it isn't), but if you don't like it, then it's not even a passable wine for your palate. Conversely, if you delight in the flavor and zest of simple Beaujolais or California Gamay at a tiny fraction of the cost of that Burgundy, then for you those are great wines, and you ought to indulge your admirably affordable passion for them on whatever occasion and with whatever foods you like. So here, before you even really start this book, is lesson number one: Just dismiss the idea that you've got to worry about "correctness" in choosing a wine. If you like it and what it does with your food, you've picked the right wine for you.

The complications in choosing wine begin when more than your own palate is involved. What do you do when other people's tastes are involved, especially when you know, or suspect, that what they like is not at all the same as what you like? What do you do when you encounter a food preparation that is so forceful it changes the taste of your regular Gamay or Beaujolais, and maybe not for the better? What do you do when you simply want to expand your enological horizons beyond your handful of familiar, favorite wines and still be sure of finding a wine that's going to taste all right with the foods you regularly eat?

That's when knowing a little something about the whys and wherefores of wine and food compatibilities comes in very handy.

This book is designed to provide exactly this kind of information. I'm going to carry you gradually from basic principles up to a pretty sophisticated level of wine and food expertise by working out the implications of a handful of fundamental ideas, first in terms of everyday eating and drinking, then in terms of more complex dinners and wines, and, finally, in the most complicated situation of all, matching different dishes and wines within the same meal in a restaurant.

Let me remind you from the outset, however, that no matter how complex, or how sophisticated, your wine and food choices may turn out to be, wine doesn't need complications to be enjoyable, any more than it needs special foods. Wine evolved with foods and as food, for peasants as well as for princes. Very great wines still show their best with very simple foods, and many of the easiest dishes to prepare match wonderfully with wines. You can enjoy wine with anything, and certainly with most of the meals that American cooks routinely prepare. Pot roast or spaghetti, hamburgers, hot dogs, chili, steak and potatoes, spare ribs and sauerkraut, corned beef and cabbage, or tofu and bean sprouts: There are wines for all of them, in greater variety than most people imagine.

The American Way of Life

Thirty years ago in the United States wine was a special-occasion thing, not an everyday drink. Aside from regular appearances as a rhyme word in songs warbled by people whose real booze of choice was clearly whiskey or beer, wine's associations ran mostly to upper-class settings and foreign cuisines—alien, hoity-toity stuff. French, Italian, or Spanish meals, sampled in restaurants or prepared for guests, parties, or to mark an anniversary, called for wine. American food—the good, solid stuff we ate every day—plainly did not. If milk, iced tea, or soft drinks weren't good enough for you, beer—domestic of course—would certainly do.

Well, we're still not a wine-drinking people—at least not compared to real wine drinkers like the Portuguese and Spanish, Italians and French—but we have come a far piece from our days of vinous innocence. Except for those who cling to the bizarre notion that the word *wine* in the Bible means unfermented grape juice, no one these days is likely to be shocked by the idea of our taking a little wine with our daily bread, whether we do so for our stomach's sake, for sanity's sake, or just because we enjoy the taste of it. Americans have grown more conscious of the foods they eat, and there has been a corresponding rise in the amount of fine wine we drink: Nothing dramatic, but a slow, steady growth in our per capita consumption of the world's most readily available civilized pleasure.

With so much serenity being daily subtracted from all the other areas of our lives, the little rituals of wine—drawing the cork, slowly pouring the first glass and watching it gleam and glisten, swirling the wine in the glass and sniffing its clean, fruity aroma, and, finally, taking the first small sip—unhurried steps like that give us at least a glimpse of the leisure we all lack. You don't need a magnificent or a costly wine or an elaborate or an expensive dinner to enjoy the sense of well-being that wine fosters. A simple meal, chosen and prepared with respect for its ingredients, and simple wine, chosen to enhance the meal, both savored for what they are: That's a formula for everyday contentment. If you haven't experienced the charm of a simple glass of wine with your weekday dinner, you're losing a major relaxant as well as a great pleasure. I'm not talking about alcoholic impact; unless you are hypersensitive to alcohol, you won't even notice the amount contained in a glass or two of wine taken with a meal. Rather, I mean the small but definite grace notes of ceremony and civility that a decent glass of wine lends to any meal, no matter how simple.

It's also a radical break from our usual eating patterns. By and large, Americans don't dine. We fuel the engine. We stoke the furnace. We even—fashionably, no less—graze. Fast food taken quickly for a maximum energy jolt, as if we were all in training for the decathlon: That's the traditional American way with food.

Underlying all our eating habits lie twin abundances: meat and sugar, used in quantities that are matched nowhere else in the world. Depending on your point of view, the dominance of these two ingredients has either exalted or corrupted every cuisine originated on or imported to these shores. Of the two, sugar is palatally the greater offender, because it masks other flavors and prevents you from tasting accurately—which is exactly why it is used so pervasively in prepared foods of all sorts. Sugar addicts—and most Americans inescapably are to some degree—have trouble adjusting to "dry" foods and drinks, which can make problems for the aspiring gourmet or wine connoisseur.

That's difficulty enough, but the worst enemy of food and wine culture in these United States isn't sugar. It's science—"food science"—with its pompous certainties-of-the-moment and its categorical health pronouncements that amount, in the end, to no more than reminders that living is a dangerous business. Our culinary history (such culinary history as we have) is largely made up of a succession of health fads, as generation after generation of "scientific facts" about food and health replaced—and usually contradicted—one another. By scaring us away from whole categories of wonderful foods, our pious following of one chimera of proper nutrition after another has done and continues to do enormous harm to our capacity to enjoy a real meal. In my opinion, so-called food science materially adds to our collective ill health—directly by depriving us of important relaxants and indirectly by adding yet one more item to life's seemingly endless list of tensions and worries. Pregnant women are now warned against taking a drink, lest it harm the fetus. My mother, when carrying me, was urged to drink stout and porter (does anyone remember stout and porter?) in order to build blood. My Neapolitan grandmother, who came from sturdy, long-lived stock, firmly believed in the efficacy of olive oil, not simply as a good food but also as a medicine, at a time when medical science "knew" olive oil was bad for us. Now, we "know," with equal "scientific" certainty, that olive oil is good for us and alcohol bad. Today's certitudes were yesterday's heresies, and may be heresies again tomorrow.

So "science" be damned. I'm casting my vote with my mother and grandmother. Anyone who is looking in this book for nutritional advice or the latest quackery about diet and health might as well stop reading right now. We'll both be happier if you just pass this book on to someone who will enjoy it, while the rest of us get on with choosing our wine.

Stop drinking water only, but use a little wine for thy
stomach's sake and thy frequent infirmities.
—*I Timothy 5:23*

PART I

Wines for Every Day

CHAPTER 1

The Rules of the Game

MATCHING FOOD AND WINE can't be much of a mystery; if it were, the human race wouldn't have made it this far. The fact is, however, that for many people today it *is* a mystery, primarily because, for the very first time, a large segment of the human race actually has a choice about what it eats and drinks. In the past we ate what our own or nearby farms grew, fatted and slaughtered our own pigs, grew and fermented our own grapes, and drank the wine of the country, whatever it might be, with whatever we ate. Now we—that fortunate portion of humanity that lives in North America, at least—can choose from the harvests of fields and forests and vineyards from all over the globe. Our food can be Caribbean or Cajun, Chinese or classic French, and our *vin de pays* can hail from New York or California, Connecticut or Texas, Europe or Australia or South America. None of the components of our dinner may ever have met one another before. They may not have dwelt on the same continent before we joined them in wedlock on a plate. No wonder choosing a wine to go with them is troublesome: They don't even speak the same language.

3

Ancient Wisdom

Those of us who are faced with this kind of "problem"—most of the world would consider it a luxury—may yearn nostalgically for that once-upon-a-fairy-tale time when life, and dining, seemed to be easier. Cooking then fell into two categories: everyday, which by definition was "plain American" and heavy on the meat and potatoes and with which it probably never even occurred to you to drink wine, and "fancy," for company or dining out, which usually meant foreign and most of the time meant French—pre-nouvelle, classic French haute cuisine, unctuous with cream sauces and wine reductions and rich, meaty stocks. Wines, in our British-derived knowledge of them, fell into three categories: claret for red, Burgundy for either red or white, and Hock for white—ample choice for any but the most exigent of gourmets. All the lore necessary for making wine and food matches was summed up in a set of simple adages: red wine with meat, white wine with fish, sweet wines with dessert. Champagne and rosé, should you choose to have them, "went with everything."

Those wonderfully simple apothegms made choices blessedly easy, at least as long as you didn't look beyond the surface. Push beyond that, however, and complications set in fast. If you let yourself get involved with trying to distinguish the characters of individual red wines from the widely different communes of Bordeaux or the divergent villages of Burgundy, or tried to sort out the varying degrees of dryness and semisweetness present in supposedly "dry" white wines like a Kabinett-class Riesling or a Vouvray, the simplicity and ease of those comfortable adages disappeared in the face of a welter of names and vintages. Ignorance might be bliss, but neither bliss nor ignorance was easy to maintain.

Then, somewhere in the 1970s, never-never land came to an end. French wine prices went through the roof, and suddenly the markets were filled with new wines from California and Argentina and Chile and newly introduced old wines from Italy and Spain. Regional American cuisines burst onto the culinary scene, as did new-to-America Oriental cuisines, and under the international impact of all these fresh and powerful influences, the seemingly petrified classic French cooking shed its old skin and transformed itself into nouvelle cuisine. In the short span of a few years, all the comfortable props of our customary food lore seemed to go right out the window. Tiny, stillborn vegetables adorned every fashionable plate. Kiwis became de rigueur. People started doing all sorts of outlandish things to food, like cooking fish in red wine and making steak sauces out of vinegar and raspberries and preparing risotto with strawberries.

As far as wine and food pairings were concerned, *the* rule—"red wine with meat," etc.: rudimentary as it was, the only one most of us had ever known—seemed to lose all its force somewhere around 1975. Ever since then people have been flapping about helplessly as if somehow the human race had lost the knack of feeding itself—at least so you would conclude if you believed everything you read in the fashionable food columns and journals.

Under all the journalistic rhetoric and hyperbole, however (to which, I confess, I have in the past contributed my share), the fact remains that it is more difficult now to know which wine to choose with which food than it ever was before—simply because there now exist more kinds of wine and more kinds of food for us to choose among than ever before. But that doesn't mean—note this well— that the principles by which you match a food and wine have changed. Not at all: The factors that cause particular wines and particular foods to partner well have remained exactly the same as they ever were. The trouble is that people had come to rely utterly on the magic formulas. No one ever bothered to learn the principles as long as they could get by with just memorizing the slogans. So the old knowledge is still good, if you can dig it out again and then figure out what it really means and has always meant.

Putting It to the Test

Take, for instance, the now fashionably neglected old standby of "red wine with meat, white wine with fish." For most of the meals that are consumed in the United States, that slogan—the rule of thumb that underlies that slogan—still works very satisfactorily as a starting place. Why? Because, at its heart and on a very general level, it has captured a single important truth about one fundamental wine and food compatibility.

You can verify that compatibility for yourself if you go to the trouble of a basic series of taste tests. Take a simple fish dish—broiled scrod or flounder, let us say—and taste with it two equally simple wines, a white and a red: a Soave for the white, perhaps, and a young, inexpensive Zinfandel for the red (I will have dire things to say about "white" Zinfandel later on). Take a bite of the fish and then a sip of the Soave. Take another bite of the fish and then a sip of the Zinfandel, then go back to the fish again. Either the red wine will taste "funny" to you, or after drinking it the fish will taste odd or the fish's taste will disappear altogether. Depending on the individual taster's perceptions and sensitivities, the red wine either overpowers the fish or is distorted by it. On the other hand, the vast majority of people will perceive the white wine as a very comforting complement to the delicate flavor of the fish. Most people also feel that the white wine freshens their palates. Perform the same sort of test with the same two wines and a grilled steak, and the white wine will all but disappear. It will taste watery and insipid in the face of the steak's more robust and assertive flavor, while the red wine now complements the flavor of the meat and refreshes the mouth and palate.

This is not absolutely true of all people at all times in all circumstances—nothing about so subjective an experience as taste is universally true—but it is true for most people most of the time and will work out pretty much the same way with any other pair of simple red and white wines and simply prepared fish and red meat. Why? Because of the comparative robustness or delicacy of flavor of the food and the wine. Red and white wines are normally fermented in very different ways, and the natural chemistry of red and white grapes—tannins and that sort of stuff, about which you will hear much more at the proper time and place—generally differs quite dramatically. Consequently, ninety-nine times out of a hundred, red wines will taste far more robust and assertive than whites. The corollary of that is that red wines will stand up to more aggressively flavored foods than will whites, whereas white wines will partner well with delicate dishes whose flavor would be obliterated by reds. This means that if you're eating a strongly flavored dish and want a wine that can contribute something to the meal, you pretty much must choose a red. On the other hand, if you only want a glass of wine to stand in for a glass of water, you can drink white or rosé with perfect pleasure. For many people that is a very desirable goal. White wines are generally lower in alcohol than reds, and a white wine then serves as a gentle but interesting flavored lubricant for their meal, more sophisticated than plain old water and less demanding of attention than a wine more thoroughly integrated with their meal would be.

It will probably come as welcome news to most people that matching wines and foods involves only a reasonably limited body of knowledge. It does require that you pay attention to some things that maybe you don't really bother yourself with now, but not a lot of them. Understanding wine and food compatibilities amounts to very little more than noticing, verbalizing, and reducing to a system what happens on your palate and in your taste experience when you eat a particular food along with a particular wine. Success in wine and food matching depends on nothing more abstruse than finding out why certain foods and wines affect each other for good or for ill and learning how to generalize from that simple information to predict the way other wines and foods will interact.

As with almost every other kind of knowledge, the key first steps involve learning what to pay attention to: what factors in the food, what elements in the wine, what facets of your taste are going to make a difference.

What is at stake in any wine and food pairing is always the same trinity of variables: the nature of the wine, the nature of the food, and the preferences of the taster. Such complications as there are arise solely from the increasing sophistication of each of the three—particularly, since this whole process is so utterly subjective, the preferences of the tasters and their awareness of them. Gustatory happiness—the "perfect meal," than which you cannot imagine anything better—comes about when all three elements mesh exactly, when the wine presents rich and complex flavors that complement the harmony of the foods, and when your palate can appreciate everything the wine and food have to offer. Just as a wine that falls below the occasion and the dishes is bound to disappoint you, so too a wine outside or beyond your palatal range will never be fully enjoyable for you, no matter how much you pay for it or how impressively it's served. The wisdom of knowing yourself, realizing as objectively as you can your own abilities and limitations, applies just as much to palatal sensitivity and aptitudes as it does to any other set of physical or mental skills.

A Decalogue for Winebibbers

Here is a set of guidelines—call them principles, if you like, or rules of thumb—to help guide your choice of wines to match with your everyday meals. They operate most strongly in the absence of any marked personal preference about wines, and they operate as guidelines only, not as inviolable laws. They are broadly valid and useful because they derive from the nature of various foods and wines themselves. The chapters of this section that follow will discuss in detail the hows and whys of this workmanly set of guides, using specific wines and foods as examples and representatives of whole categories, but for the moment here they are in all their almost-naked splendor, accompanied by only the minimal necessary exposition.

1. *There is no such animal as the single right wine for a particular food or dish.*

2. *Personal preference overrides any other rules we may generate, unless that preference makes life and dinner miserable for others at table with us.*

3. *The wines for everyday meals should be relatively simple, dry, and inexpensive.*

The first two vinous commandments stipulate that there is no such thing as a strange god. You can worship what wine you please. The wine you like is the right wine for you. As long as you're choosing only for yourself and others of compatible tastes, personal preference is the dominant consideration in any everyday wine and food pairing, even to the point of overriding the third guideline. Tastes are rarely identical, however, even within the same family, and the point at which they are most likely to divide is sugar: the amount of sweetness each individual finds pleasant or even tolerable. I, for instance, have no sweet tooth at all, and you should know this about me because the kinds of wine recommendations I'm going to make are shaped by it. I don't like very sweet desserts, and although I can relish—in small quantities—some very sweet dessert wines, I can't tolerate any sweetness at all in the wines I drink with my dinner. That is because the sugar in a sweet wine acts as a muffler of other flavors. It creates a baffle that prevents the real tastes of food from reaching your palate. Now, I like the tastes of food. I want to be able to perceive and enjoy the different flavors of the various ingredients in the dishes I choose, whether those flavors are subtle or striking, so I want a wine that will enhance those flavors rather than blur them together. Ergo, rule of thumb three: Everyday wine should be *simple* because most everyday foods are simple, *dry* so you can actually taste the good flavors that are in them and the foods you drink them with, and *inexpensive* so that you can enjoy them without pain.

4. *The nature of the food, the nature of the wine, and the preferences of the tasters form the trio of factors that dictate the choice of a wine.*

Rule four simply spells out the three factors that you have to take account of in any wine and food matchup. You may very well already do this automatically, without even thinking about it, but this trio needs to have some conscious attention devoted to it. The remaining guidelines are designed to elaborate on exactly what is involved in these three items.

5. *Self-knowledge is crucial: Tasters must be aware of their own palatal preferences, skills, or limitations.*

Number five requires you to pay attention to the nature of your own biases and blind spots, which will not necessarily coincide with anybody else's. Be aware too of the other diners' preferences or problems. For example, do they all dote on big red wines? If so, then you might want such a wine even with a dish you would ordinarily consider too delicate to serve with a robust wine. Is anybody sensitive to sulfites? Then you might have a problem with white wines. To histamines? Then you might have a problem with reds. These are gross instances. Many more subtle ones are possible—people who love or hate specific kinds of wine, like Riesling or Sauvignon Blanc or Cabernet Sauvignon for instance.

6. *Foods and wines should be matched by an analysis of their primary components, those elements in them that dominate, not in chemical analysis but in their actual taste and texture.*

7. *In the case of everyday dinners, the nature of the main dish should provide the primary referent for matching a wine with the meal.*

8. *"Red wine with red meat; white wine with white meat, fowl, or fish" still makes a useful starting place or first frame of reference but should never be taken as an absolute rule.*

9. *Strongly flavored dishes will normally need an equally strongly flavored wine to accompany them. Usually this will indicate a red wine.*

10. *Mildly flavored dishes require a more delicate wine to accompany them. Normally this will indicate a white wine.*

Guideline six gives you the key points you should look to in the foods and wines you are considering pairing, and numbers seven through ten focus with increasing sharpness on the single most important objective determinant in the whole situation, the character of the central dish or course. This, more than any other single factor (except strong personal preference), should determine your choice of wine. And when sets of taste buds other than your own are involved, this, more than any other factor, will determine the success or failure of your wine and food matching. The nature of the central dish or main course contains most of the clues you need to choose a compatible wine, a wine that "goes with" the food.

From this commonsensical observation flow all the esoteric principles you'll ever need to pair wines and foods successfully. No matter whether you want a wine that will simply accompany your dinner without fuss or fanfare, or you want a wine to dress that dinner up and make it special, or you want a dinner that will show off a particular wine to best advantage, the main dish or main course provides the clues you will need. This guideline presupposes that you will be serving only one wine with the entire meal. This will almost certainly be true for everyday dinners, though on special occasions you may very well want to serve a sequence of different wines with your different courses. We will talk later, and at length, about the problems and opportunities generated by that situation. But for most ordinary occasions, you will make your wine choice by a very simple process of matching components (or elements or characteristics, choose whichever term you like) of your main dish with similar ones in a wine. (Naturally, you can reverse the process too and choose a main dish to match the characteristics of the wine you want.) Call it component-to-component matching: Characteristic X in your food tells you to look for a wine with matching characteristic X-1. It's as simple as that.

A Closer Look

It's as simple as that, as long as you know which components of the food complement or are complemented by which components of the wine. Some of them, like flavor intensity, suggest themselves at once. Under normal circumstances, balance is what you're seeking. Ideally, you want your wine and your food to be equally perceptible and equally enjoyable. There may be exceptions to this rule of thumb in some very special cases, which we'll talk about later when we're considering more elaborate dining, but for everyday meals a genial parity between the intensity of the wine and food flavors is what you're after. Rules nine and ten above point precisely to this.

But foods have characteristics other than intensity. In fact, they even have different kinds of intensity: a dish can be intensely rich, or very sweet, or unbelievably hot, or markedly acidic. It can taste strongly of its basic ingredient—meat-sweet, or bell pepper–sweet, or carrot-sweet, as opposed to sugar-sweet, or acidic from sauerkraut, or acidic in a different way from tomatoes or citrus fruits. Even delicate sensations can vary. The gently nutty flavor of crabmeat is immediately distinguishable from the bland mildness of chicken breasts or the succulent mildness of a creamy veal stew. That marvelous abundance of impressions that foods create on our palates, pleasurable though they all are, still causes anxiety for some people. They think that choosing wines to match with them demands an encyclopedic knowledge of every wine in the world— either that, or the whole process amounts to nothing more than blind luck.

Fortunately, neither of those extremes is the case. After you've made that very simple observation about strongly flavored dish versus mildly flavored dish, and therefore strongly flavored wine versus mildly flavored, your next task is merely to take note of the dominant flavor in the dish. This deserves a bit more explanation. In most everyday dinners, in the simple, all-too-often-hurried kind of cooking that we do for ourselves most weeknights and many weekends, one element usually dominates the meal, in the fundamental sense of being the flavor that calls most attention to itself or that characterizes the meal. If we broil a steak and serve it with a baked potato and green beans, the moist, beefy sweetness of the steak makes the palatal keynote of that dinner. If the baked potato and green beans accompany broiled scallops rather than steak, the vegetables still don't furnish the fundamental flavors of the meal. The gentle sea-sweetness of the scallops provides the overall tone and character. Conversely, a good crabcake will taste predominantly of the gentle flavor of fresh crabmeat, while flaked crabmeat tossed with salad greens and dressed with strongly spiced dressing may well taste more of chili, garlic, or red pepper than of crab, and the clear palatal impression made by the whole ensemble may amount to a very assertively flavored dish despite the crabmeat's intrinsic mildness.

Even a "composed" dish, one fashioned from many different ingredients, usually presents a single, definable character to the palate. A lamb stew, for instance, unifies meat and vegetables and broth into a single, moist, and robust substantiality. A really fine bowl of chili may contain good beans and lean beef and maybe even tomato as well as onions and garlic, but what your palate notices are not the single voices of the individual ingredients but the harmony of them all that the spices bring about: a single, dominant palatal impression of spicy warmth. That kind of dominant element is exactly what you have to spot and define or describe to yourself in order to choose a wine whose characteristics will mesh with it.

It may be helpful to think of this in terms of some simple dichotomies: Does the flavor of the basic ingredient dominate in the dish or does the flavor of its condiments? And then, whichever dominates, is the flavor strong or mild? sweet or sour? Is the texture of the dish moist or dry? tender or chewy? Does the dish strike your taste buds as (choose one) rich? gelatinous? oily? pleasingly unctuous? or (choose one) austere? lean? dry? pleasingly fibrous? Each of those food characteristics has a counterpart in wine. Wines can be powerful or delicate, light or heavy, sweet or dry, fruity or acidic, soft on the palate or muscular and chewy, rich and mouth filling or lean and austere.

While it helps a great deal to be aware of all these possibilities, you don't have to run through this whole gamut of oppositions for every wine and food you consider. Normally, either the dominant characteristic of the food will already be well known to you— we're talking about everyday meals, after all—or it will leap right out at you. Moreover, the food characteristics that really matter boil down to a manageable few: the intensity or delicacy of the flavor; the nature of that flavor, which is usually a function of whether the base ingredients or its condiments (both of which you've already glanced at) dominate the preparation; and the balance of fats and acids in the dish (whether they come from the base or the condiments doesn't matter).

The last element is a crucial one: Fats and acids can make or break a food and wine match. The presence of fats in a dish at a palatally perceptible level dictates something important about the wine that will match well with it. A markedly acidic dish will scratch a "fat" wine to death (for example, spare ribs and sauerkraut will undo most Chardonnays), but an acidic wine can make a very nice counterpoint to a rich and oily meal (Sauvignon Blanc, for instance, works beautifully with deep-fried seafoods or rich sautés like sole or trout meunière). Conversely, the leaner the dish, the fuller-bodied the wine it can respond to. This is because the whole package of elements that make up what we perceive as a wine's body—alcohol and extract and acid and tannin and glycerine chiefly—often registers on our palates as "fat." They can make us taste and feel a wine as heavy or oily or rich or greasy or buttery or any of dozens of other adjectives that people use in an attempt to surround and pin down this unmistakable, unverbalizable sensation.

Practical experience shows that a lean dish can support the complement of a fat wine, whereas a dish already rich and fatty will often make a rich wine seem excessive and heavy and overblown. So roast chicken, say, or a simple veal cutlet could pair very successfully with a big, rich Chardonnay, while that same Chardonnay might very well taste flabby and heavy with fried chicken. With the roast chicken, the wine's own body would be felt on the palate and tongue as a kind of fatness, in those circumstances pleasing and enjoyably lubricant. In combination with the fats of a fried dish, that same wine fatness can seem just too much, too overpowering of any other sensation the wine may offer. With the spare ribs and sauerkraut that I mentioned earlier, the Chardonnay's nicely composed flavor would come apart in the face of the acidity of the dish, and it would once again, though for a very different reason, taste flabby, as well as probably lose most of its fruit freshness.

Another Half a Decalogue

Here are some additional guidelines for use in everyday wine and food situations, five more principles for guiding your ideas about partnering wine and food. Like the earlier ten commandments, these five all involve quite fundamental considerations about wine and food. You will find, as we go on in this book, that the principles we're discussing here will continue to operate for more complicated dining situations and more sophisticated wine choices. Which leads logically to the next principle:

11. *The fundamentals of wine and food compatibility stay the same all across the spectrum of rarity and complexity, so all the guides suggested in the decalogue (and those to be articulated below) remain valid in most if not all wine and food matchings, no matter how sophisticated the food preparation or grand the wine.*

12. *In most cases the simplest form of a dish establishes its basic wine compatibilities, which most of the time are only refined, not transformed, by elaborations of the dish's mode of presentation. This is truest of dishes built around strongly flavored basic ingredients; exceptions most often occur in the case of dishes that combine mildly flavored basic ingredients with markedly flavored condiments or seasonings.*

13. *Component-to-component matching—identifying the major flavors and characteristics of the food and the wine—is the key to even the most complex wine and food pairings, but not every component of every dish or every element in the wine has to be taken into account. In most cases one or two dominant elements will cast the deciding votes.*

14. *Three characteristics of the main dish provide the basic factors that a wine must deal with to be genuinely com-*

patible with that food: (1) intensity of flavor, (2) nature of the dominant flavor, and (3) the ratio of fats to acid in the dish.

15. *The elements in wines that answer to those ingredients are (1) intensity of flavor, (2) kind of flavor, and (3) a conglomerate of elements that work to produce the total palatal effect of the wine: body and extract, tannin or acidity, and, in white wines, relative sweetness or dryness.*

Once again, there is nothing mysterious or abstruse about any of this. To put it to use, however, you have to know a bit about the characteristics of different kinds of wines—the range of flavor intensity they present, the basic kinds of flavor they offer, and the nature of their own components, the bits and pieces that will let them work with a food's acids or fats. To that end, it's worth turning our attention for a while to an examination of some of the most popular wine varietals to see just what makes them tick, and how. After that we'll return to the question of matching these wines with compatible foods, and vice versa, and test how our principles work in actual practice.

## CHAPTER 2

The Varieties of Wine

THE SOUL OF WINE

One night the soul of wine sang in the flask:
"I bring you, man, dear disinherited,
From my vermilion wax and prison of glass,
A song all full of light and brotherhood!

I know the flaming hill where painfully
And sweating under the boiling sun you bent
To give me life and grow a soul in me;
I am not ungrateful or malevolent,

For I feel a mighty pleasure when I lave
The gullet of a man worn by his labor,
And his hot body is a cheerful grave
Which I like better than a cold wine-cellar.

You hear resounding strains from Sabbath eves
And hopes that murmur in my trembling breast?
Elbows on the table, with rolled sleeves,
Glorify me and be content to rest;

I'll light the eyes of your enraptured wife;
Give your son strength and make his pale cheeks ruddy
And for this delicate athlete of life
Will be the oil that toughens the wrestler's body.

I'll pour my living nectar, precious seed
To quicken in you, from the eternal Sower,
So that the poetry our loves may breed
Shall spring toward God like a great, strange flower."

—CHARLES BAUDELAIRE, *Les Fleurs du Mal*,
translated by C. F. MacIntyre

THE WORLD of wine can appear overwhelming in variety and
diversity, but there are usable trails through its wilderness of vines.
Variety offers not only the way into the seeming confusion but also
the way out. Varietals—the kinds of grapes used to make wines—
probably provide the easiest path into the differences and the
similarities of wines for Americans. Because of the dominance of
California in our wine production and imagination, its characteristic mode of winemaking has become the way we naturally think
about wines. That mode, of course, at the level of fine winemaking,
consists largely of the production of monovarietal wines, that is,
wines fermented entirely, or nearly so, from a single variety of
grapes. This makes for a simple naming structure that is eminently
marketable and memorable, since the name of the grape variety is
also the name of the kind of wine made from it.

Within a small region, sharing essentially the same soil types and
the same climate, varietal wines also tend—barring real eccen-
tricities on the part of the winemakers—to display similar flavors
and characteristics. So we can talk sensibly and concretely, for
instance, about Napa or Sonoma Chardonnays, and even—still
sensibly if a bit more broadly—about California Chardonnay as
distinguished from East Coast Chardonnay or Australian Chardonnay or French Chardonnay or Italian Chardonnay. Because of
their dependence upon a single varietal, these wines show enough
similarities to make the comparisons valid and useful. Because of
the differences in soil and climate, and because of national differ-

ences in viticultural tradition and winemaking techniques, these wines differ from one another in enough ways to make the distinctions important and illuminating.

An enormous number of grape varieties—certainly in the hundreds, probably in the thousands—are cultivated around the world for the explicit and often sole purpose of turning them into wine. Of these many varieties it is safe to say that most are of little or no interest unless they happen to be growing in your backyard. They make wine that is at its highest reach ordinary, with few or no virtues to warrant its export or to demand more than passing attention. Of the still large number of remaining grape varieties that make better-than-ordinary wines, only a relative handful have achieved the stature that the wine world calls "noble."

Just who confers this patent of nobility is not entirely clear, though two facts about it are pretty certain:

- If you wish to be a noble grape, you'd better be *Vitis vinifera*, the European wine grape species. All others are plebeians—especially the native American species, *Vitis labrusca* (no connection with Lambrusco, which despite the name is made from *V. vinifera*). This isn't snobbery but experiential wisdom: Wines made from *vinifera* grapes simply taste better, possess greater depth and nuance, and last longer than those made with *labrusca* grapes.
- If it's nobility you're after, you'll have a head start on it if you're not only *Vitis vinifera* but also French. The key French varietals—Chardonnay, Sauvignon Blanc, Cabernet Sauvignon, and Pinot Noir—have pretty much set the standards and even determined the techniques (though this last may be changing) for winemaking the world around.

This *is* snobbery, because experiential wisdom shows that there are many other grape varieties capable of producing equally estimable wines: to name just a few, Zinfandel in California, Nebbiolo in Italy, Tempranillo in Spain, Syrah and Grenache in many places. Varieties like these make world-class wines in Napa and the Piedmont and the Rioja and Australia and the Rhône. Some

Italian and Spanish varieties and some lesser-known varieties from the south of France, red wine grapes in particular, already make spectacular wines and give every indication that they will do so in new areas of cultivation in the near future. And some hybrid grapes—crosses between valued strains of *Vitis vinifera* and the hardy, disease-resistant American *Vitis labrusca*—show great promise. But the fact is that right now, for better or for worse (and I for one think it's worse), the worldwide production of varietal wines is dominated by a handful of grape varietals that have achieved international status. Among the whites, Chardonnay, Sauvignon Blanc, and Riesling are clearly the superstars, followed by Pinot Blanc and Gewürztraminer and, to a much lesser extent, Chenin Blanc and Sémillon. Cabernet Sauvignon stands as uncontested champion among the red wine grapes, followed by Pinot Noir and more distantly by Merlot and Syrah. In California alone Zinfandel has emerged as a serious contender. Interesting as these grapes are in themselves and fine as the wines they make can often be, that's a pretty scant handful of varieties to monopolize so much of the world's palatal attention.

A Varietal Gazetteer: Some White Grapes and the Wines They Make

THE BIG THREE

Among the dry table wines that combine the virtues of low cost with a degree of distinction and finesse, those derived from the Chardonnay, Sauvignon Blanc, and Riesling grapes stand out in terms of contemporary prestige and the intensity of the attention that has been directed toward them both in America and abroad.

Chardonnay may be the *sans pareil* grape for varietal white wines. Almost nowhere—except in the Champagne region of France, which constitutes a law unto itself—is Chardonnay ever blended.

Always it has the stage to itself. Chardonnay is a generous varietal. It seems to make interesting wines almost everywhere it is cultivated, which probably accounts for the fact that, in one or another of its many styles, it is the most prestigious and the most popular varietal among serious wine drinkers. In America Chardonnay produced some of the current California wine boom's earliest, greatest, and most consistent successes—opulent, lush wines of unforgettable richness. In France it makes the great white wines of Burgundy, wines that combine elegance and balance with reined-in power. In countless other climes it produces wines that range from light and fresh and fruity to full bodied and austere.

You may think the distinctive varietal flavor of Chardonnay provides the common denominator of all these wines, but that's not the case. Chardonnay takes much of its character from the differing soils and climates in which it is grown and from the different treatments it receives during fermentation. The most important and most readily identifiable element of these, since it directly affects the wine's flavor, is the nature and duration of the wine's contact with oak. For a while in the seventies and early eighties, pronounced oak flavors in Chardonnay seemed to command unreasonable respect in California. Chardonnays that have spent a lot of time in new oak barrels can taste of nothing but oak. Light-to-moderate oaking gives Chardonnay aromas of vanilla and taste nuances of toast, but you'll recognize what I would consider an overoaked Chardonnay by a marked aroma of vanilla and freshly sawed wood and a strong vanilla taste married to a lot of tannin, the latter a sort of overstrong tea flavor. The basic fruit flavor of the grape itself can range anywhere from applelike through melony to grapefruit or other citrus flavors or even pineapple. Generally speaking, the warmer the growing zone or season, the more pronounced and exotic the flavors that show through in the finished wine.

Chardonnays are invariably vinified fully dry—that is, fermentation is allowed to continue until all the grape sugars have been converted into alcohol by the industrious little yeasts, and no perceptible sugar sweetness remains in the liquid (though, it is worth pointing out, the rich fruit flavors in Chardonnays and other white wines may sometimes fool you into thinking there is still some sweetness left). Most Chardonnays are big wines for whites, certainly the biggest of the popular Franco-American white varietals. Giving them some degree of barrel aging has become almost a universal practice in France and the United States (except for Chablis, which cultivates a leaner style, in part dictated by the lesser ripeness achieved in its more northerly vineyards). Consequently, most Chardonnays usually carry some traces of oak in their flavors along with their basic fruit. In the mouth they feel weighty and substantial. When they are softly so, they will be described as suave or buttery. Most California Chardonnays belong to this style. When these kinds of Chardonnay are flawed, it is usually because the grapes have been allowed to ripen too much. Such Chardonnays will suffer from a lack of acidity, and the wines will taste flabby: oversoft, overfruity, inert, and unstructured.

Most French Chardonnay—Burgundy is by far the most impor-

YOUNG CALIFORNIA CHARDONNAY

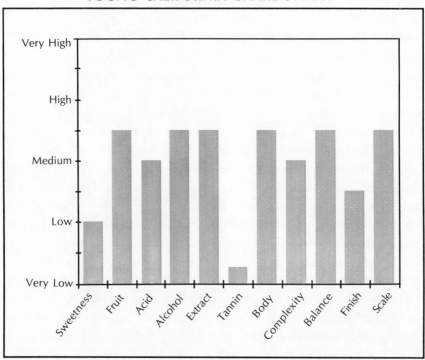

tant growing area for it—rarely attains the degree of ripeness that is normal in California, and consequently it is handled somewhat differently and yields a very different style of wine—still big, but feeling more notably firm in the mouth. This usually results from higher acidity balancing the wine's normally generous extract. In these cases the wine may be called steely or even, as in the case of Chablis, flinty. When these wines are flawed, it is almost always for reasons that are the opposite of California's problems: The grapes haven't ripened enough, and the wine's acidity dominates its fruit and its texture, making it feel sharp and almost astringent, with a sometimes unpleasant sourness.

With both French and California Chardonnay, price serves as a pretty accurate indicator not only of quality but also of style. The less expensive the wine, the less time it will have been aged in oak and the less prestigious the area or vineyard from which the grapes will have come. This means that at the lower end of the Chardonnay price ladder—the price range in which you will be looking for everyday wines—you will almost exclusively find young, essentially stainless steel–fermented wines that have been given very little or no wood aging. They will show basically simple characters—a pleasing, straightforward fruitiness, medium-to-full body (depending upon vintage), and enough acidity to keep them alive and slightly supple.

In the great majority of cases California wines of this type will be labeled with the larger geographical areas: not Napa or Sonoma or Carneros, but North Coast or even just California. French wines of this class will hail from the Mâconnais and the Chalonnais, and sometimes will bear individual village names (e.g., Montagny, Rully, St-Véran). When the dollar-franc ratio works in our favor, simple Chablis will also fall into this price range. Burgundy whites, however, even those with only village appellations, are always costly, as are Chablis *premier* and *grand crus*. Individual vineyard wines from prized Burgundy sites, while often memorable wines, are always astronomically priced, so much so as to make the most expensive California estate-bottled prizes seem quite reasonable by comparison—as indeed they were, until recently.

The lower-priced French and California Chardonnays match

YOUNG MÂCON-VILLAGES

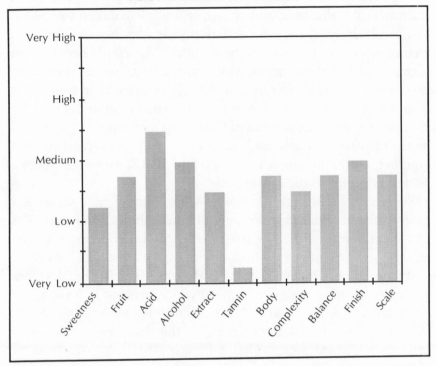

well with white-meat dinners, especially with simply prepared chicken, veal, and pork. They do not work at all well with Oriental spices or strongly sauced foods such as Tex-Mex or even with pastas with markedly flavored sauces, in the face of which all but the most acidic (and therefore least typical) specimens tend to fall apart. By and large, inexpensive Chardonnays are acceptable though not entirely pleasing with most kinds of fish. This in fact is the most common misuse of Chardonnay, because its relatively pronounced flavor, high extract, and reasonably full body will tend to overwhelm the delicate flavors of most varieties of finfish (except the very strongest, like salmon or monkfish or shark or tuna). Those characteristics, however, do cause French and California Chardonnays to work quite nicely with crab and lobster, though the latter at least is hardly everyday fare for most of us.

Chardonnays from other parts of the world tend to be vinified in imitation of either the French or the California style and to display characteristics and food affinities in the same manner. Australian Chardonnay, much of it very reasonably priced, tastes like a hyperbolic version of the California style: lots of fresh, lush fruit that makes an immediate and forceful impression on the palate. This causes Australian Chardonnays to do very well in blind tastings in competition with other wines, but to my palate it also makes them considerably less pleasing with foods, especially with fish, whose flavors they can easily obscure. On the other hand, so pronounced is the fruit flavor and the round, soft character it gives the wines that even modest amounts of acidity in the food can make Australian Chardonnays feel fat and flabby. Generally speaking, Australian Chardonnay seems to match best with foods at the extreme end of the white wine spectrum, that is, with dishes that have sufficient flavor and character of their own that you might consider using a light red wine (Beaujolais, for instance) with them.

Italy makes a few expensive Chardonnays in imitation of the California style (Gaja, Lungarotti), but most Italian Chardonnays—especially inexpensive ones from Friuli or Trentino–Alto Adige—are vinified in what amounts to a typically Italian manner to produce, a bright, fruity, light-bodied, high-acid wine. In distinction to the otherwise homogeneous—not to say homogenized—international trend, Chardonnays vinified in this almost exclusively Italian style make very pleasing quaffing with simple, light foods and all manner of fish and shellfish. They rarely achieve distinction, and they are emphatically not wines for long keeping, but they do offer very pleasant and extremely versatile everyday drinking: lighter editions of Chardonnay flavors at quite moderate cost.

Sauvignon Blanc contends with Chardonnay for the white wine fashion awards these days, despite the fact that it makes wines of less immediate appeal than Chardonnay. Markedly less full bodied than Chardonnays usually are, and never as lushly fruity, Sauvignon Blanc plays the slender, almost anorexic, fashion model to Chardonnay's buxom appeal: Twiggy to Marilyn Monroe, so to speak. As British wine expert Jancis Robinson remarks in *Vines,*

Grapes and Wines, the wine almost tastes slimming, a fact that no doubt accounts for a lot of its current popularity.

Many people have the impression that wines labeled Sauvignon Blanc are just white wine versions of Cabernet Sauvignon, but that is not so at all. Sauvignon Blanc is a distinct and important white grape varietal. There do in fact exist white versions of Cabernet Sauvignon, just as there are from time to time rosé versions of it—why I will never understand, since it wastes a perfectly fine red grape. Such wines are technically known as blancs des noirs, white wines from red grapes. White Zinfandel is another currently popular example of the generally execrable breed. The white versions of Cabernet Sauvignon are always clearly labeled (somewhere on the bottle) BLANC DE CABERNET or WHITE WINE FROM CABERNET GRAPES, so there should be no reason ever to confuse them with the true white wine from the white grape Sauvignon Blanc.

Sauvignon Blanc wines are almost always vinified fully dry and

YOUNG NAPA SAUVIGNON BLANC

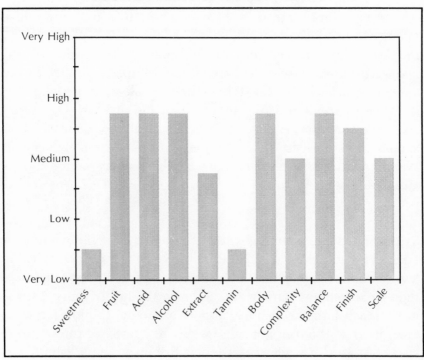

comparatively full bodied. They are not intended for use as cocktails or aperitifs, though a few of them may be adaptable that way. Primarily, they make excellent dinner companions to food of all sorts. Sauvignon Blanc by itself rarely makes really distinguished wine, though it often makes distinctive wine. It has an assertive aroma, usually described as herbal and sometimes as grassy—the latter definitely not a compliment, and usually the consequence of underripe grapes. The wine's flavor closely follows the pattern of its aroma: cool, herbal, with over- and undertones that are variously likened to steel, flint, and even gunpowder, all sustained by a vigorous, acidic attack—exactly what the French mean by a "nervous" wine, a wine characterized by *nervosité*.

Because of its marked character and its acidity, Sauvignon Blanc fills the bill as a good middle-range, all-purpose wine. It has enough aggressiveness to deal with strongly flavored finfish and shellfish, and its own acidity allows it to take acidic sauces in stride. Additionally, because of that same acidity, it can taste quite refreshing with butter-rich sauces. Most Sauvignon Blancs receive low-temperature fermentation and are aged in stainless steel to preserve their freshness and fruit. Some few California specimens receive a little oak aging to round them and smooth them a bit.

Robert Mondavi was a pioneer of this style, which he called Fumé Blanc, and much of the present status of this varietal is directly owing to his experiments with it. Mondavi chose the name to distinguish his then-novel (for California) dry, lean vinification of Sauvignon Blanc from the at-that-time dominant fatter, sweeter style. Nowadays the tide of taste has definitely swung to the dry and almost metallic style in Sauvignons, so sweet versions rarely find their way to the market, and the two names, Sauvignon Blanc and Fumé Blanc, are used almost interchangeably to designate a dry dinner wine.

Mondavi called his dry Sauvignon wine Fumé Blanc to recall Pouilly-Fumé, the more prestigious of the twin towns on the upper Loire—the other is Sancerre—where unadulterated Sauvignon Blanc makes some exceptional wine, though the best of it usually prices itself well out of the class of everyday drinking. Ironically, the Sauvignons of Pouilly and Sancerre rarely receive any wood aging, though they tend, despite that, to have the same sort of roundness and hint of softness that California Sauvignon gets only with the help of oak.

Italian vintners too have gotten fine results from Sauvignon Blanc. The northern regions of Trentino–Alto Adige and Friuli–Venezia Giulia—by far the most important white wine–producing areas in that whole vast winery of a country—turn out very stylish, lean Sauvignon, lighter bodied than either the French or the American norm, and marked by a bright acidity and fresh fruitiness. Friulians particularly have evolved a very successful style of their own with this grape, making of it a beautifully perfumed wine that tastes richly of fruit without any trace of the grape's unpleasing grassy qualities. Many of these Italian Sauvignons have a very crisp, dry feel—in some instances almost metallic or coppery. It's a wonderful package of properties, and it makes a first-rate partner to seafood and white meats, even those with fairly rich sauces.

South American Sauvignons tend to retain a sweet edge that makes the wine less companionable with most foods, though it can sometimes match well with Chinese dishes.

Sauvignon Blanc also lends itself to blending, usually with Sémillon, on the model of French white Graves (see "Inexpensive White Blends" below).

Riesling achieves its unquestionably greatest heights in German sweet wines, but its drier incarnations have also won it a loyal following in many countries. The British seem to have a much higher opinion of Riesling and its glories than American enophiles have ever held. How much this is attributable to a real or imagined indissoluble linking of "shellfish and Hock" or how much to a pervasive British passion for sweets is impossible to tell, but the fact remains that for many British connoisseurs Riesling rivals and perhaps surpasses Chardonnay as the world's great white grape.

There are many varieties of Riesling. The important one is the one known in the United States as the Johannisberg or White Riesling, elsewhere as the Rhine Riesling. Winemakers the world over produce Rieslings in either of two styles, neatly divided by the north and south banks of the Rhine. The northern, German style makes a wine light in body and low in alcohol with a delightful fruity—sometimes even minty—aroma and a delicate, fresh taste highlighted by a bright acidity. Even in the driest specimens there always lingers a hint of sweetness, and the apogee of this style can be found in the great—and expensive—sweet dessert wines, the Ausleses, Beerenausleses, and Trockenbeerenausleses of the Rhine and the Moselle (for a fuller discussion of these, see "Germany" in Chapter Five). The southern style, that of Alsace, makes a full-bodied wine of complete dryness. It retains Riesling's characteristic and beautiful aroma and flavor but weds them to a spine of steel to produce a wine that is in all key respects the antithesis of German Riesling, while clearly still its kin.

All but the very driest German Rieslings—the Kabinett classi-fication and the new Trocken wines—really do not work well with most foods (except some Oriental dishes; see "The East Is Not Red Wine Country" in Chapter Six). Their delicacy and sweetness either fight with most dishes or are smothered by them, and in both cases it is generally a waste of wine and money to pair these fragile belles with everyday foods. The sturdier Alsace style, on the other hand, matches quite well with a whole range of foods, including many dishes ordinarily thought of as too strongly flavored for white wines or too difficult for any wines—for example, classic American honey-glazed baked ham, or classic Alsace *choucroute garnie*, an elaborate dish of sauerkraut cooked with an abundance of pork products, fresh, cured, or smoked.

California produces a large amount of true Riesling (as opposed to the considerably less interesting varieties, Emerald Riesling or Grey Riesling, which are also cultivated there). The vast majority of California Riesling is currently vinified in the German style, with degrees of sweetness ranging from slight to overpowering. Vint-ners in Oregon, Washington, and New York have also had good success with German-style Riesling. Italian winemakers produce a pleasing Riesling Renano (Rhine Riesling, to distinguish it from the ordinarily quite dull Riesling Italico) very much in the style of Alsace. Food matchups for all these wines follow the broad lines of their national model—that is, German-style wines serve best as dessert, occasionally as aperitifs, and with some few Oriental dishes, while Alsace types are versatile and widely usable with the whole range of foods that want or will tolerate a white wine.

THE LITTLE EIGHT

Well behind the big three of the International White Wine Club follows a gaggle of white wine grapes that have important local or national roles but that have not yet made their mark to any great extent on the international scene. For that reason some of these wines offer American consumers quite wonderful values. The dollar-conscious wine lover—and what wine lover can afford not to be?—will look to some of these "undiscovered" varietals for the last bargains left in a rapidly upward-trending market. Here is a short list of the more important varietals, in alphabetical order.

Chenin Blanc, like most other grapes of French origin, is rarely ever bottled under its own name in France, where almost all the best-known wines take their names from their town or region of origin. (The varietally named wines of Alsace are the only major exception to this rule.) The middle Loire Valley provides the zone of most intense cultivation for Chenin, where it goes into the making of everything from simple, dry (or almost dry), and always acidic table wines to glorious long-lived sweet nectars. Its best-known appellation is Vouvray, which can occasionally be dry but is usually vinified off-dry to slightly sweet. Chenin Blanc can usually be identified by its characteristic melonlike aroma, reminiscent of a cantaloupe with a strong dose of acidity added. The slightly sweet versions, well chilled, make ideal summer quaffing, and the dry bottles match well with the characteristically fatty foods of the Loire—pork rillettes and terrines, fat river salmon, young goat cheeses. Most California versions have at least a small degree of sweetness, more or less on the Vouvray model, though there are a few completely dry versions (for example, Chappellet, Kenwood) that give some indication of what might be made of the grape if more care were taken with it.

*   *   *

Gewürztraminer is a variety whose daunting name has probably kept it from the popularity it deserves, since almost everyone who tastes a well-made Gewürztraminer likes it. It's a user-friendly wine. The name means "spicy Traminer," the latter word being the former name of the town in the former South Tyrol, now Terlano in Italy's region of Trentino–Alto Adige, where the variety is said to have originated. The first half of the name is certainly accurate. The wine generally smells and tastes spicy, without any one condiment standing out in the mélange. Some drinkers find it too much and too unsubtle, which it can certainly be, but most people enjoy the rather exotic bouquet and flavor, which suggest all sorts of extravagant ingredients without quite settling down to be any one of them.

Gewürztraminer is usually pretty full bodied, and that along with its assertive flavor makes the dry bottlings wines to match with dishes that defeat other white wines. The variety is grown in both Germany and Alsace, and the national styles differ in exactly the same way as their treatments of Riesling: German Gewürz is lighter bodied and always has at least traces of sweetness, while the Alsace bottlings are fuller bodied and completely dry. Most of California's growing regions are probably too warm for the grape. For whatever reasons, success there has been very mixed, although attempts at both the German and the Alsace styles continue to be made. The Pacific Northwest looks to be the major American source of quality Gewürztraminer in the decades ahead, though the East Coast is making some progress with it too. The grape's ancestral homeland produces rather restrained, though pleasant, versions of the wine that tame its aroma somewhat and lighten its body a trifle. They usually bear the label TRAMINER AROMATICO to distinguish them from simple Traminer, a lesser and less interesting grape.

Muscadet is the name of a dry, acidic, slightly fruity wine made in large quantities near the mouth of the Loire. (It is also the now-accepted name for the grapes that make up that wine, once known as Melon de Bourgogne.) In France, Muscadet is widely regarded as a perfect seafood wine. Its simple tang makes it an ideal companion to fresh shellfish, and many a Parisian bistro depends on a generous and well-chilled supply of it to accompany its heaping *plateau de fruits de mer*. Widely available in this country, Muscadet makes a pleasing, innocuous aperitif and a useful companion to many simple, light foods. The grape is not much cultivated outside France, though Jancis Robinson, in her authoritative *Vines, Grapes and Wines*, claims that some of what passes for Pinot Blanc in California is actually Melon de Bourgogne. If that is the case, the California vacation has done wonders for this spindly northern grape.

Muscat should be regarded as a collective noun, since so many clones and varieties of it are cultivated around the world, both as wine grapes and as table grapes. For wine purposes, the most important kinds are the French vine, Muscat Blanc à Petits Grains, and its closely related Italian cousin, Moscato Bianco. Their best products are almost always richly scented sweet wines that overflow with lush grape flavors—for example, the French Muscat de Beaumes de Venise and the Italian Asti Spumante. Despite the fact that fully dry Muscat wines can be very pleasing, few of them are made, either because the weight of tradition so heavily favors the sweet versions or, more probably, simply because the sweet versions are so luscious and appealing. For all practical purposes, the customary sweetness of Muscat wines restricts their dinner role to dessert—either with or as a substitute for.

Pinot Blanc suffers from an identity crisis. Widely grown around the world—Germany, France, Italy, Eastern Europe, Chile, Australia, and the United States are the principal but by no means only areas of its cultivation—it has nevertheless long been confused with other varieties. Some of California's Pinot Blanc may well be Melon de Bourgogne, as mentioned above, and a good deal of Australia's and Italy's is probably Chardonnay. Real Pinot Blanc is related to neither, but when given sufficient attention during vinification, it can and does make a wine very reminiscent of Chardonnay. In California it is never quite as lush as Chardonnay nor quite as big, but its gentle, applelike aroma and soft, pleasing taste—combined with a generally much more pleasing price than Chardonnay—make it a very attractive wine indeed. In all other places the style of wine made from Pinot Blanc very closely follows the national predilection. German Pinot Blanc, which is usually blended, tends to lightness, gentle fragrance, and slight sweetness. Alsace's wine is firmer, drier, fuller, very similar to the California product. Italy's Pinot Bianco is lighter than the Alsace style (though not as light as the German), crisper and more acidic. Food matchings follow according to wine style and are pretty much like those for Chardonnay.

Pinot Gris makes interesting wine in three different styles under three different names in three different locations. As Ruländer, it makes what is probably the fullest-bodied white wine of Germany. As Tokay d'Alsace and, increasingly, as plain old Pinot Gris, since Common Market regulations are phasing out the Tokay d'Alsace designation, it produces a classic, full-bodied, authoritative Alsace wine. As Pinot Grigio, it makes what may be the most fashionable white wine in Italy: light, acidic, and gently aromatic (all the Pinot Gris wines suggest a delicate Gewürztraminer), with a refreshing, palate-cleaning fruitiness.

In each of these guises it fills a slightly different food niche. The German versions are perhaps the most widely usable of all German wines with everyday foods, though the rule is still the lighter the dish, the better the match. The Alsace version, on the contrary, does very well even with dishes as strongly flavored as that regional favorite, goose—and the slight spiciness of the wine also allows it to work well with goose liver, though that would hardly count as everyday fare except in Strasbourg. The Italian style of Pinot Grigio makes both a marvelous aperitif and a good, light accompaniment to simply prepared main dishes, to various antipasti (even prosciutto), and to pastas generally.

*   *   *

Sylvaner used to be a very important grape in Germany and Alsace, though it is now losing ground—literally—in Germany to the hybrid Müller-Thurgau and in Alsace to Pinot Blanc. Sylvaner makes a pleasing and useful, if undistinguished, quaffing wine, chiefly marked by fairly high acidity. It is vinified in the dominant national styles of its two zones of production: light, acidic, and slightly sweet in Germany, and medium bodied, firm, and fully dry in Alsace. Food uses follow accordingly.

Trebbiano amounts to the blessing and curse of Italy, where its ease of cultivation and its high yields make it the base—one cannot say backbone because its flaw is a tendency toward flabbiness—of many if not most inexpensive white blends. It constitutes a major fraction, for instance, of both Orvieto and Frascati. Bottled by itself as Trebbiano d'Abruzzo, it is a useful, dry, medium-bodied, all-purpose white wine. One vintner (Valentini) gives it elaborate attention and produces as a result a wine that recalls great white Burgundy in its richness, but his price is correspondingly high, well out of the range of everyday wines. Average bottlings range from drinkable and forgettable all the way up to pleasant and forgettable.

INEXPENSIVE WHITE BLENDS

Not all wines are varietal wines, of course, and some blended wines are so popular, so inexpensive, or so useful that they deserve mention in this short list of everyday wines.

Bordeaux Blanc, Entre-Deux-Mers, and white Graves are mixtures of, predominantly, Sauvignon Blanc and Sémillon. The first two are the least expensive. White Graves can include estate-bottled classified growths, which will almost invariably cost a good deal more—unless the rate of exchange and the balance of trade are being very friendly—than an everyday wine ought to. All these appellations are dry, medium-bodied, perhaps a touch oily on the tongue, with a light, sometimes herbal flavor. Any of them makes a good, versatile dinner wine, especially with chicken or veal or slightly oily fish like shad.

Liebfraumilch started as the designation of a very specific wine (from—unfortunate name!—Worms) and has become the appellation for Germany's largest wine export. Made from Riesling and Müller-Thurgau, among other grapes, Liebfraumilch is typically very light bodied, low in alcohol, with a light fragrance and slight fruity flavor enhanced or undercut (depending on your palate) by a discernible sweetness.

White Rioja comes in two styles. The new style vinifies for freshness, lightness, and youth, and generally does its best to turn out a white wine exactly like a thousand others already on the market. Fortunately, Rioja's native Spanish grapes resist homogenization and preserve a lively prickle that keeps the wine quite interesting. What is now the old-fashioned style—the one I unabashedly prefer—subjects the wine to a little or a lot of wood aging to make a wine with deep and sometimes complex flavors. It's not at all suitable for aperitif use (unlike the new Riojas), but it's wonderful with all sorts of mild-to-middling flavored foods, from paellas to pork chops to turkey.

Soave is typical of many of contemporary Italy's inexpensive white wines: light bodied, acidic, mildly fruity in both taste and aroma, capable of taking deep chilling with little loss of flavor or bouquet—a perfect party-picnic-luncheon-and-light-dinner wine. Its ongoing popularity seems utterly unharmed by the fact that all but the very best and most expensive examples of it—single-vineyard wines, vinified with great care—are essentially character-less. Soave matches quite innocently with light foods and pastas, with canapés and picnic foods of all sorts.

YOUNG SOAVE CLASSICO

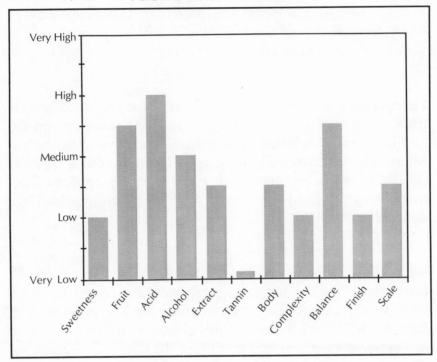

A Varietal Gazetteer: Some Red Grapes and the Wines They Make

THE MAJOR LEAGUES

As with white wines, a handful of grape varieties—Cabernet Sauvignon, Pinot Noir, Merlot, Gamay, Syrah (also known as Shiraz), Zinfandel—dominate the field in prestige and importance.

Cabernet Sauvignon unquestionably leads all other red grapes in prestige and popularity among serious wine drinkers. Its home territory is Bordeaux, where it constitutes the major component—

both qualitatively and quantitatively—in the great, long-aging wines of the Médoc, the wines that for centuries the British have known and loved under the collective name claret (see "A Gazetteer of Wines by Region" in Chapter Five). California has become Cabernet's adopted home and—along with Australia—its headquarters as a straight varietal wine. (That, however, is changing by the moment. More and more of the best California vintners are blending their Cabernet Sauvignon with Merlot and Cabernet Franc to produce a wine on the Bordeaux model.)

Cabernet Sauvignon makes distinctive wine almost everywhere, identifiable almost immediately by odors and flavors of fresh-cut cedarwood and black currants. The grape is dark and thick skinned, and so is the young wine—so much so that newly bottled Cabernet is virtually undrinkable because of its extreme tannic astringency. Even when subjected to vinification techniques designed to maximize its fruitiness and freshness, Cabernet produces a wine that remains hard and ungiving for its first few years. Cabernets from prime vineyards in good vintages that have been given the kind of vinification reserved for "serious wines"—slow fermentation, with long contact between musts and skins, and long oak aging afterward—can remain closed and unyielding for their first few decades.

With Cabernet, California grape growers normally achieve levels of ripeness—and consequently amounts of fruit in the finished wine—that Bordeaux growers see about three or four times a century. One such year for them was 1982, and the Bordelais quite openly speak of its wine as their California vintage. The California style—essentially the Napa Valley style—overlays Cabernet's youthful astringency with massive fruit, the kind of flavor that is frequently described as "rich" and "jammy." Those with lower tolerance for harsh tannins describe it as a handful of berries in a cup of cold, oversteeped tea.

There is no way that we can intelligibly discuss the flavors and styles of Cabernet without saying something about the phenomena of the California palate and the European palate. These things definitely do exist, and different individuals have discernible and consistent palatal preferences, and sometimes even tolerances and intolerances, that confine their enjoyment to or bar them from enjoying the wines of one continent or the other. As far as the California palate is concerned, a taste for lush, slightly overblown Chardonnay is its hallmark in white wines, just as surely as a devotion to fruitiness above every other quality in Cabernet Sauvignon defines it in red wines.

(In wine circles it's not considered polite to say so, but those whose palates are pronouncedly skewed in this direction are not very good judges of wines from elsewhere in the world, except perhaps Australia, which amounts to—if such a thing is possible—an exaggeration of California. The reverse is also true, of course: Tasters with a pronouncedly European palate have a great deal of trouble appreciating California wine.)

Because of the presence of all that ripe fruit, the huge preponderance of Cabernet produced in California is drunk much too young, years before the wine has fully evolved. (So is most of the claret made in Bordeaux, for that matter, but that is as much for reasons of restaurant economics as it is due to the wine's youthful attractions.) The significant consequence of this—not to mince words about it—is that it's probably a safe estimate to say that the great majority of the people who regularly drink California Cabernet haven't the slightest idea what the wine is all about—and neither does an almost as large fraction of young American winemakers.

What a Cabernet Sauvignon ought to be about, since the variety has the rare gift of living long and evolving and improving all the while, is maturity and complexity, the kind of depth and harmony of multiple flavors (as opposed to simple fruit) that make older clarets such magical companions to all sorts of foods. What in fact you get in young California Cabernet—and especially in inexpensive Cabernet, for which you must look to the so-called fighting varietals (so-called precisely because they are very competitively priced: wines like, for example, Napa Ridge, Glen Ellen, Round Hill)—is a firm, tannic wine with an overlay of curranty fruit and often other herbaceous or vegetal flavors (for example, eucalyptus, olive, pepper). In Australian Cabernets the fruit is usually even more forward, a fact that makes these still not-too-costly wines good buys in restaurants, where they are often the only affordable and ready-to-drink wines on the list.

France bottles little or no varietal Cabernet. South American Cabernets, primarily from Chile and Argentina, are marked, like Australian Cabernets, by intense fruitiness. Italian Cabernets come in two styles, one a relatively expensive conscious or unconscious emulation of the California model (the Tuscan Sassicaia, the Piedmontese Darmagi, the Umbrian Lungarotti), the other a more economical native rendering of the grape into an uncharacteristically (for a Cabernet) low-tannin, high-acid, early-drinking wine of medium-to-light body. The latter style dominates varietal Cabernet production in the Italian northeast, especially in Friuli.

All these Cabernets partner well with simple preparations of red meats, especially lamb. As the wines age and mature, they will match increasingly well with more intricately sauced dishes, especially those marked by rich and assertive flavors.

Pinot Noir: If California is the world capital of varietal Cabernet, Burgundy must be the galactic center of Pinot Noir. Red Burgundy *is* Pinot Noir—period. Nowhere else in the world does this finicky, fickle grape produce anything like the glorious nectar that in a fine vintage trickles from the vineyards of Corton and Vougeot, Chambertin and Musigny. In other places the juices of Pinot Noir don't measure up to that exalted, increasingly rare standard—not even, most years, in Burgundy itself.

There's the rub, of course. Great, great Burgundy is the only illustration of what Pinot Noir is capable of, and great, great Burgundy is an endangered species. For that matter, decent Burgundy, a wine with some shadow of the breed's potential greatness, is scarce even in an ordinary year, and expensive beyond most wine drinkers' budgets in a fine one. Most of what is sold in this country under the region's simplest appellation—Bourgogne Rouge, red Burgundy—is not worth the drinking. Harsh, thin, and sharp tasting, it is a parody rather than an echo of fine Burgundy.

The Pinot Noirs of—surprisingly—Oregon provide the closest approximation most of us can afford to the taste of classic

Burgundy—raspberries and strawberries, with an understructure of tannin and acid—but even this enjoyable wine reflects the current style of Burgundy, a lighter, simpler wine, more immediately drinkable than the great, complex, slow-evolving red Burgundies of the prewar years. And even this fresh Oregonian Pinot Noir, although a bargain by Burgundian price scales, never descends in price to the range of everyday affordability.

Most inexpensive Pinot Noirs—more California fighting varietals—will be dark ruby in color, with a dark, cherrylike fruit and a lot of stemmy tannins: a rather winy wine, so to speak, but useful with lighter meat dishes than Cabernet takes to and good too with roast fowl like pheasant or turkey. Particularly light vintages can even cross the color line and be matched successfully with such rich fish and shellfish as monkfish, tuna, crab, and lobster.

Alsace makes the best affordable Pinot Noirs for day-in, day-out use. They tend to be rather light bodied for a red wine and a bit pale, but they have fruit and they have structure, and they reflect, palely, the Pinot Noir flavor spectrum. I find them very pleasing with any food that wants a light red wine.

Merlot is almost everywhere overshadowed by Cabernet. In Bordeaux it usually takes the role of Cabernet's supporting actor, appearing as a solo and star only in Château Pétrus. This is the wine world's definitive example of starting at the top, and a role that makes up for any amount of neglect anywhere else. As that example may suggest, Merlot plays in Pomerol and St-Emilion the qualitative and quantitative role that Cabernet plays in the Médoc, being the mainstay of the softer, fruitier wine that these more easterly vineyards characteristically produce. In California some notable pure-Merlot wines are also made, though again a high proportion of the Merlot grown winds up in blends with Cabernet.

The flavors of the two grapes are similar. Cedar and black currants predominate in the young wines, but Merlot is distinctly softer and more supple, usually lacking the heavy tannin of Cabernet and therefore normally more accessible and pleasantly drinkable sooner than Cabernet. These are characteristics that ought, in strict logic, to make it the preferred varietal for California's favored, early-drinking style of red wine, but logic has little to do with wine popularity or prestige, and Merlot lags Cabernet by a wide margin both in production and popularity in California.

Merlot generally has the same food affinities as Cabernet, though its greater accessibility gives it more utility with less aggressively flavored dishes and makes it more hospitable—especially in less-than-great vintages—to milder flavored dishes that just marginally might be able to take a red wine.

Gamay really encompasses several varieties of grapes yielding similar styles of wines. The true Gamay grape makes Beaujolais, a light, fruity, acidic red wine of manifold uses and pleasures, matchable with simple foods of all sorts and drinkable at room temperature or lightly chilled at picnics, parties, and dinners. In California at least two varieties of grapes pass muster under the names Gamay, Napa Gamay, and Gamay Beaujolais (this last less and less used as an appellation), though none of the above is in fact the real Gamay of France. Nevertheless, all these are vinified in the style of Beaujolais to yield fresh, fruity wines with a bit more flesh and less acid than their French model. They are almost as versatile with regard to foods and serving circumstances as Beaujolais, which is to say that they will happily accompany light foods of almost any sort in just about any situation you can imagine.

Syrah and Petite Sirah are names that cause—or mask—another Franco-American confusion. California's Petite Sirah is not the same grape as the Syrah of the Rhône Valley (the sole grape of Hermitage, Côte Rôtie, Cornas, etc.), though it yields a wine not unlike what Syrah makes in France: big bodied and slow maturing, with deep, dark flavors—black pepper, tobacco, tar, and other mouth-filling, chewy tastes. To further compound the international nomenclatural confusion, the grape Australians call Shiraz is usually the true Syrah variety, and Australians do all sorts of things

YOUNG CALIFORNIA GAMAY

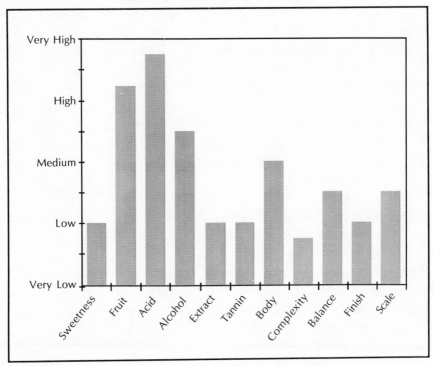

with it, including blending it with Cabernet. One last twist on this Babel of names: Most of the straight varietal wines that Australians make from Shiraz they call Hermitage, and Australian Hermitage does distantly echo the French original. Because these wines are neither well known nor cultishly fashionable in this country, they are often good buys. Any of them—French, California, or Australian—will partner well with strong meats, especially game, and with spicy stews and braises.

Zinfandel comes closest of any variety to being a California native. Without question, it's a California speciality, a red grape found nowhere else—and one with the potential, in this wine lover's opinion, to be one of the world's truly great wines, if only more winemakers could be persuaded to give it the kind of care and attention it deserves. Ridge Vineyards and a handful of other wineries have shown the way: They use mature vines, keep tight control of yields, and vinify with the same sort of care accorded to Cabernet, and the result is a wine of real nobility.

Most of the time, Zinfandel isn't given that much respect. For all sorts of reasons, ranging from indifference to sheer economic necessity—the most powerful spur of all—Zinfandel is now vinified in every conceivable style, from "white" (a blush wine made by removing the juices from contact with the skins and usually stopping fermentation before all the sugar is used up) to "Beaujolais" (light, fruity, fresh) to "claret" (wood aged, needing time to mature and deepen, in the manner of a fine Bordeaux) to "port" (the late-harvest wines, with high alcohol and high sugar, to be drunk after dinner, with or without dessert). The most useful for dinner purposes are the Beaujolais and claret styles, and the comparisons implied by the names indicate pretty accurately their dinner uses and food affinities. Both styles offer, in their different fashions, the attractive brambly and blackberry flavors that are characteristic of the varietal. Take note, however, that labeling does not always distinguish clearly between these two styles. Usually, but not always, the label will indicate if a Zinfandel has been made in the lighter Beaujolais style or the heavier, late-harvest, port style; the "white" Zinfandel of course declares itself to the eye. And usually, but not always, if the label indicates nothing about the style, it's a claret-type Zinfandel you're looking at—that is, most of the time the claret style is treated as the norm and the other styles as variants from it.

THE MINOR LEAGUES

Those are the major red varietals on the American market. As with white wines, however, there are a fair number of red wine grapes that have important local or national roles but that have not yet made their mark to any great extent on the international scene. A handful of Italian varietals, in particular, has begun to attract attention. Some of these wines offer American consumers quite wonderful values. Here is a short list of the more important kinds.

*   *   *

Barbera, though widely used throughout Italy—and California too—as a useful "filler" grape for blends, is nevertheless a varietal with a real character of its own. This shows best in specimens from the Italian Piedmont, which typically have medium body, high acidity (which makes Barbera a very versatile wine for accompanying a wide range of foods), and a lot of tarry, berrylike fruit. Some growers are experimenting with barrel aging for this grape, and a few are even trying their hand at blending it with the area's revered Nebbiolo (see below).

Cabernet Franc is widely grown in France, Italy, and the United States. In all three countries the bulk of the crop is used in blends either with Cabernet Sauvignon or with Cabernet Sauvignon and Merlot to produce claret-style wines. In France's center Loire, in and around Tours, Cabernet Franc by itself makes very pleasing, medium-bodied, soft red wines with a capacity for some aging. They usually bear the name of the town from which they come: Chinon, Saumur, Bourgueil. They partner best with foods that share some of their most charming qualities: gentleness, unaggressive flavor, smoothness, a sort of well-bred understatement—not game dishes and not barbecue either, but the middle range of meat dishes.

Dolcetto is Barbera's cousin and complement. Cultivated side by side with Barbera throughout the Piedmont, Dolcetto is fleshy and supple where Barbera is lean, soft where Barbera is muscular. Its fruit is more intense and pleasingly grapey, so much so that the Piedmontese talk of it as being their equivalent of Beaujolais, though it is nowhere near as light as the French wine. In the Piedmont, Dolcetto is the wine they drink every day, with everything except fish.

Nebbiolo, the third of the Piedmont's important red wine grapes, is also the undisputed head of the clan. The late-ripening Nebbiolo grapes make big, authoritative, heavily tannic, and slow-maturing wines—Barolo and Barbaresco the most important and prestigious of them, but also Nebbiolo, Gattinara, and Spanna. Nebbiolo can probably challenge Cabernet Sauvignon and Pinot Noir in the quality of the wines it produces and the potential for greatness the varietal possesses. Mature specimens display a huge, trufflelike aroma and a whole battery of mouth-filling flavors: tar, tobacco, pepper, leather, truffle. A great grape with a great future, Nebbiolo's least expensive bottlings usually bear the varietal name rather than any of its more exalted regional designations. Match it with strong red meats, with game, with great cheeses.

Sangiovese is Tuscany's entrant in the great-varietal sweepstakes. The principal grape of Chianti and Vino Nobile, Sangiovese has begun to receive serious attention by itself. The example of Brunello, wherein a clone of Sangiovese vinified by itself makes one of Italy's longest-lived and most expensive wines, has prompted winemakers in the Chianti district to make clonal selections of their own and to experiment with a varietal Sangiovese wine. Some of them are very good, and not all of them are overpriced. They are characteristically full bodied, with rich but austere fruit, and excellent acid-tannin balance. Use with food as you would a fine Chianti Riserva or a Cabernet Sauvignon.

INEXPENSIVE RED BLENDS

Just as with white wines, some blended red wines offer very useful and inexpensive everyday drinking. Here are a few of the major categories.

Bordeaux Rouge, including **Haut-Médoc, Médoc, St-Emilion:** These wines will predominantly be blends of Merlot and Cabernet Sauvignon, with admixtures in varying proportions of Cabernet Franc and Petit Verdot. In the St-Emilion bottlings produced by shippers and small châteaux and cooperatives, Merlot will dominate the blend and the wine will be soft, fleshy, and relatively fruity. On the other hand, wines labeled Bordeaux, Haut-Médoc, or Médoc usually depend more on the Cabernet grapes, and consequently will tend to be leaner, less fruity, and more tannic or austere. All are fully dry and medium bodied, good with red meats, especially simple grills, roasts, or stews.

Chianti is a name that covers a multitude of sins and a fair number of shining virtues. Fortunately for the consumer, the winemakers commit most of the sins against one another, in the form of ruthless competition and suicidal price slashing, which is why Chiantis can often be among the most seriously underpriced wines on the market for the value they offer. Chiantis come from several differently named zones near Florence. In labeling the producers all have the choice of designating their zone (for example, Chianti Colli Senesi, Chianti from the Sienese hills) or simply calling themselves Chianti. Chianti Classico, the designation we see most often here, refers to a specific region, the traditional heart of the Chianti country, and not to the quality of the wine. Classico here—as indeed in all Italian wine labeling—is a purely geographic and descriptive term, not an evaluative one.

All Chiantis are blends, primarily of Sangiovese, the principal Tuscan red grape, and a few other varieties, sometimes including white grapes for lightness and zest. All simple Chiantis—that is, those not designated *Riserva*—are light to medium bodied, fresh, fruity, and acidic. They match well with hot or cold appetizers and with pastas of all kinds, especially those with tomato-based sauces, as well as with roasted and grilled meats and fowl.

Côtes-du-Rhône and **Côtes-du-Rhône-Villages,** including **Vacqueyras, Rasteau, Gigondas, Chusclan:** Inexpensive wines from the southern Rhône, vinified from a mélange of grapes but usually including at least some Syrah, and very occasionally—in wines from the individual villages—predominantly Syrah. Normally, the dominant grape in these wines from the southern Rhône is Grenache, a grape much grown but little cultivated in California, though a few pioneering California winemakers have taken note of what the variety is capable of and are attempting to emulate its Rhône style. The Rhône wines are characteristically robust and fresh, with big body and lots of fruit. They are very useful with a wide variety of foods, especially those with strong flavors (e.g., grilled sausages) or spicy sauces.

Rioja is blended of several native Spanish varieties, the most important of which are the Tempranillo and Garnacha, the latter being a Spanish clone of Grenache. Rioja can usefully be thought of as a Spanish parallel to Chianti. Like Chianti, there are many makers and two predominant styles. The old style gives the wine long wood aging, which makes it somewhat tannic but gives it a fine balance. That, in turn, makes it a wonderful wine with richly sauced dishes or with dishes whose flavors don't readily resolve themselves into a single dominant element. In addition, Rioja in this style continues to match well with simple grilled meats. The new style in Rioja vinification emphasizes fresh fruit: It is lighter in body and opts for a slight acidic edge rather than perfect balance. This is still a versatile food wine, though it will not perform as handsomely as the old style with dishes of complex flavor—all just like Chianti.

CHAPTER 3

The Proof of the Pudding

It's time to taste the acme of goodness
  that goes by the name of One-Dish Madness!
It's hors-d'oeuvre-dotted-delicious with heart-of-the-briny oysters
and sea-tangy fishlets oh-so-zestfully nestled in clusters
on spry-as-the-morning, utterly udder-fresh goat-good cheese,
caressing a lip-smacking, tooth-tensing medley of goodies like these:
alabaster-bosomed pigeon with bee-sweet-honey-drenched thrush,
do-it-again-love dove and the brown-basted, burst-breasted gush
of thick-thighed chicken, the let-us-be-truly-thankful amen
of gobbet-good bloblets of squab, hard by the hit-me-again
of ever-so-finely-filleted, palate-proud mullet, new-speared,
with gusto-lusty sweetmeats, crunch-yummily kitcheneered
  to rush the most reluctant tooth to the gnash . . .
    In short, it's Heavenly
    Hash.

> —ARISTOPHANES, *The Congresswomen,*
> translated by Douglass Parker

THIS CHAPTER WILL DISCUSS the pairing of wines with a representative selection of the dishes people eat every day in these United States—a simply prepared roast beef, an equally simple roast chicken, and broiled flounder (sole if you prefer, but all American soles are flounders). On the face of it, these are the least complicated sorts of wine and food matchups, involving very unelaborate preparations and inexpensive wines. Nevertheless, the principles they involve hold true in even the most sophisticated partnerings of haute cuisine and great wines. The same basic elements that make a young Zinfandel taste good with hamburgers grilled on a backyard hibachi still hold, mutatis mutandis, at the other end of the prestige scale for mature Zinfandels or Cabernets or clarets served with a roasted and mushroom-sauced saddle of lamb. Learn the basics, and everything else follows—perhaps not with the precision of arithmetic, but with at least some appearance of logic.

Let's look at what wines and foods make good and bad pairings and try to find out why. The best way to do that is simply to take the three basic food examples I've indicated above—roast beef, roast chicken, broiled flounder—and to try matching them on the mind's palate with some of the kinds of wines we discussed in the preceding section.

A Trio of Tastes: Beef, Chicken, Fish

For the ideal diner—a person who knows and relishes good food and wine without either pretension or embarrassment—what underlies any decision about what wine to drink with any given food is a kind of quick, almost a reflex, scan of the food's character and an equally quick review of the characteristics of the wines available to choose from. It is the sort of action you learn to perform automatically, like stopping for red lights. But the ease and speed with which it's done disguise the intricacy of the act. There's nothing natural or spontaneous about stopping for red lights, after all. That's a learned behavior, involving multiple perceptions and decisions. Exactly the same is true of the "quick scan" of food and wine characteristics that is basic to any food and wine pairing. Consequently, we are now going to lay out the whole process in order and talk about its basic components, part by part and step by step.

For starters, let's consider plain roast beef and a very simply roasted chicken. Nothing fancy, no tricks in the preparation: the beef a decent cut and roasted rare, the way I like it (that's the privilege of writing the book); the chicken a bird with some flavor, cooked until the skin is crisp and golden and the flesh thoroughly done but not dried out; both meats served very plainly with a good baked potato, some fresh peas, a few spoonfuls of an honest sauce made with only water and the defatted pan drippings. Real food, basic home cooking—so what do we drink with it?

Here are some good, enjoyable wines to have with these honest everyday foods: with the beef, Bordeaux Rouge, Cabernet, Chianti, Côtes-du-Rhône, Rioja, or Zinfandel; with the chicken, Beaujolais, Chardonnay, or Sauvignon Blanc. These are not the only possibilities nor are they necessarily the very best possibilities, but, sticking for now with the most widely available and the most economical wines, these all represent good options for enjoyable, everyday wines. Even more important for our present purposes, they each embody a kind of wine that works with our representative dishes for different reasons.

This means that the slate of red and white wines named above coordinates with the beef and the chicken on the basis of no single element but for a small handful of considerations that have as much to do with qualities of the foods as the characters of the wines. For instance, roast beef has a relatively assertive and pronounced flavor and a definitely moist, chewy, and—in the most pleasing sense—fatty texture. Some people call that quality its "mouth feel," an accurate if ugly phrase. Roast chicken, on the other hand, hardly asserts itself at all. It's mildly flavored, lean, and tends toward dryness, with a texture not chewy but rather soft and (as it even sometimes seems to the eye) long stranded: Fibrous overstates the case but indicates the right direction. These differences in the nature of the meats dictate the different qualities to look for in the wines that will accompany them.

Because its own flavor is more pronounced, the roast beef will simply overwhelm delicate wines, so its companion wines must be relatively full flavored if not downright robust—just as our decalogue of principles predicts. Beyond that, however, the wines must have not merely a marked flavor, but also a distinctive flavor that will nevertheless complement, or at least integrate with, the beef's own flavor profile. In short, we've got to start performing the kind of component-to-component match counseled by our supplementary half a decalogue.

Since it's always easier to clarify these things by contrast, think of how you would describe the flavor of roast beef as compared to the flavor of roast chicken. The odds are very good that the word *sweet* will pop into your mind in connection with the beef— not sweet like sugar, but meat-sweet in the same way that we say nut-sweet—and maybe you will think even more specifically of meat-sweet with a little gamy edge (especially if your beef has been aged a bit or comes from an animal that has been allowed to browse). A flavor like that will not respond well to just any strongly flavored wine. Most people recognize almost instinctively that a markedly sweet—sugar-sweet—wine would taste quite dreadful with it, for instance. So a second definite characteristic of the wine we want with this dish, besides its strength of flavor, is dryness. In fact, as we said quite early on in this book, you're going to want your daily dinner wine to be dry about 98 percent of the time because a sweet wine's sugar will cover up the flavors of your food—and why spend good money for a piece of beef you can't taste?

Okay, what else? Well, because of beef's richness in natural fats (I wish there were a better way to say this; I'm not talking about calories or grease, but a pleasing quality of moist unctuousness that belongs in the meat—exactly, in fact, what is lost in overdone beef), roast beef requires wines that possess a certain asperity, a kind of textural strength or even roughness of their own, sufficient to rasp through the flavor of the meat and announce their own presence. The best analogy I can offer for the quality we're seeking here is the way a really fine, bitter orange marmalade cuts through the pleasing unctuosity of sweet butter. In wines, that sort of cutting edge will normally be created by either tannin or acid or some combination of the two. These are the components of most wines whose greater or lesser presence or prominence will enable the wine—to put it crudely but accurately—to degrease your palate, refresh your taste buds, and facilitate your appreciation of the other elements of the wine and the food. Usually it turns out that in red wines tannins perform this important array of tasks and in white wines acid does the job, but there are some important exceptions, of which we will speak later.

What we are discussing here is one very precise application of our guidelines about the elements of the food that influence the choice of a wine. The dominant characteristics of our main dish, the roast beef, are a relatively intense meat-sweetness and a clear preponderance of fatty flavors and textures rather than acid (the latter for all practical purposes not present at all in the beef or its accompanying vegetables). As a consequence of these characteristics, the meal calls for a wine of comparable size or mouth fillingness—what we would call body in a wine—and comparable intensity of flavor. This points to a red wine. In addition, the wine must be either tannic or acidic enough to refresh the palate and deal with the beef's unctuosity. The six kinds of red wine I listed above—Bordeaux Rouge, Cabernet, Chianti, Côtes-du-Rhône, Rioja, Zinfandel—all have that ability to penetrate the beef's richness and assert their own flavors alongside it, but all can do so for slightly different reasons.

What Makes Wine Work: Tannin

Abundant tannins constitute a hallmark of Cabernet-based wines. No matter where in the world they are made—California, New York, New Jersey, Virginia, Texas, France, Italy, Australia, Argentina, or Chile—Cabernet Sauvignons always possess a marked flavor, one of the most prized and readily identifiable in the whole world of wine, and more than enough natural tannin to match beautifully with beef and other similar meats. Tannins enter these and most other wines from two different sources: first during fermentation, from the grape skins, which are the great natural repository of tannin, and second during aging, from the wooden barrels (if they are used) in which the wine is kept after fermentation.

FOUR-YEAR-OLD NAPA CABERNET SAUVIGNON

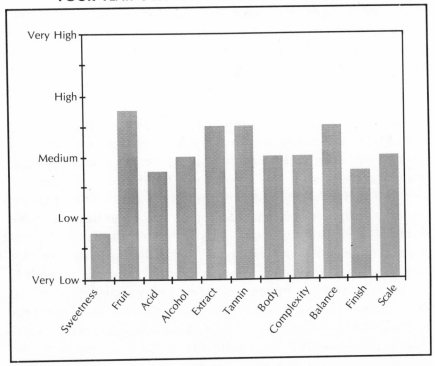

Most wines made from Cabernet Sauvignon draw their tannins from both sources. These abundant tannins give young Cabernet its characteristic rasp, a quality so pronounced that many of the world's finest Cabernets are virtually undrinkable in their youth because of it. In fact, it's almost a rule of thumb that the higher the quality of a Cabernet-based wine, the less likely it is to be really enjoyable young, precisely because of its tannin. Vintners cultivate and reinforce Cabernet's natural tannin by wood aging the wines because tannin provides them with a major component of what winespeak calls their structure. The word is at best an analogy: It suggests the resemblance of some of a wine's elements—usually tannin, alcohol, acid, and sometimes extract (more later about all these)—to the girders and beams that support a building. These support a wine and give it—variously—body or roundness or strength or firmness or depth. In these respects, tannin is particularly important. It acts as a preservative in wine and enables wines to live long and to develop over years in the bottle. Consequently, various methods of vinification have been devised to raise the level of a wine's tannin: Long contact between the musts (the pressed grape juices) and the grape skins extracts more and more tannins from the skins, and fermenting a wine in wood (especially oak) or aging it in wood allows it to draw yet more tannins from the barrels.

The result of all this reinforcement of the tannins is in many cases a wine that is only marginally palatable when first bottled or released from the winery but that blooms after some years (occasionally decades) of bottle age into a big, mouth-filling, assertive, and, at Cabernet's very best, unforgettable nectar, a fit companion not only for roast beef but also for the strongest-flavored game dishes, like venison and boar. This is because the tannins themselves change in the course of aging, losing the raw, assertive edge that often masks the fruit of young wines, and softening somewhat, surrendering their prominence in order to play a supporting role to the gradually maturing and evolving fruit flavors. The whole process transforms what started out as a relatively one-dimensional wine into a complex entity with many flavor components and consequently many modes of relating to food. But even when Cabernet's tannins soften and become less obvious to the taste, they don't disappear. They still exist in the wine, and they still work very efficaciously at cutting through fats and scrubbing the palate clean between mouthfuls of food. That's what makes the Cabernet-based wines such wonderful partners to richly flavored, unctuous meats like beef and lamb.

That marvelous evolution, it is well worth mentioning, is also why it makes so much sense to buy Cabernet-based wines when they are young—as soon as they are released—and to cellar them until they are ready to drink. These days the only thing that equals the pleasure of drinking a beautiful, twenty-year-old Cabernet is the satisfaction of knowing that you paid only $3 for it when it was released, and that it would cost close to fifty times that today—if you could buy it at all. There are no more $3 bottles of Cabernet, but wine prices, like other prices, show no sign of stopping their constant inflation, so the odds are that young Cabernets bought today will pay comparable dividends twenty years from now. Note well, by the way, that everything that has been said here applies equally to 100 percent Cabernet Sauvignons and to claret-style blends of Cabernet Sauvignon, Cabernet Franc, and Merlot.

What Makes Wine Work: Balance

In thinking about what makes a wine compatible with a strongly flavored meat like beef, it is important not to overlook the question of alcohol level, because that too affects the compatibility of the wine and the food by contributing materially to the balance of the wine. This is a crucial consideration. The balance of a wine is a very nebulous thing to talk about, though you know in an instant, tasting a wine, when it's not there. As the word itself implies, balance results from the interplay of different components in wines. In white wines fruit, acid, and the degree of sweetness or dryness the wine possesses form the three main elements that largely determine whether the wine is balanced or not. Alcohol is usually a background supporter and only rarely a prominent element in a white wine's balance, for the simple reason that most white wines are markedly lower in alcohol than most reds. In red wines balance usually comes about from the harmony of flavor intensity (chiefly varietal flavor from the grape or grapes and some additional "woodnotes wild" from the barrels), tannins, and alcohol level. A wine whose fruit flavors completely dominate everything else, or whose alcohol is deficient, will taste flabby and inert. A wine with too much alcohol tastes hot—literally: It creates a burning sensation on the tongue. A wine with too much tannin can taste like raw wood or oversteeped tea.

In Cabernet-based wines the achievement of balance determines the degree of their success or failure as wines in themselves and as companions to food. With their assertive varietal flavors and powerful tannins, Cabernets that failed to generate sufficient alcohol would be forever flabby and undrinkable, while Cabernets that were too high in alcohol would forever taste hot and agitated. The first problem—insufficient alcohol—occurs more often in Bordeaux, especially in simple wines like Bordeaux Rouge, while the second—too much alcohol—tends to be a problem in California. The canny Bordelais are able to compensate somewhat for their lack—it's usually insufficient ripeness in the grapes that causes it—by some quasi-legal chaptalization (adding sugar to the fermenting grapes to raise the alcohol level), but there isn't much Californians can do to lower the ripeness and the sugar content of their grapes except harvest earlier—but that may affect their flavor. The ideal alcoholic range for most Cabernets and Cabernet-based wines lies between 12 percent and 13 percent, with no unconverted sugars left after fermentation. That narrow band makes harvesting the grapes at the perfect degree of ripeness almost the make-or-break determinant of a vintage and explains why even a few small showers at harvest time can cause deep gloom in the vineyards.

What Makes Wine Work: Acid

Chianti and Rioja achieve their compatibility with roast beef by a slightly different route. The Sangiovese grape that forms the spine of all Chiantis and the Tempranillo that performs the same service for red Rioja are at least as full flavored and tannic as Cabernet, but traditional blending methods and fermentation practices in Tuscany and northern Spain have worked to mollify those harsh tannins and bring them more quickly into balance with other elements in the wine, thereby producing a wine that is pleasantly drinkable sooner.

The treatment afforded Chianti will serve as a useful example of how this can work. Until quite recently all Chiantis contained a fairly substantial amount of the juices of some white grape varieties blended with the Sangiovese, a practice that cut the total amount of tannin in the wine while simultaneously raising its acidity (thus, incidentally, causing no loss to the wine's ability to age well, since acid as well as tannin acts as a preservative in wine). In addition,

YOUNG CHIANTI CLASSICO

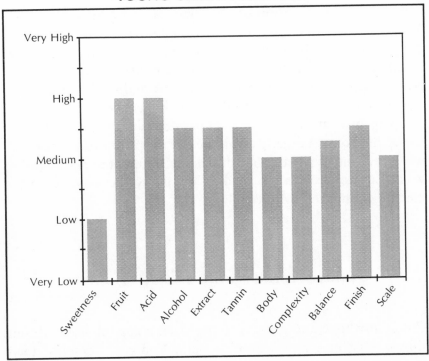

many Chiantis that were not destined by their makers for *Riserva* status (that is, to be reserved because of their high quality for special treatment, such as aging in wood, to increase their longevity) were treated to or with the *governo toscano,* a refermentation with additional, carefully saved, very ripe grapes. This had the twofold effect of markedly intensifying the youthful, fruity flavors of the wine and slightly raising its alcohol level.

The Rioja process is not identical, but it too depends on a blending of several grape varieties whose differing characteristics contribute separate components to the wine. In each case different basic grapes and different methods of treatment result in wines that are not only as distinctively and finely flavored as Cabernet Sauvignon–based wines, but also in wines whose combination of natural tannins and overall acidity provide sufficient cutting edge to penetrate the fats and richness of a dish like our nice rare roast beef. This is why drinking wines like these (Bordeaux Rouge,

Cabernet, Chianti, Côtes-du-Rhône, Rioja, Zinfandel) with such dishes gives the sensation of cleansing and refreshing the palate: That is exactly what the wines do. That good red wine strips away the fats that coat the tongue and taste buds and allows you to taste freshly each new forkful. I have a private theory, based on no data more scientific than my own preferences and cholesterol levels, that good tannic red wines do the same thing in your bloodstream, scraping away at cholesterol and fatty deposits and generally tidying up the house. I eagerly await the day that "nutritional science" will prove me as right about this as my Neapolitan grandmother was right, despite the best medical opinion of her day, about the blessings conferred by olive oil.

What Makes Wine Work: Bigness

Côtes-du-Rhône and Zinfandel approach compatibility with our simple roast beef by yet another path. You could describe their attack as exactly that—an attack, an all-out assault on your palate by the power of their flavors. If Bordeaux Rouge and Cabernet and Chianti and Rioja manage to complement the richness of the roast beef with the leanness of their tannins and acids, Côtes-du-Rhône and Zinfandel engage it head on by matching intensity with intensity, mouth-filling meat-sweetness with round, mouth-filling fruit and big body. Certainly, both wines have tannins, often in abundance, and the Rhône wines in particular also often possess a pretty high degree of acidity, but those aren't the qualities that strike a taster first. Rather, their flavors grab your attention—big, fruity, mouth-filling flavors: black cherries and tobacco and black pepper in the case of the Rhônes, blackberries and brambly, leafy, woodsy tastes in the Zinfandel. Along with those flavors, the sheer size of the wines makes itself felt. Rhône wines and Zinfandel impress you as "big" wines, big enough to elbow aside those robust beef flavors and demand the spotlight for themselves. Even when they are still very young, when the taste of fresh fruit dominates the other components of their flavors, these wines neverthe-less strike you as big, as filling your mouth and weighing on your tongue more than other red wines.

Bigness in a wine is a hard quality to talk about, but it's unmis-takable on your palate. Technically it comes about from abun-dance: intense flavors, high alcohol, rich tannins and acid, and a lot of what in wine talk is called extract, a word that sounds jargony but is actually quite precise. Extract consists of the microscopic solids that were leached out of the grape skins during fermentation and that the wine now holds in suspension. Extract contributes to the wine's texture, its "feel" on your tongue, as well as to its body and the complexity of its flavor. The more the vintner prolongs the contact between musts and skins during fermentation, the more extract the finished wine will contain. That benefit always has to be balanced against the downside possibility of at the same time drawing too much tannin out of the skins, and thereby producing

YOUNG CALIFORNIA ZINFANDEL

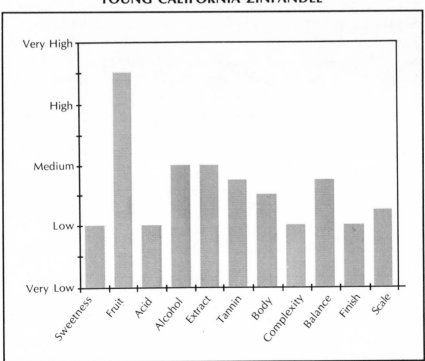

an unpleasing, undrinkable wine. Think of the puckery, almost stinging sensation you get on your tongue and the inside of your cheeks from an unexpected mouthful of oversteeped tea. That's what a wine with too much tannin tastes like. When the vinification process works perfectly—when the maximum amount and the optimum amount of extract coincide, when the kind of grapes and the quality of the harvest permit heavy extraction without building up too much tannin—the resulting wine will taste very full bodied, even weighty, without being heavy or flabby or inert.

The amount of extract in a wine is the chief determinant of the wine's scale. Wines come small scale and large scale and everything in between. A wine can be balanced and light bodied or balanced and full bodied, small and unbalanced or big and unbalanced, but in order for it to seem big or full bodied or mouth filling, or any of the other ways we have of describing a wine that presents us with an enormous amount of flavor, a wine has to contain a lot of extract. A wine can be beautifully balanced without a lot of extract, but it can't be big. It won't achieve large scale without a lot of everything in it: tannin and alcohol and especially extract. For example, a Riesling Kabinett of good vintage—let's say '83—and good village—let's say Johannisberg—and good maker—let's say Schloss Johannisberg—will unquestionably be balanced, lovely, exquisitely stylish. It will also be delicate and light bodied, its fine balance achieved on a smaller scale than that on which even mediocre red wines normally operate. The reason for this is very simple: Whereas red wines are normally fermented on their skins for at least a few days (and sometimes up to a month), the juices that make white wines are normally separated from their skins immediately after pressing. Only a very few of the "biggest"—a very relative term in this context—white wines ever receive even twenty-four hours of skin contact. No skin contact, no extract; no extract, no bulk, no size, no real bigness.

Extract differs objectively with each grape variety and with each soil condition and with each harvest. Even more important than the purely factual differences, however, are the subjective differences of each wine drinker's experience of the extract in a wine. Different tasters will not feel or describe the gustatory or palatal effect of extract in any simple, uniform way, even though the action of extract—especially extract in abundance—*is* fairly uniform. A wine that has good extract literally feels on the tongue as if it has a lot in it. It weighs on the tongue. It feels substantial in the mouth. Its flavor doesn't resolve quickly into one or two simple components. Perhaps most telling of all, a wine with good extract "finishes long": Its flavor lasts and lasts long after you've swallowed it. When people say a wine is big, that's the kind of sensation they mean, and it is emphatically high praise. A wine like that—and both Zinfandel and the Rhône wines are leading candidates to become wines like that—will complement our good roast beef by rivaling it in intensity of flavor and, at least seemingly, substantiality.

Back to the Bird

With our simple roast chicken, the difficulties in choosing a wine come from a totally opposite direction: It's not the chicken's strength of flavor but its mildness that creates the problem. We have to choose wines that will have enough flavor of their own to add something to the meal and at the same time not be so pronounced as to obscure the bird's flavor completely—a tricky balancing act and the primary reason for looking first to white wines. White wines as a class combine a broad spectrum of unaggressive flavors with relatively light body. That combination gives them a profile that works well with fish, shellfish, the lighter-fleshed fowl, and the mildest white meats and makes white wines the natural companions of delicately nuanced foods, whether they are main courses of everyday dinners or canapés at your poshest reception.

That being so, you may well be wondering what I was getting at with that short list of wines I suggested some pages back to accompany a roast chicken: Beaujolais, Chardonnay, and Sauvignon Blanc—remember? You're right to be surprised at seeing a red wine like Beaujolais in that list. It not only seems to contradict what I'm saying here but it even flies in the face of what used to be winedom's basic wisdom: red wines with red meat and white wines with fish and fowl and most white meats. I'm not trying to play any faddish games with you—like pushing you to drink red wine with fish, for instance—in order to make you modish and au courant. Far from it. What I'm trying to do is make an important point about—once again—wine components and the crucial role they play in pairing foods and wines.

The makers of Beaujolais like to joke that Beaujolais is the only white wine in the world that happens to be red, and they are not playing games either. In most vintages Beaujolais (especially the wines of the basic appellations, Beaujolais and Beaujolais-Villages) has an unusually high degree of acidity for a red wine. You will feel that acidity as a lightness on the tongue, sometimes almost a pleasing prickly sensation in the mouth, and a bright, vivid freshness in the flavor of the wine. That flavor isn't a powerful one, and it isn't understrapped by the usual red wine dose of tannin either, so most Beaujolais feel—and are—quite light bodied for red wines. That relatively high acidity and those sensuous characteristics— particularly the marked lightness of the wine's body—together create a total flavor profile that links Beaujolais, in every respect other than appearance and the distinctive strawberrylike flavor of its fruit, more closely to white wines as a class than to reds. That package of acidity and its attendant perceptible effects *plus* the pleasing, red fruit taste of Beaujolais—people almost unanimously liken its taste to cherries or berries, especially to strawberries— combine to make the wine one of the world's most versatile for use with simple, everyday foods. Beaujolais's real home, gastronomically speaking, straddles the middle range of food intensities: It has, on the one hand, just enough flavor and body of its own and, on the other, sufficient acidity and sprightliness to partner well with everything that falls between the extremes of very robust and very delicate—that is, for most simply prepared dishes you can match it with flavors whose intensities fall below the most assertive meat and rise above the mildest fish or fowl. Another way to put it is that Beaujolais and its complexionally kindred wines (some California Gamays, the not-very-common Italian wines Grignolino and Freisa, very light Chiantis and Riojas, some Barberas) overlap, in their gastronomical functions, the categories of me- dium- to light-bodied red wines and medium- to full-bodied whites.

That wonderful versatility has an obverse, however. Beaujolais doesn't have the depth to stand up to complexly sauced dishes or to particularly rich ones. If, just for the sake of contrast and clarifica- tion, we glorified our roast chicken into a *poulet aux morilles à la crème* (cut-up chicken braised with cream and wild mushrooms, which is not an everyday dish but is a relatively simple one to prepare), a Beaujolais would fall apart. Its acidity would taste sharp and bitter alongside the unctuosity of the cream sauce, and its fruit would taste either sickly sweet or flat alongside the lean, assertive woodsiness of the wild mushrooms. Any cream sauce— even a cream soup—and any richly flavored meat—say a rack of lamb—would produce the same effect on the Beaujolais: Our pleasingly light and dry red wine would suddenly metamorphose into an icky soda pop.

Go on to try our second wine, the Chardonnay, with these same two dishes and the results will be very different. A very sim- ple, fruity Chardonnay would accompany the roast chicken pleas- antly but rather innocuously, with little interaction between the wine and the food. The same wine would seem rather lost with the *poulet aux morilles,* its flavor evaporated by the lushness of the dish so that it felt more like fat water in the mouth than a real wine. Any more robust Chardonnay than that might, on the con- trary, seem just a bit too pushy and assertive with the simple roast chicken—especially if you had a really fine Chardonnay from Napa or Sonoma or Burgundy and if you had prepared the chicken very, very plainly, without herbs or other flavorings. But such a fine Chardonnay—admittedly a wine a good deal above the level of everyday drinking we are primarily concerned with here—would perform beautifully with that creamed and mush- roomed *poulet.*

Why? Because in addition to a rich, mouth-filling varietal flavor, a Chardonnay-based wine also possesses a very generous dose of extract. This combination gives Chardonnay wines a fullness of

body unusual for white wines and enables them to deal with the
sorts of lush, strongly flavored foods that most white wines can't
handle. Certainly this relative robustness (relative to other white
wines) allows Chardonnay to interact with *poulet aux morilles* and
richly flavored shellfish dishes in ways that Beaujolais's lighter
body and relatively higher acidity do not permit.

Chardonnays in fact possess the normal white wine complement of acidity, but their big body and flavor minimize and in
some cases almost erase the impact of their acidity. This reduction
of the scope or role of acidity in Chardonnay-based wines is reinforced by the ways they are treated during and after fermentation.
Sometimes they are barrel fermented, which adds to the varietal
flavor an overlay of vanilla and wood tones, plus a reasonably
hefty dose of tannin (especially if the fermentation takes place in
new oak barrels). More often, normal vinification practice in California and Burgundy subjects Chardonnay to at least a brief

FOUR-YEAR-OLD MEURSAULT

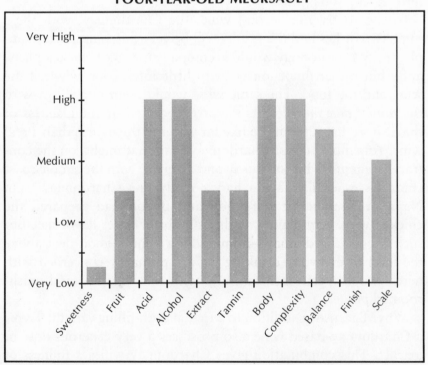

period of wood aging, which gives the wine a slight infusion of tannin and suggestions of the wood in its flavor. All these practices, by intensifying the wine's flavor and introducing or reinforcing its tannic "cut," correspondingly diminish the role and importance of the wine's acidity in its overall palatal impression or flavor profile.

Even without the help of oak, the character of the Chardonnay grape is such that it makes wines that feel fat and round and smooth on the tongue, almost as if they were thick enough to coat your taste buds and gently wrap them in flavor. The two most common descriptives applied to Chardonnay wines are buttery and nutty. Because of its generous, extract-based flavor, a Chardonnay will almost literally complement the buttery opulence of a cream sauce and create a very close harmony with it. *Poulet aux morilles à la crème* and a great white Burgundy make a partnership of heartwarming—indeed, almost heart-stopping—richness and flavor.

Our third white wine, Sauvignon Blanc, will work equally well both with our chaste roast chicken and the Gallically accented bird I've introduced to contrast it with. Most wines made from Sauvignon grapes possess a striking herbal and citrus flavor (at an extreme, it can become unpleasant; most people will then describe it as grassy) and excellent acidity. Like the Chardonnay, Sauvignon has in itself enough character and complexity to produce a wine of more than passing interest most of the time. But it is a "leaner" grape than Chardonnay, with more acid and less extract, and therefore by itself almost never makes a wine of such size or intensity that it would overpower the roast chicken. The other consequence of its relative leanness is that, lacking Chardonnay's body and extract, Sauvignon served with the *poulet aux morilles* gives you not a harmony but a counterpoint. Being a bone dry wine with marked acidity and flavors in the citrus-and-green-growing-things range rather than the red berry spectrum, Sauvignon doesn't decline into soda pop as the Beaujolais does alongside this same dish. Rather, its freshness and almost nervous vigor show through the lushness of the sauce, cleaning and refreshing the palate after it.

The Fish Story

What has been said here about white wines and fowl holds true in exactly the same terms for white wines and fish, especially for the delicately flavored ones and especially when they are simply prepared, as is our exemplary broiled flounder. Acidic, lean white wines—Sauvignon, Verdicchio, Pinot Grigio, the better Soaves, the modern style of white Rioja, Muscadet—complement without obscuring the light flavors of poached and broiled filets and whole fish of the lean, white-fleshed varieties, whether from salt water or fresh (cod, scrod, flounder, sole, bass, trout, sea bass, halibut, coho salmon, fluke). And just as Sauvignon Blanc will make a pleasing counterpoint to the rich taste of chicken in cream sauce, so too these vigorous wines will contrast flavorfully with richer, oilier fish—bluefish and monkfish, salmon and tuna—and the whole gamut of shellfish. They work well too with any of the more strongly flavored species of fowl—capons, turkeys, farm-bred (not field-grown) quail and pheasant. Not least of all, because of their acidity and comparatively light body and pleasing, light fruit, many of these wines also make quite enjoyable aperitifs. These are workhorse white wines that can be harnessed in almost any team; it is always wise to have half a dozen bottles of them around the house or bungalow or cabin.

For exactly the reasons that make wines of this character such splendid companions to our simple broiled flounder, a Chardonnay would emphatically *not* be my choice. Despite the old adage about white wine with fish, not all white wines go with all fish, and Chardonnay in particular is a wine that I think is frequently misused in this respect. Most Chardonnays are simply too big—too fruity, too assertive, too full bodied—to match well with any of the more delicately flavored finfish. You can't taste a flounder or a fluke, a cod or a halibut, alongside most Chardonnays. You have to put the punctuation mark of a pea or a potato between bits of fish and sips of Chardonnay if you want to appreciate both, and that's hardly what I would call synergy in a meal. As far as the

WHITE WINE FOOD WHEEL

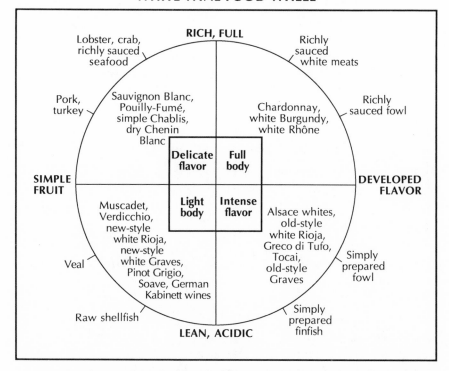

RICH, FULL

Lobster, crab, richly sauced seafood

Richly sauced white meats

Pork, turkey

Sauvignon Blanc, Pouilly-Fumé, simple Chablis, dry Chenin Blanc

Chardonnay, white Burgundy, white Rhône

Richly sauced fowl

| Delicate flavor | Full body |
| Light body | Intense flavor |

SIMPLE FRUIT

DEVELOPED FLAVOR

Muscadet, Verdicchio, new-style white Rioja, new-style white Graves, Pinot Grigio, Soave, German Kabinett wines

Alsace whites, old-style white Rioja, Greco di Tufo, Tocai, old-style Graves

Veal

Simply prepared fowl

Raw shellfish

Simply prepared finfish

LEAN, ACIDIC

denizens of the deep are concerned, Chardonnay's undisguisable authority seems to show best with the sweeter flavors of shellfish, especially crab and lobster, and with the most distinctively flavored finfish, like tuna and monkfish.

Especially since the nouvelle cuisine revolution has made many diners nervous about becoming démodé if they don't drink red wine with fish, it is well worth noting that by the very same criteria we have just been discussing, and in cases involving all but the most delicately flavored fish, highly acidic, light-bodied red wines—Beaujolais principally, but also such wines as Valpolicella and Bardolino, and even some non-Burgundian Pinot Noirs—can be utilized almost as satisfactorily as Sauvignon or Chardonnay. If you think of these light-bodied reds as—roughly—counterparts to Sauvignon Blanc and the medium-bodied reds (Alsace Pinot Noir, or inexpensive California Pinot Noir, and young, new-style Chianti and Rioja) as—equally roughly—counterparts to the lighter, less expensive versions of Chardonnay, you won't go too far wrong in your matchings.

Contrarily, the white wines that possess in themselves greater body, fatness, and complexity—such white wines as most Chardonnays, Alsace Rieslings and Gewürztraminers and Pinots Gris, the fine white Burgundies—really show their best only with the more forceful fish and shellfish or with richly or intricately sauced preparations. The situation and the logic that underlies it, the considerations that are operative, remain with fish and shellfish almost identical to those we looked at in the white wine and chicken scenario.

What Makes Wine Work: Food Characteristics

As we've seen, there are multiple ways that wines can achieve compatibility with food, even with a very simple dish like roast beef. It's worth paying particular attention to the means by which that basic compatibility comes about—by tannin or acid or powerful flavor or some combination of these elements—because as the cooking becomes more complicated, successful wine and food matchups will continue to depend on how the prominent components in the wine engage the prominent components in the dish.

Had we been dealing with, say, spare ribs and sauerkraut and choosing wines to complement the mild taste of the pork and the acid of the sauerkraut, the class of wines we looked toward would not change substantially if we glamorized our dish from spare ribs and sauerkraut to an elaborate *choucroute garnie*. The essential points of compatability would have remained intact. We would in either case be looking for wines of marked but not overpowering flavor, with firm but not necessarily full body—pork is a sweet but not strongly flavored meat, after all—and with enough acidity, or acidity sufficiently important in their flavor profile, to sustain the "scratching" of the sauerkraut. We are clearly here at the borderline of the utility of red wines. The flavor of the spare ribs themselves does not dominate this dish. Succulent and tender as the ribs may be, their taste in fact remains rather mild, not to say bland. The dominant flavor here comes from the sauerkraut, from its own acidity and its seasonings.

For this reason a white wine will generally work best with a dish like this. Because a white wine can match the sauerkraut acid for acid, it can bring to the meal a fresh, relatively delicate flavor that will neither disappear in the face of the kraut nor obliterate the gentle flavor of the ribs. You could comfortably drink a very dry German Riesling, an Alsace white, Sauvignon Blanc, or Soave with your spare ribs and sauerkraut. Owing to personal preference, you might eliminate or choose a German wine because of its almost inescapable slight sweetness or the Soave because of its comparatively mild and gentle flavor, but for most people all these white wines would fall within the range of at least acceptability, if not ravishing pleasure. Obviously Sauvignon and other acidic, medium-bodied white wines like it would work very well, as would many of the Alsace whites—Riesling perhaps best of all. Even Chablis, with its flinty taste and steely understructure, might fit the bill, but that is exceptional for a Chardonnay-based wine. Most Chardonnays would be among the last wines you should choose to accompany an acidic dish like spare ribs and sauerkraut, because the acidity of this preparation will pick apart the harmony of the Chardonnay and make it feel fat and flabby on the palate.

If, however, we kept our same cut of meat but changed the mode of preparing the spare ribs, if, say, we opted for barbecue instead, that would force us to rethink our set of wine choices completely. This change fundamentally alters the nature of the dish by substituting a different dominant element. In this case the basically mild taste of the pork would play second fiddle to the sweet/spicy flavor of the barbecue sauce and to the smokiness of the cooking technique. The acidity of the sauerkraut would, of course, be nowhere in sight, and gone with it would be our reasons for choosing the kinds of wines we did. What we would now be seeking would be wines of medium to full body, reasonably assertive flavor (the degree dependent on just how mild or sweet or hot the barbecue sauce is), and enough tannin or acidity to cut through the meat's combination of fats and sauce. This means we're certainly thinking of red wines, and depending on the exact character of that sauce, we're considering everything from some of the Beaujolais crus (they have all the fruit of Beaujolais plus more body) to Zinfandel to some Loire reds (Chinon or Bourgueil) to Barbera or Dolcetto, or maybe even a Chianti or a Rioja: All could work with such a dish.

Let's consider a few more examples and possibilities of wine and food pairings, just to spell out a little more the commonsensical nature of this whole procedure even with dishes that, because they contain many different ingredients, may seem to be complex and consequently to make complex demands on a wine.

Stews and casseroles make good cases in point, as do most braised or moist-cooked dishes. Beef and lamb stews—the basic, brown-gravy, nothing-fancy, homemade stew—actually present almost no problems for selecting a wine because they are really, despite their actual or potential number of ingredients, quite straightforward dishes. Every cook makes these differently, and each version has its own nuances, but the core of such dishes always remains the same. Moist, well-cooked meat and quite modest ancillary flavorings (onion, salt, and pepper, plus a few carrots and potatoes and a stalk of celery, perhaps a bay leaf—these are the basic regalia) don't demand any special characteristics in a wine except sufficient flavor and body to announce their presence alongside the rather assertive flavors of beef and lamb. Consequently, most white wines wouldn't work simply because they are too light of body and too gentle of flavor to really make any palatal impression at all alongside these stews. The one remotely possible exception to that is Chardonnay, since, as we've remarked before, some Chardonnays can be very full bodied and assertive. But with such bottles, you are in all probability entering a price range that takes your meal out of the everyday-dining category: At small prices you just don't buy enormous white wines. The red wine situation is the total opposite of the white: Most of the sorts of red wine we talked about in this chapter would match as decently with the stews as they would with other everyday red meat dishes (for example, flank steak, hamburgers, lamb chops, roast beef).

Not all kinds of red wine will match equally satisfactorily, however. Some of the lighter red wines, such as Beaujolais, some young Chiantis, or Valpolicella, while perfectly drinkable, will be less pleasing than heavier, fuller wines would be with the strongest-flavored of these meats or stews. Because of the food's intensity of flavor and their relative lack of it, they tend to taste light and somewhat thin alongside a hearty lamb or beef stew, even though they might work quite well with a lighter, milder dish like simple braised veal. Many people will find the lightness of such wines tolerable and even enjoyable with picnic hamburgers or even a flank steak barbecued in the backyard, but it usually appears considerably less pleasing at the dinner table. Since most stews have a rather robust and somewhat "composed" flavor (i.e., blended of several elements), you'll find their best matches, their most compatible wine partners, among the fuller-bodied and more assertive red wines, wines that can rise to a level of flavor intensity similar to their own. This usually means those red wines with a fairly plentiful tannin presence, wines such as Cabernet Sauvignon, Côtes-du-Rhône, Bordeaux Rouge, Rioja, or Zinfandel.

Other composed or complex dishes are more accommodating to light red wines. Everyday dishes that have a fair degree of acidity of their own—pizza, or spaghetti and meatballs, where the tomato sauces create a good deal of acidity, or pepper steak, where the peppers contribute the acidity—require a wine with acidity enough to meet them on their own terms. Red wines such as Beaujolais, young Chianti, new-fashioned young Rioja, and Valpolicella have a very pronounced presence of acid. In fact, the amount of acid they contain strikes most tasters as much more prominent than whatever amount of tannin they may possess and causes the impressions of lightness and freshness they create on the palate—all characteristics that make them fine partners to such bright-tasting, essentially acidic dishes as pizza and pepper steak. On the other hand, dishes with a perceptible fat content make the counterpoint of an acidic wine a pleasing option. So Beaujolais or Chianti or Valpolicella, with their combination of some of red wine's characteristic intensity of flavor with a relatively high de-

RED WINE FOOD WHEEL

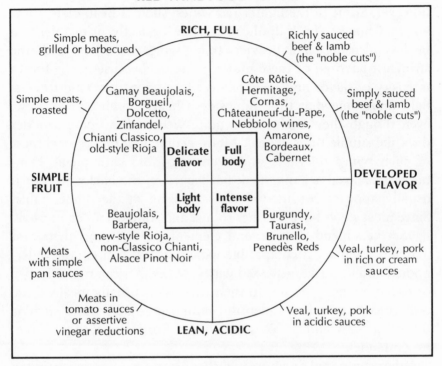

gree of acidity, can almost scrape through the unctuosity of such dishes as grilled sausages or liver and bacon and make their presence felt in a particularly refreshing and lively manner. Just as with white wines, a basically acidic character makes these three red wines and others like them very useful and versatile for either complementing or counterpointing various foods.

There are a few further points to make that belong to no single category, though they all involve wine and food relationships worth knowing about.

I've had numerous occasions so far to describe dishes as possessing unctuosity, a word I'm trying to popularize to describe a quality of pleasing fattiness in some foods or preparations. The presence of fats in a dish at a perceptible and pleasurable level (and no matter what the dietitians and nutritionists may try to tell you, fats have been pleasing the human species from before we learned to talk) dictates something fundamental about the wine that will match well with it. To state it very briefly: The leaner the dish, the fuller bodied the white wine it can respond to. This is because the whole package of elements that make up what we perceive as a wine's body—alcohol and extract and acid and tannin and glycerine and probably a fair number of other components—often register on our palates as "fat." They can make us taste and feel a wine as heavy or oily or rich or greasy or buttery or any of dozens of other adjectives that people use in an attempt to surround and pin down this unmistakable, though difficult to verbalize (I think because the diet people have embarrassed us about it) sensation. Consequently, a lean dish can support the complement of a fat wine, whereas a dish already rich and fatty will often make a rich wine seem excessive and heavy and overblown. So our roast chicken, especially if we've herbed it a bit and basted it, would stand up to an inexpensive Chardonnay, which is just about as big and full bodied a white wine as one gets in the category of everyday wines, and one of the least acidic. On the other hand, that same Chardonnay might very well taste flabby and heavy with fried chicken. The wine's own body will be felt on the palate and tongue as a kind of fatness, and in combination with the fats of a fried dish, that can seem just too much, too overpowering of any other sensation the wine may offer.

For that same reason, fried foods take very well to the counterpoint of an acidic wine. Normally that points to a white wine, and particularly to white wines marked by a characteristically high acidity: Sauvignon Blanc, for example, or Soave (most Italian white wines display bright acidity as almost a national trait). White wines are not inevitable with fried foods, however, not even with fried fish or shellfish. As acidic red wines, Chianti, Valpolicella, some other Italian reds, and Beaujolais—especially Beaujolais—constitute important exceptions to that rule of thumb.

Certain foods, too, amount to switch-hitters. Pork chops, for instance, and veal cutlets can really take a white or a red wine of all but the strongest flavor, for any number of reasons, ranging from how you've prepared them to your whim of the moment. Omelettes are the same sort of androgynous dish. Eggs, despite their wonderful flavor, are so neutral a medium (both for wines and for seasonings or additional ingredients) that you can make almost any wine work with them. I have read in perfectly reputable cookbooks that eggs make difficulties for wine, but in my experience the opposite is true: Eggs are extremely hospitable to all wines, from the most delicate whites to the finest reds. In fact, when I want to eat lightly but still drink a good red wine, the dish I most frequently turn to (when it isn't pasta) is a simple omelette, sometimes with cheese or ham, but more often than not plain.

Review and Preview

I hope you are at least beginning to see that matching foods and wines for everyday meals demands no more real expertise than deciding whether you want mustard or ketchup on your hamburger. If the United States were an essentially rural and pervasively wine-drinking nation, as France and Spain and Italy were until quite recent times, most of us would never even think about wine and food choices as problematic. Rather, they would be automatic, simple reflexes we had been unconsciously honing since childhood. Even in our present largely urban and not strongly wine-oriented reality, a very small amount of practice will convert—I hope for your sake is already converting—wine and food pairings from a chronic anxiety to an occasion of pleasure.

For everyday dining you are not going to bother about a sequence of wines. If you're not serving an elaborately graduated sequence of courses, neither do you need think about multiple wines. In all probability you will simply want one kind of wine to serve either with the main course or throughout the whole meal. This means, as we've said before, that the key to your wine choices lies in that main dish, and for all practical purposes you can think about your options as if you had to gear them to that dish only. Naturally, if you come up with half a dozen wines that will suit your entrée equally well, you ought to try to arrive at the best possible choice for the whole occasion by considering how each would taste with the other dishes in the meal, particularly if any of them should happen to be aggressively flavored. Nevertheless, in most cases you can start—and probably finish—thinking about your wine options by confining your attention to that main dish. And remember, you always have the choice, whatever food and wine you're serving as the main course, of taking a little glass of sherry or white wine as an aperitif or with your hors d'oeuvre or first course, should you be having any. No one will accuse you of decadence if you do.

Serving a single wine throughout the meal strongly implies that you want broadly usable wines for your everyday consumption: good, sound wines that will work with many different foodstuffs without either fading into insignificance themselves or causing the foods to do so. Great wine is a great pleasure, but it won't do for workday wear. Great wine doesn't serve any better as a day-in, day-out commodity than any other precious substance does. It's best saved for special occasions, when it can be served with all the appropriate panoply and fanfare and savored accordingly.

Don't leap to the opposite conclusion, however. Just because we don't want magnificent wine every day doesn't mean we want plonk. Between the two extremes lies an abundance of very good wine that may not stop your heart with its grandeur but won't stop your credit with its cost either. (See Intermezzo, p. 79.) What you want to develop for yourself is a group of reliable wines that please you and that match well with the kinds of meals you regularly prepare. You can accomplish that, after you've thought a bit more about what in the food you're trying to match with what in the wine, by the onerous expedient of buying a few sampler bottles of wines that fall within your perimeters of style and price, tasting them with your meals, and—this is crucial—jotting down their names, vintages, and a few words about what you liked or disliked about the way they interacted with your food. *This you must do.* The road to continued enological ignorance is paved with forgotten wines. We can talk about this in theory until we're both exhausted, but there is no substitute for your own empirical knowledge. That means you have to taste new dishes and try new wines and pay attention to them as you're doing it. We're all lazy, and we don't like to hear this, but in anything you do, pleasure flows from knowledge. The more you know, the more you can enjoy—so eat and drink analytically and take a few notes. This is not work; it's pleasure. And it requires neither Michael Broadbent's wine palate nor Julia Child's culinary expertise, just attention.

What you ought to be paying attention to are the most obvious and perceptible qualities of the tastes and the textures of your foods and the qualities in wines that harmonize with them. We've talked about these already in pursuing our examples of beef, chicken, and flounder: the strength or intensity of the flavor, its kind (meat-sweet or shellfish-sweet or bland or acidic like sauerkraut or spicy like pizza), the feel of the dish (moist or dry, soft or chewy). Corresponding elements in wines include the overall intensity of the wine's flavor plus such particular flavor characteristics as sweetness, saltiness, dryness, and acidity, and such textural effects as smoothness or asperity, lightness or heaviness—all very directly and usually unmistakably perceptible qualities.

These characteristics affect the way a wine and a food interact, and the more of them you are knowledgeably able to take into consideration, the more sophisticated and shrewd your pairings will be. But at bottom, most of your choices can be made on the basis of a very simple working formula. Two fundamental pairs of components of the main dish provide the base factors that a wine will have to deal with if it is to be genuinely compatible with that food: (1) the nature and intensity of the dish's flavor and (2) the ratio of fats to acid in the dish. These two packets of data provide most of the information you'll ever need to choose a wine intelligently. They serve very nicely as the shortcut that enables you to decide most of the food and wine harmonies or counterpoints you'll ever have to deal with.

Tasting for those qualities in your main dish is equivalent to component tasting a wine, except that tasting a wine is usually an end in itself, whereas component tasting a food is a preliminary step. (By the way, you don't have to actually premake or remake the dish every time to do this. Memory and imagination work perfectly well instead, especially with everyday foods that you know well.) What you discover in your food is going to point you toward the components you want in your wine. For example:

- An assertively flavored main course will need a strongly flavored wine to match it.
- A dish with a moderate amount of fat and relatively low acidity will probably take very well to a full-bodied, low-acid wine if you're dealing with whites (and you should be if it's a delicately flavored dish) or a full-bodied and somewhat tannic wine if you're dealing with reds (as you should be if the dish is robust).
- A dish rich in fats—whether they come from oil or butter, cream or animal fats—might well respond beautifully to the counterpoint of a lean, acidic wine (if it's a white wine dish) or somewhat acidic, full-flavored wine (if it's a red wine dish).
- Foods that are in themselves acidic (whether from vinegar or lemons or tomatoes or any other source) always work with an acidic wine, though other characteristics of the wine will have to be judged according to the other qualities of the food.

None of this should come as a surprise, since it all flows logically from the principles outlined at the beginning of this chapter, and they in turn derive from simple experience and observation. The "rules" I've given you aren't rules at all. They're observation and experience codified, and unless our palates differ much more wildly than is usual, they should hold as true for you as they do for me. There are no mysteries about any of this, and there is no single "right" wine for any dish. The best possibilities for wine and food combinations happily depend on a relatively limited number of characteristics, but—even more happily—the number of wines available to match those characteristics is potentially immense.

(I don't want to puncture anybody's balloon, but there is a flip side to this marvelous abundance of good wines, and it's worth remembering. To wit: Attempts to re-create a single, perfect match, whether it be one remembered or one longed for, usually fall totally flat. The glamour of a specific dish and a specific wine depends crucially on the sympathetic magic of place and time and circumstance, even on the simple facts of our own alertness or tiredness, boredom or anxiety or excitement. Our palates are constantly changing, and we can perceive the same wine utterly differently at different times and in different circumstances. "From hour to hour we ripe and ripe . . . from hour to hour we rot and rot," as Touchstone says. So if you've been fortunate enough to experience one of those miracles of wine and food serendipity, treasure the memory fondly. Tell the story as often as you like, to as many people as you can find to hear it. But don't destroy the magic by trying to do it again.)

Caveat 'Emptor

Let me enter an important reminder here: The analysis I've been making throughout this chapter, the conclusions I've been presenting are logical (I hope), but they are not exclusive and they are not rigid. Eating fish or fowl doesn't require you to drink white wine if you don't want to any more than eating hamburgers requires you to drink red. For everyday uses "drink what you like" is the only absolute rule. If you love white Zinfandel, which I regard as the public shaming of a fine red grape, an abomination of the same order as stovetop stuffings, instant mashed potatoes, nonmilk "dairy products," and "hot dogs" made of chicken lips, by all means go ahead and degrade your palate and drink it. If you love red wine but are dieting—as, at any given moment, probably half the adults in America are—and eating only skinless chicken breasts and broiled fish with lemon, you don't have to kiss your favorite potation good-bye. Far from it. Personal preference always and everywhere overrides all the wine "rules." Heaven forfend that you should have to give up red wine. You don't need the scourge of a diet—or the to-my-mind equally dreadful scourge of nouvelle cuisine—to license your drinking red wine with fish. Most red wines are far more palatally interesting than the vast majority of white wines, and a preference for red under any circumstances needs no apology, at least not as far as I am concerned. White wine makes a very fine beverage, but red is what wine is about.

A Short List of Wines for Every Day

Most weekday and even weekend family cooking is going to be fairly simple and straightforward in style, so its most satisfactory wine pairings are going to be themselves relatively simple and straightforward—wines that will complement and not challenge the direct flavors of the best home cooking. Happily, wines of this sort abound, and they usually have the extra advantage of being the most inexpensive wines around. Collectors may not be interested in such wines, but then most collectors rarely drink the wines they collect, so their opinion hardly matters.

The short list that follows offers many thoroughly enjoyable choices, from Anjou rosé through to Zinfandel. This list is not meant to be—could not be—exhaustive: It can only function as a starting point for your own palatal exploration.

Prices

A word about price is also in order here. I have tried to designate kinds of wines that normally retail at modest prices. The key terms are "normally" and "modest." Modest for Chardonnay and Cabernet can be, and often is, expensive for Chenin Blanc and Zinfandel. And the normally low price of an Italian Soave, for instance, can take a sharp jump upward when the lira strengthens against the dollar.

Remember too, with regard to price, that the wineries and brands that appear in the following lists are present because they all produce *some* simple, inexpensive, and satisfying wines. Even though a brand name or an importer's name may appear in these lists, that does not mean that every item bearing that name is going to be inexpensive—*so shop attentively*. Wine labels can be very confusing, and bottles that seem to be almost identical can differ dramatically in price.

California wineries, for example, market many variations on their basic varietal wines, and you will sometimes find a single, not-very-large producer turning out, in ascending order of price, a California Chardonnay, a North Coast Chardonnay, a Napa Chardonnay, a Chardonnay from a named single vineyard, and an older vintage reserve or proprietor's reserve Chardonnay from the same vineyard. That progression can very easily walk you from an unstressful $5 or $6 bottle to a serious $25 or $35 bottle.

With imported wines, you can travel a similar upward path with, for instance, a shipper's Bordeaux Rouge, its Médoc, its Margaux, and so on through all five classified levels of individual Margaux châteaux right up to the fabled Château Margaux itself—and that is a progression that can carry you from the comfortable $5 level up to $75 to $100 for a decent vintage of Château Margaux. So I repeat: *Shop attentively*.

One last word: Where these lists name no makers or shippers for a particular kind of wine, that means that while inexpensive bottles are available, they are not in steady supply from any one firm, so you may have to hunt a bit for them. All wines in these lists, unless otherwise noted, are fully dry. Where the country or region of origin is not part of the wine's name, it is indicated in parentheses.

Lighter-Bodied White Wines

Chardonnay (Italy): Bollini; Collavini; EnoFriulia; Favonio; Maso Poli; Tiefenbrunner

Chenin Blanc (California), very few totally dry: Alexander Valley; Almaden; Burgess; Callaway; Concannon; Dry Creek; Fetzer; Gallo; Guenoc; Hacienda; Martini; Robert Mondavi; Monterey Vineyard; Parducci; J. Pedroncelli; Preston; San Martin; Sebastiani; Simi; Souverain

Frascati and the related **Colli Albani, Castelli Romani,** and **Marino** (Italy): Fontana Candida; Fontana di Papa; Gotto d'Oro; Principe Pallavicini; Villa Banfi

French Colombard (California), often lightly sweet: Almaden; Chalone (Gavilan); Gallo

Muscadet (France): B & G; Barré Fréres; Martin Fréres; Monmousseau; Remy Pannier; Sauvion & Fils

Orvieto (Italy), some bottles *abboccato,* that is, lightly sweet: Antinori; Barberani; Bigi; Cotti; Decugnano; Le Velette, Petrurbani; Vaselli

Pinot Bianco (Italy): Favonio; Fini; Fontanafredda; Pighin; Russiz Superiore

Pinot Grigio (Italy): Bollini; Cavit; Collavini; Duca Badoglio; EnoFriulia; Fini; Molino delle Streghe; Pighin

Riesling (California), with varying degrees of sweetness and dryness: Almaden; Callaway; Chateau Ste. Michelle (Washington); Fetzer; Gallo; Jekel; Konocti; Martini; Monterey Vineyard; J. Pedroncelli; Round Hill; San Martin

Riesling (Germany), most bottlings off-dry: Deinhard; Hallgarten;

Kendermann; Langenbach; Loeb; Muller; Sichel; Zimmermann-Graef

Rioja whites (Spain): Bodegas Olarra; CUNE; Federico Paternina; Gran Condal; Marques de Riscal

Sauvignon (Italy): Angoris; Collavini; Duca Badoglio; EnoFriulia; La Delizia; Molino delle Streghe; Pighin

Soave and the related **Lugana** and **Bianco di Custozza** (Italy): Anselmi; Bertani; Bolla; Guerrieri-Rizzardi; Masi; Montresor; Pieropan; Santa Sofia; Tommasi; Visconti; Zenato

Trebbiano d'Abruzzo: Casal Thaulero; Duchi di Castellucchio; Illuminati

Tuscan white wines, including **Bianco della Lega, Bianco Pisano, Bianco Vergine della Valdichiana, Galestro; Montecarlo, Val d'Arbia,** and **Vernaccia:** Brolio; Falchini; Frescobaldi; Guicciardini-Strozzi; Pietrafitta; Pietraserena; La Quercia; Ruffino; Serristori; Strozzi; Teso

Verdicchio (Italy): Fazi-Battaglia, Garofoli; Ronchi; Villa Pigna

Vouvray (France), as dry as possible: B & G; Duplessis-Mornay; Remy Pannier

Proprietary and **jug** wines from California: Almaden; Buena Vista Chaarblanc and Spiceling; Callaway Vin Blanc; Christian Brothers Premium White; Gallo; Geyser Peak's Sonoma Vintage White; Gundlach-Bundschu Sonoma White; Haywood Linguini White; Robert Mondavi White; Monterey Vineyards Classic White; Pat Paulsen Refrigerator White; Trefethen Eschol White

Fuller-Bodied White Wines

Bordeaux Blanc and shipper's **Graves:** B & G; Chevalier de Védrines; Dourthé Fréres (Grande Marque); Ginestet; La Cour Pavillion; Maitre d'Estournel; Yvon Mau (Prestige); Mouton Cadet; Oliver de France; Alfred Schyler Fils; Sichel

Chablis and **white Burgundy** (France), the least expensive bottlings available, including **Mâcon, Mâcon Villages,** and **St-Veran:** Bouchard Père & Fils (Valbon); B & G; Chauvenet; Joseph Drouhin (Laforet); Jadot; Latour; Prosper Maufoux; Moreau; Pic; Rodet

Chardonnay (California), the least expensive bottlings available: Almaden; Bandiera; Caymus Liberty School; Columbia Crest; Corbett Canyon; Fetzer; Fisher Vineyards Everyday Chardonnay; Gallo; Geyser Peak; Giumarra; Glen Ellen; Hogue Cellars; Konocti; La Belle; Louis Martini; Paul Masson; C. K. Mondavi; Monterey Vineyards; Parducci; J. Pedroncelli; River Oaks; Round Hill Cellars; San Martin; Sebastiani; Seghesio; Weibel; Wente Brothers

Côtes-du-Rhône (France): Chapoutier; Delas' St-Esprit; Guigal; Jaboulet

Gewürztraminer (Alsace): Aussay; Beyer; Dopff; Dopff & Irion; Hugel; Josmeyer; Lorentz; Muré; Schlumberger; Sparr; Trimbach; Willm

Gewürztraminer (California): Almaden; Fetzer; Gallo; Hacienda; Paul Masson; Monterey Vineyard; J. Pedroncelli; Round Hill; Ste. Chapelle; St. Francis; Sebastiani

Lacryma Christi Bianco (Italy): Mastroberardino

Pinot Blanc (Alsace): same producers as for Gewürztraminer

Pinot Blanc (California): Fetzer; Jekel; Mirassou White Burgundy; R. H. Phillips; Roudon-Smith

Pinot Gris, also called **Tokay d'Alsace** (Alsace): same producers as Gewürztraminer

Pouilly-Fumé and **Sancerre** (France): irregular supply of inexpensive bottlings

Sauvignon Blanc (California: note that **Fumé Blanc** is the same wine): Almaden; Bandiera; Beringer; Callaway; Caymus; Christian Brothers; Corbett Canyon; Fetzer; Foppiano; Franciscan; Gallo; Geyser Peak; Glen Ellen; Guenoc; Inglenook; La Belle; Martini; Mirassou; North Coast Cellars; Parducci; Preston; Round Hill; San Martin; Sebastiani; Souverain; Wente Brothers

Sylvaner (Alsace): same producers as Pinot Blanc

Tocai (Italy): Collavini; Duca Badoglio; EnoFriulia

Lighter-Bodied Red Wines

Barbera (California): Louis Martini; Montevina

Barbera (Italy): Bersano; Ceretto; Contratto; Dessilani; Duca d'Asti; Einaudi; Fontanafredda; Pio Cesare; Renato Ratti; Vietti

Bardolino (Italy): Anselmi; Bertani; Bolla; Guerrieri-Rizzardi; Masi; Montresor; Santa Sofia; Zenato

Beaujolais (France), all types: B & G; Bouchard; Duboeuf; Drouhin; Sylvain Fessy; Jadot; Latour; Marquisat; Mommessin; Sarrau; Louis Tête

Chianti (Italy), young, non-Riserva bottlings: Antinori's Santa Cristina; Berardenga; Boscarelli; Brolio; Capezzana; Castello d'Albola; Castello di Ama; Castello di Nipozzano; Castello di San Polo in Rosso; Castello di Volpaia; Fossi; Il Poggiolo; Nozzole; Ruffino; Selvapiana; Villa Banfi; Villa Cafaggio; Villa Cusona

Gamay and **Gamay Beaujolais** (California): Almaden; Buena Vista; J. Lohr; Mirassou

Loire reds (France), such as **Bourgueil, Chinon,** and **Saumur-Champigny:** irregular supply of inexpensive bottlings

Pinot Noir (California), the least expensive bottlings: Almaden; Beaulieu; Burgess; Clos du Bois; Geyser Peak; Inglenook; Charles Krug; Louis Martini; Monterey Vineyard; Parducci; Sebastiani

Rioja (Spain), young, non-Reserva bottlings: Berberana, Campo Viejo; Domecq (Privilegio del Rey Sancho); Gran Condal; Marqués de Cáceres; Montecillo (Cumbrero); Santiago (Yago)

Valpolicella (Italy): Allegrini; Bertani; Bolla; Guerrieri-Rizzardi; Le Ragose; Masi; Montresor; Quintarelli; Santa Sophia; Tommasi; Zenato

Zinfandel (California), the young "Beaujolais"-style wines: Almaden; Bandiera; Benziger Family Winery; Buena Vista; Fetzer; Gallo; Guenoc; Charles Krug; Louis Martini; Paul Masson; Mirassou; Montevina; J. Pedroncelli; Round Hill Cellars; Rutherford Ranch Brand; Santa Barbara Winery; Sebastiani; Seghesio; Simi; Sutter Home; Wente Brothers

Full-Bodied Red Wines

Bordeaux Rouge or **Médoc** or **St-Emilion** (France): B & G; Chevalier de Védrines; La Cour Pavillon; Maître d'Estournel; Mouton Cadet; Oliver de France; Alfred Schyler Fils; Sichel

Burgundy (France), the least expensive bottles from shippers and *négociants*: Bouchard's Valbon; Cuvée Latour; Drouhin's Laforet Rouge

Côtes-du-Rhône: B & G; Bouchard; Chapoutier; Delas; Guigal; Jaboulet; Jadot; Latour

Cabernet (Italy), usually a mixture of Cabernet Sauvignon and Cabernet Franc: Angoris; Bollini; Cavit; Collavini; Duca Badoglio; EnoFriulia; Favonio; Molino delle Streghe; Pighin; Torresella

Cabernet Sauvignon (California), the inexpensive bottlings: Almaden; Beringer Napa Ridge; Christian Brothers; Clos du Bois River Oaks; Fetzer; Gallo; Glen Ellen; Hawk Crest; Inglenook; J. Lohr; Louis Martini; C. K. Mondavi (Charles Krug); Wente Brothers

Dolcetto (Italy): Bersano; Ceretto; Cogno; Conterno; Fontanafredda; Bruno Giacosa; Marchesi di Gresy; Mascarello; Oddero; Pio Cesare; Prunotto; Vietti

Lacryma Christi Rosso (Italy): Mastroberardino

Montepulciano d'Abruzzo: Casal Thaulero; Rosso della Quercia; Duchi di Castelluccio; Illuminati

Penedès reds (Spain): René Barbier; Jean Léon; Torres

Rioja (Spain): Bodegas Ellauri; Bodegas Olarra; CUNE; Federico

Paternina; Gran Condal; Marqués de Cáceres; Marqués de Murrieta; Marqués de Riscal; Montecillo; Muga; Pedro Domecq Privilegio del Rey Sancho; Viña Tondonia

Zinfandel (California), the medium-weight, "claret" style: many of the same producers as listed for Beaujolais-style Zinfandel

Proprietary and **jug** wines: Christian Brothers Premium California Red; Clos du Bois Vin Rouge; Foppiano Riverside Farm Premium Red; Gallo Hearty Burgundy; Glen Ellen Proprietor's Reserve Red; Gundlach-Bundschu Sonoma Red; Haywood Spaghetti Red; Inglenook Napa Valley Red; Kenwood Vintage Table Red; Robert Mondavi Red; Monterey Vineyards Classic Red; Raymond Vineyard Vintage Select Red; Trefethen Eschol Red; Trentadue Old Patch Red

PART II

Wines for Special Dinners

CHAPTER 4

The Occasion

There is no boon in life more sweet, I say, than when a summer joy
holds all the realm, and banqueters sit listening to a harper in a great
hall, by rows of tables heaped with bread and roast meat, while a
steward goes to dip up wine and brim your cups again. Here is the
flower of life, it seems to me!

     —HOMER, *The Odyssey,* IX. 5–11,
     translated by Robert Fitzgerald

T HE CROWN JEWEL of home entertaining is the dinner party. In
Europe, where manners remain more formal than here, an invitation to dinner in a person's home (rather than at a restaurant,
which is much more customary) really seals a friendship. It almost
approximates adoption into the family. Even here in more casual
America, an invitation to dinner is much more meaningful than a
summons to any other sort of fete. For most of the human species,
this has been so from the beginning of civilized existence: Witness
Homer's celebration of "the flower of life."

Of course, a few differences have crept in since then. Nowadays
minstrels tend to be in fairly short supply, and for cementing

friendships we tend to favor dinner parties made up of a small group of our closest acquaintances rather than a great hall full of banqueters. But we can easily counterbalance the shortage of minstrels and banquet halls with the abundance and variety of the food and drink we can set before our guests. That very abundance, of course, amounts to a true embarrassment of riches for many people and leads them through all the stages of preparty jitters and the classic have-I-made-the-right-choices vacillations and indecisions. About your guests—whether you've chosen the right ones, whether they'll have anything to say to one another—I can obviously tell you nothing. I can't even recommend a good minstrel. But about your food and wine, and how to match them well enough to approach Homer's "flower of life"—there I have a lot to tell you.

Preliminary Decisions: Goal Setting Before Place Setting

A small amount of systematic thinking beforehand about your dinner party will go a long way toward easing your hostly strain. Long before the wine starts flowing there are a few conscious decisions—strategic decisions—you ought to make about the food and wine you're going to serve.

First and foremost, have you defined to yourself the gastronomic goals of your dinner? That is, beyond whatever person or occasion may be the reason for your giving this dinner, have you considered the rationale of what is, after all, going to be the evening's main activity? Palatally speaking, what do you want to accomplish? Do you have a recipe so marvelous that the food is going to be the highlight of your occasion or a wine so wonderful that it should be the star? Or will you give them equal billing? You can assign emphases at your dinners any way you please, but if you're serving a fine and delicate old wine—say, should you be so blessed, a 1945 Romanée-Conti—you won't want to blow it away with a lamb chop coated with three different-colored peppercorns and awash in a soy and vinegar reduction. By the same token, when you're lucky enough to lay your hands on some real game rather than the usual farm-bred pap, you'll want a wine to play up to those vibrant flavors, not one that is going to cringe in the bottom of the glass and do an imitation of water. So the first strategic decision you have to make is about your own priorities in the dinner: whether the components will share the spotlight equally or whether one of them, be it food or wine, is going to be the star. If the latter, then the other component should be chosen to complement, not to compete; to show off its partner, not itself. This may seem obvious, but it needs to be said because it is too often forgotten.

The second strategic decision you need to make is almost a corollary to the first, and it's just as crucial: Determine in advance the level of opulence you're aiming for. Most of your thinking about this will rightly be generated by your assessment of the nature of the occasion and the sophistication of the participants and the states of your cellar and your finances. The degree to which your dinner will aggrandize or underplay or exactly match the grandeur or ordinariness of the occasion is, clearly, a very personal decision, but it's one that you would do well to make consciously rather than leave to habit or happenstance. As the con men and politicians so cynically but so acutely put it, suit the shearing to the sheep. Without question, wine shared is wine multiplied many times over in pleasure, but it is also true that a great wine wasted on someone who would rather be drinking cola or iced tea is a stab in the heart to a true enophile. The same appropriateness should govern the choice of food. If the guests (who are invited for their pleasure, not so you can show off) are not palatally sophisticated enough or adventurous enough to relish your favorite dishes of *cervelles au beurre noir* or *scungilli alla marinara*, don't force the issue. Make something simpler or less threatening, and gnaw your brains in private.

COMPLEMENT OR COUNTERPOINT?

Whatever level of opulence you opt for, and whether you choose to give the food and the wine equal weight or to make one of them the focal point of the dinner, your final strategic decision is vitally important. Do you want to pair your wine and food so that they complement each other or would you rather have them counterpoint each other? This is the point at which the overall strategy of the occasion starts to inform and direct the tactical choices of particular wines.

There is an aspect of what I'm suggesting here that needs to be stressed, because it is an idea that even wine professionals often lose sight of: Your options about the relation of your wine to your food are always multiple. There is never a situation in which there is only one right wine for any meal, or a single workable wine for a particular dish. You always have the option of making the wine the star or the supporting player, and that means at least two sorts of wine are possibilities. And whether the wine is star or supporting player, you always have the option of making it complement or counterpoint the food, and that's two more possibilities.

Say for instance that you've not only baked a good, earthy, country-cured ham, but you've made it elegant as well by dressing it with a fine *sauce moutarde* or *sauce au poivre vert*. What's the right wine for that dish? What sort of wine should you be looking for here? Let me suggest three very different choices to you, which will produce three very different effects.

- You can complement the food with a fruity, soft Merlot or St-Emilion. A wine like that will play under the saltiness of the ham and the tang of the sauces and support the flavors of the dish. It will be very enjoyable drinking, but it won't call a lot of attention to itself—unless, of course, you serve a very grand Merlot-based wine, such as one of the great Pomerol châteaux. So even within the broad category of complementarity, you have the further options of modest or grand.
- You could alternatively arrange an interesting counterpoint by serving a spicy, dry Gewürztraminer (preferably a nice steely one from Alsace), whose acidity would challenge the meat and its sauce and throw their flavors into sharp contrast. Here too you retain the further option of selecting a wine either modest or grand, that is, one whose quality is sufficiently fine to complete the contrast and continue to call

attention to that showpiece ham, or a wine of quality high enough—a *grand cru* perhaps, or even a Vendange Tardive —not only to contrast with the earthiness of the ham but also to become at least costar of the dinner with it.

- Or, on the third hand, you could choose a claret-style Zinfandel or a mature Chianti Classico Riserva or Rioja Reserva. Both the sharp, berry character and tannin of the Zinfandel and the tannin and acidity of the Chianti and Rioja, along with their soft fruit, offer the possibility of combining something of the attacks of both the Merlot and the Gewürztraminer in a single glass.

No one of these wines is *the* right wine with this dinner, and all of them are the very opposite of wrong. Which of them you choose is entirely up to you: It depends only on what you want to achieve in the dinner as a whole. All these wines would make good matches with that ham and all will work very satisfactorily with either of its sauces. The right wine for this dish, whether it be complement or contrast, is the wine that's right for your palate and does what you want it to do for your dinner. A memorable dinner need not— probably should not—be composed entirely of superlatives, no more than any of us could really very happily sustain a life lived at a peak of any other sensation. More, alas, is all too frequently less.

Just to clarify, here is a list of the preliminary decisions you'll want to make about your projected three-star dinner.

- Define your gastronomic goals. Do you want to

     _____highlight the food?

     _____highlight the wine?

     _____give the food and wine equal importance?

- Define your level of opulence in terms of

     _____the nature of the occasion.

     _____the sophistication of the participants.

     _____the limits of your resources.

- Decide whether you want your food and wine to complement or counterpoint each other.

Those first two points are relatively easy. All you really have to do is remember them. The third is trickier, because it involves your weighing the specific characteristics of individual dishes and wines. A few more examples of the sorts of choices it requires would probably be helpful here.

Let's consider some rich meat dishes, those with relatively high proportions of butter, oil, marrow, or animal gelatins and fats. We'll include both common and uncommon meats—dishes like steak *à la moelle* and *tripes à la mode de Caen, ossobuco alla milanese* and duck feet Szechuan style—because one of the lessons we've got to absorb is that it is the nature of the dish—its characteristics of acidity or unctuosity, mildness or intensity, and so on— and not the ordinariness or exoticness of its ingredients that guides your wine choices.

- Unctuous preparations like these can be highlighted— turned into the stars of the occasion—by serving as their complement a fat, round, high-glycerine, high-extract wine that will buttress their flavors and especially their texture. A full-bodied but not especially fruity Chardonnay would come closest to filling the bill (though it in all likelihood would not succeed with that steak *à la moelle* because the steak's own robust flavor would totally overshadow even a big white wine).
- These unctuous meats can be made to share the spotlight by equally complementary but more tannic—and therefore more assertive—soft, reasonably full-bodied red wines like a California Merlot, a St-Emilion or a Loire red, or an Italian Cabernet or Merlot (from Friuli especially).
- Finally, these same dishes could be counterpointed—harmoniously contrasted, if you prefer paradoxes—by harder, tannic red wines with a lot of very distinctive character and flavor of their own—for instance, a fine Médoc, a California Cabernet or top-flight Zinfandel, a Barolo or a Barbaresco.

In this case the wines would definitely steal the show. The only choice for a wine to counterpoint the dishes that wouldn't usurp center stage from them would be a big, full-flavored, acidic white—some California Sauvignons, for instance, or an Alsace Pinot Blanc or Gewürztraminer, or a Friulian Tocai—but such white wines wouldn't work with the steak *à la moelle* any more readily than the Chardonnay would.

Three of the meats I've chosen for examples here—tripe, veal shanks, duck feet—though somewhat uncommon, are nevertheless relatively bland in themselves, both as to taste and texture; therefore, the options for all three relationships of food and wine are workable. But because beef has distinctive and quite assertive taste and texture characteristics of its own, only the two red wine options really work well with the steak *à la moelle,* though the Chardonnay just might be interesting enough with the marrow to warrant the experiment. I think, however, that experience will quickly show that the strong flavors of the final red wine choices (the Médoc or Cabernet or Barolo) will serve best for maximizing both the steak and its dressing without losing any of the dimensions of the wine: Their strength, lean muscularity, and tannic intensity will provide a complement to the meat at the same time that they counterpoint the richness of the marrow—a "twofer," in effect, that the softer red wines of the second option can't offer.

COROLLARIES AND COMPLICATIONS

The principles at work in all these examples are only extensions of the basic principles outlined in Chapter One. Nothing really changes. The guidelines hold just as true for duck feet—or frogs or snails or sea slugs—as they do for hamburger or chicken breasts or any other food. As we move out of the realm of everyday dinners and into more exalted, or at any rate more complicated, kingdoms of gastronomy, the nature and the complexity of the problems we encounter alter only in the respect that spicing and style of preparation have a greater effect on the final flavor of the dish than they tend to in everyday cooking.

For example, as we advance, say, from the simple roast beef of our first chapters, with no spices more exotic than salt and pepper, to something like the late Raymond Oliver's Congolese pepper steak (a signature dish of his Grand Vefour restaurant: a slice of beef filet, sautéed, and then sauced with cream and green pepper-corns) or to an elaborate haute cuisine concoction like *tournedos Rossini* (a beef filet with foie gras and truffles and a richly com-posed sauce) or, in a completely different flavor spectrum, to *bis-tecca pizzaiola* (thin slices of beef sautéed in olive oil and seethed briefly in a spicy, tomato-based sauce), we present ourselves with three separate kinds of problem. In each of these cases different components in the dish affect the flavor of the beef and modify the dominant palatal sensations the beef presents.

Our first task then, in scanning for possible wine pairings, is to determine how far from the basic beef and wine compatibilities the differing preparations skew each dish. With strongly flavored in-gredients like beef, the condiments, seasonings, and other ingre-dients in differing preparations *may* sometimes indicate differing wines to match with them, but nine times out of ten the individual wines will still fall well within the guidelines of the classes or kinds of wine you would normally consider with beef. In the case of mildly flavored ingredients like pork or veal, and especially with fish and shellfish, the condiments, seasonings, or other ingredients can often add up to the dominant factors in the dish. They will furnish the characteristic that is going to point to the kind of wine you want with the dish, and sometimes they can skew the dish so strongly as to wrench it right out of the whole class of wines that you would otherwise consider drinking with it. The more mark-edly and intensely flavored the base ingredient, the less likely this is to happen, but even with a strong base meat like beef, a particular set of seasonings may dramatically alter the whole dish's flavor profile.

The most useful things to remember, however, are the guidelines we gave you back in Chapter One: The simplest form of a dish establishes its basic wine compatibilities, and these are usually only refined, not altered or replaced, by elaborations of the dish's mode of presentation. Subgeneralization one: This is almost always true with strongly flavored meats or basic ingredients. Subgeneralization two: Preparations for mildly flavored meats or basic ingredients, especially those combined with strongly flavored condiments, are more likely to provide exceptions to this rule of thumb.

Despite the possibilities of exception, these stand as some of the most fundamental guidelines for pairing wines and foods. No matter how complex the preparation of the dish becomes, the basic compatibilities suggested by its main ingredient are your points of departure, the ground from which you should begin thinking about the wines you might want to drink with it. Most of them will still satisfy most of the time. What the greater complexity of the food's preparation introduces into our simple guidelines is the slightly more complicated consideration of the degree of satisfaction that a wine compatible with the base ingredient will give in these modified circumstances. Zinfandel tastes fine with roast beef, and Zinfandel will continue to taste fine with *bistecca pizzaiola*. Chianti, however, which also tastes just fine with roast beef, will taste even better with that *bistecca*, not because both are Italian, but because the Chianti's relatively higher acidity will enable it to mesh more harmoniously with the natural acidity of the tomato-based sauce. That same tomato acidity will in all probability not harmonize really well with the tannic acerbity of a Cabernet. Because of this, it and Cabernet-based wines generally will taste a bit too harsh for most people's palates alongside this particular dish.

Such considerations lead us back yet again to one of our basic operating principles: component-to-component matching. Component-to-component matching is the key to the more complex pairings just as it is to the simplest. Remember too that not every component of the dish or every element of the wine has to be taken into consideration. In most cases one or two dominant elements will cast the deciding votes.

Component tasting is the basis of everything we have done and will do in this book. Even within the overly simplified context of the "red wine with meat, white wine with fish" guideline from which we began, component tasting plays an important role. That *bistecca pizzaiola* I just mentioned illustrates very nicely both the validity of the fundamental guidelines I'm suggesting to you and some of their limitations. *Bistecca pizzaiola* is a beef dish, but it's also a tomato dish; the sauce is at least as important as the meat. And the meat may be rich and fat in that honorable sense we talked about before (and Italians increase the fat of their lean beef by preparing this dish with olive oil), but it is also, in the Italian tradition, a small portion of meat served with an assertive, acidic sauce that dramatically changes the usual balance of components in beef dishes—so much so, that it almost (but not quite) makes this over into a white meat dish. The tomato acidity looms so large here that it becomes a—almost the—major determinant of the kind of wine called for. Because of this you could successfully pair a full-flavored white wine (like a white Lacryma Christi, for instance) with this dish, since most white wines have sufficient acidity to respond very happily to the tomato sauce. For my palate that would not be the best match for the dish by a very wide margin— an acidic red wine would taste much, much better—but it would work. Neither the wine nor the entrée would seem displeasing.

By contrast, the sauces of the *tournedos Rossini* and the Congolese pepper steak do not alter the essential nature of the beef as the tomato does, despite the fact that both of these are by any objective standards strongly flavored and in fact lush preparations. *Tournedos Rossini* essentially employs a sauce based on meat stock (reinforced, of course, with the incredible richness of the slice of foie gras that the recipe demands). Congolese pepper steak, despite the presence of those mouth-warming green peppercorns, only laves its beef filet in a sauce based on cream (itself, of course, rich with butterfats). Nothing in either preparation does anything to alter the essential sweetness or fatness of the beef itself. In fact, if anything, both preparations emphasize these qualities. Essentially both recipes add fat to fat and thereby reinforce rather than challenge the basic beef and wine compatibilities. Hence almost any big, dry, full-flavored red wine will drink very pleasingly with either of these dishes.

Some dishes, because of their components, will respond well in complement or contrast to radically different sorts of wine. Sweet-breads, for instance, possess a wonderfully smooth texture and a rich, succulent, though still essentially mild flavor. These charac-teristics remain constants however they are prepared, whether they are sautéed or poached *à blanc*, whether served with a lemon-flavored cream sauce or with a raspberry vinegar pan reduction. Simply sautéed or poached, the sweetbreads will partner very pret-tily with a fruity, not-too-aggressive, young red wine. A Chinon or Saumur-Champigny from the Loire, for instance, or a Dolcetto from the Italian Piedmont, especially a lighter-bodied, higher-acid specimen, like Renato Ratti's bottlings, would work splendidly in emphasizing the meat's lushness. Served with the sweetbreads in either of the two acidic sauces, these same wines would make a marked and very pleasing counterpoint to the food. Another case: Simply cooked, the sweetbreads will counterpoint quite pleasingly with an acidic, dry white wine of distinctive character. California Fumé Blanc or French Pouilly-Fumé would be perfect in this role, and the same two wines would just as happily complement the sweetbreads served with either of the two sauces mentioned above.

Similarly, those above-mentioned duck feet, tripe, and veal shanks, whose complementary wines we discussed a few pages ago, could also be very pleasantly counterpointed with an acidic white wine. The duck feet, because of their ginger-and-chili spic-ing, would respond best to a wine with some fruit and flavor of its own, something like a Pinot Grigio or an Italian Chardonnay. The *tripes à la mode de Caen* and the *ossobuco*, because of the substan-tial acidity of their preparations, would answer best to a muscular white like a Gavi or Pomino or a very full-bodied Fumé Blanc or Pouilly-Fumé. These are the kinds of options you ought to think about as part of the overall game plan of any elaborate dinner. Once you've made your three primary decisions about the overall strategy of your dinner, you're ready to start using these sorts of guidelines to work through the specific choices involved in your particular wine and food pairings.

* * *

Plain Food, Fancy Wine

Here's an example of what I mean. In Chapter Three I suggested a range of red wines for a simple roast beef dinner: Bordeaux Rouge, Cabernet, Chianti, Côtes-du-Rhône, Rioja, Zinfandel. Let's say we want to elevate the occasion but leave the roast beef and its honest baked-potato-and-peas accompaniments alone. After all, there's nothing shabby about a good roast beef. Rather, we'll raise the level of the dinner by changing our wines. Consider the following slate of candidates:

Chapoutier Crozes-Hermitage (Rhône) 1985
Château Gloria (St-Julien) 1979
Conn Creek Cabernet (Napa) 1984
Ridge Geyserville Zinfandel (Sonoma) 1985
Villa Selvapiana Chianti Riserva (Rùfina) 1983

Which of these could we drink with that roast beef? Any of them. Each of these five wines belongs to one of the broad kinds I originally suggested (I've omitted a Rioja from this second list). Each in fact represents a few steps up in quality—and expense, alas!—from the simpler, broader categories of the earlier list. And each wine suggested here would bring to the meal the same qualities—albeit at a higher, more refined, and more acute level— that the simpler wines provide.

- The Crozes-Hermitage from Chapoutier (a *négociant,* wine-maker, and shipper, and a good one) is a wine from a specific area of the northern Rhône and bears the appellation of its primary village.
- Château Gloria is an unclassified red Bordeaux (because it didn't exist in 1855) from the esteemed commune of St-Julien, which lies right alongside the more famous Margaux appellation.

- Conn Creek is the name of an important vineyard and winery on the Silverado Trail in California's prized Napa Valley.
- Ridge is another California winery, one of the most prestigious, and its Geyserville Zinfandel is a fine example of the claret style (i.e., balanced and long aging) of California Zinfandel.
- Finally, Villa Selvapiana is an estate in Tuscany's Chianti Rufina zone (east and slightly north of Florence), famous for the quality and longevity of its wines.

These are all first-rate wines, quite capable by themselves of lifting a plain meal out of the ordinary, and any of them would taste fine with our hardworking roast beef. But life is never that simple. In any real meal, we can't have all these wines. We've got to choose one. Which one do we pick, and why?

That makes the problem a whole lot tougher. We can't turn to obvious differences in quality as a deciding factor, because these wines are all of excellent quality. If you had a personal favorite, that might determine the issue for you, but then again, you might very well want to take the opportunity for a change of flavors. If you were in a restaurant, price might be the determining factor, in which case you might spend the rest of your life dithering between the Crozes-Hermitage and the Villa Selvapiana, caught in an endless loop of deciding which of these two wines offered the greater value for dollar.

We've reached a point, with this sort of choice, where our earlier guidelines no longer provide all the answers. We've got a whole cluster of good wines, any one of which would pleasurably accompany our meal. To choose the best wine for our dinner in circumstances like these, we've got to take into consideration another factor that we haven't yet spoken of at any great length: vintage.

WISDOM, AGE, AND GRACE

When everything else is equal, vintage can and should be the deciding factor, and unless you know that a particular wine in a particular vintage tastes spectacularly good (and therefore moves automatically to the top of your list) or spectacularly bad (and therefore automatically drops off your list), vintage probably shouldn't even enter your mind until this point. Once the question of vintage has been raised, however, make sure you deal with both important aspects of it: quality *and* maturity. Far, far too often (especially in restaurants) people order wine on the basis of vintage quality—or what they have heard about vintage quality—alone: "Ooh, this wine got a 98 and that one only got a 93!" "The 1985 vintage in Bordeaux is rated 20 and the 1979 only 17. We'll have the '85." That would make sense of a sort—presuming your palate corresponded precisely with that of the rater—if the wines were mature. But to drink a great wine too young, when it is utterly unready to show any of the character that has earned it (more accurately, will earn it) its high rating, is simply wasting wine and money. In all probability, with wines of the class and character we're discussing here, all you'll taste is tannin.

In this group of wines, all come from fine vintages, superb in some cases. Perhaps the least estimable wine of them all, considered purely from the point of view of vintage quality, is the 1979 Château Gloria. It is also, in my opinion, the one wine of the group you ought to drink with your roast beef, because it is the only mature wine in this whole lot. All the others are babies still (at the time of this writing, 1989). If you want to commit infanticide, you clearly have a lot of fellow child molesters to keep you company. Most red wines of better quality are drunk far too young, both in this country and around the world. Conventional wisdom—i.e., the opinion of those who have the most to gain by selling wine young, restaurateurs and wine sellers, at various levels of the trade—holds that this is so because American palates, modern palates, prefer the taste of young wine. I can't help wondering if it isn't also because so few Americans have ever had the opportunity to taste a really mature fine red wine. My own experience tells me that a liking for mature wine is a classic instance of an acquired taste, but one that rewards the small effort necessary to acquire it. A young wine, no matter how exalted its provenance or how fantastic its vintage, essentially offers you just one attraction: fresh fruit. It shares that with even the humblest red wines of equal youth. A mature red wine, however, even one of humble vintage, has become a whole other creature, whose attractions are a multiplicity of flavors, a complexity and depth of taste, a balance and interest that no young wine can approach.

That 1979 Château Gloria offers an excellent example of what I'm talking about. The 1979 vintage in Bordeaux got lost in the ballyhoo of the greater '78s. Most 20-point scales give 1979 a rating of 16 or 17, which is by no means contemptible, but not the grand-slam home run that everybody saw in the '78s. But lesser vintages mature more quickly than great, hard vintages like '78, and consequently they come ready to drink much sooner. The 1978 Bordeaux may not achieve full drinkability until the turn of the century, if then. The 1979s, on the other hand, have been providing pleasurable drinking for a few years now. Most people, of course, and most restaurants, used up all their 1979 claret years ago, before it was ready. But right now, a 1979 Château Gloria can show, on a slightly reduced scale, what mature claret of a great year is all about. So as much as I love all those other wines, I'll wait for them to ripen, thank you, and drink now the wine that is ready.

That Château Gloria '79 is a very fine wine, as the other four will also be in time. So fine will they be, in fact, that in all probability any one of them served at its maturity would steal the spotlight from our simple roast beef. That doesn't mean you will enjoy the beef less, only that you will enjoy the wine more. Each of these wines possesses more complexity than the meat it's accompanying, and complexity constitutes one of the great attractions of wine just as it does of cuisine.

Complex Wines, Complex Choices

In wines complexity derives from many sources. Sometimes it comes directly from the nature of the grape: Chardonnay, for instance, although it can be made into a simple wine—human beings are unfortunately ingenious—seems almost always ready and willing to make an interesting wine, no matter where it's grown. Sometimes complexity comes from the soil: California's Napa Valley, France's Côte d'Or, Piedmont's Langhe hills. Sometimes it's human intervention that does the trick: the way pleasant and forgettable Valpolicella is metamorphosed into powerful and memorable Amarone, or the ways sherry and port are cajoled into existence. However complexity is created in wines, it always means that the wine literally presents more of everything to your palate: more flavors, more individual elements of taste and texture and style. Once you are past the stage of simply relishing without distinction the pleasingness of a wine's fruit flavors, complexity becomes one of the key elements that distinguishes the best wine from the better, the better from the merely good.

Complexity, however, can make a wine dominate a meal. If you wish to savor a fine wine—to let the wine have the star turn—then drink it with a simply prepared meal. For exactly that reason, a mature bottle of any of the wines I listed—Château Gloria, Chapoutier Crozes-Hermitage, Conn Creek Cabernet, Ridge Geyserville Zinfandel, Villa Selvapiana Chianti Riserva—would show beautifully with a roast beef. The beef too will taste fine; it just won't get the lion's share of your palate's attention. When you put a complexly flavored food and a complexly flavored wine together, then you have the acme of one kind of dining pleasure.

To achieve that, you will have to make some difficult choices, based on some subtle distinctions. Just as a for instance, let's only slightly complicate the situation we were describing above. Let's exchange our roast beef for a leg of lamb, carefully flavored with garlic and rosemary, rubbed with olive oil and salt and pepper, roasted medium rare and basted while it was cooking with a little red wine: a classic *gigot*, the very essence of the French bourgeoisie's idea of a meal you'd ask a person to. Which of the following wines could we choose to serve with that *gigot*?

Château Fortia Châteauneuf-du-Pape 1985
Gundlach-Bundschu Merlot 1981
Parducci Petite Sirah 1978
Prunotto Barbaresco Montestefano 1971
Viña Tondonia Rioja Reserva 1970

This list presents some interesting and subtle problems. In theory any single one of these wines should taste just fine with a *gigot*. They are all big red wines, all totally dry, all with forceful—not to say aggressive—flavors, all with plenty of tannin. Beyond that, however, the resemblances stop. Despite all the apparent points of similarity, each of these wines differs quite markedly from the others—so much so, in fact, that in a blind tasting even wine novices could quite easily tell them apart, though they might not be able to name them.

BELOW THE DRINKING AGE

We're certainly dealing here with a level of wine that demands that we consider vintage prominently as a factor in making our choice. And beyond that, we've got to weigh very carefully the character of the individual wines. It's not going to be useful simply to think in terms of full-bodied red wine or tannic red wine or full-bodied white or acidic white, because wines have multiplex ways of being full bodied and tannic and acid. To appreciate just how much not-very-common ground can be covered by a single common noun, only consider, for instance, how differently strong tannins taste and feel in a Petite Syrah and in a Châteauneuf, or how differently the palate senses the kind and strength of the acidity in a Rioja and a Barbaresco. The same descriptor can be and is applied to wines so distinctly different from one another that only a chemist could be fooled into thinking them at all alike.

This means then that although in theory all five wines on that short list would work well with our *gigot,* in practice some would perform markedly better than others, for reasons that include their vintage—its quality and maturity—as well as their nature, the way they achieve their peculiar complexity—the precise character of their tannins and acids and fruit and extract, the exact personality those components add up to.

There is one wine here, for instance, that in practice definitely would not taste good with the *gigot* or with anything else for at least a few years yet: the 1985 Château Fortia Châteauneuf-du-Pape. Despite the fact that, as the sole French wine on the list, Château Fortia comes closest to being a wine that our French-accented *gigot* evolved with, it is simply not yet drinkable. In this case vintage maturity—rather, total immaturity—makes the difference. Hard, hard tannins, a sensation not unlike biting into a sturdily crafted oak table, is what you'd taste if you took a mouthful of this wine now. True, it has fruit in abundance, as well as plenty of extract, and good, supple acid too. But for the time being a superabundance of tannin masks everything else. All Châteauneuf-du-Papes qualify as big wines that need a long time to come around, and Château Fortia, which still vinifies the old-fashioned way (long fermentation with lots of skin contact, lots of time in wood), makes one of the biggest, slowest maturing of them all.

As I hope I've made clear by now, I much prefer the almost pruney fruit of older wines and their marvelous overlay of deeper, nearly sinister flavors—leather and pepper and tar and truffle—powerful flavors that for some people may take some time to get used to. We've been operating for a while now in an area where following my wine recommendations is going to cost you a bit of money, so I think it's only fair to let you know all the biases that shape my judgments. Briefly then; I vastly prefer:

- any wine to no wine at all
- red wine to white wine
- big wines to small wines
- mature wines to young wines
- wines with complexity to wines with fruit
- wines with character to wines with charm

If I had my druthers—an endless purse, a lifetime supply of antihistamines, and a liver of steel—I'd drink nothing but wines vinified long and slow, with lots of contact between the skins and the musts—old Pauillacs and St-Estèphes, old Côte Rôtie, Hermitage, Cornas, and Châteauneuf-du-Pape, old Amarone and Barolo and Barbaresco and Taurasi, old Zinfandel and Cabernet, old Riojas, even some old Burgundies. After drinking all these old wines, I'd take for my dessert some ancient (and preferably dry) Madeira or oloroso sherry or Vin Santo, and I would be very, very happy. If these are your preferences too, then you'll have little or no problem with any outrageous suggestion I may make. If they are not, keep my biases in mind and weigh as carefully as you can the differences of our palates.

That digression translates thus: With terrific reluctance, I will put aside my natural fondness for Châteauneuf-du-Pape and reserve this bottle of Château Fortia '85 to celebrate the turn of the century. (It's closing in fast, folks, and it is definitely not too soon to lay down wines for the big event.)

The next-youngest wine on this list, the Gundlach-Bundschu Merlot '81, also wouldn't be my first choice with the *gigot*, although Gundlach-Bundschu Merlot is a wine I normally very much enjoy. The reason here, however, is not age but the personality of the wine. Merlot yields a softer wine than Cabernet. Sometimes people think it lacks the character to stand on its own (but it makes up 100 percent of Château Pétrus, so good-bye to that theory). In some parts of California and for some vintners, it pretty consistently produces a very interesting wine that is less tannic and more initially accessible than Cabernet, with a plummy, spicy, cedar-accented flavor and a capacity for some aging. Bottles from Gundlach-Bundschu's Sonoma vineyards usually stand right near the top level of Merlot quality, and their 1981 was no exception. It is just about at perfect drinking age right now (and will be for the next five years), and the only reason I'm choosing other wines before it is because of the *gigot:* The wine is a little bit too soft to make a perfect match with that garlicked and rosemaryed meat. Generally, I find Merlot matches better with simply prepared beef than with lamb, though it does complement stews and braises beautifully. California Merlots with a small admixture of Cabernet (which gives them an extra shot of tannin) or Merlots from regions where wines develop higher acidity than they do in California would in all probability show better with lamb. New York, especially Long Island, and Italy both produce Merlots with enough fruit-and-acid complexity to be worth keeping track of as potentially very pleasing partners to dishes like this—as, of course, does almost every château in St-Emilion and Pomerol.

I won't choose the next youngest wine on the list either, but for the opposite reason: I think that the 1978 Parducci Petite Sirah is too overpowering for the lamb. Drinking that Petite Sirah with our *gigot* would be equivalent to drowning the meat in a sea of bitter chocolate. For the record, California's Petite Sirah is not the same grape as Syrah, the principal grape of the northern Rhône appellations. The probably misnamed California variety, however, does seem to derive from another Rhône grape variety, the Durif. In France this grape is mostly used as a rather unimportant filler, but in California it makes a huge wine, albeit sometimes a clumsy one. The best specimens are always hard, tannic, and unlikable when young, although even then they have an intriguing peppery aroma. The latter intensifies as the wines age and soften a bit, and their flavor opens to an unlikely but pleasing potpourri of black pepper and tobacco and leather and often, as in the case of this now-mature Parducci bottling, intense unsweet chocolate. Petite Sirah wants to take on your most aggressively flavored foods, whether the flavors come from the main ingredients—it's a great wine for game and cheeses (even mild ones, oddly enough)—or from the spices. Petite Sirah handles an all-out attack better than it deals with subtlety. It will simply smother intricate spicing, but cooperate handsomely with, for example, a strongly garlicked dish or a very peppery one. It likes good, smoky barbecue too, but it's just a touch too cumbersome for our *gigot*. (In case you're thinking that its distinctly chocolate tones might make it a good companion to chocolate desserts, forget it. All that happens is that the two chocolates cancel each other out and both the wine and the dessert wind up tasting blah.)

EITHER/OR

That leaves us with two wines to choose between: a 100 percent varietal, the Prunotto Barbaresco Montestefano 1971, and a very complex blend, the Viña Tondonia Rioja Reserva 1970. For me that's a coin toss. Otherwise I'd die of thirst while I vacillated between these two gorgeous wines, either of which would partner admirably with our leg of lamb.

Both have the kind of complexity of flavor needed to respond to the lamb and call out its best. The Barbaresco gets that complexity right from the Nebbiolo grape, a varietal that belongs to the upper strata of wine nobility. The Rioja achieves its complexity from the combination of four different varieties that go into it, no one of which seems particularly notable in isolation, but all of which work together beautifully. Both wines have the depth of flavor to match the lamb's own character, and both derive that from the same source: long aging in wood to intensify the natural flavors of the grapes. Finally, but perhaps most important, both have the ability to penetrate the layers of flavors and fats the lamb leaves in the mouth and to cleanse and refresh the palate. The Barbaresco accomplishes this primarily by means of its plentiful tannins (though it also possesses a nice acid balance), while the Rioja does the same thing primarily by virtue of its acidity (though it possesses a goodly amount of tannin).

And vintage doesn't clarify the issue here at all. The 1971 harvest in the Piedmont and the 1970 in Rioja were both excellent, and the two traditionally minded wineries, the Italian Prunotto and the Spanish Bodegas López de Heredia, took full advantage of them. Qualitatively, these are very comparable wines, both now nearing complete maturity. They will perform in very similar— and very admirable—ways with our *gigot*.

In this instance, if we absolutely had to choose between these two wines, we would have to turn to other components of the meal to help us reach our decision. That means taking into account what was being served with the lamb and the wines that were being served with preceding or following courses. If the lamb's vegetable accompaniments incline toward sweetness—if, for instance, we were doing something clever with carrots—the Barbaresco would be the better choice, because the acidity of the Rioja and the vegetal sweetness of the carrots could easily war. The reverse also holds: an acidic vegetable accompaniment—asparagus, for example— would in all likelihood prompt us to choose the Rioja, since its own acidity would enable it to respond better to the vegetable. This amounts to a one-further-remove refinement on our procedures for mating wines and foods. Nothing substantial changes in the process of component matching except our focus: We are looking for and at the same matchable elements, but in a different place. We went as far as we could with the components of the main dish, to the point where its elements could give us no reason to prefer the Rioja to the Barbaresco or vice versa. At that juncture we simply opened our eyes a little wider and took a bit more of the meal into account. That's all you'll ever have to do to get yourself through any seeming wine and food impasse.

A Useful Formula

Let me give you here a very simple schema to help you focus your attention on the important aspects of the meal. By providing a quick method of categorizing the basic nature of your food, this formula helps you direct your thinking to the elements that will determine the appropriate class of wines to serve with the dishes you're preparing. It simply divides foods into the following admittedly reductive but useful groups:

- simply cooked and sauced meats (grills, roasts, broils, the basic pan sauces or gravies)
- complexly sauced meats (ragouts or stews of all sorts, the classic French sauces, the new vinegar-fruit sauces, Oriental spicings)
- fowl cooked simply or sauced complexly
- fish cooked simply or sauced complexly

These four points cover the conventional categories of main course food: fish, flesh, and fowl. Each category is regarded in a binary fashion: Either it appears in a simple preparation or it appears in a complex preparation—the three horizontal divisions of fish, flesh, and fowl intersected by the two vertical divisions of simple preparations versus complex preparations. If it's useful to you, you can streamline this paradigm even further for your own use by reducing it to a pair of pure either/ors: Instead of fish, flesh, and fowl, think in terms of mildly flavored base or strongly flavored base, simply prepared or complexly prepared. This makes a basic four-box grid within which you can locate the kind of meal you're preparing. Whichever way you are most comfortable thinking about your meals, the grid will fulfill the same useful purpose, which is to serve as a jiffy locater of the point where the food's components and the wine's components will have to mesh.

In action, either the six-box grid or the four-box grid works simply and quickly. For example, you take ten seconds to realize consciously that the main dish you're preparing features a strongly flavored base, simply prepared, which shows that the character of the base ingredient will have to be the major determinant in selecting a wine. The same is true with a mildly flavored base, simply prepared. There too the character of the base ingredient will provide the most important clues to the wine you want to drink with it. With a mildly flavored base and a complex preparation, on the other hand, you will want to focus a good deal, if not most, of your attention on the exact character of the preparation. That, in all likelihood, will determine your choice of wine. A strongly flavored base ingredient prepared in a complex manner presents the only complications, because there you will have to pay attention to all the components of the dish. It will be the composite character they create that will provide you with the guidelines for selecting your wine.

All this amounts to no more than a preliminary winnowing of possibilities. This formula should look very much like a cruder version of the fats/acid, condiment/base paradigm we talked about in the last chapter, because that's exactly what it is. With the kind of everyday meals we were talking about in Chapter One, where you are choosing a single wine that is for all practical purposes geared to your main course or your main dish, you don't ever need to bother using this grid. When it becomes useful is in planning an elaborate dinner, when you are coping with multiple courses and multiple wines. There this simple grid functions one step earlier in your thinking than the fats/acid, condiment/base paradigm to give you a very quick fix on the problems at hand by showing roughly the broad kinds of wine each course will call for. It helps you identify the aspects of the meal that you're going to have to think more precisely about in order to choose compatible wines.

After you've found your focus by this means, then you'll go on to utilize the fats/acid, condiment/base analysis to make your specific wine choices. The "simple" preparations (I'm putting the word in quotation marks because some "simple" dishes can be quite exquisite, like steak *à la moelle*, or *boeuf à la ficelle*, while some complex preparations result in wonderful but very straightforward food, like *boeuf en daube* or *tripes à la mode de Caen*) will be the most accommodating to the greatest variety of wines.

For almost everything that falls into the category of simple preparations you can use all the classes and kinds of wines suggested for everyday dining *or* any of the finer wines suggested for the more sophisticated or expensive dishes (see the next chapter). Indeed, because of that broad receptivity, those simple preparations furnish ideal opportunities for you to try out new wines and to explore different kinds and degrees of wine and food compatibility. Simple preparations will interact quite well with many wines, but the differing ways they interact—the different components of the wines and the food that each new combination emphasizes—can provide you with an abundance of clues about your own palate and preferences *and* about what sorts of wines will match well with more complex dishes that share some of the same components. Very complex dishes, by the mere fact of their complexity, usually narrow the range of wines that can be pleasingly matched with them. A satisfactory choice for them is usually so specific to them that it teaches you almost nothing about the chosen wine's utility with other foods or about the possibility of other wines with this food. The simpler foods are the great instructors in the broad principles of wine and food partnerships.

Multiplying the Loaves and Fishes

Bear in mind, however, that several key elements in a dinner change fundamentally when we make the transition from everyday dining to extraordinary dinners. We move—or at least we should move—from plain good cooking to cuisine, and that means we enter the realm of *style,* where dishes and courses and whole meals have an individual personality and a distinctive flavor and, perhaps, an ethnic or regional character as well. Even if we stay within the precincts of sound home cooking, we are producing for our guests our concentrated best, and the format in which we present it changes importantly. We move from a single large course, preceded usually by a small appetizer or nothing at all and followed only by a simple dessert, to a proliferation of courses, any or all of which could legitimately be made important in quantity or quality. And we move—or at least we should move—from a single kind or bottle of wine drunk through the whole meal to multiple kinds and multiple bottles of wine to accompany these multiple courses. A very different situation, creating a very different set of challenges.

By the time you've determined the goals of your dinner and the level of opulence you're aiming for, you will probably have in mind a handful of dishes that would work as your main course. From there, planning the rest of the meal to lead up to and away from that main course is relatively easy. Choosing the wines to accompany as many courses as you're planning to have can also be made quite manageable.

First, how many bottles? That may depend on the number of courses, the number of guests, the state of your cellar, the state of your finances, or the happy or unhappy conjunction of all four. A decent rule of thumb about wine consumption during a long dinner suggests a bottle of wine per person, and in my experience that works out about right (except for wine writers, when it is grossly insufficient). So if you are going to be four at table to four courses, that works out nicely to four bottles of wine and allows you, if you wish, to serve a different wine with each course.

In the old days—say, thirty years ago—you would certainly have done that, progressing carefully from lighter wine to fuller, from younger to older, moving your palate to a carefully orchestrated crescendo with the best wine of the evening, a fine, fully mature red wine of good vintage, which you would have matched either with your entrée or, if your palate bends in the same direction as mine, with the cheese course. You will continue to follow a pattern like that still if you and your guests enjoy that much variety and that rather intense barrage of sensuous stimuli. Be wary, however: These are fearfully diet-conscious times, and an awful lot of people, not all of them painfully thin anorexics whose diet consists of one small can of water-packed tuna a week, will find such a dinner too overwhelming.

If you do serve multiple kinds of wine with your dinner, moving from the lighter ones to the fuller still provides the best and most enjoyable progression, for the simple reason that a full-bodied wine makes a succeeding lighter wine virtually impossible to taste and totally impossible to appreciate. This traditional sequence normally means white wines first and red wines after, but there are exceptions: Some great white wines—a handful of Burgundies and Rhônes, a few Italian and Spanish whites, some California Chardonnays—have enough body and more than enough flavor to hold their own even in the wake of many of the lighter red wines. For example, if the foods justified it, progressing from a young Chinon (red) to a mature Corton-Charlemagne (white) would make perfect palatal sense. So would moving from a fine but young Barbera to a four-year-old Vintage Tunina or a five- or six-year-old Pomino or Greco di Tufo or Fiano di Avellino, as would segueing from a young, new-style red Rioja (for example, Gran Condal) to a mature old-style white Rioja (Marqués de Murrieta, for instance, or Bodegas La Rioja Alta's Metropol Extra). Your own preferences may well suggest many more such just-as-enjoyable sequences that, despite their unconventional appearance, would still fall within the general guideline of proceeding from lighter wine to heavier.

Your criteria for selecting any individual wine depend directly on the kind of food the wine is meant to accompany and the position of the particular food in the dinner. A dish that wants a red wine may specifically want a light-bodied red if it comes early in the sequence of courses or a heavy-bodied red if it comes late. That final choice amounts to a refinement of the basic judgment you've got to make about the appropriate class of wines to serve with the dishes you're preparing.

Complex Dishes, Complex Choices

Complexly sauced dishes or dishes whose flavors are rendered complex by the inclusion of multiple, more-or-less equally important ingredients present the greatest challenges to precise wine matching. Indispensably, you must know how the dish actually tastes: whether one element predominates or whether it achieves a harmony of several, whether the flavors blend on your palate or whether they succeed one another, and—most crucially—how the dish as a single entity responds to the questions you ask of it. You have to be able to recognize the elements in the foods and wines that can be harmonized or pleasingly contrasted. Your experience with simpler dishes may give you an avenue of approach to these more intricate dishes, but at bottom there is no substitute for empirical knowledge. Unless you are a very good and very experienced cook, reading about béarnaise sauce won't give you the same information as actually tasting béarnaise sauce. This is even truer of wines: Reading about Vega Sicilia or Tokay Essencia will never convey the actual flavor of these wines. You can go a long way by extrapolating from your knowledge of simple foods and wines to making informed guesses about more complicated ones—this book is built on that premise—but nobody can successfully match totally unknown wines with totally unknown foods, except by astrology or blind luck. Such a situation isn't likely to arise at your own table, but anyone who has the good or ill fortune to be known to family and friends as "a wine expert" is sooner or later going to be called on to handle the wine choices in restaurants and other peoples' homes. If you find yourself in the position of having to choose a wine to accompany an unfamiliar dish, don't fly blind; ask what's in it, how it is prepared. If you're still in doubt, defer to your host or to the restaurant, both of whom ought to know something about what they serve (though in restaurants, alas, that is not always the case).

Everything you know about a dish becomes germane to choosing a wine to go with it. You should pull out the full battery of questions about wine taste and personality that we raised—some briefly, some more extensively—in the preceding chapter. Those questions are designed to guide your analysis of the flavor components and characteristics of the foods and wines you're dealing with, and now is the time to use them. In fact, now is the time to expand those questions and make them more particular, more exact.

First, I remind you yet again, you have to discern and describe to yourself the two fundamental pairs of components of the main dish in each course: the relation of fats to acid and of condiment (or seasonings) to base in the dish's overall impact. These two pairs of characteristics serve at every level of dining sophistication as the primary indicators of the sort of corresponding components you should be looking for in the taste of a wine—fullness or leanness, presence or lack of extract and alcohol, high or low acidity, the nature and intensity of the flavors. These constitute the most important elements in wines for you to consider in making your matches. Taste itself—the pure, physical sensation—is what counts here, not a chemical analysis of the actual fat content of a dish or the extract content of a wine or the acidity of either, all of which might differ dramatically from the way your tongue and brain perceive them.

Your procedure for the first few times you do this sort of analysis should be painstakingly methodical until you get the hang of it. Later you'll perform the whole sequence of steps automatically, without even thinking much about them. At the beginning, however, it pays to go slowly and make yourself aware of even the most minor element involved in coming to your decisions.

Initially you'll take the long view of the dish you're dealing with and ask basic questions about its overall character. Is it predominantly fatty or acidic? Don't worry about whether the fats are meat fats or dairy fats or vegetable oils; it's their impact in the taste of the dish you're concerned with. In the same way, it doesn't matter if a dish's acidity comes from citrus or vinegar or tomato; what matters is what it does to your mouth. What you're trying to determine is, simply, the basic flavor of the dish. Does its essential character, its defining characteristic(s), come from its condiments or from its base ingredient? Whichever is the case, just what is that character—spicy hot? spicy warm? sweet? meat-sweet or vegetable-sweet or nut-sweet? or just plain sugar-sweet? assertive? mild? Is the base ingredient intensely flavored? bland? warm? cool? soft? crisp? chewy? fleshy? oily? creamy? moist? dry? smooth and homogeneous? textured? lumpy? silky? abrasive? prickly? light? heavy? Does it feel in the mouth (with apologies to Lévi-Strauss) raw—succulent and fleshy like beef tartare or tuna sashimi—or cooked—a drier sensation on the palate, a warmer, more composed flavor? With most vegetables, of course, the situation is reversed. The raw forms are the drier and firmer, the cooked the moister and "fleshier."

Most of the descriptors in the paragraph above—and they are all common characteristics of food—also serve at least metaphorically and in most cases literally to characterize the sensations that wines produce. Speaking technically, sweet, sour, salt, acid, and their interactions sum up all we can really taste in anything. Everything we experience in our mouths is reducible to these four elements, plus whatever we can add to them from the purely tactile stimuli of the textures of food and drink on the surface of the tongue. This is a very limited number of basic stimuli, but they are capable of producing almost endless permutations of sensation. This is why I am urging you to confront these sensations with such a tremendous battery of questions. It is also why that multitude of questions can be concentrated into a few usable formulas such as those I've already given you.

After all is said and done, the simple act of paying attention to what you eat and drink is the major effort you are really required to make. These descriptors are here to help you verbalize and come to understand what it is you're actually tasting, and thereby make your wine choices. The characteristics to which this series of questions calls your attention directly affect the way a wine and a food will interact, and the more of them you're aware of, the apter and more pleasing your wine and food pairings will be. Above all, keep the fundamental working formula in mind: Think in terms of the ratio of fats to acid and the proportionate importance of the flavor of the base ingredient to the flavor of the seasonings—fats/acid, condiment/base. Everything else flows from there.

Back to Basics

So unless you're planning to build your dinner entirely around the wines so as to show them off to best advantage, the bedrock of all your hostly decisions is this: What sort of food are you going to serve?

Time was, there were only two answers to that question. First and most common, Standard American Cooking Gussied Up for Guests (a.k.a. *arroz con pollo*), which, according to the host's economic circumstances, might have included anything from gelatin salads with little marshmallows in them (who could forget those little marshmallows?) to one of the great roasts. Second and indispensably, for any occasion that pretended to the slightest degree of importance or style, classic French haute cuisine, or the closest approximation to it one could achieve (at least half the time this translated into beef Wellington). Anything else was unthinkable. And in either case the answer to the parallel question about what kind of wine to serve would have been—had to be—French. Until Lyndon Johnson proclaimed, sometime in the late sixties, that henceforth American wines were to be served in the White House, California had no cachet. Until the skyrocketing costs of French wine in the mid-seventies moved American consumers to explore other options, Italian and Spanish wines had only marginal presence on American tables.

Consumer consciousness of wine and the market availability of both domestic and foreign wines have expanded enormously since then. The eighties have seen even tiny mom-and-pop liquor stores offering wines from all over the world and from every part of the United States. In major metropolitan areas a not-very-exhaustive search of the shelves of larger wine shops can now turn up domestic wines from California, Washington, Oregon, Idaho, New York, New Jersey, Texas, and Virginia (closer looking can find many more states represented) and imports from France, Germany, Italy, Spain, Portugal, Austria, Hungary, Greece, Romania, Lebanon, South Africa, Australia, New Zealand, Argentina, Chile, and Mexico. There are no doubt others I've overlooked.

At the same time all these "new" wines were appearing in our shops, wave after wave of "new" cuisines were passing through our restaurants and home kitchens. Fad succeeded fad as quickly as the monthly glossy magazines and the now greatly expanded life-style sections of the daily and Sunday newspapers could write them up. In some cases the magazines and the newspapers created them, or at very least exaggerated them and their importance. In their recurring need to find some copy to wrap the ads around, the glossies and the papers with equal enthusiasm ballyhooed vaporous nothings and substantial cuisines alike: not just the skimpy, boring nouvelle cuisine and its unspeakable progeny of cuisine minceur and Spa Cuisine and the bastard *cuisine américaine*, but long-overdue discoveries such as the "other" cuisines of China (the wheel has come full circle, and Cantonese, America's original Chinese cooking, is once again fashionable) and Southeast Asia (Thai, Cambodian, Burmese, Indonesian), Japanese cooking (there is life beyond sushi), Indian cuisines (plural—there's much more to it than curry), the cooking of northern Italy (another land of plural cuisines, with many yet to be popularized here), the foods of Mexico, and, finally but not least significantly, the fascinating regional cuisines of the United States itself (for example, Tex-Mex, Cal-Mex, and most popular still, at the time of this writing, Creole-Cajun).

Even more exotic cuisines have put in at least token appearances. In New York, at the moment I write, you can dine on African cooking from Abyssinian to Zulu; Latin American cuisine from Argentine through Brazilian, Colombian, and Cuban to Vene-zuelan; and—just to pick some Yellow Pages headings—Arabian, Armenian, Greek, Israeli, Korean, Moroccan, Polish, Portuguese, Russian, Swedish, Swiss, Tibetan, Ukrainian, West Indian, and Yugoslav—not to mention kitchens specializing in vegetarian cooking, health food, seafood, macrobiotics, and dairy. I venture to guess that for each of these distinctive cuisines at least one cookbook (for some of them, obviously, far more than one) has appeared in the past ten years to make its tastes and techniques available to home cooks all over the United States. Today an up-to-date American host has all the world to choose from and almost too much culinary information to digest.

Confronted with problems relating to sophisticated wining and dining, Americans—those on the East Coast, at any rate—have traditionally turned to France for example and advice. But this doesn't work anymore. Neither the French nor any other Europeans can help us because, by and large, they have not yet arrived where we are. They have never experienced the wealth of differing, even competing, sensory and cultural stimuli that the United States offers. This may sound chauvinistic, but it is a statement of fact. The diversity of American cultures, culinary and otherwise, is a phenomenon totally outside most European experience and knowledge. The last time most Europeans had to deal with an influx of new peoples and ideas comparable to what citizens of the United States constantly confront was almost a thousand years ago, and they called it the Golden Horde and fought to keep it out. During all Europe's centuries of wars and political upheavals, European gastronomic cultures have developed in relative isolation and tranquillity. New data—like the potato and the tomato— were selectively and very gradually assimilated to produce a set of cuisines and accompanying wines that are quite internally complete and self-sufficient. Self-integrated, they do not blend well with outside ingredients, nor do they really accommodate well to altered circumstances.

This fosters in most European wine and food professionals an intense and totally sincere parochialism, an unconscious culinary chauvinism. I have seen wonderfully innocent demonstrations of this at all levels of the wine and food world. Italian winemakers from small towns in lesser enological areas, bottling their first-ever Chardonnay, proudly tell American journalists that their new wine is as good as Chablis, which they have never tasted. Seemingly much more worldly and knowing winemakers from Bordeaux insouciantly urge us to buy and drink their execrable 1977 and 1984 and 1987 vintages because, while they are not great vintages, they are useful to have while we are waiting for the great 1975 or 1978 or 1982 Bordeaux wines to mature—as if, like the Bordelais, we had nothing else to drink. Bordeaux, of course, has been selling fine wine to the world for hundreds of years. And Bordeaux, of course, scarcely ever buys a bottle from anywhere else, not even (especially not?) Burgundy. To drink anything but Bordeaux in Bordeaux is close to literally unthinkable. And it simply never occurs to the Bordelais that Americans have anything else to drink. The fact of the matter is that we have everything else to drink, and much of it at a lower price than those nasty bottles of '77 and '84 and '87, harvests that probably should have been declassified in the first place.

This is not meant to single out the French or the Italians for excoriation. These attitudes are typical of winemakers' notions everywhere. Only the names change as you move from place to place. Europeans, in my experience and speaking very generally, tend to be the most unrealistic about the American marketplace, but California winemakers are often capable of thinking the same way about New York, and vice versa. I target Europeans here only because we as a people are so used to turning to them for expert advice about food and wine. We continue to regard them as a main prop of our gastronomic thinking, while in the real here and now they have very little more to teach us. We poor Americans—poor little rich folk—are on our own now, gastronomically speaking. We're taste-bud trekkies, bravely venturing where no palates have gone before.

Unfortunately for us, we feel weighed down by what should free us, hampered by our very lack of history. We carry along all the impedimenta of our cultural insecurity, our residual fears (of the sort that induced the national nightmare of Prohibition) about the terrors of Demon Rum and his kin, our obsession with dieting, our addiction to all sorts of food quackery, our constant worry about health and healthy eating (with all the susceptibility to medical fads that leads us to), and our plain, old-fashioned gastronomic inexperience. We're dealing with all that, plus an assortment of solid and liquid culinary possibilities that might have overwhelmed the combined palates of Lucullus and Brillat-Savarin. No wonder we're confused: These are grand times.

CHAPTER 5

The Wines

Glass jars carefully sealed and coated were now brought in. Each bore this label: GENUINE FALERNIAN WINE GUARANTEED ONE HUNDRED YEARS OLD! BOTTLED IN THE CONSULSHIP OF OPIMIUS. While we were reading the labels, Trimalchio clapped his hands for attention. "Just think, friends, wine lasts longer than us poor suffering humans. So soak it up, it's the stuff of life."

—PETRONIUS, *The Satyricon*,
translated by William Arrowsmith

I HOLD THIS TRUTH to be self-evident: that wines never taste better than they do in the home. Whether you savor them as someone else's guest or revel in the host's double pleasures—you get to enjoy both the wines *and* your guests' enjoyment of them—wines taste the better for being shared, and they taste best of all when the sharing comes as part and parcel of a warmhearted offering of the best of yourself to people you care about.

The best of yourself may occasionally have to be a potluck dinner with your nearest and dearest, but most of the time it will mean a special occasion and a special effort, a party or a meal for which you will extend yourself, and this, almost invariably, will mean special foods and special wines: the best you can do in the kitchen combined with the best you can cull from your cellar. And this in turn, for all too many people, brings a replay of the old can-I-serve-this-wine-with-this-food blues.

The Beauty of Chauvinism

Moving from an everyday meal to a special dinner does in fact demand that you correspondingly enlarge the spectrum of your wine consciousness. The expansion of culinary range that is involved in the preparation of what is, after all, a feast rightly calls for equal specialness in the wines you'll drink with it. The wines you serve shouldn't be merely drinkable. They should possess flavor and character worthy of the foods you serve them with and the people you serve them to. Ideally, your wine ought to have as much—and perhaps the same sort of—style as your cuisine. If, for example, you were serving a sleek, nouvelle cuisine sort of dinner—translucent rounds of kiwi and medallions of veal *au vinaigre de framboise,* for instance—a traditionally made Barolo or a huge, seventies-style, blockbuster California Zinfandel would be utterly the wrong style of wine for that meal, whatever their virtues as wines. If you were preparing a classic paella Valenciana, with its wonderful medley of sweet shellfish and mild chicken, spicy sausage and sweet peas, all bound together by saffron rice, a great Pauillac, whatever its virtues as a wine, would be utterly the wrong style for that meal. Difficult as it may be in particular cases to pinpoint or define exactly the elements that compose a food's style, style remains nevertheless a crucial consideration for sophisticated wining and dining. A consistency of style between the foods and the wines usually produces the finest, most pleasurable food and wine harmonies. (The few exceptions are those moments of almost Zen sophistication when a single wine is deliberately chosen to violate the dominant style of the meal, the better to set off the exquisiteness of the other wine and food pairings: the flaw in the Navajo blanket, so to speak.)

In practice, you can often enough achieve consistency in style easily enough just by following through in your wine choices with the national or regional style of cooking you're using. There is a simple, down-home truism operating here whose beauty not enough people realize. *Most wines are going to show best and go best with the foods they grew up with.*

This is the useful element of the "exclusivity" and internal consistency of the various national cuisines. As a principle, it is no more or less binding than any of the other guidelines of our primary Decalogue-and-a-Half. It doesn't mean that if you're cooking a Lancashire hotpot you *must* seek out an English wine (there are a few) or drink cider or ale with the dish, nor does it require you, if you're preparing an elaborate Japanese feast, to drink sake and nothing but sake, any more than it demands that you *must* serve American Chardonnay with New England clam chowder. But, as a principle, it certainly does give you a very useful guideline for the occasions when you are working with cuisines that have already developed wine and food relationships. Even more usefully, it helps you by providing a starting place and some guidelines for considering the possible compatibilities of dishes and wines that derive from or resemble those of the wine-oriented cuisines—for example, dishes, like the rainbow of haute cuisine–*alta cucina* pizzas that now appear in upscale restaurants all over the United States, that draw as heavily on Mediterranean French cookery traditions as they do on Italian.

If you don't know anything else about matching foods and wines and achieving some sort of stylistic parity at a sophisticated level, this chauvinistic principle can serve both as your first clue and your final fail-safe. The traditional matchups may now not be the most interesting partnerships you could contrive, given the wealth of wine and food choices you have that the generations of cooks and vintners who shaped these traditions could never have envisioned. But these classic pairings will almost never disappoint you or your guests, and the partners to the matches—the particular dishes and wines you choose—will never, ever undo one another, as can sometimes happen with less tried-and-true marriages.

For example, a classic *gigot*—a leg of lamb roasted medium rare and seasoned with garlic and rosemary—has always matched beautifully with the red wines of the Médoc and will continue to do so until such time as lambs mutate into lobsters. A straightforward corollary of this fact is that leg of lamb will, without question, also therefore partner beautifully with Cabernets and Cabernet-Merlot blends from other parts of the world. So you're not forced to drink a lovely but certainly unready 1985 Château Brane-Cantenac if that's the only Médoc in your cellar. You can alternatively serve some of your eight- or ten-year-old Ridge Cabernet, for instance, or even the Mondavi-Rothschild Opus One, if you're pulling out all the economic stops, or you could try Angelo Gaja's Cabernet from the Italian Piedmont (lovely and Californian in style) if you're feeling experimental. (You can see that I credit you with either exquisite taste in your cellar or great good luck in your wine merchant.)

This essentially chauvinist (in the old nationalist sense, not the new sexist one) guideline or baseline will help you make wine selections for dinners that draw on the cuisines of countries that have developed their own wine repertoire. French, Italian, Spanish, Portuguese, and, to a somewhat lesser extent, German, Austrian, Greek, Hungarian, and Romanian cuisines all come with sets of long-established wine and food relationships. Knowledge of them is useful: These pairings still work. But you can extend your knowledge beyond such customary pairings as these national cuisines "authorize" by simply taking note of the principal elements involved in each wine and food pairing and extrapolating from them just as we did a few moments ago with the example of leg of lamb and Cabernet, and just as our primary Decalogue-and-a-Half's advice about component-to-component matching guides you.

You can, and of course should, go many steps further than that by using the principles we established in the first section of this book. Lamb, especially leg, is in its own right a strongly flavored meat, often with a slightly gamy sweetness, and garlic and rosemary further emphasize and strengthen this flavor. Cooked rare, it is moist, juicy, chewy—not a fork-tender meat like filet mignon, though a long way from tough. The strength of its own flavor demands an assertive wine, and the Cabernet grape provides that.

The tannic rasp of Médoc red wines, their strong, deeply grapey-pruney flavor (with odd, pleasing overtones, such as pepper), their full body—these elements enable the château wines of the Médoc to stand up to a meat like lamb and pair with it rather than submit to it. So wines possessing the same or comparable characteristics should do as well or better with the same or similar preparations of lamb or other strongly flavored meats. Knowing that much, all you have to do next is identify what other wines fit that description—and this is not one-tenth as tough as it may sound. To help you in your pursuit of culinary compatibility, here is a highly selective (necessarily so: completeness in this regard is impossible) presentation of some of Europe's best wines, with particular attention to their food affinities.

A Gazetteer of Wines by Region: Some Fine Wines and the Foods They Like

FRANCE

The best French wines have set the international standards for quality in wine and have, until recently, largely defined public expectations of what wine ought to be. Appropriately, then, this survey of fine wines begins where most connoisseurs' knowledge begins, and where, sadly, a too large proportion of it ends.

BORDEAUX

The red wines of the Médoc and Graves classically accompany red meats and game and strong cheeses—assertive flavors all, but essentially univocal ones. The wines themselves provide all the complexity that's needed. The red wines from the communes on the west bank of the Gironde—Graves, Margaux, St-Julien, Pauillac, St-Estèphe—contain predominantly Cabernet Sauvignon and Merlot grapes, with small admixtures of lesser varieties such as Cabernet

Franc, Malbec, and Petit Verdot. Of course there are variations in quality and characteristics from town to town and estate to estate: Pauillac wines tend to fuller body, for instance, and Margaux wines to greater softness. And of course a *premier cru* should most years give you a wine that is more exquisitely and definitively the essence of claret than a *petit château*. But overall, the red wines of the Médoc possess a marked family resemblance. The pronounced flavors of Cabernet and Merlot, plus a texture dominated by the tannic asperity of the Cabernet only somewhat ameliorated by the softness of the Merlot, are the traits that define the character of these wines and dictate their affinity, in great vintages, with what Europeans call the "noble meats"—the great roasts—and game.

In lighter vintages Médoc wines marry well even with delicate meats like veal if there is some element in the preparation with sufficient flavor or texture to act as their foil, as, for example, in a well-grilled veal chop—especially if cooked over a real wood fire—

RED BORDEAUX FOOD WHEEL

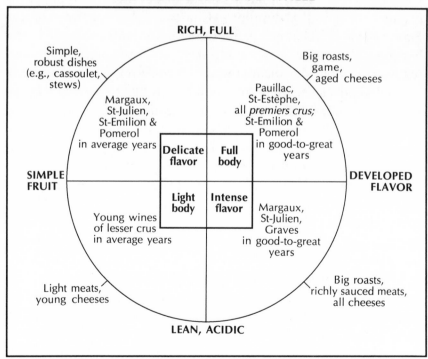

accompanied by sautéed wild mushrooms and garlic potatoes. But very light meats and young, mild cheeses will simply evaporate in the face of even middling-vintage Médocs, and the wines themselves will taste harsh or tannic or grassy, even weedy. These are wines that demand to be matched with a partner of some character and strength if they are to show their best.

St-Emilion and Pomerol make softer and fruitier and less tannic wines than does the Médoc. These wines from the fields east of the Gironde are vinified predominantly—in the case of the famous Château Pétrus, exclusively—from Merlot grapes. Though quite similar in basic flavor to Cabernet, Merlot's natural softness and more immediately pleasing fruit render the wines of St-Emilion and Pomerol more adaptable to a greater range of foods. Where the Médoc wines prefer plain meats or simply sauced dishes, St-Emilion and Pomerol will complement more composed dishes (especially if they contain a hint of sweetness) and less aggressive meats. Being less assertive in themselves, they can deal better with a variety or complexity of flavors in the dishes they accompany. For instance, a good St-Emilion—Château l'Arrosée or Château Figeac—will match much better than Médoc wines with the hearty but multiple country flavors of a dish like cassoulet. These wines really shine alongside dishes that are themselves soft and insinuating and almost sweet in texture and flavor, like the regional favorite *lamproie à la bordelaise*, in which the oily fish is poached in red wine along with leeks—a useful clue that St-Emilion and Pomerol have a so far underexploited role to play as supporters of many nouvelle cuisine fish-with-red-wine preparations. Young—and therefore still predominantly fruity—St-Emilion from a light vintage can be very pleasant drinking with as mildly flavored a dish as roast chicken, which most Médocs—even those from light vintages—would perhaps not utterly obliterate but certainly seriously obscure.

All these wines improve markedly with bottle age. They need time to develop their fullest character. The time it takes for Bordeaux reds to mature varies with every vintage. Inside the bottle the wine undergoes a series of dramatic changes that alter it from its original, simple, fruity state into a complex, many-layered, and many-flavored phenomenon. What this requires of the wine drinker is patience. The wine's ultimate maturity is reward enough for the benign neglect you invest: Mature claret is worth waiting for. (For a fuller treatment of the whole subject of bottle aging, see Chapter Eight.)

The Bordeaux area also produces a few notable white wines, dry ones from Graves and sweet ones from Sauternes and Barsac. At their best the Graves whites, vinified from a blend of Sauvignon Blanc and Sémillon grapes, offer a notable balance and elegance. As partners to food, they work best with dishes that exhibit similar qualities. Except in a purely supporting role, these are not wines to pair with very aggressively flavored recipes. In fact, their food-matching qualities are rather opposite those of their companion red wines: The whites interact best with complexly sauced dishes rather than with assertive single flavors. They will be lovely with a classic chicken fricassee, but they will fall on their faces with a heavily garlicked *poulet Marengo.*

Sauternes and Barsac, of course, stand among the greatest of the world's lusciously sweet dessert wines. In the classic cuisine, in addition to their secure place alongside sweets, they are also often served with foie gras or Roquefort cheese. With foie gras, as the start of a great dinner, they are extraordinary: Lushness calls out to lushness and is answered. There are few pleasurable palatal combinations of such concentration and intensity. I must admit, however, that I've never understood the charm of the Sauternes—blue cheese juxtaposition. For me, that never becomes a true union. The two components remain separate from each other, and none too friendly at that.

Selected Moderately Priced Bordeaux Wines
(italics indicates particularly good value for price)

Médoc Red by Commune

Graves: Château Carbonnieux, Château Haut-Bailly, Château Smith-Haut-Lafite

Margaux: *Château Boyd-Cantenac, Château Brane-Cantenac, Château Cantenac-Brown,* Château d'Angludet, Château Desmirail, *Château Giscours,* Château d'Issan, Château Kirwan, Château Lascombes, Marquis-de-Terme, Pavillon Rouge de Margaux, Prieuré-Lichine, *Château Rausan-Ségla,* Château Siran, Château du Tertre

St-Julien: *Château Beychevelle, Château Branaire-Ducru, Château Gloria, Château Langoa-Barton, Château Léoville-Barton, Château Talbot*

Pauillac: Château Batailly, *Château Grand-Puy-Ducasse,* Château Grand-Puy-Lacoste, *Château Haut-Bages-Libéral,* Château Haut-Batailley, Château Lynch-Bages, *Château Pontet-Canet*

St-Estèphe: Château Calon-Ségur, Château Haut-Marbuzet, *Château Lafon-Rochet, Château Meyney, Château Les Ormes-de-Pez, Château de Pez, Château Phélan-Ségur*

Other: Château Chasse-Spleen (Moulis), Château Clarke (Listrac), Château Fourcas-Hosten (Listrac), *Château Greysac* (Médoc), Château Larose-Trintaudon (Haut Médoc), *Château Potensac* (Médoc), Château Sociando-Mallet (Haut Médoc)

St-Emilion: *Château l'Angélus, Château l'Arrosée,* Château Beauséjour, Château Bélair, Château Canon, *Château Cap-de-Merle,* Clos des Jacobins, Couvent-des-Jacobins, *Château Larmande, Château Roudier, Château La Tour-Figeac,* Château Troplong-Mondot

Pomerol: Château Bel-Air, *Château Belle-Graves,* Clos du Clocher, *Château La Croix,* Château La Croix-de-Gay, Château Gazin, Château Petit-Village, *Château de Sales*

White Graves: Château Bouscaut, *Château Carbonnieux, Château La Louvière,* Château Olivier, Château Smith-Haut-Lafite

Sauternes and Barsac: *Château Doisy-Daene, Château Doisy-Védrines,* Château Filhot, Château Guiraud

Selected Bordeaux Wines for Extravagant Occasions

Médoc Red

Graves: Domaine de Chevalier, Château Haut-Brion, *Château La Mission-Haut-Brion, Château La Tour-Haut-Brion*

Margaux: Château Margaux, *Château Palmer*

St-Julien: *Château Ducru-Beaucaillou, Château Gruaud-Larose,* Château Léoville-Las-Cases, Château Léoville-Poyferré

Pauillac: Château Lafite-Rothschild, Château Latour, Château Mouton-Rothschild, *Château Pichon-Longueville, Comtesse-de-Lalande*

St-Estèphe: *Cos d'Estournel, Château Montrose*

St-Emilion: *Château Ausone,* Château Cheval-Blanc, Château Figeac

Pomerol: Château Certan-de-May, Château La Conseillante, Château l'Evangile, Château Lafleur, Château La Fleur-Pétrus, *Château Latour-à-Pomerol,* Château Pétrus, *Château Trotanoy,* Vieux-Château-Certan

White Graves: Domaine de Chevalier, Château Haut-Brion, Château Laville-Haut-Brion

Sauternes and Barsac: Château Climens, Château de Fargues, *Château Gilette, Château Raymond-Lafon, Château Rieussec,* Château Suduiraut, *Château d'Yquem*

BURGUNDY

It is hard to say anything about the wines of Burgundy, either of praise or blame, that hasn't already been said well and said often, so I will in fact say very little of them, and that little more in sorrow than in anger. Red Burgundy used to be the optimum choice of the whole French arsenal of wines to accompany elaborately sauced dishes. Its velvet texture and gentle, round flavor (and comparative lack of aggressive tannin) complemented cream sauces and wine reductions alike and could interact equally well with the assertive, univocal flavors of a great roast of beef and with the multiplex flavors of a coq au vin. White Burgundy from the Côte d'Or, deep-flavored and polished, matched wonderfully with almost any white meat, fowl, or fish presentation that didn't employ strong acids. Chablis—all flint and fruit, as they used to be—handled some of the more acidic dishes that the Côte d'Or whites left unpartnered.

Any of these wines in its finest manifestation—a carefully made wine from a *grand cru* vineyard of modest yield in a rare truly great vintage—once offered (and still would, were those conditions met again) a marvelous drink. But it's important to remember, amid all the rhetoric and puffery of Burgundy, amid the evocations of Saintsbury and of Napoleonic generals saluting famous vineyards, that Burgundy is neither nectar nor viaticum: It was once a very great wine, and always costly; now it is all too frequently a very ordinary wine at a staggering price. For a long time now, there has been no such thing as a good buy in Burgundy. The best consumer advice I can give you, in fact, is to bid good-bye to Burgundy. You are not losing much. Even when you pay every penny that the wildest dreams of avarice demand, you get for your money a wine that is only a shadow of the Burgundies of legend. Year by year, as Burgundy prices have escalated from joke to absurdity to farce to a whole new dimension of preposterousness, the wine has dwindled to a distant echo of its former greatness. *C'est la vie.* Save your money for wines that return more value for dollar.

The wines of Burgundy, red and white alike, are far and away the most expensive group of fine wines in international circulation. The supply of any one of them is chronically short. Their reputations are perennially high—in the case of the wines of the Domaine de la Romanée-Conti, exalted. Because there are many village appellations, hundreds of growers and *négociants,* and thousands of labels, no other group of wines presents so concentrated and at the same time so diverse a problem of value-for-dollar as the Burgundies.

Are they worth the prices they command? By and large, no. Wines that retail for above three digits a bottle at their release, such as Romanée-Conti, should not be merely good. They should make your hair stand on end. The much-vaunted 1985 vintage of these wines hasn't ravished my soul. It's good, not great, wine. More important in wines of this elevated price and reputation, they don't seem to promise much for long-term development (i.e., beyond ten years). A proportionate lack of worth reigns through most of the Burgundy price spectrum. This is, of course, one man's opinion. We all form our judgments of value in wine by a very elastic set of measures that use different scales for the depth of our purses, the height of the pleasure the wine confers, and the breadth of the ego its possession may serve.

Admittedly, when Burgundies are at their best, they are match-lessly elegant, velvety wines. Ask some wine lovers to name the best, the most memorable, wine they've ever drunk, and the odds are the great majority will name a red Burgundy. Press them further, and almost all will confess that they have since drunk innumerable indifferent-to-bad bottles of Burgundy seeking to recapture that remembered glory. Burgundies have not consistently been at their best for a great while now. Even those much-ballyhooed '85s are not consistent in quality, though they are in price.

On top of that, there is a widespread and apparently accurate impression that Burgundies simply do not taste as good in the United States as they do in Europe. Some people have wondered whether they are the same wines—that is, whether a different vat selection is shipped here from what is sold in Europe. I don't think that's the case, though it is true that many Burgundies sold here have been filtered, whereas the same wines sold in Europe usually are not. Nevertheless, most of the difference between Burgundy in Europe and Burgundy in the United States results, in my opinion, from the fact that whereas most other wines recover fairly quickly from their ocean voyage to our shores and shelves, the Burgundies simply do not. It's my guess that transatlantic shipping accelerates the aging cycle of most Burgundies and subtracts a small but unmistakable piece from the harmony that is the greatest pleasure of fine Burgundy. The aging factor in particular is something that one must take into account when choosing and serving Burgundies in the United States. I'm suggesting that you consider Burgundies here to be about two years older in development than they are in years since harvest. To obtain maximum pleasure for the money you invest in Burgundy, you'd be well advised to do most of your Burgundy buying and drinking in France, or, failing that, no far-ther from the Côte d'Or than England.

If, however, you are one of the poor unfortunates bitten by the Pinot Noir bug, and thereby doomed to a lifetime of poverty, then at least seek out the most reliable makers and the less popular or less known communes and growths. Do not covet anything from the Domaine de la Romanée-Conti or the closely related Etablisse-ments Leroy, perhaps the most overpriced wines in the whole inflated sector. Do look for first-rate *négociants* and producers like

Dujac and Jadot, the Prince de Mérode and Drouhin, and look especially for the less fashionable Beaune wines, which do not have—yet—the cachet of their more northerly brethren. Some of the Beaune whites can be exquisite—Drouhin's Clos des Mouches springs to mind—and many of the Beaune reds have retained some of the depth of flavor that enological legend attributes to the reds of the Côte de Nuits.

Selected Moderately Priced Red Burgundies

Beaune: cru wines from *Morot,* Pothier-Rieusset

Chambolle-Musigny: Henri or Michel Noellat

Côtes de Beaune-Villages: Bachelet, Bourée, *Jadot*

Fixin: Barthaut, *Clair, Faiveley,* Moillard

Gevrey-Chambertin: Bourée, P. Leclerc

Morey-St-Denis: *Clair,* H. Lignier

Nuits-St-Georges: Chauvenet

Pommard: Pothier-Rieusset

Santenay: Bachelet, Billaud, Bourée

Savigny-lès-Beaune: *Clair, Cornu,* Hospices de Beaune

Vosne-Romanée: Engel, *Mugneret*

Selected Red Burgundies for Extravagant Occasions

Beaune crus: Bouchard Père & Fils, *Drouhin, Jadot,* Remoissenet

Bonnes Mares: *Clair-Dau* (now owned by Jadot), *Dujac,* Moillard, Roumier

Chambertin-Clos-de-Bèze: Drouhin-Larose, Faiveley, Jadot

Chambolle-Musigny: *Faiveley,* Roumier

Clos de la Roche: Amiot, *Dujac,* H. Lignier, Ponsot

Clos St-Denis: *Dujac,* Ponsot

Clos de Vougeot: Drouhin, Engel, Faiveley, Jadot, Jaffelin, Moillard, *Mongeard-Mugneret, Mugneret,* Remoissenet, Tortochot

Corton: Moillard, *Prince de Mérode,* Senard

Gevrey-Chambertin: Faiveley, Moillard

Grands-Echézeaux: Engel, *Mongeard-Mugneret,* Remoissenet

Morey-St-Denis: *Dujac,* Faiveley, Roumier

Nuits-St-Georges: *Chevillon,* de Gramont, Faiveley, Gouges, *Jadot,* Moillard, *Mugneret*

Richebourg: *Jean Gros*

Vosne-Romanée crus: *Arnoux,* Drouhin, *H. Jayer, Jean Gros,* Moillard

Selected White Burgundies

All Burgundy whites worth drinking are very expensive. For comparatively good values, look for wines from Château de Meursault, Drouhin, Jadot, Lafon, Latour, Leflaive, Remoissenet, and Chablis from Auffray, Drouhin, Fèvre, Long-Depaquit, Pic.

LOIRE

The red wines of the central Loire—Chinon, Saumur, Bourgueil—are vinified from Cabernet Franc. This makes them flavorful, round, often soft, and almost always pleasing: charming accompaniments to simple foods—especially charcuterie—and to gently sauced dishes and cheeses of all sorts, especially young goat cheeses. Anjou and Touraine, in the middle Loire, produce sweet white wines that can often rival Sauternes and Barsac as dessert wines. Because not well known, they often provide very good buys—when they are available. Vouvray is the most famous appellation.

The dry white wines of the Loire—Sancerre and Pouilly-Fumé in the east, Muscadet in the west—are among the most versatile of all French whites in companioning food. Muscadet rarely rises to distinction, but its simple fruit and crisp acidity make it a welcome accompaniment to fresh shellfish and simply prepared fishes. Pouilly-Fumé and Sancerre are another story: They have some of Muscadet's acidity, to which they add the distinct advantage of the flavor—citrus to herbal to grassy—of the currently very fashionable Sauvignon grape from which they are vinified. Since they possess a fair amount of acid themselves—more than their California counterparts, less than their Spanish or Italian—Pouilly-Fumé and Sancerre (and their near-kin Quincy) probably succeed better than most French wines at dealing with acid foods. This makes them adaptable to a good many modern preparations that employ sauces based on vinegar or fruit vinegars. The somewhat spicy, racy flavor of the Sauvignon variety also makes its wines intriguing companions for some relatively lightly cured or smoked meats, like ham. They do not stand up well, however, to really aggressive flavors. Strongly smoked country hams, Oriental spices, three-alarm chilis: Foods like these will simply erase these wines.

Selected Moderately Priced Loire Wines

Muscadet: Château La Noë, Goulaine, Sauvion

Chinon and Bourgueil: Couly-Dutheil, Joguet

Vouvray (dry): Château Moncontour, Marc Brédif, Prince Poniatowski

Pouilly-Fumé and Sancerre: Chatelain, Cotat, Delaporte, Reverdy, Thomas

Selected Loire Wines for Extravagant Occasions

Chinon: Joguet's crus

Pouilly-Fumé: Ladoucette (Château de Nozet)

CHAMPAGNE

The king of sparkling wines serves marvelously as an aperitif and also makes a very adaptable dinner wine. The old cliché has it that champagne "goes with everything." Well, it's not that versatile, but it can be used with any not assertively flavored foods that will take an acidic wine. (Remember that throughout this section I'm talking about brut champagne. The sweeter versions serve more properly and more satisfactorily as dessert wines or, in some special circumstances, as aperitifs.) In fact, in most of the circumstances where you would consider serving a still Sancerre or Pouilly-Fumé, you can also give yourself the option of brut champagne or a *blanc de blancs* champagne (one made entirely from white grapes, ergo 100 percent Chardonnay). Rosé champagnes are more full bodied than others, and *tête de cuvée*, vintaged, brut rosés are usually wines as big and full bodied as champagne ever gets. They can make very substantial dinner wines, accompanying even some of the milder-flavored traditional red wine dishes very nicely.

It's become fashionable of late, in hyper-modish food and wine circles, to sneer at champagne and caviar as an unpleasing combination. Champagne's acidity, the New Wave theory holds, fights too much with the oiliness of the caviar. Piffle, I say. Harmony isn't all there is to food and wine combinations. Contrast works too. For my palate and a lot of others, that bright champagne acidity makes a beautiful counterpoint to the rich flavor and melting texture of the caviar. If you've got pots of money lying about, I can think of few things more glamorous—and palatally more pleasing—to spend it on than a *tête de cuvée* champagne and the freshest malossol osetra you can lay your hands on.

Counterpoint also provides the key to champagne's best uses as a dinner wine. Champagne's acidity is accentuated by its sparkle. The whole sought-after effect of champagne, after all, is summed up in that pleasing abrasion, that mouth-tingling prickle. Because of these qualities, champagne counterpoints moderately rich dishes better than it complements lean, acidic ones. You certainly can, if you wish, serve champagne with a classic Alsace *choucroute garnie,* and you will enjoy both, but you will enjoy the same champagne even more alongside a veal paillard and a dab of béarnaise sauce, or a lobster *mayonnaise,* or even a grilled chicken breast with tarragon butter. Once again, however, nouvelle cuisine prompts some exceptions. Many of its sweet-and-acid sauces—fruit vinegar reductions especially—respond well to champagne, extra dry as well as brut. And certain foods don't work with champagne at all, because they wipe out its flavor and reduce it to sparkling water. Strong red meats, very creamy sauces like that of lobster thermidor, strongly smoked or cured meats, and hot spices are all enemies of champagne.

Selected Moderately Priced Champagnes

Brut NV: Bollinger, *Charbaut,* Clicquot, Deutz, Jacquart, *Lanson,* Laurent-Perrier, Moët & Chandon, Mumm, Piper Heidsieck, Pol Roger, *Pommery & Greno*

Selected Champagnes for Extravagant Occasions

Brut NV: Krug

Vintage and Special Cuvées: Billecart-Salmon, Bollinger RD, Charbaut Certificate, Clicquot vintage and La Grande Dame, Dom Pérignon, Dom Ruinart, Gosset, Krug vintage and Clos de Mesnil, Mumm Cramant Blanc de Blancs and René Lalou, Pol Roger Blanc de Chardonnay and Cuvée Winston Churchill, Roederer Cristal, Taittinger Comtes de Champagne Blanc de Blancs and Rosé

ALSACE

The varietal white wines of Alsace—principally Gewürztraminer, Pinot Blanc, Pinot Gris (Tokay d'Alsace), and Riesling—yield fully dry wines of medium-to-full body and great strength of character. Occasionally they may lack a bit of acidity, which can make them taste merely heavy, but in normal vintages they balance acidity and varietal flavor and alcohol quite nicely indeed. All Alsace whites taste the better for a few years of bottle age. Like fine red wines, what they surrender in fresh fruit they more than make up in depth and complexity. In particularly good vintages such as 1983 and 1985, these wines are capable of much greater life and development, so much so that it is almost a shame to drink them before their fifth birthday, despite all the substantial attractions of their luscious youthful fruit.

Alsace has recently adopted a cru system. It is not yet foolproof, but the vast majority of Alsace *grands crus* I have tasted have been extraordinarily enjoyable wines. The producer's designation of a wine as *"Réserve"* or *"Réserve Personnelle"* can be an even more reliable indication of quality, since the winemaking situation in Alsace has proved remarkably stable, despite the region's troubled history. Many of the largest firms are also the oldest and most reputable. Houses like Hugel and Trimbach, Dopff ("au Moulin") and Dopff & Irion, with winemaking histories running back to the seventeenth century, have set time-tested standards for the entire region. If there is any such thing as a bargain left in French wines, it has to be Alsace wine generally and these cru bottlings particularly.

It is hard to overpraise the versatility of Alsace wines. Their combination of suppleness and authority, grace and weight, makes them not merely adequate but excellent companions to foods ranging from the slightest puffs of canapés to substantial cuts of meat. Quiches of all sorts (does anyone outside Alsace remember quiche?) love them, as does a fine goose liver pâté. They match marvelously with strongly flavored—and even quite acidic—white wine dishes and with "problem" meats such as strongly cured hams and smoked meats. Because many of them possess rich aromas and "spicy" flavors, they are wines well worth experimenting with as accompaniments to Oriental dishes. Many Indian dishes, I find, respond perfectly to Gewürztraminer or Pinot Gris or Riesling.

Vendange Tardive on an Alsace label indicates a late-harvest wine but not a very sweet one, and often not a sweet one at all. Such a wine—made only rarely—will be an exceptional concentration of the essence of the grape variety it is made from, frequently fully dry and fuller of body (and higher in alcohol) than the normal bottling. Such wines, even when they contain some residual, unfermented sugar, also possess sufficient acidity that the wine does not create a sensation of any marked sweetness on the palate. Sélection de Grains Nobles, on the other hand, indicates a sweet, dessert-type wine, made somewhat in the fashion of German Beerenauslese but fuller bodied and more robust.

Selected Moderately Priced Alsace Wines

Aussay, Beyer, Dopff & Irion, Dopff (especially the *Réserve* wines), *Hugel* (especially the *Réserve Personnelle*), Josmeyer, Kuentz-Bas, *Muré* (Clos St-Landelin), Schlumberger, Sparr, Trimbach, Weinbach, Willm, Zind-Humbrecht

Selected Alsace Wines for Extravagant Occasions

Beyer (1983 Tokay Sélection de Grains Nobles), Dopff & Irion (Gewürztraminer Les Sorcières), Dopff (*1983 Riesling Réserve*

Schoenenberg Vendange Tardive), Hugel (all the *Vendange Tar-dive* and *Sélection de Grains Nobles* wines), Zind Humbrecht (the single-vineyard wines)

RHÔNE

One other part of France also offers the beleaguered consumer something that approximates a just price, if not an outright bar-gain like Alsace, and that is the Rhône. Some of its wines—Châteauneuf-du-Pape for one—don't stand very high in the popu-lar imagination because of overblending and overcommercializa-tion, but that is to the canny shopper's advantage since the appellation covers many superb winemakers as well as the few industrial producers. Some Rhône wines have recently caught the public's fancy, both in France and abroad, and a few prices have consequently soared. Guigal's wines are an example of that. But on the whole, prices for excellent Rhône wines range from fair to favorable, and a shrewd consumer ought to stock up on these great wines now while that situation persists and several first-rate vin-tages are still available.

Both the northern Rhône (Hermitage, Côte Rôtie, Cornas) and the southern (Châteauneuf-du-Pape, Gigondas, Vacqueyras) make enormous red wines, France's biggest. Vinified from very localized grapes—the Mourvèdre and the Syrah are the most distinctive varieties—these wines not only have enormous aging potential but also practically demand to be left alone for a decade or so after bottling. In very great vintages like 1978, 1983, and 1985, the young wines may show a lot of fruit of the mouth-filling, rather bumptious sort, but usually they start life tannic and tough, need-ing time to collect themselves and mellow. Five years of age is pretty much as early as one ought to drink even an off vintage of Châteauneuf or Côte Rôtie, and a decade or more is about right for a fine vintage of either of these or of Hermitage or Cornas. In the case of all these wines, your patience earns the great advantage that they keep improving for some years after they reach readiness, and they are capable of living on at a high plateau of enjoyability for a very great while beyond that. Decently cared for, all but the worst vintages of Rhône wine survive nicely for fifteen years. Great vintages will outlive you.

Even in ordinary vintages, these wines make wonderful companions to strong meats and sauces, highly seasoned dishes, and strong cheeses. They are the only French wines I can imagine standing up to great Italian meat dishes such as the Piedmontese *finanziera* or the Tuscan *arista*. That is to say, these are the only French wines big enough to put on the same table with Barolo or Brunello or Amarone, with which they share as well the characteristics of longevity, slow development, and eventual, unbelievable, depth of character. For my palate, these wines deserve to be served on grand occasions, as partners to the noblest cuts of the strongest meats and game. Lighter vintages should be served with any of the foods for which you would consider using good Bordeaux or Burgundy.

The white wines of the Rhône, especially those of Hermitage and Châteauneuf-du-Pape, are built on a scale similar to the red wines of the region, and they match, mutatis mutandis, with similar sorts of food. White Hermitage is just about as big as a white wine can get without becoming clumsy or lumbering, and it would be my wine of choice to drink with an exquisitely savory dish, a dish that combined distinctive though essentially mild flavors with richness—a dish, for instance, like *poulet aux morilles* (provided the chicken has been allowed to walk around and scratch in the barnyard for food, and the morels were the tastiest, small, dark variety, and fresh from the woods). Rhône white wines, incidentally, work marvelously with cheese and cheese dishes.

Selected Moderately Priced Rhône Wines

Côte Rôtie: *Chapoutier,* Gerin, *Jaboulet, Jasmin, Vidal-Fleury* (now owned by Guigal)

Hermitage: Red—*Chapoutier,* Guigal, *Jaboulet;* White—*Chapoutier, Grippat,* Guigal, Jaboulet

Crozes-Hermitage: *Jaboulet*

St-Joseph: Red—*Grippat, Jaboulet,* Rostaing; White—*Grippat, Jaboulet, Trollat*

Cornas: Barjac, Jaboulet, *Juge, Verset*

Châteauneuf-du-Pape: Red—*Beaucastel,* Beaurenard, Chante Cigale, *Chante Perdrix,* Clos de l'Oratoire, *Clos des Papes, Fortia,* Jaboulet, *Mont-Redon, De La Nerthe, Père Caboche, Vieux Télégraphe;* White—De Nalys, De La Nerthe

Côtes-du-Rhônes-Villages: from Gigondas, *Combe* (L'Oustaou Fauquet), Guigal, Jaboulet, Les Goubert, Raspail; from Vacqueyras, *Combe* (La Fourmone)

Selected Rhône Wines for Extravagant Occasions

Côte Rôtie: Dervieux-Thaize, Gentaz-Dervieux, *Guigal, Rostaing*

Hermitage: Chapoutier, *J. L. Chave, Delas*

Cornas: *Clape*

Châteauneuf-du-Pape: Rayas

Rhône whites: Château Grillet, Châteauneuf (Beaucastel), Condrieu (Dumazet, *Guigal,* Multier, Pinchon, Vernay), Hermitage (*Chave,* Vidal-Fleury)

ITALY

Italy is a single vast winery, but really fine wines (as opposed to pleasant, drinkable, everyday stuff) come from only a few of its regions. Aside from a small handful of "eccentric" wines (literally so, because they originate outside the great wine-producing centers), the vineyards of Piedmont and Tuscany, Trentino–Alto Adige and Friuli–Venezia Giulia make most of the wines (red and white respectively) that interest the American wine lover.

Wine professionals commonly speak of a person's having a California palate or a European palate, by which they mean a settled preference for or a long-entrenched and somewhat specialized adaptation to a particular kind of wine. We say the same thing when we say we're "used to" California wine or European wine. We mean we know their characteristic flavors and palatal effects, we expect those sensations, we're comfortable with them, and on the other side of the coin, we miss them when we don't get them or when we get something different. Habit cuts down flexibility and receptivity. It's particularly important to be aware of that in approaching Italian wines, because most American wine drinkers form their palates and their expectations on either California or French wine. Indeed, when people—even wine professionals—speak of a "European palate," they're usually referring specifically to a taste for French wines. But Italian wines, although just as "European" as French, are a very different phenomenon, and the Italian palate is a third thing altogether. To appreciate properly what Italian wine has to offer requires just as much conscious adjustment of attitude and expectation as does the shift from French to California wines, and just as much conscious attention to the different modus operandi of the wine.

So here's risky generalization number 4,000 of the string of which this book is woven: Most Italian wines have more acid than most of the wines of France or the United States. But aside from the admittedly large number of white wines now being vinified in Italy for drinking very young, Italian wines don't create on the palate a primary impression of acidity. The reds particularly have sufficient fruit, and fruit of sufficient interest, coupled often with an abundance of tannin and usually with ample alcohol, so that they taste more often and more powerfully of their other components than they do of acid.

Another key difference between Italian wines and most others: By the standards of modern vinification, many Italian red wines ferment for a very long time with their skins. This means, of course, that they derive from those skins a lot of tannin and a lot of extract. This means that many of these wines achieve balance on a generous scale: They are big wines, with all the virtues and defects of bigness. Like many big wines, some of them can be very chunky and ungraceful (Barolo, for instance) or tannicly hard (Brunello di Montalcino) in their youth. Since the American wine-drinking public tends to take its wines too young, this means that most Americans, even those fairly knowledgeable about wines, have no idea what mature Italian wine is like.

Italian wines are generally very adaptable in terms of the kinds of food they will match with. They can serve very well as companions to cuisines other than their own, including dishes from other parts of Italy as well as from other parts of the world. Generally speaking, Italian wines, both red and white, will perform well with simply prepared foods of all sorts and with any foods whose character or preparation leans toward acidity. Because of their own characteristic acidity, both the reds and the whites will also perform very well with rich, unctuous foods, which they will often beautifully counterpoint. Only with very creamy sauces do Italian wines falter. Neither the reds nor the whites will show as well with dishes in which a cream-based sauce provides the dominant element. Under these circumstances, many of the biggest reds will taste harsh, tannic, and overly austere, many of the whites overly acidic.

To grossly overgeneralize (number 4,001), French and Italian wines have contrasting characters and complementary strengths and weaknesses. The great majority of French wines, both red and white, will match quite comfortably with foods prepared with cream sauces, and they will not perform as well with foods prepared in an acid medium, while exactly the reverse is true of most Italian wines. Obviously, I'm talking about degrees of success and failure rather than absolute live-or-die wine situations. And equally obviously, to generalizations as broad as these there will inevitably be exceptions. But the basic ideas do furnish one more very useful guideline for your menu planning.

PIEDMONT

The Piedmont is 100 percent varietal wine country, and predominantly red wine country to boot. A few whites are produced, almost all of them better than passable but very few of them truly distinguished, though almost all are routinely praised—probably as much for their rarity, in this sea of high-quality red wine, as for any intrinsic merit. We'll devote our attention here to the far more noteworthy reds, starting with a pair of what the Piedmont considers everyday wines but which less well-endowed parts of the world would think a lot better than that.

Barbera weighs in as probably the lightest bodied of the Piedmont red wines (though it still makes a substantial wine), and certainly the most acidic. The latter characteristic, combined with its low tannin and its distinctive dry, slightly tart, clean fruit, makes it an excellent wine with all sorts of food: Italian, French nouvelle, and what has been called, variously, American nouvelle, California modern, and—the name that seems to be sticking—contemporary American.

Widely planted throughout Italy, Barbera most of the time produces a very pleasant wine for all foods, medium to light bodied and acidic with a pleasing, black cherry tang. From particular fields and vinified with more than usual care, Barbera can demonstrate real complexity and character while retaining its basic utility-infielder attitude toward food. Experiments with aging Barbera from a month to a year in *barriques* have shown great promise, and some makers are beginning to try their hand at blending Barbera with the tannin-rich Nebbiolo, a radical departure for this very traditional area. The results so far are intriguing enough to justify further work. But Barbera by itself has still-unexploited potential. In the right hands this versatile, likable wine can get very near greatness. (See Gaja's and Pio Cesare's versions: They differ in style, but both do wonderful things with Barbera.) This is a wine that deserves a better and larger public.

In the Piedmont, Dolcetto almost matches Barbera in popularity. Dolcetto usually produces a very fruity, easy-drinking wine of deep color. It can normally take a few years of bottle age with some small loss of fruit and corresponding gain in complexity. In a few exceptional vintages, such as 1982 and 1985, Dolcetto can make an important wine of great depth and complexity while still retaining its characteristic fruitiness.

Young Dolcetto is dry, medium bodied, and intensely fruity: Think of Beaujolais with body, tannin, and fruit as its primary characteristics instead of acidity and fruit. It makes a good dinner wine with pastas, simple meats both light and dark, and not-too-aggressive cheeses. It in fact will partner well with a wide range of foods, though (because Dolcetto tastes the least acidic of Piedmont wines) very acidic dishes will upset its balance. The great Dolcettos respond to food rather in the manner of full-bodied Burgundies: Too much acid will undo them, but they have a tolerance for cream-based sauces that goes beyond that of many other Italian wines.

Both Barbera and Dolcetto serve perfectly as the introductory red wines of an important, multicourse, multiwine dinner. Interesting in themselves, they make useful, medium-bodied foils for the big guns to follow.

In the Piedmont that big gun will always be a Nebbiolo-based wine. The Nebbiolo grape is 100 percent responsible for many of Italy's noblest red wines and forms a hefty percentage of many others, both traditional blends (like the Lombard Grumello, Inferno, Sassella, and Sfursat) and innovative (Granduca's Barilot, De Giacomi's Bricco del Drago, Valentino Migliorini's Bricco Manzoni, Pio Cesare's Ornato). Wines vinified from Nebbiolo, even just within the Piedmont, bear many different place names: Barbaresco, Barolo, Boca, Bramaterra, Carema, Fara (the last four, blends of Nebbiolo and other grapes), Gattinara, Ghemme, Lessona (two more blends), Roero (95 percent to 98 percent Nebbiolo), Sizzano. The varietally named wines are Nebbiolo d'Alba (there may soon be a Nebbiolo delle Langhe designation too) and Spanna, another dialect name for the grape. The greatest of all these, without question, are Barolo and Barbaresco.

Nebbiolo produces wines of a quality and longevity to rival any in the world. These wines have full body rich with extract, a fair degree of acidity, a lot of tannin, and a very marked and assertive flavor; some describe it as black cherries blended with tobacco. These are red wines of the highest caliber, suitable for pairing with any grand dish sufficiently flavorful on its own not to be annihilated by them. Full bodied, tannic, with concentrated extract and complex fruit dry to the point of austerity, the best Nebbiolo wines make incomparable partners to red meats and roasts of all sorts as well as game—the whole category called in Italian *carni nobili*— and the great cheeses. Nebbiolo wines also match well with richly flavored pastas and risottos, particularly those incorporating wild mushrooms or the truffles whose aroma so many connoisseurs find in the wines themselves. Try them with a standing rib roast and sautéed *funghi porcini,* or with game and grilled *funghi porcini,* or simply with some excellent Gorgonzola: These are extraordinarily satisfying combinations.

In the past Barolo and Barbaresco were fermented for a month and upward on the skins and then aged for years in huge wooden barrels to produce a wine harsh and extremely tannic in its youth but big and full and austerely grand in its slowly attained maturity. Some people still make the wines this way, but most makers of both wines now shorten the time the musts spend on the skins and shorten the time the wine rests in wood (though some vintners, paradoxically, are experimenting with aging Nebbiolo wines in small *barriques*). This usually results in a wine with more pronounced fruit and noticeably diminished tannin in its youth, making it drinkable sooner. Both styles, and every conceivable stage of compromise between them, have vocal partisans both among winemakers and wine drinkers in Italy and abroad.

This situation affords a good example of precisely how and why Italy's great wines have not achieved the same degree of standardization (of normalization, you could almost say) as France's. For this reason too, and for other important considerations—because national unity came so late and because Italy's intense regionalism persisted so long after that—Italy never formulated a "canon" of its great wines, ranked by quality and associated firmly with particular kinds of food or gastronomic roles. None of its wines ever became national wines. All still remain firmly rooted in their native regions. For a Florentine, Nebbiolo is a foreign grape and Barolo a foreign wine, rarely encountered and difficult to understand.

It's well worth knowing, by the way, that Gattinara, though lighter bodied than either Barolo or Barbaresco, can achieve very great elegance. Its somewhat lesser impact in fact makes it a more useful and versatile wine, since it will match well with many foods that Barolo would overpower. For instance, you could conceivably serve a Gattinara with a *carne cruda all'albese* (a veal tartare topped with slivers of fresh white truffle), whereas a Barolo simply wouldn't work with it (too much tannin, too big a flavor). That kind of utility makes Gattinara a wine well worth seeking out.

Selected Moderately Priced Piedmont Wines

Barbera: *Gaja,* Giacomo Conterno, *Pio Cesare,* Prunotto, Vietti

Dolcetto: Aldo Conterno, Castello di Neive, *Ceretto, Dosio,* Einaudi, Gaja, Mascarello, Pio Cesare, *Prunotto, Ratti, Vietti*

Nebbiolo: Caretta, *Ceretto, Prunotto,* Vietti

Spanna and Gattinara: *Antoniolo,* Desilani, *Vallana*

Barbaresco: Castello di Neive, Mascarello, Moresco, *Pio Cesare, Produttori di Barbaresco, Prunotto,* Roagna, Vietti

Barolo: Caretta, *Ceretto "Zonchera,"* Cogno-Marcarini, Dosio, Einaudi, Fontanafredda, Mascarello, Pio Cesare, *Prunotto,* Ratti, Valentino, Vietti

Selected Piedmont Wines for Extravagant Occasions

Gattinara: Conte Ravizza (Monsecco)

Barbaresco: cru wines from Aldo Conterno, Bruno Giacosa, Ceretto, Gaja, Giacomo Conterno, Marchesi di Gresy, Prunotto, Vietti

Barolo: cru wines from Bruno Giacosa, Ceretto, Giacomo Conterno, Prunotto, Vietti

TUSCANY

To use the cliché that no wine writer can resist; the wine situation in Tuscany is in active ferment. For the wine lover who approaches Tuscan wine with an open mind and a receptive palate, the region offers the possibility of innumerable new wine experiences, ranging from enjoyable to transcendent. For the person who approaches Tuscan wine with preconceptions and prejudices—it's all plonk wrapped in wicker—well, you find what you look for. Tuscany makes so many wines in so many styles—very traditional and radically new—with so many names that the average wine buyer justifiably feels the need of a special education. It is unfortunately true that the major obstacle the unbiased wine drinker faces in dealing with Tuscan wines is confusion. The region produces everything from very mediocre wine (most of the whites, for instance, are infinitely forgettable) to excellent value, everyday potations, to memorable nectars for very special dinners—and the vast majority of the wines in all three ranges of quality are called Chianti.

The Sangiovese is the chief red grape of Tuscany, where for centuries local custom blended it with other varieties, including some white grapes, to produce Chianti and Vino Nobile di Montepulciano. Because the terrain of Tuscany is so varied and the clones of Sangiovese so numerous, Chiantis can differ markedly in quality and intensity, even within the same growing zone.

There are seven Chianti appellations: Chianti Classico, from the traditional heartland of the wine; Chianti Colli Fiorentini, from the Florentine hills; Chianti Colli Senesi, from the Siena hills; Chianti Colli Aretini, from the hills around Arezzo; Chianti Colline Pisane, from the hills near Pisa; Chianti Montalbano, northwest of Florence; and Chianti Rufina, from an area northeast of Florence. These zones differ from one another in significant ways. The Chianti of Siena, for instance, tends to be lighter bodied and fruity, while that of Rufina is heavier, with more earth tones in its flavor. But the distinction that makes the greatest difference to the consumer is that between the simple Chiantis (from whatever zone) and the Riservas (almost always from the Classico, with a few from Rufina).

A Chianti Riserva is a select wine that has been given extra care and extensive barrel aging. The best of them resemble clarets in their balance, but add a peculiarly Sangiovese juiciness and acidity that make them very versatile with all sorts of food. They mature and develop in the bottle much in the manner of clarets too, though few are as long lived as the greatest Médocs. Young non-Riserva Chianti, because of its fruitiness and high-for-a-serious-red-wine acidity, can partner with just about anything from picnic fare through aggressively sauced pastas to simply done fowl and meats. Riserva Chianti responds best to more balanced and composed foods—small game birds and, especially, rich, lean meats like squab and fine cheeses. Because of its own greater acidity, Riserva Chianti can deal quite satisfactorily with more acidic foods than can any of the clarets. Tomato-based sauces, for instance, pose no problems to Chianti, whereas they can undo most Bordeaux reds.

The Sangiovese grape is potentially a very distinguished one, with—in its best clones and harvests especially—a natural balance of tannin and acid and rich, plummy fruit. In Tuscany, where it is most appreciated, Sangiovese is turning up these days in several experimental guises in addition to its traditional use in Chianti. For instance, following the model of Brunello and the less-known Morellino di Scansano, some Chianti winemakers are trying out 100 percent varietal Sangiovese. The best of these are enormous, full-fruited wines, sort of California-style wines made with a distinctively non-California grape (though why more enterprising western winegrowers haven't tried Sangiovese is a great mystery). Other experimenters are blending Sangiovese with the "foreign" grape, Cabernet Sauvignon. The best of these add a useful polish to Sangiovese's aggressive attack. Carmignano is notable and exceptional in this regard, in that it has its own separate appellation, since Cabernet, though an interloper elsewhere in Tuscany, has been cultivated in this area for a great many years. It's also worth pointing out that several Chianti-zone growers are also experimenting with 100 percent Cabernet wines, some of which have achieved a wonderful lushness of fruit and great polish, while retaining a distinctively Italian acidity.

Neighboring Umbria also produces first-class wines on the Chianti model, both standard and the Cabernet-blend version.

Completely localized around the small town of Montalcino, about thirty miles from Siena, the Brunello grape (Brunello is a local name for a clone of the Sangiovese) makes a distinguished, full-bodied red wine of very great aging potential. It reminds one of Cabernet in its youthful tannic asperity, but the Sangiovese fruit is fuller and plummier and naturally more acidic, so over time it develops into a wine bigger in scale and surer in balance than all but the finest 100 percent Cabernets. Rosso di Montalcino is a younger wine from the same grapes, with considerably less wood aging. It can still be a very big wine and always shows enormous fruit. Here, as everywhere in Italy, old-style vintners (long skin contact, as much wood as possible) vie with new-style (shorter skin contact, cooler fermentation, less wood). So far neither style has shown a definite superiority—the new style is drinkable sooner but may not develop as well—so the jury is still out, and given the potential life span of great Brunello, it may be out for some decades yet. In average vintages a Brunello should get at least five to eight years of aging before you drink it, and more won't hurt it. In a great vintage a wine from one of the traditional makers will need twenty years to come around. If you think that is extravagant, a taste of mature Brunello will change your mind: deep and mouth filling, with an aroma of truffles and forest earth and a flavor compounded of dry plums and cedar and black pepper and sometimes hints of tar and licorice, mature Brunello combines authority and suaveness in a way that makes it like no other wine.

Brunello is a special-occasion wine. It needs big flavors as a foil—game, red meat roasts, wild mushrooms, big cheeses (especially Parmigiano). It will take complex sauces in stride, whether they be redolent of tarragon, softened with cream, or rich with marrow. Rosso di Montalcino doesn't ask so much, but is still best served with robust foods—rich stews and braises, steaks, or that humble but savory Tuscan favorite, grilled sausage and beans. In fact, Rosso di Montalcino reacts very well with the whole gamut of grilled meats and vegetables.

Selected Moderately Priced Tuscan Wines

Chianti: Antinori, *Badia a Coltibuono,* Berardenga, Brolio, Castello di Castellina, Castello di Monte Antico (not technically a Chianti, but made from the same grapes), Castello di Nipozzano, Castello di Rampollo, Castello di Volpaia, Fontodi, *Fossi,* Isole e Olena, Monsanto, Monte Vertine, Nozzole, Ruffino, Villa Cafaggio, *Villa Selvapiana*

Vino Nobile: Boscarelli, Capezzano, Fanetti, Fassati

Rosso di Montalcino: Altesino, Caparzo, Il Poggione

Brunello di Montalcino: Altesino, Banfi, *Barbi* (especially *Brusco dei Barbi*), *Il Poggione,* Lisini

Sangiovese varietal wines: Badia a Coltibuono's Sanjoveto, Vinattieri Rosso

Selected Tuscan Wines for Extravagant Occasions

Vino Nobile: Avignonesi

Brunello di Montalcino: traditionalists include *Barbi,* Biondi-Santi, Costanti; modernists include *Altesino, Banfi,* Caparzo, *Castelgiocondo,* Col d'Orcia, Il Poggione

Carmignano: *Capezzana*

Sangiovese varietal or **Sangiovese-Cabernet blend:** Antinori's Tignanello, Avignonesi's Grifi, Caparzo's Ca' del Pazzo, Cappezzana's Ghiaie della Furba, Castellare's I Sodi di San Niccolo, Castello di Volpaia's Coltassala, Fontodi's Flaccianello, Monte Vertine's Il Sodaccio and Le Pergole Torte

OTHER IMPORTANT ITALIAN REDS

AGLIANICO AND TAURASI

The Aglianico grape produces the finest red wines of southern Italy: Taurasi from the high hills east of Naples and Aglianico del Vulture from the ancient volcanic slopes of Basilicata. A very old variety (its name means Hellenic; it was brought to Italy by Greek colonists by or before 600 B.C.) whose potential is still vastly underrealized, the Aglianico can make a long-lived, full-bodied, tannic and austere but nevertheless harmonious and elegant wine. It matches well with all roasts and game, with cheese, and even— perhaps especially—with meat or fowl prepared by moist cooking with marked acidity (classic *ragù alla napoletana, brasciolone alla napoletana, pollo alla diavolo*). Like so many of the great Italian red wines, Aglianico-based wines are superb with wild mushrooms.

AMARONE

Amarone, or—to give it its full name—Recioto della Valpolicella Amarone, is a great anomaly among the world's full-bodied, dry red wines. Half of the anomaly lies in the fact that the grapes that go into the muscular Amarone are exactly the same varieties, from exactly the same zone near Verona, that go into the light-bodied and fairly innocuous Valpolicella. The other half of the anomaly lies in the process of making Amarone: One of the biggest, most powerful, nonfortified wines produced anywhere, Amarone results from very slowly fermenting carefully selected and reserved super-ripe grapes—semidried grapes of the sort that usually, in Italy and elsewhere, go into the making of sweet wines.

The wine that is produced from this unusual process manages to combine extraordinary berrylike fruitiness, enormous body, and a wonderfully elegant, velvet texture. Because of its size—its heft and authority—Amarone can be compared only to the biggest of the Rhône red wines, which it rivals in power and longevity (and value for dollar). Amarone needs a lot of time in bottle to achieve balance. My personal preference is never to drink it before it is ten years old and to keep it as long after that as my natural greed and gluttony will allow—the older it is, the better it gets. Because Amarone is so big a wine, it can be difficult to match with foods, and some people consequently prefer to treat it like port, serving it after the meal proper, with walnuts or hazelnuts. But it is also characteristic of the wine to retain a surprising freshness and fruitiness, which can balance or at least palliate its power, so it is usable with carefully selected entrées or *secondi*—chiefly either those of marked flavor themselves or composed dishes of great, balanced complexity. If you are able to obtain a chunk of top-quality eating Parmigiano, no wine in the world will do as much with it or for it as an Amarone. This is a gastronomical ne plus ultra comparable to great Sauternes and fresh foie gras.

CABERNET SAUVIGNON

The Cabernet situation is one of the most complicated in Italian wine. In some parts of Italy the grape has been long domesticated (Friuli and the Veneto). In other parts it has arrived only quite recently (Tuscany, Umbria), and in yet other parts it is still largely viewed with suspicion (Piedmont). In most of the world, whether Cabernet is vinified in blends with other grapes as in Bordeaux or in splendid isolation as in California, the winemaker intends to produce a full-bodied, deeply flavored, slow-maturing wine of complexity and character. Many northern Italian vintners, on the other hand, have consciously or unconsciously rejected that international style. Most Friuli Cabernets, for instance, go a very different direction. They may contain as much or more Cabernet Franc as Cabernet Sauvignon. If the label doesn't explicitly say Cabernet Sauvignon, you can be pretty sure there's a goodly amount of Cabernet Franc present. The wines receive little wood aging, and their vinification stresses fruitiness and accessibility rather than size and authority. Consequently, they make versatile, medium-bodied wines of no great distinction, though quite pleasant drinking.

A few exceptional houses in several different parts of Italy treat the grapes as most of the rest of the world does and produce either a very substantial 100 percent varietal wine—a sort of California Cabernet Sauvignon with an Italian accent—or a very claretlike blend of Cabernet, Cabernet Franc, and Merlot. Some superb Bordeaux look-alikes are almost handcrafted in the Veneto and in Lombardy. Tuscan, Umbrian, and Piedmontese Cabernets all resemble at least loosely the California varietal style. The food affinities of these wines are almost exactly the same as those of claret or California Cabernet, with the slight difference that their greater acidity allows them a bit more latitude in accommodating acidic foods.

Selected Quality Producers

Aglianico variety: D'Angelo, Aglianico del Vulture; Mastroberadino, *Taurasi* (especially the *Riserva*)

Amarone: *Allegrini,* Bertani (especially *older vintages*), *Masi, Quintarelli,* Le Ragose, Santa Sofia, *Tommasi*

Cabernet Sauvignon: varietal wines include Gaja's *Darmagi* (Piedmont), Lungarotti's Cabernet di Miraduolo (Umbria), Maculan's *Fratta* and Palazotto (the Veneto), and the much bemedaled Sassicaia (Tuscany); claret-style blends include Bossi-Fedrigotti's Foianeghe Rosso (Trentino–Alto Adige), Ca' del Bosco's *Maurizio Zanella Rosso* (Lombardia), and Loredan's *Venegazzu* (the Veneto)

IMPORTANT ITALIAN WHITE WINES

Italy produces scores of white wines, but few great ones. Its clean, brisk, light white wines, of which there are a superabundance, can serve as universal aperitifs. All of them will also show very well with simple pastas, seafood, fowl, and white meat dishes. But the distance between a sound, drinkable white wine and a truly distinguished one is very great indeed, and it isn't crossable by any mere technical expertise. It requires great grapes, to start with, and the talent and tact, the feel for the grapes to know what can be made of them. A few truly fine Italian white wines deserve special notice. By my estimation, those wines include:

Arneis: Ceretto (Blangé), Bruno Giacosa, Vietti
Chardonnay: Gaja, Lungarotti, Pio Cesare
Fiano di Avellino: Mastroberardino
Gavi or Cortese di Gavi: La Scolca, Pio Cesare
Greco di Tufo: Mastroberardino
Picolit: Livio Felluga
Pomino: Frescobaldi
Sauvignon: Abbazia di Rosazzo, Borgo Conventi, Gaja, Grad-
    nik, Russiz Superiore
Trebbiano d'Abruzzo: Valentini
Torre di Giano: Lungarotti
Vintage Tunina: Jermann

So markedly different from one another are the viticultural prac-
tices and traditions of the various Italian regions that even the wines on this short list differ importantly from one another. Of the internationally known varietals, the Chardonnays have a fairly evident California style: big, full-bodied fruit, a fair amount of oak overlay, and rich, almost buttery textures. (They have more acid than their California counterparts, however.) The Sauvignons, on the other hand, taste distinctively Italian. The four from Friuli (Abbazia di Rosazzo, Borgo Conventi, Gradnik, Russiz Superiore) all offer bright, live, high-acid herbal flavors, with cop-
pery, metallic, or citrus undertones and a long, dry finish—really refreshing, palate-scrubbing Sauvignon. The Gaja Sauvignon opens whole new ground for the Sauvignon grape. Its usual herbaceous quality has been metamorphosed into a rich, almost mel-
ony aroma, reminiscent of Chenin Blanc from the middle Loire, and Sauvignon's normally forthright flavor has been correspondingly transmuted into a subtle and complex blend of exotic fruits and citrus. This is a new wine, as yet in limited supply, but I think it

may well be a trailblazer for Piedmontese white wine. These two varietals will serve with all the foods you would normally turn to Chardonnay or Sauvignon to accompany, plus some dishes that you might ordinarily regard as too acidic for them to handle: *pollo alla diavola,* for instance, or lemon chicken.

Several of the wines made from native Italian grapes are varietal wines as well: Arneis, made from 100 percent of the grape of the same name; Fiano, all Fiano grapes; Gavi and Cortese di Gavi, made entirely from Cortese grapes; Greco di Tufo, vinified entirely from Greco; and Trebbiano d'Abruzzo, an otherwise indifferent-to-poor variety, transformed in the Valentini version by a unique selection of grapes from older vines and subsequent aging in wood into a round, flavorful wine of almost Burgundian character. Arneis can be made forward and medium to light bodied (the style of Ceretto's Blangé) or rounder and fuller (Giacosa's and Vietti's version). Gavi can also be vinified in these two styles, but the fuller versions seem to me to capture more of the grape's distinction, and that is what I here honor in La Scolca's and Pio Cesare's renditions. Both these wines seem to perform best with antipasto dishes or lighter or more delicately flavored *primi* and *secondi.*

Fiano and Greco are two grapes that would probably now be extinct if it weren't for the generation-spanning efforts of the Mastroberardino family, who have labored to keep alive these ancient varieties (they were introduced into Italy by the Greeks several centuries B.C.). How great a loss that would have been will be immediately apparent to anyone who tastes a mature sample—unlike most other Italian white wines, they require a few years in bottle to develop fully—of these two great wines. Greco, the less expensive of the two, offers itself a little more willingly than Fiano. Greco feels oddly oily on the tongue the first time you taste it, rather round and full bodied, but with evident good acid and a nutty aroma and taste. Fiano deceives you into thinking it's lighter than Greco; actually, for all its gentleness, it is quite a big white wine, with layer under layer of nut, fruit, and mineral flavors. Both wines need some bottle age (don't drink them at all before three years of age), and both benefit enormously from being allowed to breathe for up to an hour before serving. Greco and Fiano match well with the kinds of dishes that challenge most white wines. Greco shows its best with strongly flavored seafoods—the sorts of elaborate platters of mixed shellfish steamed in white wine and garlic and parsley so loved all through the south of Italy—and even with dishes that you might normally think require a light red wine: grilled veal chops, grilled *funghi porcini,* flavorful foods of this sort. Fiano will do well in these circumstances too, but it really puts on a show with fowl of all kinds.

In contrast to these monovarietal wines, several kinds of grapes go into the making of Pomino, Torre di Giano, and Vintage Tunina. The first two are long-established blends and near neighbors. Frescobaldi's Pomino offers the best demonstration so far of what can be accomplished with the "international" white varietals in Tuscany. A mixture of about two-thirds Pinot Bianco, one-quarter Chardonnay, and the balance Pinot Grigio, Pomino achieves a character and flavor that invite comparisons with Burgundian whites. A single-vineyard *Riserva* of this wine, Pomino Il Benefizio, contains a higher percentage of Chardonnay and receives six months' aging in wood, which gives it even greater body, depth, and complexity, while still retaining its characteristically Italian acidity. In my experience, this wine works wonders with farm-bred quail, partridge, and rabbit. Lungarotti's Torre di Giano Riserva Il Pino fills a similar gastronomic niche, though its more evident acidity makes it a better partner for more delicately flavored dishes. This wine is vinified from much more traditional grapes, Trebbiano and Grechetto, which account for much of its acidity. The regular bottling makes a lovely accompaniment to grilled or sautéed freshwater fish and herb-roasted chicken.

Vintage Tunina is a newly contrived and whimsically named blend from Friuli. Its maker, Silvio Jermann, who had studied winemaking in both Europe and North America, invented the name as a *fantasia,* "Tunina" meaning nothing but sounding exotic, and "Vintage" being a prestigious wine term in English. More pragmatic about winemaking than nomenclature, Jermann assembles the wine from undisclosed proportions of Pinot Bianco, Chardonnay, Sauvignon, and—in some equally undisclosed vintages— a tiny amount of Picolit (see below). Vintage Tunina recalls Bur-

gundian wines without quite tasting like any of them—in part
because of the nature of its blend, in part because of that omnipresent Italian acidity. It takes bottle age well and matches with all
sorts of food. Three- or four-year-old specimens deepen in flavor
and complement grilled veal chops or grilled mushrooms or small
game birds very nicely.

Livio Felluga's Picolit stands as a paradigm of a great Italian
dessert wine. Vinified from an old, indigenous Friulian variety
(now almost an endangered species because it bears so stingily),
Picolit has a golden-amber hue and a lovely, honeyed aroma. Its
typically Italian acidity interacts with its sugar to make a wine
intriguingly dry and sweet simultaneously. That complex balance
distantly recalls sherry to some tasters, but one of Picolit's additional charms is precisely the absence of sherrylike oxidation. It
leaves a final palatal impression of freshness and suppleness. Picolit
makes a perfect companion to the simplest and most characteristic
Italian desserts—nuts or fresh fruit or plain biscotti.

Finally, it's worth noting that an enormous amount of experimentation is going on right now in Italy, and the greatest amount
of it is concentrated on white wines. Italians know they have some
red wines that can stand with the world's best. Even though a large
part of the world doesn't yet share that knowledge, there is a
general sense that the time is coming, and all that is required in red
wine is perseverance at what they are already doing very well. With
white wine, on the other hand, Italians know they have a long way
to go, and they are working hard at shortening the distance. One
consequence of this is that the curious consumer can taste a whole
bevy of new white wines from producers large and small, old and
new, from all parts of Italy and from all sorts of grapes. In keeping
with overriding Italian tradition, however innovative these wines
may be, they all work well with foods. Here are a few names to
bear in mind:

Ronco delle Acacie, from Abbazia di Rosazzo, in Friuli
Cervaro della Sala, from Antinori's vineyards in Orvieto
Libaio, from Ruffino's Tuscan plantings
Fontanelle Chardonnay from Villa Banfi's holdings in Mon-
    talcino

SPAIN AND PORTUGAL

The wines of Spain and Portugal present an oddly jumbled picture
to the connoisseur. Each country possesses unusual fortified wines
that are famous the world over and readily available almost everywhere, though they are of limited utility as dinner wines. Each also
possesses a host of drinkable-to-excellent unfortified wines that
would be marvelous accompaniments to many dinners, if only they
were better known and more easily available outside the Iberian
peninsula. International markets and parochial wines set the pattern for both countries. Native and highly regional wines remain
important in both Spain and Portugal, and in both countries, too,
methods of making wine have been heavily influenced by
foreigners—notably, in the north of Spain, by the French. But the
English, of all unlikely influences, have had the heaviest hand in
shaping Iberian wine and are directly or indirectly responsible for
the two countries' only genuinely national—and international—
wines, sherry, port, and Madeira. These three wines might never
have come into being, or continued to exist, without English tastes
and English wine merchants and the English market.

But the unfortified wines of Spain and Portugal should be our
main interest, for several good reasons. First, for economics: They
are among the last inexpensive fine wines in the world—a condition that will not survive much longer now that both countries
have entered the Common Market. Second, because throughout
the peninsula, cultivation of the traditional and native grape varieties has long been influenced by French styles of vinification and
by the importation and naturalization of French grape varieties.
The wines have consequently developed a character that partakes
of some of the finesse and elegance of French wine while preserving
a rock-hard Mediterranean spine. In the terms in which we have
been so far talking about wines, this makes Spanish and Portuguese
bottlings very useful and very versatile. Not only do they serve well
with those awkward dishes that don't seem fully comfortable with
either a French or an Italian wine—*pissaladière* springs to mind, as
well as the classic Spanish dish, paella—but they will also match
nicely with all but the creamiest and butteriest of French cuisine
and all but the most acidic of Italian cooking—not to mention, of

course, how marvelous they taste with their own native dishes. They will serve just as happily with most of the dishes of the standard American and regional American cuisines.

There is a catch, however. Unfortunately for most of us, Spanish and Portuguese wines, like fine Spanish and Portuguese cuisine, are neither widely known nor readily available in many parts of the United States. Consequently, I'm going to limit what I have to say here about them to those few of their many wines that are fairly readily obtainable in the United States.

Spanish Table Wines

Two major districts dominate Spanish exports to these shores, the Rioja and Penedès. You won't go too far wrong if you think of them as somewhat analogous to Bordeaux and Burgundy in the general character of their wines and in their gastronomic uses.

Rioja

The Rioja region, like Bordeaux and like the Chianti zone in Italy, varies widely in soil quality and microclimate and is divided, like those other two districts, among many estates that produce wines of widely differing styles. The finest Rioja wines, like the best Bordeaux and Chianti, are elegant, full bodied, and tannic. Many connoisseurs, in drawing their mental maps of the wine world, in fact see red Rioja as standing about midway between Bordeaux and Chianti in taste and style, neither as tannic as the French wine nor as acidic as the Italian. A fine Rioja needs time to lose its youthful asperity and to mellow and deepen and gain complexity and resonance. Properly matured red Rioja possesses enviable depth and authority, quite enough to accompany all but the deepest-flavored game dishes. It belongs in exactly the same sort of dining circumstances that call for either claret or Chianti, though of course it doesn't taste exactly like either.

The white wines of the Rioja are made from strictly Spanish varietals, and different houses vinify them either in the modern way— low-temperature fermentation in stainless steel or fiberglass—or following the traditional Spanish preference for slightly fuller-bodied white wines with a hint (sometimes a heavy hint) of wood. The modern-style whites make excellent aperitifs and cocktail wines and match well with hors d'oeuvres and light, simply prepared dishes. The old-fashioned Riojas beautifully accompany more complex and more assertively flavored dishes. The greater roundness and the slight vanilla flavors that their barrel aging bestows on them make them recall Burgundian whites (at least, Burgundian whites as they once were).

PENEDÈS

Penedès reds, like Burgundies, offer more luscious fruit earlier—even though they too are capable of aging gracefully—and they tend to feel softer and rounder on the palate. The premier maker of Penedès wines is the Torres family, whose specialty is the gracefully aged and richly flavored Gran Coronas Black Label, a blend of the "foreign" Cabernet Sauvignon and Cabernet Franc. Despite the Bordelais grapes, the analogy with Burgundy continues to hold true, for gastronomical purposes, for most Penedès wines.

The Penedès also produces a goodly amount of champagne-method sparkling wine, most of which retails at considerably less than champagne prices. The best production can rival good champagne at its own game—and will, of course, cost you almost as much. The less costly sparkling wines can be very pleasing drinking for large parties and receptions, but don't really have the interest or quality to sustain a whole meal.

The still white wines of the Penedès are worthy of attention and useful with many sorts of food. The Torres firm cultivates both traditionally Spanish and new "international" grape varieties (Chardonnay, Sauvignon Blanc) and vinifies them all in a thoroughly modern manner (low-temperature fermentation in stainless steel). Most of these wines display fresh, lively fruit and a bit of roundness and depth: European wines with a California education, so to speak. For my palate, they serve best with simply prepared foods, especially the richer-tasting seafood items—crab, for instance, or tiny bay scallops.

VEGA SICILIA

For your pull-out-all-the-stops feast, the only Spanish wine that will really do is Vega Sicilia. A wine in such limited supply that for most wine lovers, inside or outside Spain, it is only slightly less mythical than the unicorn, Vega Sicilia is still made on a single large estate in the Duero district in exactly the way it has been produced for more than a hundred years. Three French varietals (Cabernet Sauvignon, Merlot, Malbec) blended with three Spanish varieties (Tinto Aragonés, Garnacha, Albillo) provide the almost free-run juices—the grapes are subjected to only the lightest pressing—that, after fermentation, age for ten years in oak barrels and two more in bottles before being released for sale. The resulting wines possess tremendous depth and body and flavor, and as a consequence work best with strongly flavored foods, especially cheese, game, and what Europeans call the "noble meats"—the great joints and roasts. Vega Sicilia is so prized in Spain that its sale is strictly controlled, and it rarely appears at retail within the country. Most of it goes to the grand hotels and restaurants and to the state, with a small amount reserved for export.

Selected Moderately Priced Spanish Table Wines

Red Rioja: Bodegas Lan, Campo Viejo, CVNE, *Faustino,* Gran Condal, *Vina Tondonia, Marqués de Cáceres, Marqués de Murrieta, Marqués di Riscal,* Montecillo, *Muga,* Olarra, Paternina, La Rioja Alta

White Rioja: CVNE, Marqués de Cáceres, Marqués de Riscal, Paternina

Penedès: *Jean Léon, Torres*

Selected Spanish Table Wines for Extravagant Occasions

Rioja: Bodegas Lan's Vina Lanciano, Muga's *Prado Enea,* La Rioja Alta Reserva

Penedès: Torres *Gran Coronas Black Label*

Vega Sicilia Unico Reserva and *Valbuena*

PORTUGUESE TABLE WINES

Like Spain, Portugal produces many fine unfortified wines not well known or well distributed in our country. Probably the best known are the *Vinhos Verdes,* or green wines; actually they are white wines, but are so named because they are vinified from scarcely ripe grapes. Light flavored and acidic, they are vinified both still and *pétillant* (also called *frizzante,* or crackling)—that is, nearly sparkling, striking the tongue with a pleasant scratching sensation. Vinhos Verdes appear in the United States as an almost-compulsory beverage in Brazilian restaurants, where they make a pleasant, light accompaniment to seafood dishes.

Fine red wines originate in Portugal's best known region of appellation, Dão. They tend to combine rather full body with an old-fashioned Burgundian smoothness and elegant fruit, a set of attributes that makes them very versatile dinner wines, usable with even aggressively flavored dishes. Wines from the Dão are usually the best distributed of all Portugal's reds, and the region also makes some hefty whites that occasionally manage to find their way to these shores. The best alternative to a Dão wine—and really the only practical one, given the rarity of Portuguese wines in the American market—is a Garrafeira, a term that roughly designates a shipper's private reserve (often blended and frequently very fine). Since very few estate-bottled Portuguese wines ever come to market, most reputable Portuguese wine firms pride themselves on the quality of their Garrafeira. Usually, both Dão red wines and Garrafeiras are quite full bodied and tannic (from long aging in wood), and frequently of pretty high alcohol content. In matching them with foods, you should therefore treat them pretty much as you would the big reds of the Rhône or as you would Barolo or Barbaresco.

Aside from Vinhos Verdes, Portuguese white wines tend to resemble old-style Rioja whites, with a lot of oak flavors and not too much of the lush fresh fruit that is now so sought after in white wines. If you like this style of white wine—and I for one wish more vintners would revert to it; the world is awash in white wines that are aspiring to become 7-Up—you'll find it a marvelous partner to the richer white meats, turkey and pork particularly, and often to cured ham as well. (This holds true, by the way, for almost all markedly flavored white wines, whether they've received long wood aging or not. Try an Alsace Gewürztraminer, for instance, with a Virginia ham, or even with the Burgundian *jambon persillé*. The more flavorful your ham, the better white wines like these will interact with it.)

SHERRY

Sherry and port are probably the best-known fortified wines in the world. Of the two, sherry has by far the greater role with food. It can fit any meal at least twice; once as aperitif and again as digestif. Beyond that, all-sherry dinners are at least thinkable. They occur fairly frequently in Spain, and even the English have been known to so indulge their passion for the wine of Jerez. But the practice has never caught on in the United States, and given the moment's obsession with caloric lightness and alcoholic moderation, it doesn't seem likely to in the near future. Nevertheless, few wines can match a dry fino or amontillado sherry as an aperitif with all sorts of canapés and hors d'oeuvres. Even the dry oloroso sherries can make wonderful before-dinner drinks, but they tend to be so rich and satisfying in themselves that they want only the simplest food accompaniment. The sweet olorosos, by the way, though all too often overlooked in America's current passion for port, stand on a par with any of the world's great dessert wines. And if you are monitoring your alcoholic intake, a dry oloroso makes a wonderful substitute for an after-dinner brandy.

PORT AND MADEIRA

Portugal produces not one but two great fortified wines. One is the undeservedly neglected Madeira, from an island off the coast of Africa. Once one of the world's most honored wines, Madeira went into eclipse in this century and is only now beginning to show signs of recovery, riding the coattails of the revived interest in port and Sauternes. Madeira unfortunately needs a very long time in the bottle to ripen to its glorious maturity, a fact that seems to work strongly against its ever achieving the recognition it deserves as the peer of any of the world's great dessert wines. If you come across a bottle of old Madeira, by all means try it. It will be a revelation to you.

The other of Portugal's fortified wines suffers from no such neglect. Port, from the Iberian mainland itself, is known the world over. It is currently riding a new wave of popularity with American and British connoisseurs, despite what is for me the very serious drawback of its often unbearably intense sweetness. It is fascinating the way our sweet tooth, very much a part of our British culinary (?!) heritage, manifests itself in austere halls of gourmandise. In any event, most port fans agree that the wine is best enjoyed by itself after dinner, with at most simple biscuits or nuts to accompany it. In France it has become something of a fad to take a glass of port as an aperitif, but that's a practice I suggest you follow only if you expect a really dreadful dinner.

GERMANY

Germany presents us with a great oddity in the world of wine, producing distinguished wines that have evolved without a great popular cuisine to interact with them. This has made German wine markedly different from that of other countries (Austria excepted) and has created great divergences between the German wine scene and that of the rest of the world. These divergences are reflected in the classifications of German wines and the kinds of information their labels give you. German wine law incorporates several provisos that distinguish it sharply from that of the other major wine-producing nations: Not only geography and grape varietal but degree of sweetness as well determine a wine's legal appellation. In fact, sweetness often counts as the most important single quality. The very finest German wines (which, by general consent, are the very sweetest) don't serve well for everyday drinking. Rather, they are precious nectars whose sweetness and scarcity decree that they accompany your best desserts or be drunk by themselves *as* your best dessert. Accordingly, all German wine labels bear very prominently an indication of the exact degree of sweetness of each wine.

The traditional Gothic script that German wine labels sport in such abundance looks very confusing to the uninstructed eye, but amid all its foliage lies a wealth of information. Vintage of course is clearly and unambiguously displayed. After that, look for the level of the wine: Tafelwein, the lowest level, which is rightly not often exported; Qualitätswein, often abbreviated QbA; and Qualitätswein mit Prädikat (QmP, or Fine Wine with a Descriptive, to render the succinct legal phraseology somewhat ham-handedly).

Within the QmP classification, which offers the level of wine quality that most consumers will be interested in, the Kabinett Prädikat is the driest and comes closest to conventional dinner wine. Sometimes fully dry, more usually with just the slightest touch of sweetness (for many people imperceptible) to emphasize the fruit, the Kabinett Rieslings are the most useful German wines on a day-in, day-out basis. The ascending degrees of sweetness achieved within the other QmP categories are indicated by the descriptives Spätlese, Auslese, Beerenauslese, and Trockenbeerenauslese. The last two are usually referred to simply as BA and TBA, for obvious reasons. A Riesling Spätlese, if it has sufficient acidity to balance its sugar, can be used as a dinner wine, particularly with dishes whose ingredients or sauces combine sweet-and-sour or sweet-and-piquant elements in a way that makes trouble for totally dry wines. But usually all the gradations sweeter than Kabinett are regarded as dessert wines, and some examples of them are among the very greatest wines of this category.

In addition to degree of sweetness, the label will show the large geographical region from which the wine comes: Ahr, Hessische Bergstrasse, Mittelrhein, Nahe, Rheingau, Rheinhessen, Rheinpfalz, Mosel-Saar-Ruwer, Franken, Württemberg, and Baden. The most important German wine regions represented on the American market are Mosel-Saar-Ruwer (usually just called Mosel and often spelled the French way, Moselle) and the three Rhine areas, Rheingau, Rheinhessen, and Rheinpfalz. They always come in brown bottles, and the Mosels always come in green. Why, I haven't a clue; tradition probably. Tradition also holds—and this is verifiable by experience—that the Mosel wines are a bit lighter and more delicate than the Rhines.

After that, German label information is more or less like that of

France. You get more precise geographical and vineyard names. For example, Bernkasteler, a wine from Bernkastel (town names are turned into adjectives and hence usually end in *er*); more precisely, Bernkasteler Doktor, "Doktor" being the vineyard name. As in Burgundy, one vineyard can be divided among many owners, not all of whose winemaking skills may be equal, so the label will also tell you the name of the vineyard owner or winemaker.

Since the German wine-growing areas are very northerly and the Riesling grape (which is Germany's most important) is a late ripener, the amount of QmP wine produced varies tremendously from harvest to harvest. In good years grapes intended for QmP are left on the vines as late as possible to concentrate their sugars and acids, and sometimes they are helped along by *Botrytis,* the "noble mold" that reduces the water content of grapes and reinforces their sugars. Repeated hand pickings, often selecting individual grapes from a bunch, are the key to the greatest German wines, and one of the reasons they will never be cheap.

Nevertheless, Kabinett and even Spätlese wines, the driest classifications, often appear on the market at quite reasonable prices, and they can make wonderful companions to many Oriental meals whose peculiar blends of spices and herbs defeat more conventional wine choices. These wines have an intriguing combination of flavors typical of the best handling of the Riesling grape. In good vintages they possess a delicate but pronounced fruit, mixed with spice and just a touch of sweetness. In the hands of producers like Graf Matuschka of Schloss Vollrads, this is in turn balanced by an acidity that sustains and almost dries the wine, so that the palate records a series of alternating and not-quite-merging flashes of lushness and austerity. Wines like these are sui generis: They do not fit any of the categories that we've been dealing with so far in this book, because their delicacy is so extraordinary—so much so that it is easily lost in a poor harvest, and even the best makers wind up with a wine that tastes simply acidic or merely sweet. For wines like these to work with food at all, their acid balance is crucial. Without it they are merely pleasant, sweetish, light wines; with it they have the equipoise to match exquisitely with delicately flavored and complex foods.

As for the sweeter classifications, although normally dessert wine means a wine to accompany dessert, you will do much better to think of these great wines *as* dessert. In that role they will maintain their character and their worth against even the lushest Sauternes. If you are looking for a light ending to a rich and elegant dinner, you could hardly find a better conclusion than a glass—or two or three—of these nectars, whose delicacy contradicts the tongue-blocking clutters of syllables that name their makers and villages and estates and quality: Steinberger Trockenbeerenauslese; Schloss Groenesteyn Rudesheimer Berg Rottland; Deidesheimer Hohenmorgen; Rauenthaler Langenstuck; Prüm's Wehlener Sonnenuhr, Langwerth von Simmern's Erbacher Marcobrunn and so on through all the length of the Rhine and the Mosel.

Selected Moderately Priced German Wines

Rhine: Kabinett, Spätlese, and Auslese bottlings of middling to fine vintages from such villages as Deidesheim, Eltvil, Erbach, Forst, Hattenheim, Hochheim, Johannisberg, Nierstein, Oppenheim, Rauenthal, Rudesheim, Winkel and from producers such as Dr. Burklin-Wolf, Deinhard, Heinrich Braun Hahnhof, Langwerth von Simmern, Lingenfelder, Schloss Johannisberg, Schloss Vollrads, Von Buhl, Dr. R. Weill.

Mosel: Kabinett, Spätlese, and Auslese bottlings of middling to fine vintages from such villages as Bernkastel, Brauneberg, Erden, Graach, Ockfen, Piesport, Trittenheim, Wehlen and from producers such as Deinhard, Dr. Fischer, Egon Muller, J. J. Prüm, Reichsgraf von Kesselstatt, Max Richter, Dr. Thanisch.

Selected German Wines for Extravagant Occasions

Rhine: Estate bottlings or individual vineyard wines bearing the designations Auslese, Beerenauslese, or Trockenbeerenauslese, in good to excellent vintages, from such top-rated areas as those mentioned above (for example, Schloss Vollrads, the Staatsweinguter Eltville's Steinberger, Hochheimer Konigin Victoriaberg)

Mosel: Estate bottlings or individual vineyard wines bearing the designations Auslese, Beerenauslese, or Trockenbeerenauslese, in good to excellent vintages, from such top-rated areas as those mentioned above (for example, Bernkasteler Doktor or Graacher Himmelreich from Dr. Thanisch, Trittenheimer Apotheke from Friedrich-Wilhelm-Gymnasium, Wehlener Sonnenuhr from J. J. Prüm)

Dessert Wines

Dessert wines have been enjoying a well-deserved renaissance of late, and at least some of them have become downright popular. A few classic Sauternes never lost their cachet, of course. Even non–wine drinkers always knew that Château d'Yquem was something to be impressed with, and recently ports have rejoined that very select group of prestigious postdinner wines that people actually order and drink rather than merely mention. Far too many other fine wines, however, remain in Limbo—Barsac and Vouvray and Beaumes de Venise, Madeira and oloroso sherry and P.X. sherry, Vin Santo and Picolit and Recioto and Passito, Trockenbeerenauslese and Eiswein, Alsace Vendange Tardive and California late-harvest wines and Cyprus Commandaria, even Asti Spumante and the doux and demi-sec champagnes.

I love most of these kinds of wine, but I'm probably the worst person in the world to recommend them. Most people like them for their sugar, and that's what interests me least about them. I have no sweet tooth. I can't stomach pronounced sweetness unalloyed by other qualities. For a sweet wine to win my vote, it has to have acidity to tone its sweetness and brighten it, fruit to give it personality, complexity to give it interest, body to give it support, even contrasting flavors—a dry or sour finish, for instance—to keep it from being monotonous or cloying. Sometimes even wines with all these qualities fail to please me—even though other wine enthusiasts whose taste buds I respect assure me that the wines contain all sorts of wonders—because their sweetness is simply quantitatively too great for me to taste anything else. As far as I am concerned, most ports fall into that class; others around me rhapsodize, and all I can taste is sugar. In fact, I have long suspected that port in particular is a British conspiracy, a way for otherwise mature adults to indulge the palatal equivalent of a taste for party crackers and whoopee cushions. With very, very few exceptions, California late-harvest wines strike me much the same way. A tidal wave of sugar obliterates every other taste sensation, leaving nothing but a quick sugar fix.

So how can I say I love these wines? Let me count the ways. I love them:

- in moderation
- in their place
- *as* instead of *with* dessert

Let's take these considerations in order.

In moderation: Because sugar in any discernible concentration, no matter how masked or modified by other elements, is a palate killer. It builds up on the taste buds and hides every other flavor, even the other flavors present in the wine itself. That's why making a dessert wine that doesn't merely taste of sugar is so extraordinarily fine an accomplishment. If sweetness were the only consideration in great dessert wines, they could be made in factories and sold as cheaply as Mars bars and Hostess Twinkies, and they would no doubt be as popular with people whose palates, like children's, recognize no taste but sugar.

In their place: That means, for the most part, at the end of a meal—again because of what sugar does to your palate. You can with pleasure drink a sweet wine after a dry one, but not vice versa. A dry wine will taste not dry but bitter, even vinegary, after even a modestly sweet wine, and that, for all practical purposes, confines the sweet wines to the end of the meal. There are a few pleasing exceptions. We have already talked about the role of some sweetish wines with Oriental foods. The wines at the less sweet end of the German wine spectrum—Kabinett, Spätlese, sometimes even Auslese if their acidity is good—can make wonderful light aperitifs or cocktails or simple afternoon refreshers all by themselves. This is as true too of the drier range of Vouvrays and Chenin Blancs as it is of the best of that class of lightly sweet wines that Italians call *abboccato* (Orvieto *abboccato,* for instance, can be lovely). But in most of the cases where this works, it does so because the wine is not heavily sweet, and its sweetness is usually balanced by a significant acidity. I know that the French occasionally take a perverse pleasure in drinking port as an aperitif. This, like the preference of the nineteenth-century French for sweet champagne, is a taste that I can neither explain nor condone, but *chacun à son goût.*

As *instead of* with *dessert:* This isn't just my lack of a sweet tooth dictating austerity to the sugar-loving hordes of America. I very seriously suggest to you that you ought to drink the great dessert wines by themselves rather than as accompaniments to desserts for one very sound palatal reason: Sweet on sweet doesn't work. They cancel each other out. Match a pronouncedly sweet wine with a markedly sweet dessert, and you're going to lose one or another of them, maybe both. This means that if you have a really glorious wine—an old, old Madeira or a mature Château d'Yquem or Rieussec, for instance—whose every drop and nuance you want to relish, your best bet will be to drink it in solitary splendor. Either that or serve it with a very simple, nearly unsweet dessert—simple butter cookies, nuts, even dried fruit will work. Simple foods like these will let a dessert wine sing. A sweet dessert or even an elaborate-though-only-moderately-sweet confection will interfere with any sweet wine worth drinking. They will compete with its flavors and upset its necessarily highly fragile balance, leaving you with only the empty husk of a great wine on your palate. Dessert wines are prima donnas, and like all great divas they perform their best only when they have undisputed control of center stage.

Dessert wines fall into several broad divisions: sparkling and still, fortified and unfortified, botrytised and unbotrytised. Most of the unfortified wines are vinified from white grapes—almost the only significant exception is Recioto della Valpolicella—but aside from this, generalizations fail entirely. Dessert wines are made from every conceivable grape variety in every conceivable style and just about everywhere grapes are grown.

SPARKLING DESSERT WINES

There are two principal sparkling dessert wines: the sweet champagnes and Asti Spumante.

The sweet champagnes all bear rather paradoxical indications of dryness—extra dry or extra sec (with 1.2 percent to 2 percent sugar), sec, and demi-sec (with 3 percent to 5 percent sugar). This results from the gradual drying of champagne over the course of the nineteenth century. As you may infer from these names, the basic champagne consumed at the beginning of that period was quite sweet, probably resembling today's rarely seen doux classification. As wines, they share the great breed and finesse of all true champagnes, but the essential austerity of their acidic northern grapes is veiled by varying degrees of sweetness. At their most successful—and for my palate this means the lighter range of sweetness, extra dry or sec—these wines offer a refreshing effervescence that seems to renew the palate's vigor. I find they work well with very simple desserts but tend to disappear with complex ones. They serve best of all, I think, as an intermezzo, a kind of palate scrubber between courses: after salad and before dessert, after dessert and before coffee. The sweetest champagnes simply don't work for me. They just come apart on my palate into two unrelated effects, sparkle and sweetness.

Most Asti Spumante lacks the great finesse of champagne, but all Asti Spumante possesses the great advantage, for a dessert wine, of the Moscato grape. Though much overused in wine writing, luscious is the only word that does justice to the flavor of top-quality, ripe Moscato and the wines that can be made from it. So intensely flavored is the variety, and so naturally high in sugar, that knowing how to rein it in is the skill most needed for making a good dessert wine from it. It must be harvested while it retains enough acidity to balance its sweetness, and it must be vinified very carefully to preserve its fragile freshness. In recent years the introduction of temperature-controlled fermentation in stainless steel has made a tremendous difference in the quality and character of this wine. Some years ago many Asti Spumantes were oxidized or flabby or straight-sugar cocktails, the essence of ick. These days the vast majority of Astis are bright, fresh, and clean sweet wines with a lively sparkle and a refreshing underlying acidity that keeps them supple and graceful, and they still have that wonderful Moscato flavor. Italians will drink Asti Spumante with almost any dessert, but far more commonly they simply drink it by itself, as a festive— and still happily not expensive—conclusion to a convivial dinner.

FORTIFIED DESSERT WINES

There are only four kinds of fortified wines that occupy any serious place in a meal: Madeira, Marsala, port, and sherry. Of these, port is always sweet to very sweet. The other three wines can range from nearly completely dry to quite sweet, and their uses will vary accordingly.

Madeira is probably the least esteemed of these wines today, a once-great wine tragically fallen from popularity. Some few examples of fine, old-fashioned Madeira can still be found, and they give a hint of what the wine may once again become. Madeira's vineyards were all but destroyed in the last century by phylloxera. Subsequently they were replanted—where they were replanted at all—with heavy-bearing, inferior varieties. Now Portugal's entry into the European Common Market is forcing a dramatic conversion of Madeira's vineyards back to the original varieties. It will of course be some years before we taste the fruits of these efforts, especially with so slow maturing a wine as Madeira, but we can at least look forward to a time when the words Sercial, Verdelho, Bual, and Malmsey will once again designate wines made from distinctive grape varieties with markedly different characters and not just indicate—as they do today—almost dry, semisweet, sweet, and very sweet.

Marsala has shared Madeira's fall from grace, but for more immediately remediable reasons. The makers of Marsala killed their own market by manipulating the wine, adding all sorts of gimmicky flavors to a basically sound wine. For years it was easier to buy a Marsala flavored with coffee or bananas than to find a simple, unadulterated Marsala. Happily, the flavored glop is disappearing from the market, and the best Marsalas are once again finding their audience. Marsala comes in three styles: *Fine,* the basic grade, dry or sweet (mostly sweet); *Superiore,* dry or sweet, normally a large jump in quality above the *Fine;* and *Vergine,* always dry, and produced by a method similar to sherry's solera. Marsala *Vergine* can be exquisite, but it is better suited to use as an aperitif or a cocktail than as a dessert wine. The best dessert Marsalas come from the sweet *Superiore* category from such reliable makers as Florio, Pellegrino, and especially Rallo.

Port is booming right now, and after years of slumbering on the shelves, bottles of port—especially vintage port—have become big-ticket items in the trendy wine shops. There are many very reputable makers, for port has had an uninterrupted and discriminating British market since the eighteenth century: Cockburn, Croft, Delaforce, Dow's, Ferreira, Fonseca, Graham, Quinta do Noval, Sandeman, Taylor Fladgate, and Warre are only some of the best. Ports come in several designations:

Ruby: The least expensive category, aged two years in wood. Young tasting, sweet.

Tawny: The best of these—and they can be very fine—are so called from the color they turn after many years of cask aging. The least of them are blended from red and white ports to reach the desired shade. Age and price are the key indications of quality in this very miscellaneous category. All are sweet.

Vintage: Vintages in port, as in champagne, are declared by individual houses when they think the quality of their grapes justifies it. Vintage ports never receive less than twenty-two months or more than thirty-one months of wood aging before bottling. Regarded by connoisseurs as the finest of all ports. Sweet.

Vintage character, vintage reserve: Essentially ruby port of good quality given extra barrel aging before bottling. These wines do not develop in the bottle as do the true vintage ports. Sweet.

Late-bottled vintage: Port from a single harvest, aged in wood for double the time given vintage port. Sweet. Because of the scarcity of true vintage port, the makers have created these last two categories to meet market demand with an approximation of their best product.

White port: Usually the driest of all the ports, though that is a very relative term. Vinified much like ruby and intended by its makers for consumption as an aperitif.

Most ports respond much better to simple cheeses, nuts, and fresh fruits as accompaniments than they do to complex or sweet desserts.

Sherry is the most varied of all these wines, including in its range dry, pale, and essentially light-bodied aperitif wines as well as dark, syrupy, dry, or intensely sweet after-dinner wines. Many sherries are marketed under proprietary names, but their labels will almost always, even if only in very fine print, reveal what class the wine belongs to. The principal sherry groups are as follows:

Fino: Normally the driest of the sherries. Best consumed as an aperitif or a cocktail, though the Spanish, and occasionally the English, will also drink it with dinner. Good commercial brands: Gonzalez Byass's Tio Pepe, Pedro Domecq's La Ina, Hartley & Gibson, Wisdom & Warter.

Manzanilla: The favorite of sherry aficionados, but often hard to find in the United States. Pale, light bodied, tangy. Devotees claim to be able to smell and taste the ocean in it (it's vinified near the sea). Legend also has it that manzanilla goes especially well with seafood, though that must mean canapés, since most people drink it as an aperitif.

Amontillado: The bait in Edgar Allan Poe's classic tale, amontillados are essentially darker, slightly heavier, nuttier-tasting versions of fino. Excellent aperitifs. Lots of good ones from Byass, Domecq, Hartley & Gibson, Sandeman, Williams & Humbert, Wisdom & Warter.

Oloroso: This group contains dry wines and sweet ones, golden wines and deep amber ones. These are the most varied and the most potentially rewarding of all the sherries. Read the labels carefully to determine the degree of dryness (oloroso is rarely more than medium sweet). All are good after-dinner drinks, but the driest olorosos also make wonderful aperitifs. Names to look for include Domecq's Rio Viejo, Sandeman's Royal Corregidor and Imperial Corregidor, Williams & Humbert's Dry Sack and Dos Cortados.

Palo cortado: A rarity. Palo cortado stands about halfway between an amontillado and a lightly sweet oloroso, heavier than the first, more supple than the latter.

Cream sherry: Essentially, these are very sweet olorosos. In fact, they are usually olorosos *sweetened*—normally by the addition of Pedro Ximénez grapes (see next item), sometimes Moscato. Harvey's Bristol Cream provided the original model and remains the most famous of them. Other good ones include Byass's Nectar Cream and San Domingo Pale Cream, Domecq's Celebration Cream, Hartley & Gibson's Cream, Wisdom & Warter's Delicate Cream.

P.X.: A sherry made entirely from Pedro Ximénez grapes, or nearly so. They are relatively rare: dark, full bodied, almost syrupy in texture, of a sweetness so intense that sometimes all sensation of sweetness is lost. A wine for connoisseurs and adventurous palates. If you're curious, look for Domecq's Viña 25 and Venerable, Hartley & Gibson's Argüeso Cream.

With sherries of whatever kind, and whether I am drinking them before or after dinner, I much prefer—and I believe the wine does too—only the simplest accompaniments. Fresh or fresh-roasted nuts, especially walnuts, almonds, and hazelnuts, work beautifully with all sherries.

BOTRYTISED WINES

Some of our most glorious dessert wines get their start in life from an inglorious—in fact rather repulsive-looking—mold, *Botrytis cinerea*. It infects ripe grapes, consuming their juices and thereby concentrating their flavor elements and at the same time adding an almost unmistakable "honeyed" note of its own. This "noble rot" (*pourriture noble*), as it is called, may appear spontaneously on the grapes as they ripen. So may other less desirable molds. And some bunches of grapes develop no mold at all. The mixed vineyard situation requires careful hand picking and, usually, multiple passes through the vineyards, spread out over days or weeks as the weather holds or threatens. This means that the finest botrytised wines will always be scarce and always expensive. The very best of them are unquestionably worth their high prices. Even for those of us who do not relish sweets, these wines are nectars. Here are the major kinds:

Sauternes and Barsac: Château d'Yquem has all the glory, but the Sauternes district produces many other fine wines, as does its sadly neglected sister zone, Barsac. Made predominantly from the Sémillon grape, with varying small amounts of Sauvignon, and in the very best years with almost all the grapes at least touched by *Botrytis*, the wines of this Bordeaux area rank as the supreme dessert wines of the world: thick, with a silken, almost syrupy texture, golden hued, and tasting simultaneously of fruit and nuts and honey, a whole dessert in themselves. Of the two, Barsac tends to be a little less sweet and less forceful, but still very impressive.

Bonnezeaux, Quarts de Chaume, Vouvray: These long-lived dessert wines come from stretches of the Loire Valley in Anjou and the Touraine. They are vinified from Chenin Blanc grapes, and they capture the rich, melony taste of this grape beautifully, enlivening it always with Chenin's characteristic acidity. In years when *Botrytis* is prominent, the wine also displays lovely honey flavors as well. Like Sauternes and Barsac, these wines improve with bottle age. The best structured vintages can live forty years and more.

Alsace Vendange Tardive and Sélection de Grains Nobles: The two French terms amount to exact translations, respectively, of late harvest and Beerenauslese, which should tell you a fair amount about these wines already. The grape varieties involved are those we normally associate with the German wines Riesling and Gewürztraminer (sometimes Pinot Gris, a.k.a. Tokay d'Alsace), but vinified in a thoroughly French manner to produce full-bodied sweet wines that overwhelm rather than seduce. The years 1983 and 1985 had high summer temperatures that forced the grapes to an unusual degree of ripeness and made possible some wonderful Vendange Tardive bottlings. Nineteen seventy-six brought *Botrytis*, which in turn brought some spectacular bottles of Sélection de Grains Nobles. Vendange Tardive wines range from lightly to medium sweet, and Grains Nobles are usually distinctly sweet. Because of their body and acidity, these wines partner well with sweet or complex desserts, though my personal preference is still to drink them by themselves.

German Auslese, Beerenauslese, Trockenbeerenauslese, and Eiswein: If there are any contenders or pretenders to Barsac's and Sauternes's crown as the premier dessert wines, they are these German select pickings, individual grape pickings, individual dried grape pickings, and the rare ice wines—wines made from the scant juices that run from grapes frozen on the vine at the peak of ripeness. Vinified mostly from Riesling, occasionally from Gewürztraminer, these wines are the polar opposites of Sauternes and Barsac. Light and delicate on the tongue, their flavors have depth and complexity, but you would never describe them as lush. Ethereal comes closer to the truth. Have them with fruit, or have them by themselves.

Vin Santo, Passito, Picolit: Italy offers an oddly varied lot of dessert wines. Picolit, from the province of Friuli, and made from the grape of the same name, superficially resembles Sauternes. But it lacks Sauternes's lushness, though it shares its silky texture and adds a suppleness that comes from higher acidity. Italians call it a *vino da meditazione*, a wine for meditation, and that seems to sum it up nicely.

Passito is wine made from partly raisined grapes. In some parts of Italy, especially the south, the grapes are left to reach this stage on the vine. This gives us Passito of Moscato from Sicily and of the island of Pantelleria, which can be superb, and a Passito of Malvasia from the island of Lipari, which can be matchless. In the north of Italy the traditional way with Passito selects bunches of grapes to be left to dry in the sun on straw mats and then fermented. This gives us the two Recioti of Verona, Recioto di Soave and Recioto della Valpolicella, white and red respectively. The Soave has great delicacy and charm, the Valpolicella a rich authority and tremendous fruitiness. Passito, north or south, can develop *Botrytis* if harvest conditions permit, and those wines that are touched by it add its characteristic smoky-honey tones to their attractions.

Finally, Vin Santo is not a single wine, but many. It should be regarded as a collective noun, because there is vast disagreement about what it is—even whether it is sweet or dry—among the various vintners and regions that produce it. Consensus holds that the best Vin Santo comes from Tuscany, but you can get your throat cut for preferring that of Siena to the Vin Santo of Florence, and vice versa. Very ripe Malvasia grapes are fermented in small, sealed barrels, which are stored under eaves and in attics where for anywhere from one to many years they pass through extremes of heat and cold. When finally bottled, the wine may be anything from pale amber to deep brown in color, sweet or dry or some indescribable mixture of the two. Definitely an acquired taste for most Americans, but the best examples—Avignonesi's, for example, or Barbi's—are well worth the trouble of acquiring. All these wines—Vin Santo, Passito, Picolit—are traditionally served accompanied only by the simplest dry cookies, especially the sort known in Tuscany as *biscotti di Prato*.

American late-harvest wines: It is flatly impossible to generalize about wines made everywhere from Southern California to northern New York from every imaginable variety of *Vitis vinifera* and some of its hybrids as well. The only advice I can give you is to read the label very carefully to try to determine what has been the model for the individual wine you're considering—Sauternes, TBA, port—and what its sweetness and acidity are. California labels especially are usually very good about providing this kind of information. Once armed with as much as you can learn about the characteristics of your particular wine, you'll then have to judge by analogy—by how much it resembles the more conventional or more established types of dessert wines—whether you want to drink it and what you want to drink it with. One clue: Late-harvest Zinfandel usually resembles port in its attack, and several of its makers swear it's delicious with peanut butter!

CHAPTER 6

The Food

At the dinner table, in between bits of deviled grilled lamb kidneys with a sauce he [Nero Wolfe] and Fritz had invented, he explained why it was that all you needed to know about any human society was what they ate. If you knew what they ate you could deduce everything else—culture, philosophy, morals, politics, everything.

—REX STOUT, *The Final Deduction*

T HE PRINCIPLE THAT "Wines show best and go best with the foods they grew up with" deserves more attention than we were able to give it in the last section. When, in the process of choosing wines to drink with particular foods, you find yourself confronted with novel or unanticipated circumstances, it's important to remember what you already know and to look for ways to use it. Always get down to basics. New recipes don't necessarily mean new problems in choosing wines. Remind yourself of the truisms, the old never-fail combinations. This is exactly why and where the conventional wine and food pairings of the various national cuisines have so much to teach us.

180

Understanding the underlying rationale, the—broadly conceived—animating spirit of each cuisine in terms of its own internal consistencies and goals is an important conceptual stage in mastering the skill of appropriately matching food and wine. Each of the major European wine-oriented cuisines has its own set of internally generated elective affinities between foods prepared in its peculiar way and wines vinified in its own style. Each of those sets, each individual pairing, contains seminal information about a theoretically infinite number of wine and food combinations. Exploring just some of the implications of those traditional relationships can teach us an immense amount about the art of marrying wines and foods. (Trying to work out all the implications of the ever-so-easily-stated "Wines go best with the foods they grew up with" would make a worthwhile and enjoyable lifetime project for an omnivore of refined sensibility.)

Wine with French Meals

French wine and food partnerships are the most thoroughly codified and documented of all the various national cuisines, a consequence of the scrutiny that both connoisseurship and scholarship have applied to French cooking over the past three hundred years. Few cuisines and their attendant arts have been as rationalized as the French, a fact that has in no way pruned it of delight or surprise or eccentricity. Descartes in the kitchen turns out to be another person than Descartes in the study. Clear and distinct ideas may rule in some areas, as in the classification of the great French sauces—but only until dethroned by unruly romantic impulses. How else can you account for the existence of *soufflés glacés*?

In French cooking there seem to be rules for everything, even for breaking the rules, and so for French food and wine professionals, even the originally daring innovations of the now-no-longer-new nouvelle cuisine rapidly became fairly regularized. All nouvelle cuisine really accomplished, in terms of wine and food pairings, was to show the limitations of a too-rigid application of the "red wine with meat, white wine with fish" rule. Maybe this came as a revelation to the mass media, but it wasn't really news to anyone who had strolled beyond the tourist centers of gastronomy. But despite the journalistic hoopla and incomprehension, nouvelle cuisine's seemingly frivolous playing with fish poached in red wine and blood meats seasoned with raspberry vinegar had the very healthy effect of sending people back to examine first principles, the very principles we're grappling with in this book. Nouvelle cuisine started people looking anew at condiment, food, and wine combinations that they had been taking for granted. It started them thinking again about *why* some wines succeed with some foods while others fail.

As a result, even in popular perception (maybe especially in popular perception) the "rules" for wine to accompany dinner have altered dramatically. The old haute cuisine and its conventional, seemingly invariable battery of wines have totally lost their authority, and what were once heresies are now fashionable. But freedom exacts its price: If you can't fall back on the old truisms, how can you tell what to drink with what? Especially when the "what" might be veal breast with Armagnac sauce, or sweetbreads with a lemony cream sauce, or lamb shanks braised with garlic, tomato, and vinegar, or a warm beef salad flavored with lime and chilies and Thai fish sauce, or carpaccio dressed with a basil béarnaise, or salmon poached in red wine. These particular examples aren't whimsically chosen rarities. All are dishes that nouvelle cuisine and America's increasingly internationalized appetite have called into being on the menus of French restaurants (French restaurants in the United States, that is; French cooking on its home turf continues to go its own many ways, some of them quite traditional).

Always bear in mind the simple fact that changes in gastronomic style, no matter how dramatic, have no effect on the laws of nature. Take red wine with fish as a case in point. This is a currently infamous pseudo problem that seems to send a lot of people into an unnecessary tailspin. Fish poached in red wine normally takes a red wine as a natural and appropriate accompaniment because the mode of cooking—the prominence of the condiment, red wine—

has substantially shifted the so-to-speak "power center" of the dish. The flavor profile of delicately flavored fish is altered significantly by an aggressively flavored condiment, just as our basic Decalogue-and-a-Half of guidelines warned you it would be. The only real questions generated by such a preparation are what kind of red wine and how big, and there are precedents for determining this in the traditional cuisine.

It may come as a surprise, but the practice of cooking fish in or with red wine has been around a long time, at least since the Middle Ages, maybe since Roman times (Apicius isn't clear on the subject). *Lamproie à la bordelaise*—lampreys braised with leeks in red wine—isn't a new dish but a very old one, a classic and delicious specialty of French regional cuisine. A fish cooked in red wine, especially if it is a strongly flavored, fatty fish such as salmon or tuna or eel or lamprey, behaves remarkably like chicken or veal braised in red wine, and it generally follows pretty closely the same pattern of wine compatibilities. This means that your best choice of wine, for all the reasons we've discussed in earlier chapters, would be a light- to medium-bodied, dry, soft red wine, not very tannic and with a reasonable degree of acidity. It also indicates that an assertively flavored, rather full-bodied white wine could also work with the dish, despite its red wine cooking medium, if the particular white wine possessed sufficient acidity. *Lamproie à la bordelaise*, for instance, works very well with St-Emilion (its softness complements the dish beautifully), young red Graves (a cedary, acidic wine, leaner than St-Emilion), and middle-aged (about five years old) white Graves. This is simply because in cooking all wines, white or red, create an acid presence that, unless it is counteracted or masked by other cooking steps, your wine choice must be able to deal with. In *lamproie à la bordelaise* the red wine acidity of the sauce is counterbalanced by the sweetness of the leeks, thereby creating an almost neutral medium for the lamprey and the dinner wine. A fish's own fats can often have exactly the same effect.

You don't have to be a slave of fashion to want red wine with fish. Richly flavored fish—tuna, for instance—and richly flavored preparations like the one discussed above provide in themselves ample warrant to try something potentially more interesting than the conventional white wines. And even if the fish and its preparation are conventionally mild, you don't have to stifle any pronounced desire for red wine you may be feeling. You can achieve a very workable compromise between what the dish wants and what you want by choosing a lighter-bodied red wine either with relatively abundant acidity (like a Beaujolais or Barbera) or with the kind of stemmy tannins whose action can mimic acidity (some non-Burgundian Pinot Noirs). Alsace and California both produce quite decent, inexpensive Pinot Noirs that show a marked tendency toward lightness of body and exactly the sort of acidlike, stemmy tannins that are needed to complement a simple fish preparation without conquering it. This will let you taste both the wine and the fish, especially if the fish is one like salmon or tuna that possesses its own fair share of body and flavor.

The combinations of ingredients in dishes like these may come as surprises or novelties to you, but the working principles by which you select a wine to accompany them remain exactly the same as those we have been dealing with all along. And for exactly that reason, your crucial first reactions, in the face of any new gastronomical data, should be to discern their basic components or flavor elements and to recall what you already know about them and their wine affinities. In the case of a dish clearly rooted in a specific culinary method or national culinary style, such as an inventively sauced nouvelle cuisine preparation, you should also bring to bear all that you know about the wine and food affinities that usually obtain within that style, its normal way of connecting the two. The sum total of everything you know about the spirit of a cuisine— what used to be called its "genius"—is relevant to every particular decision you make about it.

THE MOTHERS OF INVENTION

You find the soul of French cuisine in its sauces. No other Western cooking style has so many of them or uses them so abundantly and prominently. By their importance, their number, and their character, French sauces differentiate French gastronomy from every other national style in the world. Within its classic cuisines, both haute and bourgeoise, most of the elaborate dishes fall into a few kinship groups, however different from one another they appear. These kinship groups are formed not by the base ingredients used (which they share with most of the other nations of Europe) nor by the methods of cooking them (though these are obviously important, they are limited in number and shared by most of the world) but by the sauces that dress them: They impart the flavors and nuances that all of us think of as characteristically French.

Almost all classic French sauces descend, by various steps of elaboration and refinement, from a very few "mother sauces." The brown sauces derive essentially from *demi-glace* or *espagnole,* the white sauces in large part either from some form of *velouté* or from *béchamel.* So sauces as variously named and ingrediented as *bigarade* and *bordelaise, charcutière* and *chevreuil, diable, Madère,* and *périgourdine* all branch out from an underlying *espagnole,* just as *ravigote, Albuféra, Bercy,* and *normande* are all varieties of *velouté.* A genuinely new and different sauce is very hard to discover. Even the antitraditional sauces of the nouvelle cuisine descend in large part from these august *mères,* in many cases with only the flour removed and more meat or fish stocks added. The supposedly revolutionary sauces employing various fruit vinegars grow from even simpler dressings, such as *beurre blanc* and especially *beurre noir.* They also have very firm roots in classic sauces, such as *hollandaise, béarnaise,* and *mayonnaise,* all sauces achieved by bringing an acid into suspension with other liquids and flavorings. Diners have been successfully matching wines with these sauces and the simpler vinegar-accented dressings with little difficulty for a good many years. The difference between the most modern and the most traditional French sauces is one of degree rather than kind, and recognizing that fact can go a long way toward helping you choose compatible wines for them.

A TRIO OF TASTES

Even within the confines of the classic sauces, recognizing this common thread that links apparently dissimilar dishes makes your component matching of wines and foods that much simpler. Duckling with *bigarade* sauce, venison with *sauce grand veneur,* or beef filet in a *sauce italienne* sound wildly different from one another, but look again. In each case you are dealing with:

- a strong-to-gamy tasting meat
- tender in texture
- cooked moist
- sauced with an intensely flavored liquid
- which is produced by concentrating a *demi-glace*
- and adding vinegar, citrus juices, or other acids

So similar are the preparations, in fact, that you could very easily and successfully serve the same wine with them all: A mature St-Estèphe would be perfect, because it has its own intensity and balance to match those of the three dishes. Within that single category, there are still plenty of choices. To list some options in ascending order of excellence (and cost):

- Château de Pez and Château Les Ormes de Pez are moderately priced selections. The 1975 or 1978 vintages would be very drinkable now as well as top quality. Alternatively, consider the 1981 vintage—perhaps a bit unready still, but balanced and fresh.
- As yet more opulent alternatives, consider Château Montrose—the first-rate 1970 is just ready to drink—or Château Cos d'Estournel, whose 1966—an almost legendary vintage in the Médoc—is now nearing its peak of maturity.

These wines would show gorgeously with all three dishes. A St-Estèphe's deep flavor and full body, coupled with its lean, tannic muscularity, ensure that it will have the intensity to match the flavors of the meats and the necessary burr to penetrate the richness of their sauces. The acidic elements in each preparation are balanced by meat-sweetness and herbs, so the wine's tannins will not clash with them unless you choose too young a bottle.

This is an example of how to approach these dishes and their appropriate wines emphasizing their similarities—the sort of exercise you might well have to perform in a restaurant, for instance, when the members of your party order different meals. But there is another approach as well, an opposite one, that concentrates on what distinguishes these sauces from one another and seeks a much closer mesh between a wine and a particular dish. This requires more analytical effort on your part, but it can yield a match that will please you much more than the common-ground approach. Enjoyable though a St-Estèphe would be with all these dishes because of the qualities they share, the wines you might pair with each of these dishes individually, by paying attention to their differences, could be even more pleasing.

The *boeuf à l'italienne,* for instance, has the gentlest, least intense flavors of the three, as well as the lushest, softest textures and the lowest acidity. For these reasons, you could match it very well with a softer, lighter, less intense wine—a good but not transcendent Burgundy perhaps. The red Burgundies have been tending toward lighter and lighter body over the past two decades. The winemakers say this is because the vines are field mutating (the grapes are changing character and losing intensity), but many people think, despite the professionals' denials, that the Burgundians have deliberately changed their methods of vinification to produce lighter, faster-maturing wines. Some cynics also believe that the growers are overcropping, i.e., not pruning the vines severely enough, which produces more grapes of less intense flavor, which in turn results in more but lighter wine at ever higher prices: a salesman's dream and a wine lover's nightmare. Whatever the truth of the matter, a red Burgundy that is six to ten years old would taste marvelous alongside that piece of beef. Try that old favorite Pommard or a Beaune village like Pernand-Vergelesses for moderately priced wines, remembering always that moderate means something different with Burgundies than it does with other wines. For an expensive, exquisite wine, try a fine single-vineyard Burgundy, such as the superb Beaune Grèves Vigne de l'Enfant Jésus. In good vintages all three are wines of middling body but great elegance and balance, at their best displaying a velvety texture that would nicely complement the tenderness of that beef filet.

Your venison in *grand veneur* sauce is another story, however.

Real venison always stays chewy and always retains an intensity of flavor that reminds you that those graceful creatures with the soulful, big brown eyes—Bambi look-alikes though they be—are really wild animals. Here the sheer depth of flavor of the preparation dominates every other consideration, and the cream and currant jelly in the *sauce grand veneur* eliminate any problems that might arise from an overemphatic acidity. So you don't need a wine with assertive tannin or acidity of its own, but rather one whose own flavors can match the intensity of the venison and its sauce. Within the French repertoire, that description points one way: toward the Rhône. Côte Rôtie, Hermitage, Cornas, and Châteauneuf-du-Pape all produce powerful, long-lasting red wines of intensity and depth sufficient to accompany any game. For a great wine at moderate expense, I would look to the Châteauneuf-du-Pape from Château Fortia, Château de La Nerthe, or Domaine du Mont-Redon. Slightly more expensive (largely because the producing area is small) but well worth it is Cornas from Delas Frères or, if you are lucky enough to be able to find some, from Clape. If expense were no object, I would seek out one of Guigal's single-slope Côte Rôtie wines, La Mouline or La Landonne, or the matchless Hermitage from Chave. Among the larger Rhône houses, both Chapoutier and Jaboulet make lovely Hermitage.

To complete this set, consider the Duckling *bigarade* in isolation. Any of the St-Estèphes suggested earlier would taste perfectly fine with it, without question, but since we are in all probability eating a soft-fleshed and more delicately flavored Long Island duck, i.e., a Pekin, rather than a *rouennais* or anything gamier, how about a softer, richer Margaux to complement the lushness of the bird and its bitter-orange sauce? Château Margaux itself stands alone, the commune's sole *premier cru,* at the pinnacle of excellence and expense, but there are many thoroughly enjoyable lesser growths that step down the ladder of cost with little diminution in quality. For an amplitude of fine choices at several levels of expense, consider, for instance, the second growths Rausan-Ségla and Brane-Cantenac, the third growths Palmer, Kirwan, and Giscours, the fourth growths Prieuré-Lichine and Marquis-de-Terme, and the unclassified d'Angludet and Siran.

WINE AND FOOD CORRELATIONS: BEEF

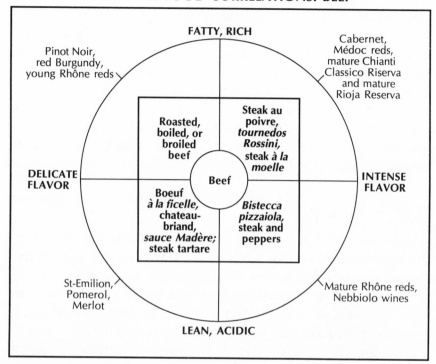

In all these examples I've consciously confined the wine choices for these dishes to the most classic French growths, following that fail-safe guideline with which we started: Wines always show best and go best with the foods they grew up with. But we can very readily extrapolate from that kind of pairing. You could certainly replace our workhorse, go-with-all-three St-Estèphe with a Cabernet Sauvignon or Cabernet-Merlot blend from just about anywhere in the world, provided it was built on the same big scale as the red wines of Bordeaux. This includes all the California Cabernets, most of the Australian, and some of the Italian (mostly those from Tuscany, plus one—Gaja's—from Piedmont). And you could break out of the Cabernet group entirely (as we already did with the Rhône wines) by simply seeking out full-bodied, assertive, and somewhat tannic wines from anywhere. This opens the door to California Petite Sirah and claret-style Zinfandel; to top-of-the-line, old-style Rioja Reserva (Muga's Prado Enea, Bodegas Lan's

Viña Lanciano; López Heredia's Viña Tondonia); to Barolo and Barbaresco as well as to Chianti Classico Riserva and Taurasi. Think how the fruit of a Zinfandel would play with the flavors of that duckling, or how satiny a foil a fine Barolo would make for the venison, how a great Rioja could surround and support the beef. The world of wine is rich with possibilities, and a very decent percentage of them are wonderful. There is very little risk of choosing a red wine that simply won't integrate with your food when you work outward in this manner from a traditional match to wines that share similar qualities.

WHITE WINE SUBTLETIES

Note, however, that that great assurance and ease is limited to red wines. When it comes to white wine meals, you lose a bit of that marvelous latitude. Because the range of flavors in white wines is itself narrower than in reds, and because so many of the wines are relatively delicate and the foods they accompany so gracefully nuanced, it is, alas, much easier to really come a cropper in matching a white wine with a French dinner—even within the confines of French wine alone. The spectrum of flavors in the red wines and in the foods they pair with as well as the multiplicity of components each contributes to the matchup give you some shelter from partial mismatches. With white wines and their corresponding foods, the flavor spectrum is much narrower. Everything lies right out in the open. There is no place to hide. Because there is so much less to work with in the first place—smaller scale flavors, much lower intensity, and consequently greater importance of slight gradations of difference—nothing can mask or blur the clash of tastes or styles if the wine and the food don't fit together well.

This narrowed spectrum produces one advantage for your decision making. It reduces the number of components of the food and the wine you have to worry seriously about. In a decision involving a white wine, one factor should get most of your attention: the acid/fat ratio. The main ingredient may be fish, flesh, fowl, vegetable, or eggs, and its sauce based on cream or tomato or broth: The chief elements that will determine whether your wine selection complements the food, or fights it, or surrenders to it will be the way the wine's body and acidity get along with the food's unctuosity or acidity.

Let's consider another classic trinity of dishes, this time for white wines: *suprêmes de volaille Nantua, Poached Sole with sauce Bercy, raie au beurre noir*. Once again, looking for common factors is the best way to proceed, and when we look we find that all three dishes:

- use white, mild-flavored meats
- that are somewhat dry and stringy, or long-stranded, in texture
- all cooked by a moist method (braising or poaching)
- and served with an abundant sauce that does not alter, but rather enhances, the delicate taste of the main ingredient

Beyond the inherent differences in flavor of chicken breasts, Dover sole, and skate, their sauces account for the major differences between the dishes. *Nantua* is béchamel-based sauce, a smooth, creamy sauce flavored with shellfish. *Bercy* adds fish stock and white wine to sautéed shallots and binds them with a fish-based velouté to produce a thinner, lighter, and more archetypally "fishy" sauce than the average Nantua. *Beurre noir* is technically not a sauce at all, but a parsley, capers, vinegar, and butter liaison used piping hot.

So what do we need in a wine to accompany these dishes?

- First, it must fall in the right range of flavor intensity, neither so strong that it will obliterate the food nor so light that it seems tasteless alongside the dishes it's meant to accompany.
- Second, it will have to be fully dry: Sweetness will fight with the unmodified fish flavors in the sauces and the main ingredients.
- Third, it will have to possess sufficient body or acidity or asperity to cut through the flavors of the creamy sauces and to stand up to or complement the vinegar and caper acidity of the *beurre noir*.

Within the French repertoire, a good many wines happily meet these requirements. Muscadet, Graves, Pouilly-Fumé, Sancerre, or Chablis for whites and Alsace Pinot Noir for a red will serve well with these dishes, though no single one of them will integrate as happily or as effectively with all three as our St-Estèphe did with its three meat preparations. This is because these dishes and most white wines simply operate on a finer scale of flavor differentiation and consequently demand much more precise correlation than do more strongly flavored red wines and their foods. It's my guess that by far the greatest portion of the difficulty people imagine to be intrinsic to matching wines and foods arises from white wines and the meals that need them, and precisely for this reason. (Of course, this is yet one more argument, if any rational soul needs one, to drink more red wine.)

The Dover sole offers the least challenge to your matchmaking skills. The fish itself, soft fleshed and with some but not excessive natural oiliness, enters completely into the medium of its sauce, which possesses proportions of "fat" and delicate fish flavors comparable to its own. Because this whole preparation presents itself so gently to the palate, no single element needs to be compensated for or mitigated by the wine. As a consequence, almost any white wine of good quality will marry happily with this dish, from the acidic counterpoint of a Pouilly-Fumé, through the complementary balance of a fine Graves (a three- or four-year-old Château Carbonnieux would be lovely), to the more emphatic presence of a Burgundy. For the latter, consider anything from a first-rate Chablis (a *grand cru* still costs less than any other white Burgundy of comparable quality) to a Meursault (a shipper's or an individual vineyard, depending on the level of expense you can stand). The only wines to avoid here, to my thinking, are the great whites of the Rhône, which by their sheer size and intensity would overpower this dish.

That same gentleness of flavor also makes it relatively easy to select a wine outside the French repertoire to pair with this dish. Again, a really big wine should be avoided, which means we should be very wary about California Chardonnay, but California Sauvignon or a fully dry Chenin Blanc from a first-rate producer would be lovely with the sole, as would some of the California Graves-like blends (Vichon's graceful Chevrignon, for instance). Italian Sauvignon and Pinot Bianco would also serve more than satisfactorily.

Those Rhône whites that are too mighty for the Dover sole—especially Hermitage or Châteauneuf-du-Pape—might work very well with the *suprêmes de volaille Nantua*, particularly if the sauce were a forceful one. *Sauce Nantua* can be made in many degrees of flavor intensity, depending on the amount of shellfish used and how far their essence is concentrated, but it is always rich because of its béchamel base and its mandatory infusion of cream. Chicken breasts, a lean and somewhat dry meat, make a wonderful underpinning for this sauce, and the whole dish presents a fascinating interplay of fish and fowl flavors lusciously bound together by a rich, creamy liquid. Because of that character, the richest, fullest white wines—the Rhônes and the Burgundies—best complement this dish. Also because of that character, you could arrange a very interesting counterpoint between your wine and food by choosing a high-acid wine of lesser, though still respectable, body: a Pouilly-Fumé or a Sancerre. Muscadet, though acidic enough, I would judge to be both too light of body and too simple—coarse even—in flavor to stand up to this food preparation. (There are a few single-estate Muscadets of very interesting character that are well worth trying, if you are lucky enough to find them, with somewhat less demanding dishes.) A Graves would not harm this dish any, but neither would it do much for it. The richness of the sauce would somewhat muffle the Graves's flavor, while the wine is so thoroughly balanced that it has neither the strong acidity nor the forceful flavor nor the body required to break through that envelope.

The same considerations of course reveal the kinds of non-French wine you could use to complement or counterpoint this dish. To complement: California Chardonnay for openers, and as big as they make them. Those lush California fruit flavors and that typical buttery roundness would match perfectly with the richness of *sauce Nantua*. A big, oleaginous, full-flavored Italian white like Greco di Tufo, though much more acidic than California wines, would still provide a beautiful complement, as would a fine, old-style white Rioja. For a fine acidic counterpoint, consider a Washington or Oregon Riesling, or a really bright Italian Sauvignon (Gradnik's or Russiz Superiore), or a Gewürztraminer from Alsace or Trentino–Alto Adige.

A RAIE OF LIGHT

Raie au beurre noir is at once the simplest dish of these three and the most exotic, and not because it's made with skate. Skate is a wonderful fish, firm fleshed and slightly oily-gelatinous in texture (not unlike monkfish or scallops), with a distinctive briny-fleshy flavor. In this preparation its dressing combines a rich fat—the browned butter—with the sharp, acidic flavors of capers and vinegar. On the face of it, such a combination sounds unlikely to yield anything even edible, but the dish in fact tastes wonderful. Everything comes together in a bright, clean palatal harmony. In less calorie-conscious times, when people were also less squeamish about what their food looked like when it was alive, *raie au beurre noir* appeared regularly on the menus of Parisian bistros and family restaurants all across France. These days the dish has become something of a rarity, but for us an instructive one, since its butter-and-vinegar sauce creates exactly—we should probably say archetypally—the same kind of difficulty in choosing a wine to accompany it as do any of the fashionable fruit-and-vinegar or meat-glaze-and-vinegar sauces of the new cuisine.

The big surprise is that there isn't any difficulty. *Raie au beurre noir* matches quite well with a number of white wines, from simple Muscadet through Pouilly-Fumé and up to the grand Rhônes. Acidity is the key here. For all the butter in the sauce and the natural oil of the fish, acetic acid from the vinegar becomes the binder that links and holds the disparate flavor elements together. Note well: This same fact is true of a very large number of the new sauces that result from using flavored vinegars or fruit vinegars in combination with fats (butter, oil) and fruits, meat glazes, highly concentrated broths, or other intensely flavored ingredients. Unless the recipe calls for a large enough amount of sweetness to constitute a dominant flavor in the sauce—and this is relatively rare—

the vinegar's acetic acid is going to be the key flavor component for determining the kind of wine to drink with the dish.

The wines that work best with any dish using this sort of attack are those whose own acidity is high enough that the dish's does not distort them. This means that, generally speaking, the great white Burgundies won't succeed with these kinds of sauces. Their acids simply pull apart the fat, round flavor and rich extract the Burgundies draw from the Chardonnay grape, making the wine taste unstructured and inert. And the good Graves whites fail here for a similar reason. Their balance of acid and fruit and alcohol is easily upset by the marked acidity of the sauce, so that they taste flabby and uninteresting. Muscadet, on the other hand, although its flavor is rather one dimensional and far less interesting than that of Graves, shows well with *raie au beurre noir* precisely because acidity provides the chief element of its attack. Pouilly-Fumé also builds on the natural acidity of the Sauvignon Blanc grape (aided

WINE AND FOOD CORRELATIONS: FISH

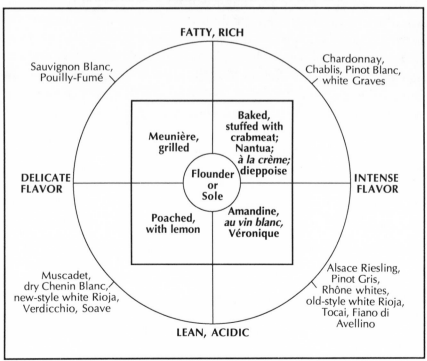

and abetted by careful vinification), but it has the added advantage of a naturally complex and interesting flavor. Finally, the Rhône whites possess not only a pretty high acidity of their own but also by far the most assertive and interesting flavors of all the wines mentioned here. Both these factors make them a wonderful match for this dish.

Raie au beurre noir also points a way out of the conventional "white wine with fish" box and into a much larger set of options. Even within the confines of an exclusively French wine list, a fair number of red wines—specifically, lighter reds vinified from Pinot Noir—will taste just fine with the acidity of this dish. The reason is, as I remarked earlier, because they tend to contain high proportions—directly tasteable proportions—of "stemmy" tannins that mimic the action of acid on the palate. (This is my own particular, unscientific hobbyhorse. Whether or not these tannins originate in the stems I really don't know. I call them stemmy tannins because they taste to me as if I had just bitten into a green stem. It is a fact, however, that in vinifying Pinot Noir some stems are often included in the fermentation, whereas most other wines are made from completely destemmed grapes.)

So the Pinot Noirs of Alsace and the lighter red Burgundies—especially those from lighter vintages, of which there are many in Burgundy—will work very well with *raie au beurre noir* and with many nouvelle cuisine dishes. California Pinot Noirs, which have not succeeded in emulating red Burgundies in other respects, have achieved at least parity if not superiority in the stemmy tannin league, and as a consequence many of them work much more successfully with fish and fowl preparations and nouvelle recipes than they do with the dishes that traditionally call for a red wine. The combination is well worth a try for those who don't want to surrender the pleasures of a serious red wine even when they're eating fish.

You can, in fact, draw one more very large and valuable corollary from the way *raie au beurre noir* interacts with wines. To wit: Everything we've concluded here about wines that work well with this dish will also apply to a great number of nouvelle cuisine preparations, especially those employing various sorts of vinegars or other acidic substances (for example, citrus fruits, tomato). So with such dishes you can avail yourself of all the sorts of white wines mentioned here, the lighter Pinot Noir wines, and also—lest we forget—the dry rosés, like Tavel and Lirac, which behave very much like substantial white wines.

And since the nouvelle cuisine itself draws so much of its inspiration from sources outside the French repertoire, it also gives us our absolute entitlement to step completely outside that repertoire to choose our wines. The possibilities are almost unimaginably wide:

- acidic, flavorful white wines like California Sauvignon Blanc or New York Riesling
- Italian Sauvignon or Pinot Grigio or even Verdicchio (single-vineyard bottlings such as Le Moie can be splendid)
- bright, acidic Spanish sparkling wines
- even medium-bodied, acidic reds like young Barbera and Chianti and Rioja as well as the previously mentioned Pinot Noir

It is particularly useful to know that, since Italian food often tends to be quite acidic, a great number of Italian wines (having evolved in symbiosis with that acidic food) will often partner even more happily with the dishes of the nouvelle cuisine than French wines will. It is that same marked presence of acidity in the wine that accounts for the gastronomical myth that you can serve champagne with everything and also for the gastronomical fact that champagne is a very versatile wine that does in fact match well with many diverse foods.

Big generalizations are always dangerous, but it is not this book's task to shy away from them. Rosé, too, is supposed to go with everything, but believing that will ruin a fair number of meals for you. Despite the pitfalls of this kind of misinformation, a broad sense of the culinary compatibility and utility of large classes of French wines is both obtainable and useful. Because the norms for the major categories of French wine have been firmly established, it is possible to generalize accurately about their affinities for classes of food in a way that we really can't for less settled wine-producing regions.

Wine with Italian Meals

Matching wines with elegant Italian meals and extrapolating from those matches to other uses are tasks in one sense easier and in another sense more difficult than performing the same operation with French meals. Simply finding *a* pleasing match is easy, because so much of Italian cooking remains highly regionalized, and the wines of the foods' native regions unfailingly go well with them. Our axiom "Wines show best and go best with the foods they grew up with" works like a dream here. But the extrapolations from this axiom are much harder to generate and take advantage of, because Americans know too little of Italian wine and food, and much of the little they know is wrong.

STEREOTYPES AND STANDARDS

Stereotypes about Italian food and wine abound, most of them shaped by Italian-American cooking, which is a very different creature from any of the cuisines of Italy's twenty-two regions. So different is it that food writers are starting to treat the Italian-American tradition as a separate entity, a kind of a Creole cuisine or an "Italian colonial" cooking, distinguished from its homeland cousins by radical differences in the raw materials available to it and by its hundred-year development in isolation from its native roots. Italian-American cooking is wonderful stuff, flavorful and nourishing, but it's not the material of formal dinners, and it's not what native Italians or foreign gastronomes have in mind when they envision a grand Italian dinner. Unfortunately, what they do have in mind remains largely unknown outside a few urban centers—New York, Boston, Philadelphia, Chicago, Los Angeles, maybe San Francisco. In most of the rest of the country, Italian food still translates into the old spaghetti-and-meatballs stereotype.

Italian wine also suffers widely from the same sort of negative stereotyping, almost certainly the heritage of generations of

Americans encountering it first as dubiously cheap "Chianti" or "Frascati" or "Orvieto," poured from wicker-wrapped flasks in inexpensive spaghetti joints everywhere. Of course, without that experience many Americans would probably never have been exposed to the idea of wine with dinner at all, but that good deed has been punished, as all good deeds must be. Americans have decided, in the main, that Italian wine is cheap and raw and must come in big jugs or wicker flasks. Well, it has been so long since real Chianti came in wicker that some Chianti makers are beginning to talk about reviving the old flasks as a piece of nostalgia. The gulf between the reality of Italian wine and the American perception of it yawns about that wide in every other respect as well.

Because of the two sets of erroneous stereotypes, talking to an American audience about fine Italian wining and dining amounts to a major exercise in translation and persuasion, and this holds true despite the enormous popularity of "Italian" food in the United States. Right now, for instance, something called "northern Italian cooking" is riding a wave of fashion. But what "northern Italian cooking" actually turns out to be most of the time is very little more than fresh pasta made with eggs appearing in place of dry, eggless commercial pastas, and cream and butter substituting for olive oil and tomato in the sauces. This does at least break the spaghetti-and-meatball stereotype, but it still leaves a long way to go before Americans understand that Italian cooking is capable of the sort of elegance and impressiveness they automatically identify with French cooking.

The wine situation is identical. French wine is widely perceived as the benchmark against which all wine should be measured. In large part this is just. France's finest wines have a centuries-long record of achievement, whereas, as the late Renato Ratti—an eminent winemaker and wine historian—so wryly put it, the Italian discovery of wine is quite recent. His irony is well pointed. Despite more than two millennia of making and consuming wines, it's only recently that Italy has begun taking its own wines seriously. In that short time, Italians have taken great strides in raising the quality of their everyday wine and in protecting, proliferating, and publicizing their great wines (of which, happily, there exist more than a few). The converse of Ratti's quip also deserves careful notice. If Italians have only recently discovered fine wine as an object of *virtú*, of connoisseurship, they nevertheless have 2,500 years of experience of good wine as a daily beverage, as what California only this morning (by Italy's time scale) happened upon and proudly announced to the world as "food wine."

FINE DINING ALL'ITALIANA

All right then: What constitutes an Italian meal fine enough, as Doctor Johnson would say, to ask a man to? Just to give some sense of the possibilities, here's the menu from an Italian banquet given at a private New York club. This particular dinner lends itself quite comfortably to our interests here because it was expressly organized for the benefit of a group of people generally knowledgeable about good food but not about Italian cooking or wine, and it was carefully designed to show the shape and character of fine Italian dining.

Assorted Small Antipasti
Ca' del Bosco, Dosage Zero Spumante, Metodo Champenois

Sweetbreads and Shiitake Mushrooms,
over a Salad of Mesclun
Jermann, Vintage Tunina, 1986

Combination of Home-Made Pastas
Gaja, Barbera d'Alba Vignarey, 1985

Stewed Rabbit with Sage and Balsamic Vinegar,
served with Savoy Cabbage and Seasonal Vegetables
Ceretto, Barolo Riserva Bricco Rocche Bricco Rocche, 1982

Grilled Gorgonzola over Fried Polenta
Valentino, Barolo Riserva, 1979

Chocolate Zabaglione Cake

Hazelnut Cookies
Livio Felluga, Picolit, 1984

Coffee and Grappas

This dinner, even though markedly regional in its orientation (predominantly Piedmontese), embodies the typical structure of a gala dinner anywhere in Italy. Where the French service places hors d'oeuvre, the Italian places antipasti, which in Italy can comprise many different kinds of dishes—raw vegetables, smoked or pickled or boiled or fried fish, miniature omelettes or sausages and beans, prosciutto or salami or pâté, artichokes *alla romana* or zucchini *al funghetto*. The antipasto course can be one serving or it can be up to fifteen (that's the most I've ever been served) different dishes. In this menu the antipasto is represented both by the canapé-like assortment and by the warm sweetbread-and-mushroom salad.

The next course in the classic French service—it has all but disappeared from the modern—would be soup. In Italy this corresponds to the *primo,* and far from disappearing, it thrives. *Primi* include the true soups (*zuppe, minestre,* and *minestrone*) as well as pastas, rice dishes, and gnocchi, and can even include *pizze* and *focaccie,* or everything that falls under the broad heading of a farinaceous base dressed with a sauce. In an Italian feast there may be many different dishes of these also. Depending on the region's or the host's specialties, you might be served several pastas or several risottos, or a long-strand pasta and a stuffed pasta like tortellini and a risotto. In less formal dining situations than the menu above represents, *primi* may very well be the climax or center of the meal. In this particular dinner Italian exuberance was reined in, and assortments of both antipasti and pasta were presented rather than multiple dishes of them, to provide the diners with a hint of what a full-scale Italian feast would be like.

In its placement, the next course corresponds to the entrée or main course, but in Italian it is simply called *secondo,* which quite accurately indicates that it doesn't have to be conceived of as a *main* course in either size or importance. It is simply one more dish in the whole configuration of the meal. "Configuration" is in fact an important part of the Italian conception of a meal, which in its ideal form is rounded and harmonious. Thus, the vegetables served alongside the *secondo* are called *contorni,* or "contours," literally dishes that "round out" the course and the meal.

The *secondo* may be followed by salad or cheese or both. After those courses, dessert follows, but it is rarely elaborate and not often very sweet. In the case of this menu, and in deference to the great American sweet tooth, two desserts were served. But in an authentic Italian context, the real dessert would probably not have been the chocolate cake but the simple hazelnut cookies and the exquisite Picolit, a very scarce and lovely wine from Friuli. In Italy espresso is served only after the dessert has been removed (the only exceptions are very simple dry cookies). Grappa—a pomace brandy that can be very fine indeed—may be taken with espresso, in it, or after it.

In authentic Italian service no one of these courses need be any larger or any more important than any other. Any one of them can be multiplied in the number of dishes or aggrandized in quality to turn it into the star of the meal. In that respect the structure and flow of an elaborate Italian dinner is more like that of a Chinese feast than it is like our American dining pattern of appetizer, main course, and dessert. Of course, this means too that the wines to match the various courses must also reflect the importance being attached to them. The whole concept is much more variable than the classic French sequence of wines. In theory you could build an important Italian dinner around a proliferation of antipasti, serving your finest wines with them, and proceeding from there by a graceful diminuendo to the end of the meal.

Using our by now tried-and-true method of looking for common factors, reading between the lines of this menu gives us some clues about the nature of authentic Italian cooking. The sweetbread-and-mushroom dish (shiitake were used in place of unavailable *porcini*), despite its exotic ingredients, was in composition a very straightforward, almost unadorned, salad, dressed only with extra-virgin olive oil and wine vinegar. One of the pastas had a bright, fresh tomato sauce on it. The rabbit was cooked with balsamic vinegar. Grilling the Gorgonzola brought up its sharpness and strength. The common element in all these foods is acidity, and it is very safe to say that, for all the great diversity of Italian cooking, acidity is a common denominator of all its cuisines. You'll find that acidity in the wines of this menu too, pronouncedly in the whites—the Ca' del Bosco Dosage Zero, the Jermann Vintage Tunina, the Picolit—but also in the Barbera. Italians eat bright, acidic foods, and if the current enthusiasm about the health benefits of the Mediterranean diet means anything at all, a lot more Americans will soon be eating such foods too.

ANOTHER EXAMPLE

A menu like this one, instructive as it is for our purposes, is probably beyond the reach of the average home cook, not because the recipes are complex, but simply because of the multiplicity of them. Right now, we need some more specifics to work with. Here is a somewhat less elaborate and eminently more doable, though still very elegant, Italian dinner.

Torta Verde
Crustless Spinach and Rice Pie

Carne Cruda all'Albese
Veal Tartare

Tajarin
Home-Made Tagliarini with Sage-Tomato Sauce

Pollo ai Peperoni alla Piemontese
Braised Chicken with Red and Yellow Bell Peppers

Formaggi
Cheeses: Parmigiano, Taleggio, Caprini

Pesche al Forno
Baked Peaches

Once again, this is a Piedmontese menu, for no other reason than that the region affords us some marvelous wine choices to accompany its foods. This menu should reinforce for you several noteworthy points about the character of authentic Italian food. Numerous elements yet again contribute acid to the meal: the spinach, which is the main ingredient of the first antipasto; the lemon, which brightens and "cooks" the veal tartare; the sage-and-tomato sauce on the pasta; the bright flavor of the peppers with the chicken (sharpened by a bit of anchovy in the sauce); perhaps even the peaches. Every course is thus marked by strong acidity.

Moreover—and this is important because it points to the under-lying character of Italian cooking—acidity is a quality not just of the dressings or sauces, but also of the base ingredients themselves. In the *secondo,* the peppers are as important to the dish as the chicken (and the anchovy commonly used in cooking this dish brings additional tang to it). In the *primo,* the acid of the tomatoes and the bright zing of a very large quantity of fresh sage make them the predominant flavor element of the dish, the pasta serving pri-marily as vehicle and texture for them. This is absolutely typical of Italian cooking, which is not a cuisine of sauces but rather a cuisine characterized by the primacy of simply presented basic ingredients, usually either acidic in themselves or acidic in their condiments. A simple veal scallop is not an acidic food, but no simply cooked veal scallop ever comes to table in Italy unaccompanied by a plate of lemon wedges to squeeze over it and brighten it. The genius of a whole cuisine is synopsized there.

The different palatal range in which Italian wines and foods operate doesn't change any of the principles of component match-ing we've been working with. The generally high levels of acidity common to both Italian food and Italian wine might seem likely to create special problems, but in practice they simply compensate for each other almost automatically and scarcely have to enter your thinking (unless, of course, you're matching Italian foods with non-Italian wines). You can turn your primary attention to other key components of the foods and wines you're dealing with.

For some practical examples, let's turn back to that last menu. The first antipasto, the spinach torte, would want a reasonably substantial but not overpowering white wine. Smooth texture, delicate vegetable flavor, the omnipresent acidity all point to a wine of character, medium body, and freshness. In still wines either Gavi or—to be very regional—Arneis (Ceretto and Giacosa make fine ones) would suit admirably. But a good brut sparkling wine, made by what Italians call *metodo champenois,* would probably taste even better—Cinzano, say, or Riccadonna, or Ferrari, or Ca' del Bosco.

The second antipasto, Veal Tartare, presents a classic set of Italian food characteristics. The dish depends entirely on the finest, freshest ingredients for its success. With them—with pale, lean veal, minced *al momento;* fresh, firm mushrooms (the usual substitute for scarce and very expensive white truffles); young, nutty Parmigiano; top-quality extra-virgin olive oil; and ripe, juicy lemons—*carne cruda all'albese* is, simply, transcendent. With anything short of them, it is ordinary, a cutlet that had a bad accident. Despite the presence of the lemon juice and the delicacy of the mushrooms, this dish will work with a reasonably big white wine, so the first remove's Gavi or Arneis or sparkling wine would still match quite nicely, should you wish to continue with white wines. But because of the rich fleshiness of the veal, moistened in addition with extra-virgin olive oil and further enriched with thin slivers of young Parmigiano, you could easily take a red wine with this dish. All these flavors combine in the dish to a delicate harmony, so you don't want a powerhouse of a wine, but rather a red of medium body and some subtlety, fruity rather than tannic, a top-flight Barbera, say, or a Dolcetto, from Ceretto or Gaja or Giacosa or Pio Cesare or Prunotto or Vietti.

Because of the vivid acidity of the tomatoes and the strong character of the sage—the sage is so concentrated it almost has an exotic, orange quality—you could very well serve the same red wine with the *tajarin,* or use the two courses to start up a ladder of fullness by progressing from a Barbera to a Dolcetto.

In either case the *secondo,* wherein the essentially mild flavor of chicken is augmented by the savoriness of its preparation and sauce, presents the opportunity to ascend to a really fine, full-bodied red wine. In the Piedmontese tradition, you would move to a Barolo or Barbaresco (from any of the same makers mentioned for Barbera and Dolcetto). The peppers and the condiments (herbs, prosciutto, garlic, anchovies, red wine vinegar) create and imbue the normally bland chicken with a symphony of forceful flavors that is buttressed by the acidity of the dish rather than submerged in it. The palatal consequence is that the flavors of the dish don't merely stand up to aggressive and tannic wines, they demand them to match their own appealing richness.

With the cheese you have once again the option of either con-

WINE AND FOOD CORRELATIONS: CHICKEN

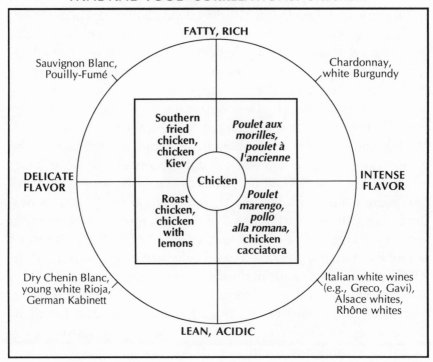

tinuing to serve the same wine you drank with the *secondo* or establishing a progressive increase in vinous body by moving from Barbaresco with the chicken to Barolo with the cheese. If you're being completely Piedmontese, with your dessert you'll drink either Asti Spumante or a still Moscato, and with or after your espresso you'll take as a *digestivo* a little glass of grappa, or that rare, oddly pleasing specialty of the Piedmont, Barolo Chinato, a Barolo fortified and aged with an infusion of quinine.

THE SPIRIT OF THE COOKING

These northern dishes, despite their regional particularity, share and show the characteristics that mark all the cuisines of Italy. They present the flavors of their primary ingredients forthrightly. The tastes of individual components of the dishes are pronounced and clear. With the exception of pasta and rice dishes, sauces never dominate the other elements of a recipe but rather integrate with them, usually by way of an acid bond, to produce the culinary equivalent of an orchestral *tutti*. Even when particular recipes exhibit great elegance—as does, for instance, the Veal Tartare— the component flavors remain clear, sharp, distinct. They retain their individual identity within the achieved harmony of the whole dish. Such foods make wonderful partners with all sorts of wines, but especially with wines whose own flavors can match them in forthrightness and distinction. At that particular game, the red wines of the Piedmont excel.

Italy has more cuisines than just northern ones, however, and a great many more fine wines. A very nonofficial count reports well over two thousand different wines being made in commercial quantities—many of them, obviously, extremely localized in production and consumption. As for cuisines, traditional Italian usage counts one for every administrative region. There are twenty-two of those for political purposes, but as far as culinary purposes are concerned it might be truer to count one cuisine for every village or valley, or perhaps one for every family. For the non-Italian, both the enological and the gastronomic situations look hopelessly confused. While I'm not prepared to say that in fact everything is as clear as day, I can reassure you that understanding Italian wine and food isn't nearly as complex as it looks.

In the case of the cuisines, you already know some of the avenues by which to approach the situation. Acidity is a major key, though far from the only one. All Italian cuisines, north, south, and center, share the same stylistic goals: freshness, simplicity, directness. These are culinary aims antithetical to the more familiar (to most connoisseurs) style of the French classic cuisine, and they produce a style of cooking utterly opposite that of haute cuisine, whose goals are to transform, to elevate, the raw materials it deals with. In clear contradistinction to that, the working philosophy of generations of Italian cooks could be stated in one short phrase: Do nothing to interfere with the natural flavor of the ingredients.

French cuisine, as we have come to know it in this century, derives ultimately from the cooking of the court and the noble houses. It passed through the kitchens of a comfortably well-off bourgeoisie and almost two centuries of urbanized and partly *déraciné* restaurant professionals before it got to us. In the process, French cooking adopted as one of its goals the erasure of a food's regional roots, its "rusticity." Cooking was to be, and in fact became, cosmopolitan. Italian cooking underwent no such unified national development as the French, in part, of course, because there was no unified nation until quite late. Rather, Italian cuisine remained rooted in the home and the countryside until quite recently. Despite the recent efforts of a few inspired restaurateurs (like Luigi Morini at San Domenico in Imola), there simply is no Italian national cuisine equivalent to the French haute cuisine. For this reason, *cucina casalinga* and *cucina contadina*—home-style cooking and country-style cooking—are still the very highest terms of culinary praise in Italy. For this reason too, among others, Italy never formulated a "canon" of its great wines, ranked by quality and associated firmly with particular kinds of food or gastronomic roles. None of its wines ever became national wines. Even now, all remain firmly rooted in their native regions.

And even now Italian cooking does not depend on complex dishes with elaborate sauces (even that multi-ingredient, long-simmered tomato sauce that so many Americans think of as the essence of Italian cooking is a red herring; that dish is as American as chop suey), but rather on relatively simple dishes using comparatively few ingredients of the highest possible degree of quality and freshness. This emphasis on the individual character of specific foods has necessitated the creation of wines that adapt readily and well to a great variety of food circumstances, however marked and distinctive their own character may be. One does not have to be a rigid Darwinian to conclude that versatile grapes and adaptable wines are the kinds that have survived and prospered in Italy over the course of the two-millennia-long, parallel, and symbiotic evolution of Italian food and wine.

This adaptability provides an important bonus for modern wine lovers. It means that Italian wines serve very well as companions to cuisines other than their own, whether preparations from other parts of Italy or from other parts of the world. Speaking very generally, both red and white Italian wines will match well with simply prepared foods of all sorts and with foods whose character or preparation leans toward acidity. Because they themselves are characteristically acidic, both the reds and the whites will also work well in counterpoint to rich, unctuous foods. They falter with very creamy sauces, of which there are very, very few in the Italian repertory. With them, neither the reds nor the whites show their best.

Wine with Other International Meals

Of all the European wine-oriented cuisines, those of France and Italy have had the widest and deepest impact on American ideas of fine dining. For this reason I have dealt with these cuisines and their wine affinities at greater length than I will those of Spain, Portugal, and Germany, which, so far in our history, have had only minimal influence on the way we eat when we want to eat grandly. Recently, however, other foreign cuisines—most notably Asian—have entered our culinary arena in a very significant manner. They have introduced new ingredients into mainstream American dining and have in some cases dramatically altered the ways familiar ingredients are cooked or combined within a dish or a meal. So in addition to talking about the food and wine affinities of the "traditional" European cuisines, this section will pay particular attention to the ways different styles of Oriental cooking respond to wines.

SPAIN AND PORTUGAL

In the style and character of their food and wine, Spain and Portugal fall almost exactly midway between the poles of France and Italy. Their cuisines are neither as heavily influenced by aristocratic styles as France's nor as deeply marked by regional distinctions as Italy's. Put another way, the cooking of the Iberian peninsula employs some of the sophisticated sauces and artful blendings of flavor that are the hallmarks of French cuisine (this is more notably true of Spanish cookery than Portuguese), while at the same time it preserves some important ethnic and regional traditions—most significantly, Catalan and Basque. Neither Spain nor Portugal possesses a single national style such as exists in the classic French haute cuisine, but neither is their cooking as distinctively and as much divided as is Italy's.

Their wines too seem to occupy the same sort of halfway house. They have a character that combines some of the polish and sophistication of the best French wine with the earthiness and strength of more southerly, Mediterranean wines. For gastronomical purposes, that makes Spanish and Portuguese bottlings useful indeed. Their versatility allows them to serve well not only with their own native cuisine—some of which can make very awkward demands on a wine (paella, for instance)—but also with any characteristically "Mediterranean" dish, from couscous to *pissaladière*. They will match nicely with all but the creamiest and butteriest of French cuisine and all but the most acidic of Italian cooking. They will serve just as happily with most of the dishes of the standard American and regional American cuisines.

It is generally a mistake, by the way, to assume that Spanish wine matches well with Mexican food, especially if what is really meant by Mexican food is Tex-Mex or California-Mex. It's hard to tell whether this idea arose simply because Mexicans speak Spanish or because several large Spanish wine houses have established an important presence in Mexico as exporters and, lately, as winemakers. Domecq, for instance, seems to have succeeded in placing its wines on every wine list in Mexico, and has also begun producing wines from extensive vineyards in Baja California. But young red Rioja suits heavily chili-peppered dishes no better than young Chianti or Zinfandel, and probably not as well as several simpler wines would (including some jugs). The cuisines of Mexico vary as much as the cuisines of France or Italy or Spain, and stand about as distant from what is popularly known in the United States as Mexican cooking as the genuine cooking of Italy stands from the Italian-American style. The very best Mexican cooking, of course, is as subtle and fascinating as any other distinguished cuisine, and it takes wines to partner it on exactly the same principles as all the others we've been discussing.

GERMANY AND AUSTRIA

Both Germany and Austria are important wine-producing countries, and in both, the reputation of their sweet dessert wines
dominates the field. Both nations also possess highly developed
folk cuisines that are caricatured in the popular imagination as on
the one hand *Wurst* and on the other hand *Schlag*. The home
cooking of Germany and Austria—the equivalent of the *cucina
casalinga* or *cuisine bourgeoise*—has in fact developed largely
without interaction with wine. Beer rather than wine has shaped it
and consequently given it a general character not particularly
friendly to its own wines. This evolution in isolation from the
popular cuisine means that some of the finest German wines really
show their best by themselves, with no food at all to distract the
palate from their delicate harmonies.

But there is a great difference between the popular table and the
aristocratic table in both Germany and Austria. Where the popular
cooking is direct and forthright, the dishes of the upper classes and
old nobility are more subtle and complex. They take their lead
from the popular cooking, but accentuate particular tendencies
within it. For example, the sweet-and-sour spicing of sauerbraten
is either an ancestor of this subtler upper-class cuisine or a descen-
dant of it (in a particular dish it's almost impossible to tell which
way the influences run). The elegant and festive cookery of both
Austria and Germany typically combines sweet-and-sour elements
in very sophisticated and very "modern" ways. Consider, for instance, preparations like fish poached in wine with allspice and
cloves and served with a mustard sauce, or beef with a sauce of
lemon and capers, or cured vegetables and meats cooked with
fruits—especially apples—or long-cooked game dishes, such as
hasenpfeffer, that combine wine and fruit or acids and sweets.
Even though heavier and more substantial than is now fashionable,
such dishes, for all practical purposes, long anticipated some of the
liaisons dangereuses of the nouvelle cuisine. This fact may help
create a brand-new gastronomical role for German wines in
twentieth-century dining.

In many nouvelle preparations and *cuisine américaine* recipes, fruit-sweetness (and sometimes even wine-sweetness) predominates in the flavor of the sauce. Even more often, acid from vinegar or wine reductions and sweetness from either fruits or wine stand very much on an even footing, the balance of flavors tilting neither way. As a quick example of this, think only of the widespread use of sweet mustards in "California-style" dishes. Some meats or fish possess in themselves a degree of sweetness that the cook can choose to suppress or to express. Oxtails are a good case in point; think of the meaty sweetness of oxtail soup. Or think of the flavor harmonies of a dish like green pea soup with mint, or poached rainbow trout with a sauce made from Riesling and saffron.

All these dishes and many more like them in the contemporary culinary repertoire can be extremely difficult to match with wine because they combine in a precarious balance such polarities of sweetness and acidity, insubstantiality and solidity. Precisely those qualities that make dishes like these uncomfortable partners with more conventional wine choices point to German wines as their natural mates. A Kabinett will complement the driest, most acidic of these preparations, and a Spätlese will play up beautifully to those with a perceptible element of sweetness. Be reassured: This will not turn the meal into a sugar fest. Nine times out of ten, the sweetness of the food will simply cancel out the sweetness of the wine on your palate, leaving you with a delicately fruity, dry-tasting but not austere partner to what has become, to your perception, only a lightly sweet-tasting preparation. The tenth time may reverse these polarities and give you a lightly sweet wine accompanying a dish that you will perceive as dry, but the interplay of wine and food should still be thoroughly pleasing. This kind of wine-food pairing, I think, constitutes a great and potentially expanding place for German wines in contemporary dining.

German wines in general and the Kabinett wines in particular have one other special vocation in the kingdom of culinary matches. Many people (I am one) find these wines partner beautifully with Chinese cuisine, where the spicing of the dishes, unusual to Western palates, seems to echo many of the nuances of the Riesling grape. For my palate, German wines rarely work with Indian dishes—they are often too delicate for the food—and inconsistently with Japanese—sometimes too sweet, sometimes too delicate—but with many Chinese dishes, the combined acidity and sweetness that the Kabinett and even the Spätlese Rieslings can bring to a meal simply makes as fine a pairing as you could hope for. Only with the most heavily chili-peppered Szechuan dishes does this unlikely combination seem to break down. But with cuisines that specialize in and exploit delicate harmonies and contrasts, that achieve their effects (like nouvelle cuisine) with careful balances of sweet and sour, sweet and acid, sweet and spicy, with, in short, Mandarin cooking, or Shanghai, or—best of all if you can find it—top-flight Cantonese cooking, the flavor marriages are superb.

THE EAST IS NOT RED WINE COUNTRY

All of which brings us, logically enough, to the question of the right wines to drink with the panoply of Asian cuisines that have begun to significantly influence American dining patterns: Japanese, Chinese, Burmese, Malaysian, Thai, Indonesian, Indian, Pakistani, Bengali.

As far as the relations of wine and food are concerned, the nations of the Far East present a problem that is precisely the reverse of the German situation. In India, in China, in Japan, in the many nations of the Pacific Rim, rich and varied cuisines have evolved in the absence of great wine. These cuisines, varied within themselves, differ from one another in the basic ingredients they employ, in the spices they flavor them with, in the ways and sequences in which they serve their dishes. For wine lovers who also relish Oriental food, this situation presents probably the greatest difficulty in the whole realm of wine and food matches.

As we have already had numerous occasions to point out, the way to proceed in thinking about these kinds of problems is to look first for common factors that will simplify and clarify the situation. For the sake of simplicity—and also because it's true—we'll consider the cooking of India, China, and Japan as the three basically distinctive gastronomic "archetypes" of Asia. Despite their national differences, common factors among them abound. All three, no matter how luxurious they can become, begin as cuisines of scarcity, cuisines in which a small amount of food—particularly of meat—is made to go a long way. Also, in all three nations traditions of vegetarianism play a very important role. These facts have worked to create styles of cooking in which richness in the dish or satiety in the diner is attained by intensity of flavors—usually spices—rather than by abundance of food. Meat is often entirely omitted from a dish or a whole menu, and fish, bean curd, starches such as rice and noodles, and a wide array of vegetables play the most prominent roles in much of the cuisine. So radically limited is the role of meat, especially beef, that even their by-products, the fatty dairy foods—cheese, butter, milk—are almost totally absent in Chinese and Japanese cooking, and in Indian menus they play a limited role.

Cooking techniques also bear a family resemblance among the three cuisines. In all three, short, intense cooking of precut, small pieces of ingredients is the predominant mode. Long-cooked dishes—and especially long-baked ones—occur rarely if at all, and large pieces of meats never. Fish seem to be almost the only animals ever served whole. One other gross generalization is possible: All three cuisines strongly favor moist cooking over dry. Obviously there are exceptions to this—the Indian tandoori technique, for one—but by and large, the major dishes of India, China, and Japan present a main ingredient or ingredients in a broth or an abundant sauce. It is only with liquids—and indeed, even there only by contrast rather than in any absolute sense—that Oriental cooking becomes at all profuse. Otherwise these cuisines embody the lessons of centuries of scarcity and millennia of philosophic and religious teachings about asceticism.

Preparations of individual dishes demonstrate similar qualities of leanness. Even when sauces are thick, they have not been fattened with meat stocks, butter, or cream. This impression of leanness is further reinforced by the prominence of the spices and condiments rather than the base ingredients in many Eastern preparations. (Once again, there are obvious exceptions: sushi and sashimi, for instance, though I find it hard to think of those two dishes without soy sauce, wasabi, pickled ginger, or *oshinko,* those wonderful, palate-scrubbing Japanese pickles.) The condiments that flavor the basic ingredients of dishes themselves tend toward taste extremes: very salty (soy sauce), very sweet (plum sauce, tamarind, some chutneys), very sour (lemon pickle), very hot (wasabi, chili peppers), or a very non-Western combination of all (*garam masala*).

The principle of contrast plays a very large part in Asian cookery. Many dishes employ contrasts in texture (for example, crunchy and soft, as in the use of water chestnuts and straw mushrooms in the same dish) as well as contrasts in flavor. The strong spices, for instance, contrast markedly with bland or mild base ingredients, and often even the base ingredients counterpoint one another, either texturally (sea scallops and pork, for instance) or in flavor (chili peppers stuffed with a paste of shrimp, cabbage, and water chestnuts).

Far Eastern cookery, because of its innate leanness, or because of the nature of its distinctive flavorings, or because of these two characteristics combined, all but prohibits your matching red wines with it. Most red wines, no matter how distinguished, simply flatten out alongside these cuisines. All most tasters can perceive of them in the context of Oriental meals is their tannin, and that is not the most pleasant sensation to set alongside a good moo shu pork or *kung pao* chicken or *tonkatsu* or *shabu-shabu* or lamb pilaf. In a few cases a small number of red wines can partly integrate with these kinds of food. Beaujolais, because of its acidity, can sometimes work with such dishes, and so can young Zinfandel or Chianti or Rioja or even Barbera. At an extreme, you could even try a very light Pinot Noir—one from Alsace would be best—with the most mildly and conventionally spiced recipes. But the most interesting red wines, the biggest and fullest and most complex, simply fade away with these kinds of foods.

Some fine white wines, however, show spectacularly well with these three Asian cuisines. Not just indiscriminately: This is not simply the broad spectrum, "any white wine will go with any Far Eastern dish" notion some people may try to pass off on you. Each of these three cuisines has a marked proclivity for the white wines of one particular region, and those regions and their wines differ clearly for each cuisine.

In my experience Alsace wines—especially Gewürztraminer and

Pinot Gris—match beautifully with many Indian preparations. The relatively full body and the assertive, dry fruit of Alsace wines respond particularly well to curries in the middle range of heat intensity and to other moist-cooked Indian dishes. Pinot Blanc also succeeds with many of these dishes, and for what appears to be much the same reasons—body and fruit. Pinot Blanc does especially well with tandoori preparations, though overall the natural spiciness of the Gewürztraminer varietal gives it, to my taste, a distinct advantage over other Alsace whites in complementing the characteristic flavors of Indian cooking. Alsace Riesling does not work as well with Indian dishes as you might expect it to on the strength of Gewürztraminer's performance. It seems to almost wash out, to lose its basic character. Alsace's one red wine, Pinot Noir, is worth trying with the gentlest and most conventional-tasting, in Western terms, of these dishes—some of the Moghul lamb dishes like *shahi korma* or *gosht kari,* for instance. Most young red wines will taste all right with *biryani* (pilaf) and *korma* (braised) dishes, but only all right. In my experience Zinfandel is the most satisfactory. Most red wines won't really interact with the food. They remain separate from it, pleasant enough in themselves, but rather more like bystanders than integral parts of the meal.

Chinese cuisine, with its own completely different range of flavorings, presents a radically distinct wine situation. Chinese dishes can call out wonderful nuances in the drier German wines, the Kabinetts and the Spätleses. The heavy reliance in Chinese cooking on contrasts in texture and on the mixture of sweet-and-sharp or sweet-and-sour elements creates a perfect foil for the balance of sweetness and acidity, lightness and substance, that the best German Kabinett wines exhibit. The Spätleses sometimes tip the balance too far to the sweetness side for my palate, though many people who have a greater tolerance for sweetness than I thoroughly enjoy them with dishes where I would choose a Kabinett wine. I find the Spätleses work best with Chinese recipes that either are themselves somewhat on the sweet side or have textures that strike Westerners as rather bland or rubbery (depending on the mode of presentation, that could include anything from squid to jellyfish, snails to duck feet, bamboo shoots or mushrooms). The very delicate Mosel Rieslings in particular, even more than their slightly more robust cousins of the Rhine, seem to respond to the subtleties of Chinese cooking as to a long-lost friend. They sometimes can even—despite that lovely delicacy—manage to hold their own against the many chili-peppered dishes of the Szechuan and Hunan styles, though at those extremes of sensation I find the driest possible Kabinett wine works much better than any Spätlese, whose sweetness in that context becomes far too marked for my pleasure. (With the very hottest Szechuan dishes, I have to admit that I really prefer beer, just as I do with the hottest Indian and Mexican dishes.)

Japanese cooking, though it has clearly drawn much from the Chinese, differs both from that and from Indian cooking in its far greater insistence on what, for lack of a better term, I have to call purity of flavor. Even when it makes use of contrasts, Japanese cooking techniques insist that they be starkly simple. They are made to depend on the juxtaposition of sharply differentiated flavors and textures: the fatty, fleshy richness of raw tuna versus the salty tang of soy and the bite of wasabi. Like a Zen rock garden, those dishes disguise great sophistication as simplicity and innocence, and my palate tells me that they don't respond very well to wines that wear their sophistication openly, as do most European white wines. Perhaps that's why Japanese dishes tend to work so well with American West Coast white wines. Those wines are innocent, sometimes to the point of naïveté. They wear their heart on their sleeve. Their clear varietal flavors and straightforward intensity respond directly to the artful purity with which Japanese cuisine presents its components. Combinations like California Chardonnay or Sauvignon Blanc with sushi or sashimi or shrimp tempura and Northwest Gewürztraminer or Riesling with vegetable tempura or *chirinabe* or *udon-suki* (noodle sukiyaki) make the best of both the food and the wine.

Let me summarize the general rules of thumb I have been able to discern for matching wines with Japanese foods:

- Drink white wines only. Reds are far too tannic to be pleasurable with these kinds of dishes, with the possible exception of *tonkatsu*.

- Chardonnay and Sauvignon Blanc work best with the simpler preparations and those with brief (or even no) cooking time.
- Gewürztraminer and especially Riesling match well with more complex preparations and those involving longer cooking times.

Why American wine works best with Japanese food I don't know, any more than I have any idea why Alsace wine goes so well with Indian, and German wine with Chinese. I didn't deliberately set out to find these national linkages, but the process of trial and error very quickly showed them to be real and effective, despite the fact that I can't come up with a theory to explain them. I'm grateful for them, however, as I am grateful for everything that simplifies life and unclutters memory. These neat national pairings make very concise and memorable formulas.

Other Home Entertaining

HOME ENTERTAINING these days embraces a wide range of activities of every conceivable degree of formality and informality. Depending on what part of the country and its crazy quilt of climates you inhabit, your parties may range anywhere from a blue-jeans-and-Bermuda-shorts backyard barbecue to black-tie dinner, or the other way around, from black-tie barbecue to super-casual buffet dinner.

Wines exist in plenty for all these activities and for all degrees of seriousness or frivolity. All the ground rules that work for choosing foods for dinner parties work just as well for any other festive occasion. The only thing that changes from the situation of a conventional dinner party is the nature of the event itself, and all that means is that in addition to thinking about matching your wines with the food you're serving, you want to think also about matching them with the occasion you're creating and the people you're inviting. As I've said before, appropriateness to the occasion ought to be the first and overriding criterion for matching wines with events.

219

Let me give an example of what I mean. A fresh, young
Beaujolais-Villages will taste just fine—charming and casual,
properly nonsignificant—at a fifty-guest, ask-all-the-neighbors,
Fourth of July cookout. Everyone will love it, and rightly so. That
same Beaujolais served to four or six intimate and valued friends at
a dress-up, Saturday-night dinner party will fall flat on its face, for
all the same reasons that caused its success at the cookout. The flip
side of that coin holds true too. A great wine—let's say a 1982 Cos
d'Estournel or a 1977 Taurasi Riserva—will captivate everyone at
an important dinner, but it will be utterly lost, and maybe even
actively unpleasant, at a cookout. It will be too big, too austere, too
tannic, too demanding of attention. It just won't fit the circumstances in which it's being served.

Those wines are the wrong scale, in cost and importance and
complexity, for their respective occasions. They err either through
deficiency (the wine's style is beneath the occasion) or excess (the
wine's style is uncomfortably above the occasion). What is involved here is an issue of taste and tact, a question of what an
earlier age would have called decorum. That word unfortunately
has a terribly dated and puritanical sound to it in this I-want-what-
I-want-when-I-want-it age, but the idea it expresses remains em-
barrassingly sound.

Preliminary Decisions

Whatever kind of home entertaining you're planning, you've got to
make a few preliminary decisions before you call the caterer. First,
think about the nature of the event itself and what it involves in
people, pomp (or lack thereof), food and wine. Often the reason
you want to entertain in the first place also supplies the nature of
the event and even the guest list for it. At the simplest level, the
number of people involved either allows or prohibits different
kinds and degrees of elaborateness in cuisine and wine service. The
differences between a brunch and a formal dinner, between what
you'd serve at a buffet dinner and what you'd set out at a cocktail

party, mandate some dishes and wines and eliminate others: no egg salad at the formal dinner, no Château Pétrus beside the cheese dip.

The individuals you invite dictate other decisions and preparations. It might be a bit tactless, for instance, to serve Captain Ahab leg of lamb or pigs' feet. If Fred and Ginger are strict vegetarians, you're not going to offer them a huge cut of prime rib. If the guests-to-be are very close friends, you may tell them to dress casually no matter how elaborate or formal a meal you want to serve them. You may also know that they have a pronounced preference for simple food, though they love good wine, or vice versa. In either case that could mean that for that evening, out of deference to your guests, you'll have to stifle your desire to make lobster thermidor or your thirst to open a bottle of 1929 Lafite. It's far too late to discover, after you've put your pièce de résistance pork loin stuffed with prunes on the table, that one of your guests keeps kosher and the other is allergic to prunes.

Most of this involves little more than common sense and a decent consideration for the people you're asking to your home for their pleasure. A third factor is involved, however, and it, more than anything else, determines success or failure in any home entertaining. That third factor is the host: you, with your whole package of skills and inabilities, knowledge and ignorance, wealth and poverty. If you are entertaining not just to satisfy social debts but because you genuinely want to give your friends a memorable evening, then you're going to have to play devil's advocate with yourself. You'll have to become your own prosecuting attorney, to make yourself think realistically about your skills and limitations —physically, psychologically, economically, circumstantially. Think about what you can realistically do with the time and space, skills and money available to you. Self-knowledge allows people to succeed as hosts as much as it helps at anything else. Do you handle large groups of people well, or are you more comfortable with a small number of friends? Can you organize your culinary and bartenderly activities (or get professional help with them) so that food and drink will be ready when needed? Have you ever prepared a multicourse dinner for more than four people? Or made canapés for fifty? How much can you afford to spend for wine? Do you have a realistic notion of how much wine is enough for a small but lengthy dinner party or for a fifty-person, four-hour cocktail party or reception?

I hope I don't sound like Perry Mason badgering a hostile witness, but these are all real concerns for anyone planning even a mildly elaborate party. Far better to be ruthless in your self-examination and modest in your undertaking than to have your guests walk around empty handed and glassy eyed and unspeaking because you didn't realize that all your canapé choices need elaborate last-minute finishing and you therefore are busy being hysterical in the kitchen rather than refilling glasses and introducing people.

Glorious parties can be done on a shoestring, but what such parties lack in costly food and drink, their hosts supply with hard work in the preparations, with care and thought about what would give their guests pleasure and with their own evident delight in the giving. I'm talking here about a sense of welcome and openness that no amount of money spent on caterers and booze can ever simulate. Either guests perceive it immediately and bask in it, or else they suffer the lack of it for the duration of the event. This is the final piece of self-examination all hosts should perform: If—for whatever good or bad reasons: financial straits, personal problems, just plain too-busyness—you can't bring yourself to be comfortable giving the best of yourself, your time, your cellar (even if it's just six bottles of Cabernet that you've squirreled away), and your larder, then either scale back the event or postpone it until you can do it right. To do otherwise will only cheat yourself and disappoint your guests.

Particular Parties

All this applies to any home entertaining. Now it's time to get to some specific forms of home entertaining. Obviously, there's no way I can talk here about the wines and foods appropriate to all the conceivable forms of entertaining we perpetrate on one another, so I will use as examples of the two possible extremes of formality and informality the brunch and the backyard barbecue. You should be able to triangulate to your particular needs from these two points.

THE BRUNCH

Increasingly popular as a form of home entertaining, the brunch as an event is as hybrid as its name. Large cocktail party in everything but name, or intimate dinner party in everything but hour and menu, the brunch straddles times and meal categories, formality and informality, elegance and simplicity. Most of us have attended brunches that have run the gamut of everything from hangover breakfasts to elaborate buffets, at early hours of the A.M. and early hours of the P.M., with dress ranging from Bermuda shorts to formal wear to whatever you still had on from the night before. A phenomenon like this isn't flexible; it's chameleon. Trying to pick wines for it, therefore, means first determining the level and style of the particular brunch. That is to say that here as elsewhere, the hosts have to define to themselves beforehand exactly what sort of event they want to produce.

For the sake of clarity, we'll divide brunches into three styles. The first is the simple and straightforward. The intention is to give a party, to exercise some hospitality, to gather together some friends and relatives you want to see. The choice of the brunch format is merely incidental to that, a neutral factor: The event and the time are selected primarily for reasons of the mutual convenience of guests and hosts.

The middle range of brunch involves more complications in selection and planning. The event and time are chosen because it is a season for entertaining, such as the New Year or Christmas or Labor Day weekend, and others of your friends and neighbors will also be entertaining or receiving guests at more conventional party times. Even more often, a brunch is chosen to mesh into other events, to serve as a prologue or epilogue to some other central event.

Finally, the formal/elegant brunch is itself the main event. This is the brunch conceived of and designed to be An Important Occasion, in its own way as elaborate as a formal dinner.

The levels of the wines to be served at each of these kinds of brunch ought directly to reflect, in their complexity and in the level of their palatal interest, the levels of the events themselves. The simple brunch is also the easiest to make wine choices for. Because the event is straightforward and unpretentious, you want relatively simple and uncomplicated wines to accompany an array of foods that can run anywhere from scrambled eggs to the lighter and less spicy cocktail canapés. Because the event is early in the day, you want light wines (or at least wines that feel and taste light).

White wines tend to be more popular at brunches than reds, sometimes by as much as two to one in consumption, which is a factor very much worth knowing about when you're doing your menu planning and shopping. Almost certainly, the fact that people perceive white wines as being lighter than reds—whether they really are or not—constitutes the main reason for that preference, just as it seems to be the main impulse behind the continuing thirst for white wines of the American public at large. That emphasis on light wines means that you can readily use at a simple brunch the same sorts of wines you would use for picnics—essentially wines with clean, fruity, uncomplicated flavors—though it would be wise, because of the different circumstances, to eliminate any sweetish wines and emphasize dry choices: less expensive California Sauvignons and Pinot Blancs; Alsace Pinot Blanc or Riesling, Mâcon, Mâcon-Villages, and shippers' Chablis from France; white Rioja (especially the lighter new style) from Spain; good Kabinett Riesling from Germany; good Soave and less expensive Sauvignon and Pinot Bianco and Chardonnay from Italy's Friuli and Trentino–Alto Adige regions. Red wines should be of similar nature, though you could also use slightly fuller-bodied wines such as simple shippers' St-Emilion or young Côtes-du-Rhône from France, some inexpensive California Merlot, young new-style red Rioja, and Dolcetto from the Italian Piedmont.

The middle-range brunch will characteristically lean more toward lunch than breakfast in the array of foods it offers. If breakfast foods do predominate, they will tend to be of the heartier, more substantial sort. Consequently, the right wines too will have to rise up a step in heft and complexity to match the food. For this sort of brunch you can happily choose from any of the upper level of the wines suggested for everyday dining. There are few surprises here, because the dishes served at this sort of brunch depart least from the standards of normal eating (except perhaps in juxtapositions; dishes that wouldn't normally be on the table at the same meal—Swedish meatballs and bagels and lox—do wind up cheek by jowl at brunches). These are the kind of foods that companion beautifully with many American wines and allow their wonderful fruit flavors to really stand out. Some of the most pleasing wines will be found among the California Chardonnays (but watch the prices) and claret-style Zinfandels, Washington and Oregon Rieslings and Pinot Noirs especially. Fine choices from Europe would include almost any of the Alsace white wines and, if you are lucky enough to find them, the Cabernet Franc–based Loire reds (Bourgueil, Chinon, and Saumur-Champigny) and Italian Cabernets from Friuli or the Veneto, which are usually made from a blend of Cabernet Sauvignon and the softer Cabernet Franc grapes.

The formal brunch in many important respects resembles nothing so much as the elegant midnight supper, with which it shares many characteristics. Notably both events, in their most sophisticated manifestations, provide perfect settings for a full-scale champagne service: i.e., top-flight champagne (vintage at least, and *tête de cuvée* would be even better: Clicquot's Grande Dame, Krug's Clos du Mesnil, Moët's Dom Pérignon or Dom Ruinart, Mumm's René Lalou, beautiful champagnes all) accompanied by warm, lightly buttered (sweet butter, of course) toasts and the freshest possible caviar (I suggest osetra) and thin, thin slices of silky smoked salmon. Jaded palates may think that sounds trite, but no one I know has tired of it yet, and nothing else comes near it for superlative simplicity.

Perhaps you won't want to opt for that much simplicity or that much expense, but the realm of foods and wines over which caviar and *tête de cuvée* champagne reign is the one appropriate to an important brunch. Essentially, you'll be making your selections from among the lightest—and lightest is here very definitely a relative term—wines and dishes that furnish the materials of your most important dinners.

In foods, this points to elegant trifles like fish and vegetable mousses and terrines, tiny puff pastry canapés filled with cheese or delicate meats, airy soufflés and the thinnest, most delicate fresh pastas. In still white wines, because Chardonnay and Chardonnay-based wines are often too full bodied and assertive, it indicates the very finest Sauvignons or Sauvignon-based blends from California (Vichon's lovely Chevrignon, for example) or Pouilly-Fumé from France (the wonderful but preposterously expensive Baron de L from Ladoucette, for example), exquisite high-acid Spätlese from Germany (Schloss Vollrads, for example), the finest Italian white wines (the Gavi from La Scolca, or Mastroberardino's Fiano di Avellino). Among red wines, these are the sorts of circumstances where the Pinot Noir grape really comes into its own, and you can choose between supple Pinot Noirs from Oregon and Washington and velvety wines from Burgundy (especially the lighter-bodied Beaune wines). If your table inclines to slightly meatier, more substantial foods, smaller châteaux from the Médoc (such as Château de Pez or Les Ormes de Pez), the best claret-style Zinfandels (Conn Creek or Ridge Vineyards' Geyserville or Paso Robles Zinfandels for instance), and good Chianti Classico Riservas (Monte Vertine is an excellent example) will round out the repast quite successfully and elegantly.

There are, quite obviously, many more options than these few, but they should give you at least a rough idea of the quality of wine appropriate to this sort of occasion. The crucial thing to remember here is that, just as with an excellent meal, the success of the wine depends on the food it has to interact with, so the style and nature of the dishes you serve will in large part dictate the style and kind of wines you choose to go with them. The same basic principles of food and wine pairings operate here as operate in any dinner situation. The only substantial difference is that most brunch foods, like most cocktail party foods, tend to resemble the first courses or appetizer courses of a formal dinner and therefore to take lighter wines than those that would accompany a dinner entrée. Otherwise, judge just as you would for the most elaborate of your dinners.

THE COOKOUT

Let's bracket entertainment by moving from the elaboration and formality of The Important Brunch to what is often the most casual event to which we invite one another—the cookout. Obviously, this too can be turned into a formal occasion, but what we want to focus on right now is the basic barbecue or backyard picnic or around-the-pool party. Call it what you like, as long as you see it as casual, relaxed, very informal and easygoing.

The first rule with this sort of entertaining, as with all the others, is "respect the occasion." Here that translates into "don't swank it." This is not the time to try to impress family and friends with the subtlety of your palate or the depth of your wallet. Simple foods call for simple wines. Almost everything we said about the wines that accompany everyday dinners applies here, with only one further restriction. These are supposed to be lighthearted occasions. Many of them, because they are outdoor events, can take place only in warm-to-hot weather. These two facts mean you want to serve wines that can be chilled without harm (the unsung hero of many a picnic is the ice bucket) and that will be perceived by your guests as light, refreshing, unserious. At times like these, to serve a big, complex red wine amounts to utter waste. Even among white wines, the more full bodied (California Chardonnays, Burgundies, Rhône whites, for example) are going to make demands on your guests' attention that they are simply not going to want to comply with. Even if they are too polite to tell you so directly, they will react to such wines as too heavy or too strong or in some other vague way excessive and unpleasing (too dry or too sweet, too tannic or too fruity, and so on).

For cookouts and barbecues and all similar occasions, the best wine choices are the simplest: anything from jug wines to the simpler domestic varietals and the less complex imported wines. Wines of that rank offer uncomplicated, pleasant drinking as well as, in most cases, a reassuring quality of near-familiarity. Even if your guests don't recognize a specific name, they will know the wine's type and find it unthreatening.

Obviously, some wines work much better than others in these circumstances. Specifically, wines that come across as light bodied (whether in fact they are or aren't) and wines that taste very fruity (even those with a very small, minimally perceptible trace of residual sugar) make ideal cookout wines. If they happen in addition to possess enough acidity to continue to taste fresh and lively even under heavy chilling, so much the better. Among white wines, those made from the Chenin Blanc grape can be absolutely charming in these circumstances. Those from California will bear the name of the grape; the best-known and most readily available of those from France is Vouvray (both Vouvray and California Chenin Blanc can be very sweet, so read their labels carefully). Italian Pinot Grigio and Frascati, Alsace Pinot Gris (sometimes labeled Tokay d'Alsace), and the driest classifications of German wines, the QmP Kabinett or the simple QbA (*Qualitätswein*), would also serve very well in these circumstances. All these are light and fruity. For somewhat more austere, totally dry, light white wines, select Muscadet or Verdicchio or some of the inexpensive California Sauvignons. Most of these wines, fully dry or slightly sweet alike, possess the kind of acidity that keeps them alive even under an otherwise numbing load of ice cubes.

Most reds just don't possess the same degree of acidity and so cannot, without mortal harm, be that heavily chilled. Beaujolais and Italian Barbera and young Chianti bear up best under icing and still possess sufficient fresh flavor to please. Young Zinfandel and California Gamay, though not as acidic as those three, have such an abundance of fruitiness—berry-tart and refreshing in the Zinfandel and succulent in the Gamay—that they too shine as picnic wines (especially Zinfandel in its Beaujolais-style incarnations).

Many people like "white" Zinfandel, but then many people have also come to think that Zinfandel is a white grape. Most white Zinfandel is very sweet—for my palate, much too sweet to drink with food of any kind. You will have to read labels very carefully to find a fully dry or even near-dry white Zinfandel. I grudgingly admit, however, that many of your guests may enjoy white Zinfandel as a picnic wine.

Finally, you can crank the festivity one notch higher and still preserve the informality of the occasion by offering a good but inexpensive sparkling wine. Spain, Italy, California, and even parts of France other than Champagne produce quite decent bottles of party-style bubbly, Charmat or transfer-method sparkling wines that will not tax your palate or break your budget. They will take all the cooling the hottest summer requires and fizzle and bubble sufficiently to lend your get-together some extra effervescence.

Review and Preview

The formal brunch and the casual cookout between them bracket the style possibilities of home entertaining, outside the spectrum of dinners. You've got under your belt all the guidelines you'll ever need to make your wine choices for any of these. What you need now is some practice. Nobody was ever genius enough to perfectly match foods and wines he'd never tasted. The philosophers tell us there is nothing in the mind that didn't start in the senses; sensual experience is the beginning of wisdom. Whether that's true or not of other kinds of knowledge, there's no question it's true of wine lore. Just to pick one example, nothing I've said anywhere in this book about the red wines of Burgundy or Alsace or Oregon is going to really mean anything to you until you taste a few Pinot Noir–based wines and experience for yourself some of that variety's delights and disappointments, its food compatibilities and irreconcilabilities.

Your own home is the best place for such testing, because there you can take as long as you like to savor and to think, to compare and to take notes. And wine is nowhere less expensive than at home, a fact by no means to be ignored. A restaurant may offer you the opportunity to taste rare wines or unusual ones, but it's not a very good place—certainly not an economical one—to learn the basics of a category of wines or the rudiments of wine and food compatibilities. You should look on restaurants rather as your baccalaureate exams, the place to test the skills you've been acquiring. That's where we're going and what we're going to do next.

PART III

Wines for Special Uses

CHAPTER 7

Wine in Restaurants

FOR WINE LOVERS, choosing wines to match with restaurant meals is the final exam in their most important course. Picking wines at home is just a warm-up for this main event, triple-A ball compared with the restaurants' big leagues. At home you have all the time you need to brood over your wine and food matchups. After all, you're in charge: You're choosing the menu from your own repertoire, and you're picking wines from your own cellar or your regular wine shop. Learn the basic principles of food and wine compatibilities, and you are quite literally home free.

In a restaurant, on the other hand, the first and biggest problem you encounter is that you're rarely choosing a wine to coordinate with a single dinner. Usually you're trying to pick a bottle or bottles that will mesh with two or three or four different appetizers and an equal number of divergent entrées. The wine list may very well contain a lot of wines that you've never tasted, that you know only from hearsay. Moreover, you may not be entirely familiar with the restaurant's cuisine, which certainly increases the difficulty, and you don't have all the time in the world to study the wine list. Even if the restaurant staff is very cooperative and willing to talk to you at length about how the food is prepared or what an individual wine is like, you and your party do want to actually eat and drink something, and sooner rather than later is usually the desired time.

A good restaurant can ease this process immensely. A competent sommelier can go a very long way toward narrowing your range of sound wine choices quickly, even if the list contains a lot of names you don't recognize. A knowledgeable and well-trained captain and serving staff can convey the pertinent wine-oriented information about the food clearly and concisely. Most helpful of all, and most fundamental, is a well-thought-out wine list or, if the restaurant has a particularly strong cellar, a short list culled from all the available wines. That is to say, not a list composed by formula—X many white wines and 2X many reds, Y many sparkling wines and 3Y still wines, Z many American wines and Z many Italian and 2Z French—but a list especially chosen by a caring and knowledgeable person to correlate broadly with the kind of food the restaurant cooks, and particularly with the evening's (or the week's, or month's, or season's) menu. Such a list, in itself, is one of the surest and most reassuring signs that you are in good hands, that the restaurant cares equally about the quality of its food and its wine.

Some problems, however, even good restaurants can't alleviate. If you're looking forward to drinking a really fine wine with your meal, price shock verging on cardiac arrest is almost unavoidable. The structure of the American restaurant business is such that wine drinkers subsidize everybody else's dining. Restaurants charge 200 percent to 300 percent above retail for wine, and restaurants do not pay retail prices for their wine. At the time and place of this writing, the $25 Beaujolais has become a restaurant commonplace; that translates into a profit of anywhere from $12 to $20 per bottle of Beaujolais. Prices go up accordingly for more prestigious wines. Very, very few restaurants—treasure them when you find them!—see any reason to limit their take on wine to a flat rate per bottle. If it costs them $20, it costs you $40 to $60, to yield a profit of $20 to $40; if it costs them $120, it costs you $240 to $360, to yield a profit of $120 to $240. Let me emphasize that 100 percent to 200 percent is the *normal* profit margin. Markups higher than these are not at all uncommon, and prices below them are sighted as rarely as ostriches in Iowa.

Aside from the fact that it is offensive to be asked to pay such an exorbitant *agio* in order to enjoy some wine with our meals, restaurant wine prices compound the difficulty of satisfactorily matching food and wine for all except the very few who are totally free of financial constraints. Far too often diners simply cannot afford the wine that would really make their meal memorable but are forced instead to drink Beaujolais rather than the *petit château* or fine Chardonnay their meal ought to have. This is a deplorable state of affairs, but until customers start making their displeasure about restaurant wine prices known to their waiters and especially to the management, it is more than naïve to think that restaurateurs are going to give up this gold mine voluntarily.

Enough of the bad news. Let's remind ourselves that we go to restaurants in the first place seeking pleasurable experiences, to taste dishes that we either can't make at all or can't make as well and to drink wines we don't have at home. We're out to give ourselves a treat, and we'll put our economic concerns on the back burner for the time being—not that, canny shoppers that we are, we won't be happy to snap up a bargain or two should any appear.

The fact that we're not dining at home is, ironically, the source of most of the difficulties we face in restaurant wine selection. At home we operate, in theory, with the absolute freedom to choose our matchups from all the foods and all the wines of the world. In a restaurant we must work within the real constraints of *this* particular menu and *this* particular wine list. These restrictions make it crucial that we understand thoroughly and work comfortably with the ideas that govern wine and food interaction. This chapter takes all the principles and information we've been acquiring and puts them to the test—this really is a final exam—in the context of several real menus and their accompanying wine lists. I've chosen establishments with different styles of cooking and different ambiences. The four sets of documents we'll be looking at embody four different but equally valid, equally satisfying visions of the ways wine and food can be presented and related to each other in a restaurant. Each mode has limitations simply because each is finite, but each establishment manages to find its own way to integrate its food and its wines and to offer its patrons a manageable diversity of food and wine combinations.

Even with a well-integrated menu and wine list, it still isn't all that easy to make good matches in the limited time you have to ponder and choose. To expedite that process, I'm going to give you some suggestions and examples of how to go about reading a menu and a wine list: how to size them up quickly so you can make a dinner choice and a wine choice that will satisfy your palate and your pocketbook, free you from total dependence on the waiter's or sommelier's opinion, and still leave you time to talk to your dinner companions. By showing you how to make a quick assessment of the broad characteristics of the dishes on the menu and an equally quick analysis of the kinds of wine on the list and their general natures, I'll be giving you the data you need either to make your matches entirely on your own or to use the sommelier's expertise most effectively—the latter because you'll be able to ask the sommelier the kind of specific questions about the dishes and the bottles that will exploit his familiarity with the restaurant's cellar and kitchen, rather than simply confronting him with the tabula rasa of "we'd like a good bottle of wine."

A special caution is owed both to the reader and to the four fine restaurants that graciously allowed me to use their menus and wine lists: Café Provençal in Evanston, Illinois; The Four Seasons in New York; Sofi in New York; and Valentino in Los Angeles. What you are about to read are not restaurant reviews: They are analyses of the ways four top-flight establishments integrate their food and their wine. They are strategies for your use, ways you can take best advantage of these and similar wining and dining situations. Because this is all based on real menus and real wine lists, the bare facts will be unavoidably dated by the time you read this. Wines and vintages will have changed, menus will have altered, prices will no doubt have gone up. Chefs leave (Seppi Renggli is no longer at The Four Seasons), houses try a new style (Café Provençal is now more contemporary French than country French in emphasis), even—sadly—mortality takes its toll, as it did with the unexpected death of Café Provençal's Leslee Reis. Those changes or others yet to come in no way affect the validity of what you can learn from these examples and analyses. But it would be the worst repayment I or any of you could make these generous and forthright professionals to fault them for no longer offering any of the items discussed here, or for not offering them at the same price.

Stylish and Personal: The Short, Selected Wine List

Our first restaurant is Sofi, a very promising medium-sized establishment that, alas, closed as this book was going to press. Its menu and wine list, however, remain an instructive example of a restaurant that strove for a comfortable mix of downtown casual and uptown elegant in its ambience and clientele.

THE CHARACTER OF THE COOKING

As you read through this, or any other, menu, what you ought to be keeping an eye out for are indications of the style of cooking the establishment does, the accents its foods will bear. One of the first things to look for, for example, is what the house does with veal. Veal is a mild and delicate meat that takes whatever coloration the restaurant wishes to give it. Ninety percent of the restaurants in the United States offer at least one veal dish. All the bad ones will give you the same overbreaded cutlet, but all the good ones will vary the cut and the preparation according to their own lights. What the house does with simple foods like this will tell you more about their style than any other factor. After that, look at the kinds of basic ingredients and condiments the kitchen likes to use. Notice which ones show up in more than one item on the menu. This conveys the next most important information about the restaurant's culinary style.

Sofi's menu is very revealing in these regards, and the revelations

Sofi
Dinner
Summer 1988

First Course ~ hot

   Asparagus Parmeggiano   7.

   Sauteed Fresh Mozzarella with Tomato Pesto
     and Garlic Croutons   8.

First Course ~ Cold

   Mixed Green and Fresh Herb Salad with Vinaigrette 7.
     with Roquefort and Vinaigrette   8.

   Vegetable Tart of Eggplant, Tomato and Zucchini
     with Tomato Thyme Coulis   7.

   Gardener's Salad   9.

   Vegetables Milagro : Braised Escarole, Fried Zucchini
     with Mint ; Roast Peppers, Grilled Eggplant,
     Fennel Salad, Stuffed Mushroom, and More'   10.

   Asparagus Gribiche   7.

   Lobster Salad with Marinated Celery, Tomato
     and Avocado Puree   15.

   Sea Scallops Marinated and Poached, Served with
     Broccoli and a White Bean, Osetra Caviar Salad 15.

Pasta Course

   Pasta of the Day   priced accordingly

   Cold Fettucine with Fresh Tomato Coulis and Pesto 15.

   Rigatoni Stuffed with Swiss Chard and Ricotta
     with Fresh Tomato and Fontina Cheese   18.

       Please Refrain from Cigar and Pipe Smoking

Second Course

Fish of the Day   priced accordingly

Grilled Sushi-Grade Tuna with warm Eggplant,
Zucchini, Roast Pepper and Arugula with a Cold
Garlic, Chive and Tuna Consommé   25.

Lobster Castlebay with julienned Vegetables and
Dried Ginger, garlic and Shallots in Lobster Sauce   29.

Sauteed Striped Bass with a Compote of Fennel,
Parsley and Orange Zest, Beurre Monté   24.

Sauteed Salmon with Swiss Chard, Thyme, Basil   25.
and Balsamic Vinegar; Sauce Vin Blanc and Chard Puree

Sea Scallops Poached with Carrots, Zucchini, Mushrooms
and Celery Root in a Lobster Broth   19.

Filet of Beef in Garlic Port Sauce with a Gorgonzola Souffle   25.

Roasted Breast of Muscovy Duck with Tapenade,
Endive Confit and Vermouth Sauce   28.

Marinated Grilled Squab with Brandy, Madiera,
Ginger and Peaches   24.

Sauteed Chicken with Fresh Herb Vinegar Sauce,
Market Vegetables and Straw Potatoes   17.

Sauteed Veal Medallions with Tuna and Scallion
"Tartare", Marsala Sauce   24.

Grilled and Herb Marinated Chicken Breast
with Roast Mushrooms, Leeks in Vinaigrette,
Tomato Herb Concasse   17.

Executive Chef - Dennis Mac Neil

	Champagne	and
	glass	bottle
Piper Sonoma Brut, 1985	7.	27.
Schramsberg Blanc de Blancs, 1984		36.
Perrier Jouet Brut, N.V.		40.
Deutz Champagne Brut, N.V.		46.

White Wines

Italian
Soave Classico, Anselmi
    Capitel, Foscarino, 1986 ... 7.25 ... 29.
Terre Alte, Livio Felluga, 1986 ... 7.50 ... 30.

Sauvignon Blanc
Kendall-Jackson, 1987 ... 5. ... 20.
Sancerre, Dom. La Moussiere, 1986 ... 23.
Frog's Leap, 1987 ... 24.
Pouilly Fumé, Denis Gaudry, 1986 ... 7. ... 28.

Chardonnay
Macon Villages, J.J. Vincent, 1985 ... 5. ... 20.
St. Veran, J.J. Vincent, 1986 ... 5.75 ... 23.
Kendall-Jackson Vintner's Reserve, 1986 ... 24.
Sonoma Cutrer Russian River, 1986 ... 7. ... 28.
Rully, Antonin Rodet, 1986 ... 25.
Chablis Bouchard, 1985 ... 7.50 ... 30.
Newton, 1986 ... 30.
William Hill Gold Label Reserve, 1986 ... 32.

Sparkling Wine

	glass	bottle
Veure Clicquot Brut, N.V.	9.	50.
Moet and Chandon Brut Imperial, 1982		52.
Krug Grand Curee, N.V.		95.
Krug Rose, N.V.		135.

Red Wines

Rhone
Côtes du Rhone Villages,
Dom. Sainte-Anne, 1986 — 5. — 20.

Beaujolais
Julienas, Collin and Bourisset, 1986 — 5. — 20.
Fleurie, Collin and Bourisset, 1986 — 23.

Sangiovese
Chianti Classico Riserva,
Badia a Coltibuono, 1968 — 44.

Zinfandel
Summit Lake, 1982 — 5. — 20.

Pinot Noir
Sea Ridge, 1983 — 6. — 24.
Beaune Jeurons, Bouchard, 1983 — 42.
Pommard-Epenots, Drouhin, 1981 — 60.

Merlot/Cabernet, France
Chateau Lapelletrie, 1982 — 7. — 28.

Cabernet Sauvignon
Chateau Jourteran (Haut-Medoc), 1981 — 6. — 24.
Viansa, 1984 — 23.
Simi, 1984 — 6.50 — 26.
Chateau Gruaud Larose, 1979 — 36.
Mondavi Reserve, 1983 — 62.

point to three related conclusions. First, the style of cooking: If you'd never dined at Sofi and knew nothing about it, the menu would tell you that the house's culinary predilections were eclectic American, or even what is called *nouvelle américaine*. Look at the telltale veal, here served with a conventional-seeming Marsala sauce and a very unconventional tuna tartare. Look at the prominence of vegetables and fresh fish—and especially fish in combination with vegetables—in every course. Notice too the importance of grilling as a cooking technique. These are all also results of the fact that this is a summer menu, but then it's always summer in California, which is the spiritual home of much of the new American cooking.

Second, the dishes show that the kitchen is both sophisticated and willing to experiment, to combine techniques and ingredients in ways that derive from more than a single gastronomical tradition: Witness the visible presence of influences from the French tradition (for example, *gribiche*), the Italian (rigatoni with ricotta and Fontina), and the Japanese (the various uses of tuna, poached sea scallops). Also noteworthy in this regard is the combination of some of these very different influences with one another in a single course: for example, a Gorgonzola soufflé accompanying a filet of beef in garlic port sauce, a single dish that manages to combine ingredients or techniques from Italian, French, British, and general American traditions.

Third, you can see evidence of Sofi's serious interest in wine in the number of different wines employed in sauces, each one apparently selected for the particular properties it brings to the particular sauce: a simple white wine sauce with a chard puree; port with the beef; vermouth with a Muscovy duck breast; Madeira and brandy with the squab; Marsala with the veal and tuna.

Taken all together, these observations point to a consistent house style in the food and its preparation, a clear preference for bright, forward flavors made more emphatic by a profusion of fresh vegetables. These vivid flavors are especially highlighted by carefully selected acidic accents in their preparation: vinegars and vinaigrettes, tomato and tomato *coulis*, bitter vegetables like endive and arugula, and herbs like mint, chive, and basil—even orange zest.

Just a quick skim of a menu as stylistically distinctive as this conveys a wealth of information to a wine-conscious reader. The most important broad conclusion to be drawn from it is that, by and large, these foods are going to want wines that are lean and somewhat acidic themselves rather than wines that are fat and luscious. Like most nouvelle cooking, these dishes need an answering brightness and—for lack of a better word—agility in the wines that will companion them. Really big-bodied wines may overpower the food or be wrecked by the food's acidity unless they have enough mature tannin or acid of their own. So before you've even picked up the wine list, you should already have at least a general idea of the kind of wines you're going to be looking for. It's important to keep an open mind about this. A good wine list or a good sommelier can always suggest a wine you never thought of that will work spectacularly with what you're eating. Nevertheless, even a loose sense of the kind of characteristics you want in your wine will considerably reduce the amount of time you have to spend poring over the wine list.

THE CHARACTER OF THE WINES

When you turn at last to that wine list, if it is of any manageable size, give it a double reading: a quick scan to determine the broad categories the wines fall into and to locate the ones with the sorts of characteristics you've judged you're looking for, and a closer, more careful appraisal of the wines that seem like candidates for your dinner.

Sofi's wine list is just as revealing as its menu. It exhibits the same kind of eclecticism, sophistication, and willingness to experiment. It's a short list, and it bears clear signs of thoughtful selection.

- California, France, and Italy provide all the wines, three dozen in total. That's not a remarkable range, but a short list can't represent the whole world and shouldn't try to. This one focuses on the three currently most interesting wine-producing areas.
- About half the wines are available by the glass, a courtesy that is happily becoming more widespread and eliminating a lot of problems for people who want more than one wine

with a meal or who want to taste a new wine before plunging for the cost of a whole bottle. Before the Cruvinet and its kin—nitrogen-cap bar machines that prevent oxidation of opened wines—half-bottles were the only resort for such problems, and not many restaurants bothered to stock them in any variety. These days the presence of a nitrogen-cap machine is in itself an important indication that a restaurant is taking more than routine interest in its wines.

- The wines are arranged by grape variety, a mode of listing that conveys a lot of information about the wines in an economical manner. The conventional way of grouping wines by country keeps you hopping all over a wine list looking for wines of similar characteristics. This list's Châteaux Gruaud Larose and Tourteran do in fact have more in common with the California Cabernet Sauvignons from Mondavi and Simi with which they are grouped than they do with the two French Beaujolais on the list.

- The list displays an admirable assortment of wines in generally very fair price ranges. The eight sparkling wines represent not only a healthy percentage of the list as a whole but also a wide spectrum of prices, from a quite reasonable Piper Sonoma 1985 Brut ($27) up to an expensive Krug N.V. Rosé ($135; I love Krug champagne, but both Krug and Sofi overvalue this particular wine). The fourteen whites are priced from a low of $20 to a high of $32, an excellent price range with several good values but, alas, no real stars. The fourteen red wines are priced from $20 to $62. Nine of them are available between $20 and $28, including some with five or six years of bottle age. That by itself would make quite a decent selection for many restaurants, but the five most expensive reds ($36 to $62) listed here also offer some striking values. They include that great rarity in restaurants, some red wines that have been properly matured and may actually be ready to drink: to wit, a Pommard Epenots 1981 (marginal as to age, but a lightish year and therefore worth trying); Château Gruaud Larose 1979, which should be just about perfect right now; and Badia a Coltibuono 1968, a fine, long-lived vintage from a great estate.

- The list also includes a few uncommon selections, such as the Schramsberg '84 Blanc de Blancs and the '83 Bouchard Beaune Teurons. It even risks a few wines that at first glance might seem overpriced, for instance, Anselmi's Soave Classico Capitel at $29 and a Chianti, the '68 Badia a Coltibuono, at $44. The first is a rare, single-vineyard Soave that has spent a while in oak. It is all in all a very substantial wine and not what one ordinarily thinks of as Soave, though $29 may still be a bit much for it. On the other hand, the Badia may be the best buy on the whole list (with some stiff competition from the 1979 Château Gruaud Larose at $36).
- Finally, reading this list with an eye toward matching the wine with the menu rather than appraising the list in itself very quickly reveals that the vast majority of the wines listed possess the kind of acidity or the kinds of tannins needed to mesh with the bright, acidic character of the kitchen's dishes. All the sparkling wines, the Italian whites, all the Sauvignon Blancs, most of the Chardonnays, and all the red wines with the possible exception of the California Cabernets will partner happily with most of the menu. Whatever problems this list is going to present us with, paucity of choices won't be among them. It may be short, but it is very well integrated with the style of Sofi's cuisine.

In fact, this brief list could force us to some agonizing choices. How do we decide between ready-to-drink claret like the '79 Gruaud Larose and twenty-year-old Chianti Classico Riserva of the caliber of Badia a Coltibuono? Either would be lovely, and much—everything in fact—would depend on the food to be eaten with it. When I come across values like either of these on a wine list, I tend to pick my wine first and then choose the food to suit.

PRIORITY TO THE WINE

Let us assume for the moment that we are going to do exactly that, that you and I are dining together and have agreed that, whatever we may choose for our dinner, we want to taste—coin toss here to decide—the '79 Gruaud Larose.

Fine. We've got our dinner wine, so logically we're going to put our meal together backward, from main course to appetizer. If we're being a little spendthrift, I'd suggest that while we mull over our options we sip a glass of Veuve Clicquot, perhaps the best nonvintage brut champagne on the market now. It's always easier to think about food and wine while you've got some in front of you.

Gruaud Larose is a St-Julien, a second growth from a commune that the 1855 classifiers awarded no first growths, though many wine lovers today would dispute that ranking. It is a big, fruity wine. Some people call it "chunky" in its youth, but like other fine St-Juliens it matures into a silky, elegant wine of reserved power.

In choosing a food to match with it, you want to find a combination of elements that will call forth both its fruit and its complexity. Lamb, the reflex response and traditional partner of all the wines of the Médoc, is absent from this menu, and the next most obvious choice, the Filet of Beef in Garlic Port Sauce with a Gorgonzola Soufflé, is a workable but not exciting prospect with this wine: That Gorgonzola soufflé (really a kind of Gorgonzola popover) might prove just a bit too sharp and make the wine taste a bit thin and underflavored. That soufflé would, of course, work splendidly with the more acid Badia a Coltibuono Chianti. The Roasted Breast of Muscovy Duck is questionable for a similar reason. Lovely as the duck itself would be with the Gruaud, its accompaniments of Tapenade, Endive Confit and Vermouth Sauce might well be too sharp for the wine. So too the otherwise promising Grilled and Herb-Marinated Chicken Breast with Roast Mushrooms; that much would be fine, but its accompanying Leeks in Vinaigrette and Tomato Herb Concassée would undercut the wine.

This is not to say that the Gruaud Larose wouldn't be enjoyable with these dishes. It emphatically would, but you would not be getting everything out of the wine, nor the best of it, because of that slight acidic discord caused by the various garnitures. Besides, there are at least two offerings on the menu that will call out everything the wine has to give: the Marinated Grilled Squab with Brandy, Madeira, Ginger and Peaches, and the Sautéed Veal Medallions with Tuna and Scallion "Tartare," Marsala Sauce. In the first case the dark, deeply flavored, extra-lean flesh of the squab in combination with that rich, fruity, ever-so-slightly sweet sauce will make a perfect complement to a mature St-Julien. The flavor components of the food and the wine will match almost perfectly, item for item and strength for strength. In this case the food and the wine will claim equal shares of your attention and enjoyment. The other dish—the veal and tuna combination—will provide a glorious counterpoint to the Gruaud Larose, to which it will probably surrender the spotlight. Already counterpointed within itself by the juxtaposition of raw and cooked, lean and fleshy, the veal and tuna together with their slightly sweet sauce will play beneath the wine's power, emphasizing the wine's complexity and size and their own complexity and delicacy. Without the richness of the tuna and the Marsala sauce, veal would have a hard time competing at all with a wine like this. It is the combination of components within the preparation that allows the successful matching.

The choices of first course to precede these dishes are very wide indeed. In fact, what we select will depend mostly on whether we want to drink our bottle of Gruaud Larose all the way through the meal or whether we'll take a glass of something else with our first course. If we're sticking with the Gruaud, then we could hardly do better than either the vegetables Milagro or the sautéed mozzarella. The concentrated but delicately flavored fats of the cheese will make the wine taste beautifully round and full. It will feel leaner but more assertive and complex with the interestingly mixed flavors of the vegetable dish, and it will probably pick up and respond to elements like the sweetness of the roast peppers and fennel and zucchini, the smokiness of the grilled eggplant, the fleshy richness of the stuffed mushroom. If we're opting instead to have a glass of another red—say something simple and young like the Côtes-du-Rhône-Villages or the Juliénas—then we can widen our horizons somewhat. For instance, the vegetable tart, the lobster salad, and the sea scallops would all work well with the fruit and acid vivacity of the Juliénas. The Rhône, because of its greater body and relatively lower acidity, would work better with the sautéed mozzarella, the vegetable tart, and the vegetables Milagro. You might even consider having a half-portion of the rigatoni. Its two cheeses would tame the tomato's acidity, and the total combination would interact very pleasingly with the fresh, fat fruit of the Côtes-du-Rhône.

If we take a glass of white wine, especially if it's one of the more acidic ones like that Soave or the Pouilly-Fumé, then we can take our pick of the menu quite free of constraint. Any of the appetizers or pastas would taste fine with these two wines, or even with the Mâcon, St-Véran, or Rully. The Chablis and the California Chardonnays would require a bit more selectivity because of their greater body and flavor and the pleasing fatness that is so much a part of Chardonnay character. For this reason, they would match best with the least acidic of these dishes, and especially with very flavorful but delicate dishes like the lobster salad or the poached scallops. They might even be very fine with the Cold Fettucine with Fresh Tomato Coulis and Pesto. If the olive oil in the dish is sufficient in flavor and quantity to produce the sort of rich unctuosity that pesto should ideally possess, then one of those bigger Chardonnays will be magnificent with it.

PRIORITY TO THE FOOD

That's all well and good if we have picked our wine first, which is really the easiest way to go about things in a restaurant. But our problem and our choices would be very different if the food took priority over the wine, if, let us say, we two entered Sofi with our hearts and our palates set on lobster or salmon.

Let us assume that you have chosen to start your dinner with the vegetables Milagro and go on to the lobster Castlebay, while I have opted for lobster salad followed by the sautéed salmon and its vegetable accompaniments. Perfectly safe and satisfactory wine choices would include all the sparkling wines on the list, with the possible exception of the Krug rosé, which might be just a touch too full bodied and austere for the lobster; much would depend on just how rich or light the lobster sauce actually was. All the still white wines would also perform well with these dishes. My purely personal inclination would be to opt for the Pouilly-Fumé, because its combination of roundness and acidity would enable it to interact differently and freshly with each dish. Any of the Chardonnays would certainly bring more strength and character to the meal, but the strength that Chardonnay possesses is precisely its weakness too. The food must bend to fit it: It won't adapt to the food. If we were both eating the striped bass, for instance, any of the Chardonnays would be fine. The same is true of the grilled chicken, but with the sautéed chicken and its herb vinegar sauce, a Chardonnay would be as chancy as it is with this sautéed salmon and its accompaniments of white wine sauce and vegetables in balsamic vinegar. Most wines made from the Chardonnay grape respond much better to fatty, creamy sauces than to those with any sort of marked vinegar presence. Certainly if our party were larger and the dishes even more diverse than the four we've chosen, a wine with acidity and suppleness, like the Pouilly-Fumé, is the kind of wine I would look to as disserving none of the dishes and being potentially very pleasing with all of them.

I would be remiss if I didn't say something here about the possibilities for drinking red wines with any of these fish dishes. By now the principles governing these options should be pretty familiar to you, but this is the final exam, so they're worth going through once again.

With the grilled tuna: If push came to shove, you could drink any of the red wines on this list with the tuna. I think the California Cabernets would be the least successful bottles, because they just don't have the kind of acidity I want with a dense-fleshed fish like tuna. For my money, the best choices would be any of the Pinot Noir–based wines or—and this is where my heart is—the Badia a Coltibuono. If I had pots of money, I would choose first of all the Krug rosé, whose body and acidity and distinctive Pinot Noir flavor would be ideal with the tuna and its accompaniments—far better than any of the still white wines, in fact.

With the lobster Castlebay: Lacking the body and robustness of the tuna, this dish needs a milder-mannered wine altogether. My choices here for a red wine would be restricted to the Sea Ridge Pinot Noir or—and I believe this would be better—the Juliénas.

With the sautéed striped bass: I would make the same choices as for the lobster and for the same reasons. One further possibility:

the '81 Pommard Epénots from Drouhin, a very smooth and elegant wine, very light on the tongue.

With the sautéed salmon: The best wines from which to choose include all the Pinot Noirs, the Beaujolais, and the Chianti, and I honestly don't know which I would prefer among them—perhaps either of those cru Beaujolais, which have all the fruit and acidity of their kind plus some body and breed.

With the poached sea scallops: If you want to continue tasting the scallops, only the gentlest of reds will really work. This means either of the Beaujolais or, at the very extremest reach, the Sea Ridge Pinot Noir.

IN SUM

One of the most pleasing aspects of this menu and wine list is how well they are coordinated with each other. The bright, acidic flavors of the foods coordinate beautifully with the carefully selected, largely acidic accents in the wines. As a result, most of the wines, red or white, will match quite happily with any dish on the menu, fish, flesh, or fowl. This makes for maximum security for everyone—wine novice, wooden palate, or nervous connoisseur. With a list and menu like these, you would have to work hard to choose a "wrong" wine. The house's aim, clearly, is to come as close as possible to making every wine the "right" wine for every dish. This requires a lot of care and a lot of self-awareness in drawing up a wine list, but it furnishes a model of what restaurants that cannot afford or do not want a large, diversified cellar can do with the small number of wines they do stock.

American Classic: The Eclectic, Balanced Wine List

Let's turn our attention now to a totally different restaurant situation. If, by making an advantage of the small size of its wine selection, Sofi is able to come close to eliminating the possibility of error for wine novices, The Four Seasons takes full advantage of the depth of its cellar to create a cornucopia of possibilities for people who are knowledgeable or more experimental about wine. Yes, you could make "wrong" choices here—wrong in the sense of not being the optimum wine, out of all the possibilities The Four Seasons offers, for the meal you've chosen—but you won't get a bad wine, and rarely even an uninteresting one. Following is a summer menu and its companion short wine list (the full list, though as fascinating to enophiles as fumets to King Pellinore, is much too long for us to deal with here) from the Grill Room of this landmark restaurant.

THE CHARACTER OF THE COOKING

Even a quick look at the menu reveals that The Four Seasons's cuisine is, once again, what we would have to call American eclectic. A European influence shows through in items like the Carpaccio with Grana and Arrugola (an Italian dish, though the word *arrugola* is strictly American Italian), the gazpacho, and the Sautéed Filet of Striped Bass with Grapes, but the New World makes an emphatic entrance with many specifically regional ingredients (for example, that striped bass or the Louisiana shrimp) and recipes (Crabmeat Cake with Mustard Sauce, and the Blackened Shrimp, Salsa Fria). Oriental influences show up obviously in dishes like the three curries, more subtly in combinations like multiethnic shrimp with a definitely New World corn cake and a definitely Chinese cilantro ginger sauce, or an international Escalope of Veal accompanied by a clearly Japanese-influenced Soy and Wasabi Sauce, or the Breast of Pigeon with Rice Noodles (Chinese? Japanese?). Such a congeries of influences points definitely to nouvelle cuisine or its *américaine* cousin as the dominant style in the kitchen. Even The Four Seasons's self-evidently minceur-inspired Spa Cuisine shows a clear touch of nouvelle in its Summer Fruits with Mango Puree.

The variety of cooking techniques mirrors the eclecticism of ingredients: grilling, roasting, braising, sautéing, even serving meat raw (carpaccio). There is a discreet reminder, at the top of the menu, that dessert soufflés take time. Such a combination of influences and styles would, in many lesser restaurants, justifiably cause

THE GRILL ROOM AT THE FOUR SEASONS

For Your Convenience We Request That You Order
Dessert Soufflés
At The Beginning Of Your Meal

* available as a Main Course
** available as an Appetizer

APPETIZERS

* Carpaccio with Grana and Arrugola 16.50

* Spinach Pasta with Crabmeat 15.00

Chilled Gazpacho 8.50

SPA CUISINE ^R : Summer Fruits with Mango Purée 11.50

Belon and other Oysters 11.50

Little Necks or Cherrystones 10.50

*Blackened Shrimp, Salsa Fria 15.50

* Shrimp and Corn Cake, Cilantro Ginger Sauce 15.50

THE GRILL ROOM CURRIES

** Mussels, Mild Yellow 27.50

** Louisiana Shrimp, Spicy Red 35.00

** Beef, Extra Spicy Green 32.00

MAIN COURSES

Sautéed Filet of Striped Bass with Grapes 34.00

** Frogs' Legs with Tomato and Basil 34.50

** Crabmeat Cake with Mustard Sauce 35.50

Escalope of Veal with Soy and Wasabi Sauce 33.50

Médaillons of Lamb with Zucchini and Eggplant 35.50

Breast of Pigeon with Rice Noodles 34.00

SPA CUISINE ^R : A Skewer of Marinated Shrimp and Chicken 34.00

Fish Grilled on Charcoal 30.00

Lamb Chops, Sirloin Steak or Filet Mignon 35.00

WINES

Tonight's Wines by the Glass 5.75

Chardonnay, Groth, Napa 1985
Chardonnay, Sonoma Cutrer 1986
Merlot, J. Phelps 1986
Moulin a Vent, L. Latour 1985

THE GRILL ROOM AT THE FOUR SEASONS
* Bottles of the Week

AMERICAN

Reds
518 Dominus, C. Moueix 1984 72.00
515 Daniel Estate, C. Moueix 1984 36.00
529 Cabernet Sauvignon, Hanzell 1982 45.00
506 Cabernet Sauvignon, Montelena 1983 48.00
603 Cabernet Sauvignon, J. Luper 1983 44.00
* 512 Cabernet Sauvignon, La Jota 1984 34.00
531 Grenache, Clos du Gilroy, Bonny Doon 1987 18.00
514 Merlot, Joseph Phelps 1986 31.00
241 Merlot, Duckhorn 1985 65.00
524 Zinfandel, York Creek, Ridge 1985 24.00
527 Pinot Noir Reserve Chalone 1983 75.00

Whites
586 Chardonnay, Mayacamas 1985 55.00
585 Chardonnay, Reserve Simi 1984 55.00
550 Muscat Canelli Vin de Glaciere, Bonny Doon 1987 42.00 half
569 Chardonnay, Château Woltner Reserve 1986 51.00
572 Sauvignon Blanc, Sanford 1986 18.00
532 Pinot Blanc Chalone 1986 36.00

ITALIAN

Reds
600 Sassicaia, Tenuta San Guido 1983 75.00
418 Tignanello, Antinori 1982 45.00
278 Cabernet Sauvignon, Darmagi, Gaja 1983 54.00
* 428 Cabernet Sauvignon, Maurizio Zanella 1984 36.00
293 Grattamacco 1985 33.00
433 Balifico, Volpaia 1985 41.00
* 437 Le Vignacce, Villa Cilnia 1985 27.00
298 Le Pergole Torte, Monte Vertine 1983 45.00
* 416 Vinattieri Rosso 1983 25.00
411 Corbulino Rosso, Scarpa 1985 27.00
337 Bricco Dell'Uccellone, G. Bologna 1984 48.00

Whites
420 Gavi dei Gavi, La Scolca 1986 45.00
574 Montecarlo Bianco, F. Mazzini 1983 23.00
563 Arneis, Bruno Giacosa 1987 38.00
* 551 Meriggio, Tenuta Fontodi 1986 16.00
434 Bianco Imperiale Berlucchi n.v. 12.00
319 Chardonnay, Marzocco, Avignonesi 1986 25.00
429 Recioto Dei Capitelli, Anselmi 1985 45.00

FRENCH

Reds
266 Château Clerc Milon, Pauillac 1982 45.00
* 310 Château Latour, Pauillac 1980 56.00
286 Château Talbot, St. Julien 1978 51.00
245 Château Mouton Baronne Philippe, Pauillac 1982 45.00
353 Nuits St. George, Premier Cru, Faiveley 1983 65.00
252 Julienas, S. Fessy 1985 15.00

Whites
389 Chablis Pic Premier 1985 65.00
360 Beaune, Clos de Mouches, J. Drouhin 1986 81.00
376 Clos Blanc de Vougeot L'Heritier-Guyot 1985 75.00
425 Puligny Montrachet, Premier Cru, Leflaive 1983 85.00
427 Chassagne Montrachet Premier Cru Lequin-Roussot 1985 65.00
581 Châteauneuf du Pape, Château de Beaucastel 1986 53.00
584 Muscat Beaumes de Venise, J. Vidal Fleury 21.00/half

Champagnes and Sparkling Wines
* 466 Billecart-Salmon, Rosé 55.00
467 Henriot Cuvée Baccarat 1979 110.00
452 Taittinger Comte de Champagne Rosé 1982 150.00
453 Moët & Chandon, Dom Pérignon 1982 135.00
457 Mumm, Cordon Rouge 1982 60.00
592 Krug, Grand Cuvée 85.00
593 Iron Horse, Sonoma Brut 1983 39.00
476 Perrier-Jouët Brut n/v 40.00

Tonight's Wines By The Glass $5.75

you to fear you had wandered into Calvin Trillin's infamous Maison de la Casa House. Here, it simply betokens the serene control The Four Seasons has of its métier.

More than that, in fact: A second look will show that for all the apparent exoticism, The Four Seasons's menu essentially offers real food: straightforward meats and fish presented for the most part straightforwardly, adorned essentially by their intrinsic freshness and quality. Nothing else, after all, distinguishes The Four Seasons's oysters from anybody else's—ditto the carpaccio, clams, lamb chops, and steak. In cuisine as in any other art, there is a level of style so high its hallmark is a bold simplicity. That's what this menu shows as its governing principle. Robert Courtine, the most exigent of gourmets and Parisian restaurant critics, used to order tomato salad as the ultimate test of a fine kitchen, on the rather Zen-paradoxical theory that attaining excellence in the simplest things is the most difficult art of all. He was, of course, correct, and the barebones listing of dishes on this menu conceals exactly that kind of artistry. It all makes an interesting counterpoint to the evident sophistication of the wine list, of which more will be said below.

One last general reflection on the menu: The Four Seasons also reveals in it the seriousness and pervasiveness of its concern with fine wine by listing on the menu itself four daily changing wines that are available by the glass. Besides being an unobtrusive, yet effective way of guiding diners who don't automatically think of wine toward one of the house's great strengths, such a listing is a great kindness to the tired winebibber who wants a little glass of something decent while he composes himself to the serious task of choosing his dinner. A small service like this always makes me, at least, feel that I've landed safely and that my dinner is in good hands.

THE CHARACTER OF THE WINES

The wine list itself completes my sense of well-being. For convenience's sake, we'll work here with The Seasons's short list. It displays a spirit just as eclectic—ecumenical is probably the truer word—as the menu, a characteristic that becomes all the more admirable when you remind yourself that this list in fact contains only a fraction of The Four Seasons's cellar. Here are some of the things that seem to me striking and notable about it:

- Its visual presentation and organization are totally straightforward and classic. The wines are organized into three large groups by nationality—American, Italian, and French—each subdivided into red and white, with a small tail of "Champagnes and Sparkling Wines," all but one French, wagging along behind.
- This short list is big. It contains fifty-six different wines. With the four wines that are listed on the menu proper, that makes sixty wines the happy enophile can play with, to twenty menu items. Three to one: Those are good odds.
- Not only is the list big, but it favors big wines. Full-bodied red wines set its tone. Even among the whites and sparklers, there is a remarkable paucity of light, aperitif-style wines. Bold, forthright flavors predominate.
- The dinner menu offers four wines by the glass—two fine California Chardonnays, a California Merlot, and a Moulin à Vent—at a very reasonable flat price. On the wine list itself seven selections—five red wines, a white, and a rosé champagne—are specially marked as wines of the week, all of them in very fair price ranges.
- The general pricing pattern too is quite remarkable. While there are several wines on which you could happily blow the budget (and many more such on The Seasons's full list, should you be so inclined), there are also five wines under $20, and thirteen more under $40, not to mention a nice champagne buy—Perrier-Jouët—at exactly $40. This short list reflects a conscientious attempt to correlate value and price.

All this is very attractive, but not what truly distinguishes this wine list. To be purely tautological, what distinguishes this list is distinction. This list isn't particularly going to impress a wine novice, and it may not make the merely casual wine drinker's choices any easier. That, after all, is why restaurants that have good cellars also have sommeliers. But it will arrest the attention of connoisseurs and serious wine lovers. For the knowing wine drinker, reading through the wines on this list becomes a series of happy encounters: Oh, the Dominus! Oh, Zanella's Cabernet! Oh, Drouhin's white Clos de Mouches! Even the list's lone Beaujolais rates an Oh! It's a very stylish Juliénas from Sylvain Fessy, at a remarkably fair price.

This is a wine buff's list. It has clearly been selected by people who are passionate about wine for people who are passionate about wine. There is scarcely an obvious wine on it. Well, maybe the Dom Pérignon. But just look at some of the other sparklers it's sharing space with: the little known but exquisite Billecart-Salmon (rosé yet), the beautiful Henriot Cuvée Baccarat, the full-bodied and authoritative rosé from Taittinger's Comtes de Champagne, and so on down from *têtes de cuvée* to a very nicely priced N.V. brut from Perrier-Jouët and the lone California sparkler, the interestingly chosen 1983 Sonoma brut from Iron Horse. That's a handsome range of quality and style and price, and it requires an individual or a staff who possess real familiarity with all the wines to select them that way.

The more you know about wines, the more intriguing this list is. It starts you off with a rush, with the well-chosen second vintage (it's more forward than the '83) from Dominus, a Bordeaux-like blending of Cabernet Sauvignon, Cabernet Franc, and Merlot that is the fruit of a much-talked-about collaboration between native Napa talent and Napa vines and the winemaking skills of the proprietor of Château Pétrus. That little gem could easily serve as the diamond solitaire of many wine lists, but this one follows it immediately—and at half the price!—with the less publicized but potentially even more interesting 100 percent Cabernet Sauvignon from the same vintage and the same makers.

In fact, the whole cluster of California reds constitutes an object of interest for the contrasts of standard-setting—and standard— wines and rarities it presents. Among the Cabernets, for instance, it juxtaposes such longtime benchmark wines as Chateau Montelena with newcomers like La Jota, and a Cabernet from an estate better

known for its Pinot Noir and Chardonnay—Hanzell—with one of
the first wines released under his own name by Jerry Luper, who has
served as winemaker at several important California estates, including Montelena. The two Merlots also differ interestingly from each
other: One comes from a longtime champion of the variety, Duckhorn, another from a longtime California pacesetter, Phelps, which
only occasionally makes a varietal Merlot. The single Pinot Noir
comes from Chalone, one of the earliest California winemakers to
master this touchy grape and one of the most consistently successful
with it. The 1983 vintage was a fine one for Chalone's Pinot Noir,
and the particular bottling offered here is one of their much-sought-
after, hard-to-get Reserves, in its own way a small rarity. The list's
single Zinfandel is similarly well chosen, from Ridge Vineyards, the
acknowledged California master of that "native" varietal. The
York Creek Zinfandels almost always contain 5 percent to 10 percent Petite Sirah, which gives them a delightful spicy-peppery edge.
The final red wine in this group amounts to another rarity: a single-
vineyard Grenache from Bonny Doon. In California, Grenache
usually disappears into inexpensive blends, rosés, and ports. In
southern France and northern Spain it blends with other varietals to
make big, full-bodied red wines. The Bonny Doon Vineyard carries
the banner of Rhône Valley grapes and blending techniques, which
are uncommon in California, and this varietal bottling of Grenache
is unusual even for Bonny Doon.

These unconventional California choices set the tone for the
whole wine list. Snobs and label drinkers may think they're on safe
ground when they see Dominus heading the parade, but the rest of
those California wines are calculated to give such folk a severe case
of the uneasies. The French selections, especially the reds, will
compound the effect. You might well expect The Four Seasons to
be the sort of place that offers you *premiers crus,* period, and lets
you find the bucks to pay for them. The cellar certainly has those
wines if you want them, and in multiple vintages. But look at what
the house proposes: only six French reds (as compared to eleven
from California and, what we will talk about later, eleven from
Italy), one a very inexpensive—and good—Beaujolais; a solitary
red Burgundy, neither a *grand cru* nor estate bottled; and four
Bordeaux, two fifth-growth Pauillacs (Clerc Milon and Mouton

Baronne Philippe), a fourth-growth St-Julien (Château Talbot), and Château Latour, the only *premier cru* of the lot, and that from an off year, 1980.

This is a very modest slate of French wines for a place that could, if it wished, bowl you over with acute accents and circumflexes. It is partly, no doubt, due to The Four Seasons's long championing the cause of California wines; the restaurant's much-missed annual California Barrel Tasting was for years the East Coast's center for information about California wine, a kind of combination carnival and consciousness-raising session. But it also seems due to an admirable house policy about the relation of value and price in wines. This Four Seasons's list creates a remarkable situation: Whether you are a label drinker or a connoisseur or blissfully unaware of the differences of one wine from another, whether you are a recent lottery winner or recent entrant into Chapter 11 or just an average citizen on an average budget, this is a wine list from which you can order by price with absolute impunity. Take the California wines as an example. Choose the most or the least expensive—Chalone's Pinot Noir or Bonny Doon's Clos du Gilroy Grenache—and you have in both cases good and interesting bottles of wine. Go a step in either direction—Dominus and Ridge York Creek Zinfandel—and neither the quality nor the interest fades. You can safely suit the wine to your budget without worrying about outraging your palate.

Among the French wines, that lone Bordeaux *premier cru* exemplifies once again what I'm suggesting about quality and value scales at work in this wine list. Château Latour 1980 stands as the only representative of the small group of wines that, in reputation at least, sets the winemaking standards of the world. Why? Why this wine? Why this year? Here are the reasons we can infer from the list's overall shape.

- Too much first-rate Bordeaux is consumed too young.
- The *premiers crus,* of all the Bordeaux wines, are consistently among the slowest to evolve.
- The Pauillacs, which include three of the fabled first growths (Latour is one, Lafite and Mouton the others), are notoriously hard and tannic in their youth.

- Château Latour is famous for being the hardest and slowest of them all.
- Château Latour is also famous for making good wine even in off years. It is, you might say, a specialty of the house.
- Therefore, if average American restaurant patrons are ever going to have a chance to get any idea at all of what a mature *premier cru* tastes like, it is going to have to be an off-year bottling. Such bottlings are the only ones that come ready to drink quickly enough, and they are the only ones that are remotely affordable.
- And if those same average American restaurant patrons are to draw from their off-year *premier cru* an accurate indication of what all the fuss is about and why people who are wine lovers and not wine snobs are willing to pay megabucks for the first growths, then for all practical purposes the wine must be Latour. Nobody does an off year better.

So if you're choosing, for reasons of price and value, to put only one first growth on your wine list, an almost ineluctable logic dictates that an off vintage of Latour should be the one.

The same sort of logic eliminates—from your short list if not from your cellar—Burgundy *grands crus,* because they cost too much money. The prices of the Bordeaux *premiers crus,* the Burgundy *grands crus,* and some individual wines—Château Pétrus and Guigal's La Mouline and La Landonne, for examples—have reached obscene levels. That would be bad enough in itself, but spectacular prices like theirs act as a gravity well, drawing along other, lesser wines. This phenomenon has already happened in Burgundy, where a fairly priced wine—one asking a price in some way proportionate to its level of quality—has all but disappeared from the landscape. It is well under way already in Bordeaux, where the prices of the so-called Super Seconds have begun inching up to the Legendary Firsts. Can the Thrilling Thirds be far behind? Or the Fabulous Fourths? the Fantastic Fifths? the Coruscating *Crus Bourgeois*? Perhaps we will at least be spared the Asinine Artisans, but I doubt it if we don't right now stop unquestioningly paying any price that's asked for a wine. Great wine deserves to be costly, just as any fine craftsmanship deserves generous recompense. But costly doesn't mean—or at least we wine consumers shouldn't allow it to mean—that there is no upper limit.

If in the late seventies and early eighties the California Barrel Tasting embodied The Four Seasons's enthusiasm for all that was experimental and innovative in wine, the action right now—as displayed by this particular wine list at any rate—is in the Italian section, especially, once again, the red wines. Perverse as it may seem to say this of a country that has been making wine for at least two-and-a-half millennia, winemaking in Italy today is in just about the same situation it was in California in the late sixties. Everything is changing, all the time (I'm fighting hard the impulse to talk more about ferment in Italian winemaking), and somehow The Four Seasons is attuned to it and is offering it all to whoever is interested. The Italian portion of this Grill Room list presents as august a gathering of unconventional Italian wines as you are ever likely to see in so short a space. It is less a *carta dei vini* than it is a corralful of mavericks. The list offers eleven Italian red wines—not one of which has the DOC (the official designation of the traditional wine kinds). No Barolos, Barbarescos, or Brunellos: All on the list are experimental wines, wines that according to Italian wine law can bear only the humble designation of a *vino da tavola*. This has become a catchall category that increasingly embraces the least interesting and most interesting, the most backward and most advanced of Italy's wines. A wine can be classified *vino da tavola* because it is judged not qualitatively worthy of a DOC, or it can in effect lose its DOC and be relegated to *vino da tavola* because it violates the regulations in any number of ways, either by blending grapes that are approved only for making 100 percent varietal wines, or, at the opposite pole, by making varietal wines from grapes that are approved only for blending, or by planting and vinifying nontraditional varieties of grapes, or by treating traditional varieties in new ways. Each one of the Italian wines on this short list violates the existing DOC regulations in at least one of these ways. While this says something significant about the limitations of the DOC, it says even more about the excitement and revolution that characterize winemaking in Italy today.

This section of the list begins with the wine that began it all in

Italy, Sassicaia, a Cabernet Sauvignon that drew attention to the new Italian wine scene by sweeping an international tasting in London in the seventies, much the way some Chardonnays started the ball rolling for California by besting some Burgundies in French tastings around the same time. Italy, with two thousand–plus years of winemaking tradition to unlearn, was not as quick to apply the lessons as California, nor half as good at p.r. As a consequence, Italy is only now exploiting the lead of Sassicaia. That lead pointed to Cabernet Sauvignon and to several other things new to Italy. Sassicaia comes from Tuscany, and Tuscan tradition blends grapes. Sassicaia is 100 percent Cabernet. Tuscany did not grow Cabernet; it was not one of the region's traditional grapes. And Sassicaia is not made in one of the traditional wine zones, but in a nearly seaside location that Tuscan enological tradition declared unlikely at best. Sassicaia is aged in the French manner, in new, small oak cooperage; Tuscan wines, when they age at all, do so in large, old oak barrels. That combination left a lot of sacred cows mooing unhappily, and the general tendency in Tuscany, especially in the Chianti region, was either to dismiss Sassicaia as a fluke or simply to pretend it wasn't there. For a lot of small landowners and winemakers, the lessons of Sassicaia were simply not economically feasible, even if they were observable.

Antinori started cautiously applying them. After all, the maker of Sassicaia was the uncle of the present generation of Antinoris. So next in time as next on The Four Seasons's wine list came their Tignanello, ten years ago a revolutionary wine—a wine made in the Chianti zone, on prime land in fact, that forfeited the right to call itself Chianti by omitting all the compulsory white grapes and using instead some unprovided-for Cabernet Sauvignon. Now, because of changes it inspired in the Chianti DOC, the Antinori could label it a Chianti if they wished. But why should they? Tignanello has won its own prestige.

Tignanello and Sassicaia between them opened many avenues for Tuscan winemakers—not just the use of Cabernet, but Cabernet in blends or Cabernet by itself. And if Cabernet by itself made a fine wine, why not the region's indigenous grape, the Sangiovese? Some of its clones had already shown, in Brunello di Montalcino, that by themselves they could make a spectacular wine. The wine scene in Tuscany today covers all the possibilities, from the most conservative (traditional Chianti) to the most innovative. The latter are well represented on this list. Le Pergole Torte and Vinattieri Rosso are 100 percent Sangiovese wines aged in *barriques*; the first is a single-vineyard wine as well. Castello di Volpaia, which also makes a fine traditional Chianti, blends Sangiovese and Cabernet Sauvignon to make its Balifico. Near Arezzo, which has its own Chianti DOC, Villa Cilnia blends Sangiovese, Cabernet Sauvignon, and the usually lowly Montepulciano d'Abruzzo grape to produce the still-experimental Le Vignacce. Grattamacco is the estate name for a vineyard in the less-than-esteemed area near Livorno. The red wine (there is a white wine also) blends Sangiovese with other local grapes (non-Chianti varieties). The winemaker there has also been experimenting with Cabernet, and some of it is doubtless finding its way into his basic *vino rosso*.

The experimentation was not long confined to Tuscany. In the Piedmont Angelo Gaja, a winemaker who admires French wine and has learned much from California, planted both Chardonnay and Cabernet among his prized Nebbiolo vineyards in the heart of the Langhe hills. The resulting Cabernet, Darmagi (the name means "what a shame," which is what his father said when he saw Cabernet being planted rather than Nebbiolo), doesn't have Sassicaia's track record but can certainly give it a run for the money. In Lombardy, Maurizio Zanella established a winery deliberately to make French-style wines—claret blends, Burgundy-varietal reds and whites, champagne-method sparkling wines—as well as the French do. Other northern winemakers began experimenting with their native grapes, aging them in *barriques* or blending them even though the northern tradition customarily made pure varietal wines. One example of that is Giacomo Bologna's brilliant Bricco dell' Uccellone, a single-vineyard, oak-aged Barbera. Another is Scarpa's Corbulino Rosso, a brand-new blending of Nebbiolo and Barbera. From Sassicaia to this wine, this short list also amounts to a short history of the modern opening up of Italian wine.

WHAT'S FOR DINNER?

For all the intrinsic fascination of a wine list that offers so much novelty, its ultimate virtue remains that of any good wine list: that it is so satisfyingly fitted to the cuisine. All those full-bodied, robust wines suit exactly the clear, distinctive flavors of The Four Seasons's artfully simple cooking, a proposition we are about to put to the test right now.

Suppose you start with the Carpaccio with Grana and Arrugola and I begin with an assortment of oysters. You will then have the Veal with Soy and Wasabi Sauce and I will have the Crabmeat Cake with Mustard Sauce. Okay, now what shall we drink? Much depends, of course, on whether we are going to drink one wine throughout, or whether we will opt for different wines with each course, or whether, in this case, each of us will choose a different wine to accompany our very different meals. It will be instructive, I think, to look into all three possibilities and see what the wine list offers us for each.

ONE WINE THROUGHOUT

Despite the diversity of the dishes we've ordered, choosing one wine for the entire meal is surprisingly easy: Everything points to a very full-bodied white wine. Oysters, crabmeat, veal—the only remotely discordant possibility is the carpaccio, which is after all raw beef. But the carpaccio preparation gentles the beef by slicing it paper thin and serving it chilled. Even its usual accompaniment of thin slivers of Parmigiano is in this presentation toned down by the substitution of the slightly less assertive Grana and the addition of the licoricy-bitter leaves of Arugula. By the time you add the customary extra-virgin olive oil and squeeze over it all the mandatory lemon juice (not forgetting a generous sprinkling of salt and grinding of pepper), you have a dish of rich flavor, harmonious rather than aggressive. It could easily take a red wine, but it doesn't *need* a red wine.

The list offers a wonderful range of white wines to match with all these dishes. Any of the California Chardonnays would serve admirably, though my personal taste leans toward the richness and balance of the Simi Reserve. But if we want to go the California route here, opting for big, robust flavors, I think I would incline toward the 1986 Chalone Pinot Blanc, in part because it is a less common wine that Chalone does very well, in part because the flavor of the Pinot Blanc is a bit more restrained than that of Chardonnay and will give the food a little more elbow room.

The French whites listed here also give us many options, though they are again predominantly Chardonnay wines. If price were no object, we could not do better than that beautiful Beaune Clos des Mouches, a lush, elegant wine that is a specialty of the Drouhin firm, which excels in white Burgundies generally. The remaining white Burgundies—the Chablis, Clos Blanc de Vougeot, Puligny-Montrachet, and Chassagne-Montrachet—are absurdly over-priced, not because of the restaurant's markup, mind you, which in this case is standard or less, but because of the price commanded at the source for wines of this caliber. The hyphenated Montrachets in particular almost always disappoint me. All too often they turn out flabby and unstructured, lacking any of the elegance and charm of great Burgundy. The Drouhin Clos des Mouches, on the other hand, has never failed to give me the true Burgundy elegance and balance—a very salutary reminder that *some* of these wines genu-inely deserve high prices. Still, one repines—at least this one repines—at their being quite this high. *C'est la vie.*

Just for the record, I wouldn't order the Château de Beaucastel with the dishes we've chosen because I fear a white Rhône, espe-cially a forceful one like Beaucastel's, would be too powerful a flavor for them, even for the soy-wasabi sauce. Besides, I like my white Rhônes, especially forceful ones like Beaucastel's, much older.

The Italian white wines offer us the fewest possibilities. The Chardonnay, though very good, doesn't have anything we can't get as well or better in California. The Gavi and the Montecarlo are too delicate and too acidic for my total pleasure with the foods we're having, though if you do want lighter-bodied wines, these two are excellent choices. The Arneis from Bruno Giacosa is our best bet. It's made from an old Piedmontese grape that had almost died out until resurrected by a handful of winemakers. Giacosa's handling of it produces a wine relatively soft and full bodied, with fine fruit and a distinctive, dry tang. It should work splendidly with both the crabmeat and the veal, even allowing for the bite of the wasabi.

So much for whites. But what if, perverse though it may be, we wanted a single red wine with all these dishes? One more time, let's work through our red wine options with fish or white meats.

The carpaccio presents no problems for a red wine. The impact of its lemon juice is minimal. The meat and cheese flavors set the tone for this dish. Oysters would seem to be a source of trouble, but like most seafood they can deal quite well with lighter-bodied red wines, especially fruity ones, as long as the wines possess perceptible acidity and a moderate-to-modest amount of tannin. The veal dish too will handle red wine easily. Although the meat itself has a delicate flavor, the sushi-inspired soy and wasabi sauce will give it a pleasing accent and a bit of bite. Crabmeat, of course, presents a wonderful combination of richness and delicacy. Add the mellow bite of the mustard sauce, and the dish cries out for a wine with good fruit and good acid, whatever its color.

So where does all this lead us? I would say that it eliminates all the California reds at a stroke. They are all too big, and the Cabernets and Merlots—and probably the Ridge Zinfandel also—are additionally too tannic. Neither the Pinot Noir nor the Grenache has the high acidity that's needed to match with these particular dishes, though the rich fruit of the Grenache at least puts it in the ballpark.

That same stroke also takes the four Bordeaux reds and the one red Burgundy out of contention. Again, they have too much tannin and not enough acid. A lighter Burgundy than a Nuits-St-Georges might work very well, but that particular commune makes rather robust wines for Burgundy, and Faiveley produces the biggest of them all. That leaves the Fessy Juliénas, which would, I think, be apotheosized alongside these dishes. They have just the right combination of delicacy and forthrightness, in just the right range of intensity, to call out all the fruit and vivacity and the full allotment of Beaujolais depth (not profound, to be sure) this particularly elegant Juliénas possesses. If there were such a thing as the single right wine to have with a particular meal, this Juliénas and this combination of dishes would be it. And of course it doesn't hurt at all that this is the least expensive wine of the whole list.

Normally you would expect that Italy would provide a fair selection of light-bodied and acidic red wines to pair with dishes of the kind we're dealing with here, but, as I said before, this is a highly unusual list of Italian wines. The same criteria that took so many of the California and French reds out of consideration also eliminate a lot of these Italians. Those Sangiovese wines and Sangiovese-Cabernet combinations are just too big bodied, too tannic and hard, for the flavors we want to match them with. The one real possibility among these Italian reds is the Bricco dell' Uccellone, a *barrique*-aged Barbera. A conventional Barbera—one aged in large, old cooperage or in steel—has excellent black cherry–tasting fruit with discreet tannin and high acidity, which would make it perfect for our present purposes. Unfortunately, aging Barbera in small oak cooperage changes its balance. It makes the wine more complex and elegant, but it does so by increasing the amount of tannin it contains, thereby reducing the impact of both the fruit and the acid. So this particular Barbera, distinguished as it is, remains a gamble with these particular dishes. Much here will turn on the differing sensitivities of individual palates. If you are strongly sensitive to the presence of tannin, this Bricco dell' Uccellone will almost certainly not work for you.

A final reminder: Either of the rosé champagnes, Billecart-Salmon or Taittinger Comtes de Champagne, would serve more than satisfactorily throughout this whole meal. The Comtes de Champagne especially has the big body and acidity and the marked Pinot Noir flavor to interact splendidly with these dishes.

ONE WINE PER COURSE

Choosing a different wine with each course multiplies the variables and introduces the problem of sequence. Our second wine not only has to match well with our food, it also has to follow agreeably in the wake of whatever wine we choose for our first courses. In each course we still confront the problem of picking a wine to go with both a meat dish and a shellfish dish, so we still have a clear option of white or red with either course. Whichever combination of colors we choose, the wines ought to progress from lighter bodied to fuller bodied if we are going to derive maximum pleasure from them. For most people, that will translate into a fairly conventional sequence, light-bodied white leading to fuller-bodied white, or light- to medium-bodied white leading to light- to medium-bodied red. Within this group of wines, the Juliénas offers the single possible exception to that sequence. You could very pleasurably drink it with our first courses and take with our main courses one of those big Chardonnays or white Burgundies, or even the Arneis. But let's examine the more conventional choices.

With the carpaccio and the oysters: For a white wine to precede another white wine, I would look for a bright, high-acid wine with a lot of fresh fruit so that I could follow it with a fuller-bodied, more structured and complex bottle. The Sanford Sauvignon Blanc could fill the order, but either the Gavi dei Gavi from La Scolca or the Montecarlo Bianco would make better choices because of their greater acidity. La Scolca's Gavi is a reliable wine of decent body and cool, flinty feel. Montecarlo Bianco, a wine new to the American market, might offer some pleasant surprises. From near Lucca, in Tuscany, it is vinified from the normally less-than-exciting Trebbiano grape, blended with a diversity of "foreign" varieties—Pinot Bianco, Pinot Grigio, Roussanne, Sauvignon, Sémillon, Vermentino. The results vary widely from producer to producer, but its presence on this list offers the chance to taste a new and potentially very exciting wine.

For a white wine to precede a red wine with the second course, you could use any of the wines named above plus the Arneis, the Chalone Pinot Blanc, or the Pic Chablis. These last three are more full bodied than the wines I suggested above, but not so big or so assertive as to either overpower the dishes we want to drink them with or upset the balance of the progression we're establishing.

With the crabcake and the escalope of veal: For a white wine, you could use any of the whites suggested for accompanying the whole meal—the California Chardonnays and Pinot Blanc, the

Giacosa Arneis, the white Burgundies—plus one other possibility, the white Châteauneuf-du-Pape, Château de Beaucastel. While I think this wine is too assertive to serve for the whole meal, it might work very intriguingly with the sauces of these two dishes, both of which add a lively, warm tang to the rather sweet flesh they accompany. Certainly a less formidable white Châteauneuf than Beaucastel would succeed here. A lighter, new-style wine, such as Domaine de Nalys, for instance, would be fine. It's only Beaucastel's bravura style that raises any questions at all. For all practical purposes, the château makes a white wine to drink with red meat—which is a useful thing to know in circumstances somewhat the reverse of these.

ONE WINE PER DINER

The conditions for choice alter quite seriously if you and I decide to go separate ways, each choosing a wine for his own dinner. The center of each of your courses is a gentle-flavored meat dressed with significantly sharper, more assertive ingredients (Grana, arugula, soy and wasabi sauce). My courses center on sweet-fleshed shellfish (oysters, crab) with rather minimal adornments (mustard sauce). Your meal will tolerate a degree of tannin in a red wine that would kill mine. My meal demands a delicacy of flavor in its wine that in all likelihood would simply evaporate into nothingness with yours. While I could make a light red wine work with my meal, my best bet by far is clearly to choose a white wine. You could pleasurably drink a big white wine with your meal, but why should you when a red would show so much better?

With carpaccio followed by escalope of veal: Three reds practically volunteer themselves: the 1983 Chalone Pinot Noir Reserve, 1984 Bricco dell' Uccellone, and 1983 Faiveley Nuits-St-Georges. The two Pinot Noirs and the Barbera share similar characteristics: relatively restrained tannins that have a rather acidic effect in the mouth; rich, cherrylike fruit with suggestions of pepper and tar; and a mouth-filling flavor that owes more to good structure and balance than to real size. They are elegant and persuasive wines rather than powerhouses. All these qualities complement perfectly these two gently flavored, sharply accented dishes, creating, for my palate, marriages made in heaven.

With oysters followed by crabcakes: Classically simple dishes call for classic wines, and for me this combination of flavors demands Chardonnay, either the '84 Simi Reserve, for the extra touch of wood and age to emphasize the big dimensions of its balance, or the '86 Clos des Mouches, for the freshness of its fruit and the distinctive balance of acidity and extract that the finest white Burgundies display. Other wines from other grapes would underplay and consequently highlight these dishes, which can produce a very pleasing effect, but to achieve a complete synergy of wine and food, the Simi Chardonnay and the Beaune Clos des Mouches are the wines to choose.

IN SUM

Despite the fact that the menu offers many dishes whose wine affinities we haven't explicitly touched on, there is nothing there that you aren't equipped to handle. You've got the basic principles to figure out even the dishes that to the untrained eye—and yours is no longer that—look difficult. The curries will behave with wines just as curries in an Indian restaurant would. With the wine choices available to you here, that points toward the lighter, more acidic whites—Sanford Sauvignon Blanc, La Scolca Gavi, Montecarlo Bianco, perhaps the Berlucchi Bianco Imperiale, the Pic Chablis. The Blackened Shrimp, Salsa Fria, will respond to wines just as any other spicy seafood dish would—just as, for instance, the crabcakes and mustard sauce that we've been discussing did. Breast of pigeon, medallions of lamb, grilled lamb chops, and grilled steaks cry out for the big, forthright red wines with which this wine list abounds, and your choices are limited only by your wallet and your preferences. Believe it or not, you already hold the key to all the mysteries. Certainly it's true that the level of sophistication embodied in the fifty-six choices on this list makes it a more complex proposition than Sofi's shorter, almost foolproof selections, but it is nevertheless a list just as carefully designed to correlate solidly with the kinds of food the house prepares and designed beyond that to give more developed wine palates the thrill of the hunt and the pleasure of discovery. It's a list put together with intelligence and imagination, and it generously repays intelligence and imagination in its use.

Heart of the Country: The Specialized Wine List

Under the late Leslee Reis's direction, Café Provencal offered food prepared with a distinctly southern French accent and a spectacular list of French wines in what was once the teetotal capital of the United States, Evanston, Illinois. I hope the following pages will serve, among their other uses, as a small memorial to her generous spirit and *joie de vivre*.

THE CHARACTER OF THE COOKING

Café Provençal presents a much more specialized cuisine and, appropriately, a much more specialized wine list than either Sofi or The Four Seasons. Its southern French touch shows more strongly in the fish dishes and the vegetables than in the meat selections, but that is as it should be. What distinguishes Provençal cuisine from that of more northern parts of France is precisely its dependence on fresh Mediterranean fish, abundant fresh vegetables from its lowland farms, and the deeply scented herbs of its hills. You'll readily see, smell, and taste those characteristic Provençal accents in dishes like the vegetable torte or lobster ravioli or Marseillaise fish soup, but they're present too in that typically southern French grilled breast of duck and in the herb-infused saddle of lamb. Bright, sprightly flavors, a light treatment of meats, and heady herbal aromas are the hallmarks of the cooking of Provence and Café Provençal.

THE CHARACTER OF THE WINES

The substantial wine list dovetails nicely with the house's emphatically French style of cooking. Indeed, our adage about wines

Hors d'oeuvres et Potages

Torte aux Legumes Provençal   6.95
*Vegetable torte — layers of artichoke mousse and
sautéed Provençal vegetables, served chilled with
a fresh tomato coulis seasoned with garden basil.*

Saumon Fumé aux Blinis   8.95
*Smoked salmon with creme fraiche, American sturgeon
caviar and chives, served with warm corn pancakes.*

Foie Gras Chaud   13.95
*Fresh New York State foie gras sautéed, served with
warm young vegetables and a champagne tarragon sauce.
Accompanied by grilled bread.*

Raviolis de Homard aux Thyme   8.95
*Ravioli of Maine lobster served in a light, full-flavored
sauce of white wine, saffron and fresh thyme.*

Canard Roulé   8.95
*Breast of duck and foie gras roulade, garnish of
sweet and sour wild cherries and a confiture of onion.*

Soupe de Poissons Marseillaise   4.95
*Provence style fish soup, seasoned well with saffron,
tomato, garlic, fennel and garnished with a variety of
fresh seafoods.*

Specialités du Jour   prices vary
Seasonal specialities.

Salades

Salade Maison   ----
*Our house salad of mixed greens with a light vinaigrette
is included with each entree.*

Salade de Saison   prices vary
*California farm-grown greens prepared according to
the tastes of the season.*

Since opening Café Provençal, I have welcomed the adventure of developing each and every new menu.

The changing seasons provide a continuous source of inspiration. Spring, with its fresh asparagus and sprigs of chervil ... summer's bounty of perfectly ripened fresh fruits and vegetables ... fall's cooler weather beckoning long, mellow simmerings of meats and sauces ... winter's rich indulgences of fresh black truffles and wild game.

Transforming these seasonal inspirations into dinner at Café Provençal is a personal passion. It is a pleasure and a privilege to share this with you.

Leslee Reis

Poissons et Crustacés

Fricassée d'Homard et Saint-Jacques   market price
Sautéed Maine lobster and sea scallops with saffron noodles and a lightly buttered lobster jus. Subject to availability.

Poissons et Fruit de Mer   prices vary
Seasonal fish and seafood specialties.

As a courtesy to fellow diners, please do not smoke pipes or cigars in the dining room. We will be happy to accommodate you across the hall in our salon. Thank you.

Rôtis et Grillades

Magret Grillée, Salade Rustique   24.95
*Grilled breast of duck served with a warm salad of
potato, duck sausage and fresh herbs with a sauce of
tomato, honey, vinegar and duck glaze.*

Selle d'Agneau Rôti Cote d' Azur   29.95
*Roast saddle of American lamb infused and garnished
with Mediterranean vegetables, herbs and spices.*

Filet de Boeuf Grillée, Garni Mireille   26.95
*Grilled filet of beef with a light white wine sauce
flavored with mustard, shallot and tarragon.*

Côte de Veau Grillée au Printemps   26.95
*Wisconsin milk-fed veal chop marinated in olive oil
and fresh herbs, grilled and served with lightly creamed
Swiss chard and a Chateauneuf-du-Pape sauce.*

Faisan Roti   27.95
*Young Wisconsin farm-raised pheasant, roasted and
served with wild mushroom ravioli and a natural sauce.*

Plat du Jour   price varies

Desserts Maison

"Shortcake" aux Fraises a' l'Italienne   6.50
*Fresh strawberries marinated in a dash of Grand Marnier
and balsamic vinegar served with lightly peppered Italian
shortcake.*

Tarte au Sabayon Citronée   5.95
Lemon sabayon tarte with a fresh blueberry sauce.

Fruits Frais du Jardin, Sorbet et Crème Anglais   6.95
Seasonal fruits, sorbet and light custard sauce.

Sélection du Chocolat   price varies
One of our pastry chef's chocolate specialties.

Pâtisseries Maison   prices vary

THE WINE SPECTATOR
1985
AWARD OF
EXCELLENCE

GRAND
AWARD

Cafe Provençal

*One of my real pleasures is tasting and selecting wines
that will complement your dinner. I am proud that
these selections have earned The Wine Spectator's
"Award of Excellence."*

*The front section of this list features our most popular
wines. I choose these with both value and taste in mind,
looking for wines from a good vintage that exemplify
a particular region.*

*The second section is our cellar list of rare and
older wines — my personal favorites.*

*The last section lists after-dinner drinks. Travels
in France have sharpened my appreciation for small
producers of Armagnac and Cognac. It is my pleasure to
offer you these special selections as well as ports,
sherries and eaux de vie.*

274

Champagne and Sparkling Wine

# 27	Veuve Clicquot Brut N.V.		38.00
# 1		half bottle	20.00
# 38	Joseph Perrier Brut N.V.		42.00
# 35	Möet & Chandon Brut Imperial N.V.		40.00
# 37	Pol Roger Blanc de Chardonnay 1979/82		55.00
# 190	Cuvée William Deutz 1979		75.00
# 39	Perrier - Jouët Fleur de-Champagne 1982		95.00
# 110	Taittinger Comtes de Champagne Rosé 1981		130.00
# 51	Dom Perignon 1982		110.00
# 189	Cuvée Winston Churchill 1979 (Pol Roger)		85.00
# 34	Domaine Chandon - Napa Valley Brut		26.00
# 82	Schramsberg Blanc de Noir 1983		35.00

White Wine - Alsace

# 24	Riesling - Cuvée Fr. Emile 1983 (Trimbach)	26.00
# 26	Gewürztraminer 1983 (Trimbach)	
	Cuvée des Seigneurs de Ribeaupierre	21.00
# 198	Riesling-Clos St. Hune 1976 (Trimbach)	95.00

White Wine - Germany

# 12	Piesporter Goldtropfchen Riesling Kabinett	
	1985 Moselle (St. Josefskellerei)	16.00
# 63	Schloss Vollrads Kabinett Blau 1985 Rheingau	21.00

White Wine - Loire

# 17	Pouilly Fumé 1986 (Dom. des Chailloux)		22.00
# 25		half bottle	12.00
# 41	Muscadet 1986/87 (Dom. de la Fruitière)		13.00
# 15	Vouvray 1985/86 (Marc Bredif)		15.00
# 76	Sancerre 1986 (J.M. Roger)		18.00

White Wine - Rhone

| # 145 | Condrieu 1985 (Paul Jaboulet Ainé) | 40.00 |
| # 136 | Ch. Grillet 1981 (Condrieu) | 50.00 |

White Wine - Burgundy

# 3	Macon Viré 1987 Les Acacias		16.00
# 21	Saint-Veran 1985 (M. Vincent)		24.00
# 75	Clos du Chateau 1985 (Chateau Meursault)		28.00
# 18	Chablis 1er Cru 1985/86 Vaillon (Droin)		30.00
# 19	Pouilly - Fuissé 1984 Ch. Fuissé		
	Tête du Cru (Vincent)		45.00
# 78	Pouilly-Fuissé 1985 Ch. Fuissé Vielle Vignes		
	(Vincent)		55.00
# 29	Meursault 1986 (Drouhin)		42.00
# 30	Meursault 1985 (Latour)	half bottle	25.00
# 149	Meursault-Clos de la Barre 1984 (Lafon)		60.00
# 158	Meursault-Perrières 1983 (Lafon)		65.00
# 31	Puligny - Montrachet 1er Cru 1985 (M. Boillot)		38.00
# 43	Chassagne - Montrachet 1986 (Thévenin)		38.00
# 44	Chateau de Meursault 1985		
	(Dom. Ch. Meursault)		65.00
# 33	Puligny-Montrachet 1983 (Dom. Leflaive)		55.00
# 94	Puligny-Montrachet Les Pucelles 1983 (Leflaive)		75.00
# 88	Chassagne-Montrachet 1er Cru 1986		
	(J.M. Morey)		65.00

White Wine - California

# 2	Johannisberg Riesling 1986 (Jekel)		15.00
# 16	Sauvignon Blanc 1985/86 (Flora Springs)		15.00
# 32	Fumé Blanc 1986 (Robert Mondavi)		21.00
# 40	Chardonnay 1985 Belle Terre (Ch. St. Jean)		28.00
# 28	Chardonnay 1986 Russian River Ranches		
	(Sonoma-Cutrer)		23.00
# 48		half bottle	13.00
# 14	Chardonnay 1986 (Neyers)		23.00
# 36	Chardonnay 1985 (St. Andrews)		25.00
# 49	Chardonnay 1986 Proprietor's Reserve		
	(Kendall-Jackson)		30.00
# 13	Chardonnay 1986 Alexander Valley		
	(Ch. Montelena)		35.00
# 42	Chardonnay 1983 (Robert Mondavi)		38.00

Red Wine - Bordeaux

# 151	Ch. Langoa - Barton 1970 (St. Julien) Eng. Btl.		75.00
# 154	Ch. Les Forts de Latour 1976 (Pauillac)		49.00
# 157	Ch. Ducru-Beaucaillou 1976 (St. Julien)		60.00
# 53	Ch.Talbot 1979 (St. Julien)		33.00
# 52	Ch. Grand Puy Lacoste 1979 (Pauillac)		40.00
# 73	Ch. Pichon Lalande 1979 (Pauillac)		70.00
# 91	Ch. Haut-Brion 1979 (Graves)		90.00
# 50	Ch. Gruaud-Larose 1980 (St. Julien)		27.00
# 71	Ch. Gruaud - Larose 1981	half bottle	20.00
# 164	Ch. La Mission Haut Brion 1981 (Graves)		78.00
# 67	Ch. Clos l'Église 1982 (Pomerol)		35.00
# 66	Ch. Cote Puyblanquet 1985 (St. Emilion)		20.00

Red Wine - Burgundy

# 74	Gevrey Chambertin 1er Cru 1978 (Faively)	60.00
# 84	Nuits St. George 1er Cru 1980 (Gouges)	32.00
# 85	Vosne-Romanée 1er Cru 1980 (Mongeard)	33.00
# 87	Chapelle-Chambertin 1980 (Trapet)	35.00
# 81	Morey St. Denis 1er Cru 1981 (Faively)	28.00
# 80	Morey St. Denis 1982 (Dom. Dujac)	30.00
# 83	Clos de Vougeot 1982 (Mugneret)	38.00
# 57	Nuits St. Georges 1er Cru 1983 (Faively)	40.00
# 54	Cote de Beaune Village 1983 (Tollot-Beaut)	23.00
# 77	Volnay 1er Cru-Clos de la Bousse d'Or 1983	45.00
# 79	Gevrey-Chambertin 1er Cru 1983 (Faively)	45.00
# 121	Mazis-Chambertin 1983 (Faiveley)	70.00
# 124	Clos de la Roche 1983 (Dujac)	75.00
# 55	Volnay 1er Cru-Santenots 1984 (Lafon)	44.00
# 72	Bourgogne Pinot Noir 1985 (Faiveley)	25.00
# 56	Pomard 1985 (Dom. Andre Mussy)	50.00
# 132	Corton-Grancey 1985 (Latour)	63.00

Red Wine - Rhone and Provence

# 23	Cotes-du-Rhone 1985 Dom. de la Berthete	15.00
# 96	Hermitage la Chapelle 1982 (P. Jaboulet Ainé)	55.00
# 142	Côte-Rôti 1983 (Guigal)	38.00
# 178	Domaine Trévallon 1984	18.00
# 59	Chateauneuf-du-Pape 1984 (Beaucastel)	32.00

Beaujolais

# 60	Beaujolais - Villages 1986/87 (Jean Bedin)		14.00
# 61		half bottle	8.00
# 11	Morgon 1987 Jean Descombes (Geo. DuBoeuf)		19.00

Red Wine - Italy

# 107	Le Pergole Torte 1985 (Monte Vertine)		39.00
# 146	Barolo Riserva 1978 (Pio Cesare)		36.00

Red Wine - America

# 68	Cabernet Sauvignon 1979 (Robert Mondavi)		40.00
# 147	Cabernet Sauvignon 1982 Opus I (Mondavi/Rothschild)		80.00
# 45	Cabernet Sauvignon 1983/84 Alexander Valley (Silver Oak)		33.00
# 47	Cabernet Sauvignon 1983 Napa Valley (Raymond Vineyards)		22.00
# 62	Cabernet Sauvignon 1985 (Caymus)		21.00
# 70	Cabernet Sauvignon 1983 (Rutherford Hill)	half bottle	14.00
# 22	Cabernet Sauvignon 1983 Napa Valley (Spottswoode)		30.00
# 20	Cabernet Sauvignon 1984 (Lyeth)		27.00
# 64	Merlot 1984/85 Napa (Chateau Chevre)		26.00
# 65	Zinfandel 1985 (Chateau Montelena)		20.00
# 159	Pinot Noir 1984 Jensen (Calera)		38.00
# 46	Pinot Noir 1984 (Edna Valley Vineyard)		18.00
# 86	Pinot Noir 1985 (Oak Knoll)		23.00

Rosé

# 69	Anjou Rosé 1986/87 (Gautier Audas)		10.00

Dessert Wine

# 152	Johannisberg Riesling 1982 Late Harvest (Chateau St. Jean)	half bottle	32.00
# 58	Muscat de Beaumes de Venise 1984 (Jaboulet)	half bottle	10.00
# 137	Ch. Rieussec 1970 (Sauternes)		95.00
# 131	Ch. d'Yquem 1975 (Sauternes)		170.00
# 138	Ch. Rieussec 1976 (Sauternes)		60.00
# 194	Ch. d'Yquem 1976 (Sauternes)		150.00
# 175	Ch. d'Yquem 1980 (Sauternes)	half bottle	80.00
# 150	Ch. d'Yquem 1981 (Sauternes)	half bottle	85.00
# 176	Ch. Rieussec 1983 (Sauternes)		65.00
# 177	Ch. Rieussec 1983 (Sauternes)	half bottle	35.00
# 195	Ch. d'Yquem 1983 (Sauternes)	half bottle	125.00

CELLAR LIST

Bourgogne Blanc

1961 Meursault - Charmes (Ponnelle)	78.00
1964 Meursault (Ponnelle)	50.00
1976 Clos Blanc de Vougeot (l'Héritier-Guyot)	110.00
1978 Corton Charlemagne (Latour)	150.00
1978 Puligny-Montrachet-Folatières (Bouchard Père)	85.00
1978 Bâtard-Montrachet (Latour)	150.00
1978 Meursault-Perrières (P. Morey)	90.00
1982 Corton Charlemagne (Latour)	140.00
1982 Meursault Charmes (Cômtes Lafon)	85.00
1982 Bâtard - Montrachet (Dom. Leflaive)	130.00
1982 Meursault-Perrieres (Cômtes Lafon)	90.00
1982/83 Puligny-Montrachet Clavoillon (Dom. Leflaive)	90.00
1984 Le Montrachet (Cômtes Lafon)	300.00

California White Wines

In addition to what is listed below, very small amounts of some older Chardonnays are in our cellar. Please ask the maitre d'.

1979 Chardonnay - Private Reserve (Mondavi)	68.00
1982 Chardonnay - Napa (Chateau Montelena)	
Magnum	130.00
1983 Chardonnay - Napa (Chateau Montelena)	60.00
1985 Chardonnay (Long Vineyard)	55.00

Bordeaux Rouge

1942 Ch. Haut Brion (Graves)		200.00
1945 Ch. Bourgneuf (Pomerol) Eng. Btl.		260.00
1953 Ch. Siran (Margaux)		150.00
1953 Ch. Baret (Graves)		70.00
1953 Ch. Lafite-Rothschild (Pauillac)	half bottle	125.00
1955 Ch. Latour (Pauillac)		270.00
	half bottle	145.00
1959 Ch. Mouton-Rothschild (Pauillac)	half bottle	185.00
1961 Ch. Siran (Margaux)		190.00
1961 Ch. Lynch Bages (Pauillac) Eng. Btl.		160.00
1961 Ch. Lynch Bages (Pauillac)		200.00
1961 Ch. Léoville-Las - Cases (St. Julien)		205.00
1961 Ch. Millery - Papelletrie (St. Emilion)		90.00
1961 Ch. La Rose - Pourret (St. Emilion)	half bottle	45.00
1966 Ch. Gruaud-Larose (St. Julien)		125.00
1966 Ch. Clos l'Église (Pomerol) Eng. Btl.		80.00
1966 Ch. Palmer (Margaux)		210.00
1967 Ch. Latour (Pauillac)		115.00
1970 Ch. Lafon-Rochet (St. Estephe)	half bottle	40.00
1970 Ch. Gazin (Pomerol)		65.00
1970 Ch. Brillette (Moulis)		65.00
1970 Ch. Talbot (St. Julien) Eng. Btl.		90.00
1970 Ch. Talbot (St. Julien)		110.00
1970 Ch. Lynch Bages (Pauillac)		120.00

Bourgogne Rouge

1949 La Tache (D.R.C.)	425.00
1953 Vosne - Romanée - Dr. Barolet	120.00
1964 Échézeaux (D.R.C.)	155.00
1966 Clos de Vougeot (Coron from Coquard)	85.00
1969 Charmes - Chambertin (Ponnelle)	100.00
1969 Ch. Corton - Grancey (Latour)	125.00
1971 Grands - Échézeaux (D.R.C.)	215.00
1971 Chambertin (Tortochot)	115.00
1972 La Tache (D.R.C.)	190.00
1976 Musigny - Vielle Vignes (Comte de Vogüé)	110.00
1976 Nuits St. Georges - Vignes Rondes (Rion)	88.00
1976 Bonnes Mares (Faiveley)	110.00
1978 Mazis - Chambertin (Faiveley)	88.00
1978 Volnay Santenots-du-Milieu (Comtes Lafon)	60.00
1980 Clos de la Roche (Ponsot)	85.00

California Red Wine

1968 Cabernet Sauvignon - Private Reserve Georges de Latour (B.V.)	210.00
1970 Cabernet Sauvignon - Private Reserve Georges de Latour (B.V.)	188.00
1973 Cabernet Sauvignon - Private Reserve Georges de Latour (B.V.)	70.00
1973 Cabernet Sauvignon (Phelps)	60.00
1974 Cabernet Sauvignon - Private Reserve Georges de Latour (B.V.)	150.00
1977 Cabernet Sauvignon - Insignia (Phelps)	70.00
1977 Cabernet Sauvignon - Bella Oaks Vineyard (Heitz)	70.00
1978 Cabernet Sauvignon - Private Reserve Georges de Latour (B.V.)	90.00
1984/85 Merlot-Napa Valley (Duckhorn)	55.00

Other Red Wines

1974 Sablet or Rasteau Côtes du Rhone (Chateau de Trignon)	35.00
1978 Torres Grand Coronas Black Label (Spain)	50.00
1978 Chateauneuf-du-Pape (Beaucastel)	65.00
1978 Chateauneuf-du-Pape (Dom. Font de Michelle)	40.00

An 18% service charge will be added to the check.

As a courtesy to fellow diners, please do not smoke pipes or cigars in the dining room. We will be happy to accommodate you across the hall in our salon. Thank you.

Armagnac

Danflou	5.50
Danflou Extra	6.00
Danflou Exceptionnel	10.00
Baron de Casterac Trés Rare	11.00
Domaine Lafitte Reserve Speciale	6.00
Janneau Reserve	5.00

Bas Armagnacs of Francis Darroze:

Dom. de Hourtica (Labastide)	1942	40.00
	1970	10.00
Dom. de Bonnefin (Escagnan)	1959	18.50
Dom. de St. Aubin (La Houga)	1964	12.50

Calvados

Danflou	6.00
Jules Duret 1964	16.00

Cognac

M. Ragnaud Grande Champagne V.E.	4.00
M. Ragnaud Grande Champagne V.S.E.P.	4.50
M. Ragnaud Grande Champagne Grande Reserve Fontvielle	9.50
Danflou Fine Champagne	6.00
Danflou Grande Champagne Extra	10.00
Leyrat Brut de Futs	11.00
R. Ragnaud Grande Champagne Reserve Extra	5.50
R. Ragnaud Grande Champagne Heritage	32.00
Leopold Gourmel Age d'Épices Extra	10.00
Jules Duret Grande Champagne Bronze	11.00
Jules Duret Grande Champagne Silver	21.00
Jules Duret Grande Champagne Gold	30.00

Eau de Vie

Framboise (Danflou)	6.00
Poire William (Danflou)	6.00
Kirsch (Trimbach)	5.00
Marc de Bourgogne Grande Reserve (Danflou)	6.50

Port

Croft's Tawny Distinction (10 yrs.)	4.00
Late Bottled Vintage Port: Graham 1981	4.00
Dow's Rare Tawny (30 yrs.)	8.50
Vintage Port: Warre 1970	11.00
Dow 1963	25.00

Sherry

Harvey's Bristol Cream	3.75
La Riva Oloroso Extra (21 yrs.)	6.50
Emilio Lustau - Old East India (Oloroso)	5.50

Café Provençal also offers a selection of premium liqueurs.

showing best with the foods they grew up with is obviously held in honor here. Aside from a healthy clustering of California wines (36 items, mostly Chardonnays and Cabernets), the list contains two German whites, two Italian reds, and one Spanish red. All the rest of the bottles—134 of them—are French, and a good many of those—what Café Provençal calls its cellar list—are older bottles. Indeed, even the house's regular list is notable for its paucity of too-young wines. Half its red Bordeaux, for instance, come from the 1976 and 1979 vintages, which are quite ready to drink right now. The white Burgundies on the same section of the list predominantly come from the vintages of 1985 and earlier, while the cellar list has two Meursaults from the sixties and several other white wines from the seventies. If there is any criticism to be made of the list's overall design, it is only that the wines of Provence itself and of the Rhône are not more strongly represented, though that is a small cavil in the face of the quality of the Bordeaux and Burgundy selections the list provides.

No less noteworthy are Café Provençal's very fair wine prices. Five sparkling wines are offered for under $50, plus a thoughtfully added half-bottle of Veuve Clicquot at $20. Thirteen white wines appear at $25 or less, and an even larger number of reds at $30 or less. The primary list offers a string of red Burgundies—including a batch of *premiers crus* from some very fine shippers like Dujac, Faiveley, and Latour—with a ceiling price of $75 and all but four available at under $60: these would qualify as bargains in 90 percent of the restaurants in this country. And on top of that, the cellar list adds a whole other dimension to Café Provençal's wine selections. Consider its major groupings: white Burgundies dating back to 1961 and red Burgundies to 1949 (including a couple from the fabulous 1969 vintage); red Bordeaux from the vintages of 1953, '55, '59, '61, '66, and '70; and twenty-year-old California Cabernets—and all these at prices that in many cases fall below current retail prices of these wines in the few shops where they are available. Café Provençal is a treasure-house of fine French wines. This cellar may be limited in its scope, but it is finely concentrated in its quality and value. Indeed, in these terms, this too is a wine list from which you can't make a wrong selection.

GUESS WHO'S COMING TO DINNER

I think you and I have had enough tête-à-tête dinners by now. It's time to complicate the wine selection process to more common and more realistic dimensions. This means we will now be four at dinner and have four different dinners to choose wines for. *Moi,* I will start with Raviolis de Homard aux Thyme and go on to Magret Grillée, Salade Rustique. You, self-indulgent devil that you are, have decided to pamper yourself with Foie Gras Chaud and Faisan Rôti. Our two guests, a little less venturesome, have opted for the Provençale vegetable torte and the smoked salmon as starters and, for their main courses, the Fricassee d'Homard et Saint-Jacques and Grilled Sea Bass with Provençale Spinach and Tomato Coulis, a special this evening.

How Many Wines?

Four diners and four different dinners complicate dramatically the problems of choosing wines. This meal generates questions not only about what wines to order but also how many wines to order and whether the number of bottles needed and the number of kinds needed coincide.

For example, we clearly need at least two wines to accompany that selection of dishes for four people, but it's not certain that only two wines will be able to deal with all the issues. One easy if inequitable solution to the problem would be for us all to drink a white wine with our first courses—if it were full-bodied enough it wouldn't mishandle your foie gras—and for our guests to continue with that or another white wine with their seafood main courses while you and I go on to a red wine with our birds (thereby giving us the lion's share of the wines, which we no doubt deserve). Alternatively, we could order two wines from the start. A red would do quite nicely with both your foie gras and the vegetable torte, and a white would accompany the smoked salmon and my lobster ravioli quite happily. The two diners who have chosen fish could then continue with the white while we, with our duck and pheasant, went on with the red. Neither of these solutions gives us what I would call an abundance of wine, but it is a sufficient if lean ration, and appropriate to the dishes we've chosen.

The real difficulty generated by these dishes is that they include only one emphatically red wine starter, the foie gras, and one emphatically red wine entrée, the *magret de canard*. The sautéed foie gras ideally wants a medium-bodied, soft, fruity, lightly tannic red wine to complement its own lushness. (If more than one of us were eating foie gras, we could of course allow ourselves the sybaritic pleasure of some fine Sauternes with it. The wine list offers some very lovely bottles of Château d'Yquem and Château Rieussec.) The roast pheasant does not absolutely demand a red wine—it is, remember, a farm-bred bird, not a game bird—though it could tolerate the same red wine as the foie gras. And the Provençale torte could work with that same wine, even though—because of its artichoke mousse and tomato coulis—it would really prefer a flavorful and acidic white wine. The duck breast and its robust accompaniments unequivocally need a strong red wine, full bodied and assertive, to deal with their own pronounced flavors. That is clearly not the same red wine that the other dishes will work best with. So in this particular selection of dishes, the duck diner is distinctly the odd man out. What this usually means in real restaurant situations—especially as I am a charming chap and not one to stand on protocol—is that the duck diner either changes his order or agrees to drink white wine with everybody else.

Indeed, one more satisfactory solution to this particular menu puzzle would be to drink white wine throughout, moving from a lighter, more acidic white with the first courses to a full-bodied white with high extract to accompany the entrées. The 1986 Pouilly-Fumé from Domaine des Chailloux would serve adequately with all the first courses—its acidity would do some of the work of a red wine's tannin with the foie gras—but better all around would be either of those 1983 Trimbach wines, the Cuvée Frédéric Emile Riesling or Cuvée des Seigneurs de Ribeaupierre Gewürztraminer. Both would bring to the match good body and acid and, even more important, exciting spicy or herbal flavors to interact with each of the appetizers. The other significant shove in their direction is their vintage: 1983 produced great white wines in

Alsace, and all of them have grown wonderfully in depth and character with a few years of bottle age. To follow any of these wines and complement the main courses, I would choose either the 1985 Condrieu or—and given my fondness for older wines, this would probably be my preference—the 1981 Château-Grillet. Both are white wines vinified from the Viognier grape at sites a few kilometers apart along the northern Rhône. Both are full bodied and distinctively flavored, often of high alcohol—big wines, with layers of flavor. Condrieu is more forward, more accessibly fruity in its youth than Château-Grillet, though the latter ages better, maturing into a wine of subtle power. The fact that 1985 produced magnificent wines all through the Rhône just makes the final choice here that much harder, though Château-Grillet's rarity—it's France's smallest appellation—and its very fair price here would probably tilt me toward it. Certainly both these wines will do as much justice to the duck breast as any white wines can, and they will have no problem whatever with the pheasant or the shellfish fricassee. They are also of a level of quality and an intensity of character to remove my usual reservations about all-white-wine dinners.

PRIORITY TO THE WINE

None of these wines, however, really draws upon the greatest strengths of Café Provençal's wine list, which are its red Bordeaux and red and white Burgundies. Selecting from among these wines and then picking foods to match, we could put together quite a memorable feast for four kindred spirits. This seems to me to be always the best possible strategy when you encounter a wine list that has, as this one does, conspicuous strengths in well-defined areas. That way, whether your meal is only the first of many you will have at that particular restaurant or the only one you will ever have there, you will sample the best of what the kitchen and cellar can do.

Here, for instance, we could start with a 1985 Château de Meursault, which would taste marvelous with the smoked salmon or lobster ravioli, smoked tuna or soft-shell crab—just the right combination of acidity and body and extract in the wine to match beautifully with the sweet-fleshed delicacy of these appetizers.

Alternatively and more expensively (though by Burgundy standards far from outrageously, alas), we could begin with a 1978 Corton-Charlemagne, one of the world's most distinctive white wines. Current fashion would prefer the 1982 bottle (at only $10 less!) for its fresher fruit, but if fresh fruit is all you turn to white wine for, you might as well drink Soave all the time and save yourself a bundle of money. Older Corton, especially from an initially hard vintage like '78, develops an intense aroma and a vivid, muscular flavor undergirded by a spine of steel. No other white wine resembles it. In my experience, it loves rich shellfish preparations, especially lobster. (If there is one right wine in the universe to serve with lobster thermidor—another classic dish too long missing from restaurant menus—it is Corton-Charlemagne.) The ideal dish to have with it from this menu would be the Fricassee d'Homard et Saint-Jacques, which would make a splendid choice if we were to drink this wine with our main courses—that is, after the Château de Meursault rather than instead of it. As a wine to drink with our appetizers, however, the Corton has one glorious complement here: the Canard Roulé, with its combination of lean breast meat and lush foie gras and its garnishes of sweet and sour cherries and sweet onion. That battery of flavors and textures would call out everything a Corton-Charlemagne has to offer. It's hard to tell which would feel more substantial on the palate, the solid or the liquid.

Selecting another wine to follow either the Corton-Charlemagne or the Château de Meursault amounts to a substantial challenge. Certainly, after the Corton-Charlemagne there is no real alternative to switching to a red wine. Besides, there are simply too many attractively priced and attractively aged red wines on this list for us to ignore them any longer. Take for instance the very first red wine listed: a 1970 Château Langoa-Barton at $75. You would be very hard put to find this wine at retail at this price, even if there were any of it left in the market, which there isn't. Granted it's an English bottling rather than an estate bottling, but the practice of shipping wines from Bordeaux in barrels to be bottled in England used to be perfectly commonplace for all the Bordeaux châteaux, including the *premiers crus*. As late as the early seventies it was still quite normal for many of the lesser growths, especially for those, like the two Barton châteaux (Langoa and Léoville), with strong English ties. So unless you are a relentlessly suspicious type who believes the whole world is out to swindle you, all "English bottling" implies is that you've lost the cachet of estate bottling. *Tant pis.* The wine remains an excellent choice at an excellent price: a very well-regarded third growth, known to be slow maturing, and a vintage as good as any Bordeaux has seen since World War II. This wine could complement the *magret*, the saddle of lamb (I've said enough already about the magic of combining lamb and the red wines of the Médoc), and the *filet de boeuf*. This last dish and its wine reduction sauce, flavored with mustard and shallot and tarragon, would work particularly well with the Langoa-Barton, which itself combines qualities of gentleness and suppleness with strength and intensity. The component-to-component complementarity should be very exact and very pleasing.

Café Provençal offers many attractive buys among the Bordeaux wines, both on its primary list and its cellar list. If not all bargains, the 1979 Château Talbot at $33, '79 Grand-Puy-Lacoste at $40, Haut-Brion of the same year at $90, even the '82 Clos l'Eglise (an unclassified small Pomerol estate) at $35 are all very fairly priced and all thoroughly enjoyable wines. Among the older Bordeaux, 1955 Latour, 1961 Lynch-Bages, and 1966 Gruaud-Larose—a favorite of mine—all stand out. At $115, the 1967 Latour is an exceptional value for an exceptional wine, now at its peak. The prices asked for the 1970 Talbot and Lynch-Bages are also very favorable. Any or all of these wines will happily match with the characteristic way the house handles duck, lamb, and beef (which is, for the most part, dry cooked—grilled or roasted—but moistened with a sauce composed of both sweet and herbal or spicy elements).

The generous selection of red Burgundies will complement better the gentler-flavored meats: the grilled veal chop, the roast pheasant, the grilled poussin. With these dishes, several of the younger Burgundies will shine, because of their typically lighter, less tannic, and more velvety style than that of red Bordeaux. The Domaine Dujac 1982 Morey St-Denis, the Mugneret Clos de Vougeot of the same year, and Faiveley's 1983 *premier cru* Nuits-St-Georges offer the kind of rich Pinot Noir flavors and balance to complement delicately flavored meats, richly prepared. One or two bottles among these younger wines—notably the Domaine Dujac 1983 Clos de la Roche and the Latour 1985 Corton-Grancey— have the size and the depth of flavor to match really well with dishes like the grilled filet of beef and perhaps even the grilled breast of duck, given its sauce's combination of acid and sweet elements.

Among the older Burgundies, the 1969 Corton-Grancey offers both an outstanding value and a top-quality Burgundy evolved enough to be able to handle very happily strong flavors such as those of the duck and the beef. The same would be true of the 1953 Vosne-Romanée from Dr. Barolet's estate: Almost every wine I have drunk from that great connoisseur's collection has been out-standing of its kind. The '76 Vieilles Vignes Musigny from the Comte de Vogüé, a superb wine from an ancient house, and the '76 Bonnes Mares from Faiveley both offer fine value for wines that can only be described as suave. To my palate, they make perfect accompaniments to the roast pheasant, accentuating its suggestion of gaminess while not overpowering its delicacy. All these wines are examples of classic Burgundy, Burgundy as it is supposed to be rather than the thin, acidic grape broth it all too often is.

IN SUM

Café Provençal provides us an example of a restaurant whose cooking bears an unequivocal regional and stylistic stamp, with a strong cellar (the largest wine list we have chosen to deal with so far) selected to match the foods; the cellar is not broadly diver-sified but fine and deep in its chosen range. Such restaurants typ-ically offer you the chance to taste dishes and wines you simply won't find elsewhere, and the wisest course of action and the surest source of real dining pleasure is to let your choices be guided by the house's strengths rather than to order your food and wine according to any predetermined program. Gifted with a menu like this one, you'd be crazy to ask the kitchen for moo shoo pork. By the very same token, it's foolish to repine over the absence of Zinfandels or Riojas from the wine list. Enjoy what is there instead, and don't fail to finish up with one of those exquisite Armagnacs.

Westward Ho! The Overwhelming Wine List

Los Angeles's glamorous restaurant Valentino offers us another kitchen producing a specialized Old World cuisine—marvelous Italian food this time—matched with a cellar epitomizing New World abundance. Valentino confronts the happy winebibber with the kind of wine list that is, in theory, every insecure diner's or slow reader's nightmare: the dreaded telephone-book-thick tome. More than one thousand different wines are available from a cellar stock of more than 100,000 bottles. While that prospect may daunt non–wine drinkers, real enophiles will revel in it: all those possibilities, and all yours for the asking, and often enough at very reasonable prices. Italian wines are present in squadrons, as you would hope to find them in such a restaurant. Valentino offers almost five full pages of Barbaresco and Barolo listings alone, for instance. Not surprisingly, this being Los Angeles, California wines are at least as strongly represented, especially in the red wine division. There are ten pages of standard-size bottles of Cabernet Sauvignons alone, plus another page for Cabernets in magnum.

Beyond that, in a casual display of just what the phrase *international restaurant* really means, Valentino also provides a battery of French wines that could easily be the envy of several serious restaurants in Bordeaux and in Beaune. Picture a whole page of Meursaults, in vintages from '77 forward and from a dozen different producers; or four solidly typed pages of red Bordeaux, including all the *premiers crus,* all the great postwar vintages, and even some nineteenth-century vintages; and eight or so pages of red Burgundies—including all the Domaine de la Romanée-Conti wines—at prices that run from $32 (for a Gevrey-Chambertin and a Nuits-St-Georges) to $1,500 (for 1961 Romanée-Conti).

If we had world enough and time, and space to reproduce it here, such reading would be our delight. Alas, we don't, neither here nor in our imagined visit to Valentino, where our two companions— we are four for dinner again—are hungry and want to look at the menu.

THE CHARACTER OF THE COOKING

The cooking at Valentino is self-evidently and classically Italian, not confined to the traditions of any single region, but pan-Italian, with dishes exemplifying the differing culinary styles of the Italian north (for example, Carpaccio di Manzo e Parmigiano, Risotto di frutta di mare), center (for example, Zuppa di Orzo, Fagioli, e Pancetta or Tortellini ai Quattro Formaggi), and south (Rotelle con Pomodoro, Melanzane, e Mozzarella or Pesce Spada cipollato). And the sequence of courses is archetypally Italian: antipasto, *primo, secondo,* and maybe we'll get to dessert, but don't think about that until later.

Now is the time to remind yourself of all the things we said about Italian cooking and its preferences in wines, because, confronted with a wine list of the size we're dealing with here, if you actually want to choose a wine for your dinner rather than undertake an evening's casual reading, you've quickly got to map out whole classes of wines and their characteristics in your head. Before anyone in your group even chooses a single dish, you should be thinking in terms of broad categories of wines that will or won't work with this kind—or these kinds—of cooking. Remember what we said about the overall traits of Italian cooking: that much of it is lightly to markedly acidic. Look for the telltale common factors in the dishes offered here that will point to wine affinities. For instance, in the first two courses at least, meats are not at all prominent. Seafood yes, vegetables even more so, and cheese is very important, particularly in the pastas. Cheese remains important too in the *secondi,* and spicy elements come to the fore there along with a barrage of acidic ingredients or condiments: aspara-

Let's Start with...

Orzo, Fagioli e Pancetta	8	Calamaretti e Frittelle	10
Barley, Tuscan beans, Bacon Soup		Fried Squids and Ricotta fritters	
Zuppa di Verdure e Cubetti di Vitello	9	Scampi e Fagiolini al Pomodoro	12
Minestrone with Julienne of Veal		Shrimps and Stringbeans in Tomato Garlic	
Piatto di cose rustiche	10	Brodetto di Frutti di Mare	11
Egg plant, olives, peppers, cold cuts		Variety of Seafood in broth	
Caesar Salad	8.50		
Insalata calda d'Aragosta	12	Tonno, Zucchine, Capperi al Crudo	10
Warm Lobster Salad		Slices of fresh Tuna marinated with vegetables	
Carpaccio di Manzo e Parmigiano	10	Insalata Valentino	9
Beef carpaccio, cheese and aromatic oil		Our mixed Vegetable Salad	

Primi Piatti

Canelloni d'Aragosta	12	Lasagna d'Anatra e Porcini	13
Lobster canelloni		Duckling and Mushrooms	
Fettuccine al Mascarpone	11	Pennette all'Arrabiata	10.50
Linguine alle Vongole	12	Chili pepper, mushrooms, tomato	
Clams Sauce		Agnolotti di Fonduta, burro e salvia	11
Tortellini ai 4 Formaggi	11	Ravioli with cheese, butter and sage	
Rotelle Pomodoro, Melanzane		Risotto di frutti di mare	15
e Mozzarella	11	Risotto, sweet corn and peppers	13
with tomato, eggplant e mozzarella cheese			

Secondi Piatti

Scaloppine di Vitello	20	Costoletta di Porcello ai	
Veal of your choices		Peperoni dolci	19
Costoletta alla Valdostana	24		
Veal Chop, Asparagus, Fontina		Tagliata d'Agnello alle erbe	23
Pollo con Salsiccie e Peperoni	19	Slices of Lamb loin, lemon, herbs aromatiche	
Chicken, Sausages, peppers		Animelle con capperi e olive	19
Galletto alla Griglia, piccante	18.50	Veal sweetbreads, capers and olives	
Grilled baby chicken, spicy		Casseruola di Melanzane	
Osso Buco e Gnocchi	21	e Formaggio	12.50
Veal Shanks		Eggplant parmigiana	
Medaglione di Manzo all aceto			
balsamico	21	Pesce Spada cipollato	20
Loin of Beef in balsamic vinegar		Grilled Swordfish, lemon and onions	

gus, peppers, vinegar, lemon, capers, olives. This adds up to a cuisine of bright, vivid flavors and forceful accents, and this means you'll want wines that can match these flavors and tolerate their acidic vehicles. This in turn means that your first choice for wines is, *senz'altro*, Italian. Don't say you're surprised. Remember, wines show best with the foods they grew up with, and vice versa.

PRIORITY TO THE WINE: BURGUNDY

Before we order our dinner, however—we have time; the others are still studying the menu—let us consider the hypothetical question of what we would do had we come to Valentino with our hearts and palates set on tasting some of its best French or California wines. Giving priority to the wine in this way always simplifies the process of putting together a meal, even when you are opting for wines that have not been custom-made for the particular style of cooking you're dealing with. Let us assume two different scenarios: In the first we've decided we want some French wines, especially those of an elegant and somewhat delicate character rather than powerhouses. In the second we've set our appetites for California wines with the opposite characteristics, big, forceful wines that overwhelm rather than seduce. Given the strengths of this wine list, our first scenario points us directly toward the Burgundies, both white and red. Our second scenario has an equally clear thrust: We'll go with two of California's—and Valentino's—strong suits, Chardonnay and Cabernet.

· The general intention of our first scenario—to choose grace rather than power—suggests a further narrowing of our search before we even get to specific wines. Folk wisdom about Burgundies has it that if we're seeking delicacy in a red wine, we should be looking in the Côte de Beaune rather than the Côte de Nuits, and of course for a white Burgundy, there is no other place to look. While it is not always true that all the red wines of the area are always more delicate than their northern cousins, it tends to be true of Volnay most of the time. So I suggest we examine what Valentino offers us in the way of white and red wines from the neighboring towns of Meursault and Volnay and see which of the restaurant's dishes will match best with those wines.

White Burgundy
Meursault

	Vintage	Bottle
Poruzots	1979	42.00
Leroy	1980	56.00
Louis Jadot	1981	45.00
Louis Latour	1982	50.00
Louis Jadot	1982	42.00
Ballot-Millot	1984	47.00
Bouzereau-Emonin	1984	48.00
J. Monnier, *Charmes*	1979	45.00
P. Morey, *Charmes*	1981	45.00
R. Monnier, *Charmes*	1982	47.00
Comte de Moucheron,		
Château de Meursault	1984	65.00
Moillard, *Clos de la Barre*	1979	43.00
Lafon, *Clos de la Barre*	1980	45.00
R. Manuel, *Clos des Bouches Chères*	1982	50.00
Labouré-Roi, *Clos du Cromin*	1984	50.00
Lafon, *Désirée*	1977	46.00
Lafon, *Genevrières*	1979	50.00
J. Boillot, *Genevrières*	1981	44.00
Louis Jadot, *Genevrières*	1981	50.00
Jaffelin, *Genevrières*	1982	50.00
R. Monnier, *Les Chevalières*	1979	42.00
P. Bouzereau, *Les Narvaux*	1984	47.00
P. Bouzereau, *Les Narvaux*	1985	58.00
Morey, *Perrières*	1985	49.00
F. Jobard, *Poruzot*	1980	40.00

Red Burgundy
Volnay

Bouchard Père et Fils	1978	40.00
J. Drouhin, *Clos des Chênes*	1978	48.00
Hospices de Beaune, *Blondeau*	1978	58.00
Ballot-Millot, *Santenots*	1983	46.00

In the Meursaults, Valentino's holdings are particularly rich. Volnays are less amply represented, but the quality of the choices is just as high, and the range of prices just as attractive. Neither of these wines, in the examples listed here, has rocketed into the economic stratosphere, so we can promise ourselves some very nice drinking at expensive but not bankrupting price levels. This leaves us free to choose our wine entirely by vintage and maker rather than price differential—a luxury we're rarely given with Burgundy, so let's enjoy it.

The Meursaults offer us wide scope for indulgence: 1980, '81, and '82 wines from fine *négociants* like Jadot and Leroy, single-vineyard wines from the *domaine* Lafon and the *négociant* Labouré-Roi, and several different first growths in several different vintages—Charmes, Genevrières, Perrières. In choosing Burgundies, you've always got to consider a combination of factors: the intrinsic quality of the vineyard or commune (vineyard in this case, since we've already opted for our communes); the reliability of the grower, shipper, or *négociant*, plus whatever you know about the vintage in terms of its intrinsic quality, rate of maturation, and longevity. Taking these elements into account, we should find ourselves settling on something like the 1981 Genevrières from Jadot, which has everything we're looking for, including maturity—and, on a restaurant scale, the price is quite right.

Our choice among the Volnays, though smaller, will be no easier. Three of the wines come from the classic vintage of 1978; the other is a 1983—an iffy year to be sure, but in individual wines sometimes quite magnificent. Two of our choices come from ancient and prestigious Burgundian *négociants,* Bouchard Père et Fils and the Hospices de Beaune, and two are from *premiers crus* vineyards, Clos des Chênes and Santenots. All are tempting, but my advice is to choose mature Burgundy every time you can get it at a price you can afford, so that eliminates the '83 Santenots, and always to choose a *premier cru* from a reliable *négociant* in preference to a simple village wine. These considerations point us unarguably right at the '78 Clos des Chênes from Drouhin.

Now that we've chosen some lovely and elegant French wines for our first scenario, what foods will we match with them? That's easy enough: Look to the least aggressively flavored, least acidic items you can find within this broad style of cooking, not, for instance, the Piatto di cose rustiche. The marinated eggplants, peppers, and olives would all be too acidic for the Meursault. Consider rather the warm lobster salad, which is likely to be seasoned with a light sprinkling of lemon juice rather than vinegar, and in which, in any event, the sweetness of the lobster will predominate. Consider the carpaccio, which admittedly offers some marked flavors, but they are all flavors highly compatible with any kind of wine. Consider above all the Calamaretti e Frittelle, in which the lightness and delicacy of the seafood and the freshness and sweetness of the cheese would call out all the best in a fine white wine. If you're going to continue drinking the Meursault with your *primo,* there is even less problem. The Risotto di frutti di mare stands out as the perfect companion for all white wines, with the Agnolotti di Fonduta, burro e salvia not far behind. The Fettuccine al Mascarpone would also work well, as would the Canelloni d'Aragosta if the lobster was bound and sauced with a *balsamella* (béchamel) rather than tomato (tomato would be too acidic for the Meursault).

The same considerations hold for the Volnay: Avoid the markedly vivid and aggressively flavored dishes. Almost any of the veal dishes will work, for instance. Scaloppine can be prepared any number of simple ways that will enhance a red wine, and the classic Marsala style would be perfect. Osso buco, though sometimes prepared with tomato, is never dominated by it, and the succulence of the veal shank meat and its ambrosial marrow make ideal foils for the kind of velvety softness and roundness a Volnay can give. The Costoletta alla Valdostana might look like trouble because it includes asparagus, but the quantity is small and the antiwine tendencies of asparagus are amply balanced by the wine receptivity of Fontina. The Medaglione di Manzo all aceto balsamico would also work nicely with our Volnay, since the *aceto* in question is balsamic vinegar, which lacks the high acidity of the conventional item, and in fact tends to be rather winelike and nearly sweet. What wouldn't work with this wine are all the dishes with peppers and lemons and capers and olives. The acid attacks of those ingredients would cause any Burgundy to fall apart on your palate.

PRIORITY TO THE WINE: CALIFORNIA

So much for scenario one. Now for our second round of wine choices, full-bodied California Chardonnays and Cabernets. These two categories make up the bulk of Valentino's American wine list, so unless we're going to sit all night reading and dithering, we'd better institute some principles for narrowing our range of choices. Obviously, when you're actually confronted with a situation like this, you're going to be guided largely by your own tastes and preferences and those of the people you're with. But to prevent yourself from always drinking the same old thing (no matter how good it may be) and to taste some wines that you might not otherwise get to, try every now and again to be as arbitrary as I'm going to be now. We'll choose our Chardonnay from Sonoma rather than from Napa, and we'll take our Cabernet from Napa, but only from either the now-fabled 1974 vintage—since Valentino offers us a rare chance to sample it—or the very slowly developing 1980. This cuts the choices down dramatically and saves us a good hour of indecision.

Here is Valentino's list of Sonoma Chardonnays:

Chardonnay
Sonoma and Alexander Valley

	Vintage	Bottle	Tenths
Ferrari-Carano	1985	28.00	
Sonoma-Cutrer	1985	32.00	
Dolan	1984	24.00	
Iron Horse	1985	24.00	
Kistler, *Dutton Ranch*	1985	25.00	
Meeker	1983	25.00	
Simi	1984	22.00	
Jordon	1984	27.00	
Chateau St. Jean	1984	24.00	13.00
Chateau St. Jean, *R. Young*	1984	31.00	
Kalin Cellars	1985	26.00	
Matanzas Creek	1984	24.00	
Joseph Swan	1979	36.00	
Lambert Bridge	1985	23.00	
Sam J. Sebastiani	1985	24.00	

As much as I generally love older wines, I find my taste in Chardonnay runs to much younger wines than I would choose in white Burgundies. Perhaps this is because the huge, fresh fruit of California Chardonnays forms so major a component of their appeal, or perhaps it is because they just don't evolve in the bottle as well, or in the same way, as Burgundies. Whatever the reason may be, California Chardonnay at three, four, and five years of age generally provides me the greatest pleasure, so on this list I would be looking primarily at the youngest wines, the 1985s. That cuts us down to seven wines: Ferrari-Carano, Sonoma-Cutrer, Iron Horse, Kistler's Dutton Ranch, Kalin Cellars, Lambert Bridge, and Sam J. Sebastiani. These are all fine wines, but the ones that immediately catch my interest are the two from makers that could almost be described as Chardonnay specialists, Iron Horse and Sonoma-Cutrer, both of which turn out very big, lush wines. It's really a coin toss to choose between them, but I'll go this time with the Iron Horse, which is, for those of us who live on the East Coast, a wine less frequently encountered than Sonoma-Cutrer.

Valentino's Cabernet listings are even longer than its Chardonnays, and they include many vintages of the sixties and seventies. Here are the choices of 1974 and 1980 bottles culled from the house's offerings of Napa Cabernets.

Cabernet Sauvignon
Napa

	Vintage	Bottle	1/2 Bottle
Beringer	1980	23.00	
Louis Martini, *Private Reserve*	1974	30.00	
Rubicon, *Niebaum-Coppola*	1980	37.00	
Beaulieu Vineyards	1974	27.00	
Beaulieu Vineyards	1980	17.00	
Beaulieu Vineyards, *Private Reserve*	1974	120.00	66.00
Beaulieu Vineyards, *Private Reserve*	1980	42.00	20.00
Chateau Montelena	1974	95.00	
Chateau Montelena	1980	31.00	
Cakebread	1980	26.00	

	Vintage	Bottle	¹/₂ Bottle
Raymond	1980	24.00	
Joseph Phelps (*Tenths*)	1980	14.00	
Joseph Phelps, *Insignia*	1980	42.00	
Inglenook, *"Cask"*	1974	25.00	
Robert Mondavi	1974	46.00	
Robert Mondavi, *Reserve*	1980	46.00	
Trefethen	1980	26.00	
Stag's Leap Cellars	1980	24.00	
Mayacamas Vineyards	1980	30.00	
Mayacamas Vineyards	1974	85.00	
Newton	1980	24.00	
Diamond Creek, *"Red Rock"*	1980	34.00	
Diamond Creek, *"Volcanic Hill"*	1974	100.00	
Diamond Creek, *"Volcanic Hill"*	1980	34.00	
Diamond Creek, *"Gravelly Meadow"*	1980	34.00	
Opus One, *Mondavi-Rothschild*	1980	120.00	
Johnson Turnbull	1980	23.00	
Flora Spring	1980	23.00	
Vichon, *Fay Vineyard*	1980	27.00	
Neyers	1980	27.00	

This still leaves us thirty wines to choose from—twenty-two 1980s and eight different '74s, every single one of the latter a California classic. So the idea of narrowing the choices by looking at only two vintages doesn't, in fact, get us very far in a restaurant with these rich resources. So let's now be logical rather than arbitrary. We're here to enjoy a great dinner, right? Okay then, we'll take one of the '74s. Why? Because the 1980 vintage, which *may* turn out to be monumental, is still developing—rather slowly in fact—while the 1974, which *is* monumental, has arrived. It is not merely ready to drink; it is in most cases at its very best. Not only that; there are bargains on this list. Louis Martini Private Reserve 1974 at $30? Inglenook Cask 1974 at $25? Excuse me please, but I'll have one of each, every day until the cellar runs dry.

So, these will be our wines. Now for the food. Given the nature of these wines and the nature of Italian cooking, we don't have to worry about any of the food flavors being too aggressive or too powerful for the wines to handle, but we do still have to watch out for some of the dishes being too acidic to achieve a really happy complementarity with these bottles. Specifically, that Iron Horse Chardonnay would probably match none too well with any of the salad-style antipasti, except perhaps the rustic platter, in which the meats might sustain it, or the lobster salad, in which the sweet lobster meat could do likewise. It would taste just fine with that hearty Tuscan bean soup and with the fried squid and ricotta fritters. Dishes like these would emphasize its roundness and fruit. The fresh tuna might do the same, but a lot would depend on the kind of marinating it received: Too vinegary, and the wine will lose its integrity; lightly lemony, or with balsamic vinegar or wine, and the wine will lose a bit of its freshness but show all its power and elegance. Perhaps the ideal antipasto for this kind of Chardonnay, however, is the carpaccio, in which the sweetness of raw beef, the richness of top-quality Parmigiano and olive oil will elicit everything the wine has to offer.

Similarly, if you continue drinking Chardonnay with your *primi,* choose simple, forceful dishes without much acidity, so that their strength can complement its strength: the fettuccine with mascarpone without question, the tortellini with four cheeses, the agnolotti with fonduta, the lobster cannelloni (if not made with tomatoes), or even, with this wine, the lasagna with duck and porcini.

To match with the Cabernet, choose dishes with pronounced flavors: Spices, herbs, strong meat, and marked vegetable flavors will make great foils for the intensity of the Cabernet. Even peppers, which can create problems because they are often as acidic as they are sweet, will work well here because the Cabernet's tannins are sufficient match for them. So choose from dishes like the chicken with sausage and peppers, the spicy grilled chicken, the pork chop with peppers, or (best of all, and you knew it all along, didn't you?) the herbed lamb. And if you have any wine left at the end of your *secondo,* ask the house to bring you a little piece of Parmigiano to finish the Cabernet with: They will sing to each other.

PRIORITY TO THE FOOD

So much for assigning priority to the wine. Let us now consider the even more likely possibility that we have come to Valentino with our palates set for a fine Italian dinner and our minds prepared to choose appropriate Italian wines to match whatever appeals to us most on the menu. So, first we order our food. I will start with Valentino's Calamaretti e Frittelle, go on to Pennette all'Arrabiata, a wonderfully spicy Roman pasta, and conclude—in all proba- bility—with the pork chop and peppers. You, in an orgy of cheeses, have chosen the carpaccio, the tortellini with four cheeses, and the Valdostana veal chop. One of our guests has opted for Valentino's rustic plate—what most of America thinks antipasto must be—Linguine alle Vongole, and eggplant Parmigiana, and the other has chosen the lobster salad, seafood risotto, and grilled baby chicken. This is an eclectic group of choices to say the least, but a set that, because of its conjunctions of acids and spices and cheeses and sweet vegetables, points unequivocally to Italian wines as the only wines able to deal happily with all these varied and pronounced palatal demands.

This of course may be very comforting to know, but it doesn't advance our wine choices very far, given the depth of the restau- rant's Italian wine list. How do we narrow our choices down to a manageable range? We know that, as a dining strategy, we ordi- narily want to proceed from lighter wine to heavier, from younger to older, and there is nothing in our dinner choices here to counter- indicate that sequence. So we will want a white wine, or at most a very light red wine to start. In fact, since we're indulging ourselves in a proper Italian meal, with three equally important courses— antipasto, *primo, secondo*—we might do well to think of choosing three different wines, moving in an ideal sequence from white to light, fruity red to full-bodied, austere red. If we decide to proceed in this fashion, then our task defines itself more narrowly. First we must pick a white wine to drink with Calamaretti e Frittelle, carpaccio, *piatto rustico,* and warm lobster salad; then a light red (or very big white?) to partner Pennette all'Arrabiata, Tortellini ai Quattro Formaggi, Linguine alle Vongole, and Risotto di frutti di mare; and finally a full-bodied red to match with Costoletta di Porcello ai Peperoni dolci, Costoletta alla Valdostana, Casseruola di Melanzane e Formaggio, and Galletto alla Griglia, piccante.

So let's get to work. We'll ignore all the sparkling wines, in part because that's too easy a cop-out and I'm not going to let you off the hook like that, and in part because all serious sparkling wines are imitations of champagne (even some champagnes are) and that's the wrong flavor and attack—too austere, too stripped—for these foods. Similarly, we'll ignore all the Italian Chardonnays on the principle of not carrying coals to Newcastle. That still leaves us with a nice list of white wines to choose from.

Italian White Wines

	Vintage	Bottle
Arneis delle Langhe, *Voerzio*	1986	20.00
Arneis, Blange, *Fratelli Ceretto*	1985	25.00
Gavi dei Gavi, *"La Scolca"*	1985	30.00
Gavi, *Liedholm Carlo*	1986	20.00
Gavi, *"Principessa"*	1984	21.00
Gavi dei Gavi, *"la Giustiniana"*	1984	18.00
Gavi, *"La Merlina"*	1986	25.00
Soave, *Pieropan, Classico Superiore*	1985	16.00
Soave, *Cru Monforte, Roberto Anselmi*	1985	18.00
Soave, *Bolla*	1985	15.00
Verdicchio, *Macrina, Garofali*	1985	15.00
Verdicchio, *Fratelli Bucci*	1985	14.00
Vernaccia di San Gimignano, *Riccardo Falchini*	1984	14.00
Franciacorta, *Azienda Ca del Bosco*	1985	20.00
Pinot Bianco, *Ronco di Fornaz*	1985	16.00
Pinot Bianco, *Vigne del Leon*	1985	16.00
Pinot Bianco, *Abbazia di Rosazzo*	1985	15.00
Pinot Grigio, *Angoris*	1985	15.00
Pinot Grigio, *Santa Margherita*	1985	24.00
Pinot Grigio, *Marco Felluga*	1985	16.00
Pinot Grigio, *Livio Felluga*	1985	20.00

	Vintage	Bottle
Pinot Grigio, *Collavini*	1985	16.00
Pinot Grigio, *Franco Furlan*	1985	18.00
Pinot Grigio, *Ronco dei Gnemiz*	1985	18.00
Pinot Grigio, *Vigne del Leon*	1985	17.00
Pinot Grigio, *Tiefenbrunner*	1986	18.00
Russiz Superiore *di Marco Felluga*	1985	21.00
Breganze Bianco, *Maculan*	1986	24.00
Montevertine, *Bianco di Toscana*	1984	20.00
Tocai, *Ronco di Fornaz*	1986	16.00
Tocai, *Vigna del Leon*	1985	15.00
Vintage Tunina, *Jermann*	1985	35.00
Ronco Acacie, *Abbazia di Rosazzo*	1984	24.00
Foian Blanc, *Bortoluzzi*	1985	20.00
Terre di Tufo, *Teruzzi & Puthod*	1985	20.00
Orvieto, *Antinori*	1985	15.00
Orvieto, *Ruffino*	1986	17.00
Orvieto, *Vaselli*	1985	15.00
Orvieto Classico, *Decugnano*	1985	16.00
Est Est Est, *Antinori*	1984	14.00
Frascati, *Fontana Candida*	1985	13.00
Marino, *Colle Picchioni*	1984	16.00
Chiaro di Villa Pigna, *Rozzi*	1985	15.00
Fiorano Bianco, *Ludovisi-Boncompagni*	1983	25.00
Lacryma Christi Del Vesuvio, A. *Mastroberardino*	1983	16.00
Fiano di Avellino Apianum, *Mastroberardino*	1983	24.00
Corvo di Salaparuta, *Casteldaccia*	1984	15.00
Regaleali, *Conte Tasca*	1984	15.00
Nozze D'Oro, *Conte Tasca*	1985	20.00

What we should be looking for is a wine subtle yet rich enough to complement the shellfish-sweetness of squid (deep fried at that) and lobster, the meat-sweetness of tissue-thin slices of raw beef, the fresh cream–sweetness of ricotta fritters, the nutty-sweetness of Parmigiano, sufficiently flavorful to match the meats of the *piatto rustico*, yet acid-bright enough to hold together despite all the lemon and vinegar that dresses the fish and carpaccio and the vegetables of the rustic plate. On the score of acidity, there are no problems. Every wine on this list qualifies. Strength of flavor and subtlety coupled with richness will be the deciding factors. The Soaves, Verdicchios, Orvietos, Frascatis and their kin all possess subtlety but for the most part lack richness or any sort of intensity. Many of the Pinot Grigios and Pinot Biancos, on the other hand, have all the intensity one could ask for, but lack the subtlety and the complexity that enable them to respond equally well to radically different dishes. Not, mind you, that any of these wines wouldn't be completely pleasant drinking with these dishes. They emphatically would, but you would not be *bouleversé*. And we want to be bowled over. We want a dinner and a wine to remember, so we'll look to the more uncommon and more distinguished wines: Arneis and Gavi, Tocai and Vintage Tunina, Fiano di Avellino and Nozze d'Oro.

The two Piedmont wines, Arneis and Gavi, probably bring the greatest amount of acidity to bear, combined with interesting citric-range flavors. The Ceretto Blangé and the La Scolca Gavi are both excellent of their kind and would match well with these foods, though to my palate they would fall somewhat short in body and roundness for dealing with the carpaccio and the lobster. The Friulian entries, Tocai and Vintage Tunina, amply make up that deficiency and add an intriguing spiced-nut flavor of their own, which comes from the Tocai grape. These wines are too little known, and this would be a fine set of dishes with which to make their acquaintance. The southern wines, Nozze d'Oro and Fiano di Avellino, will probably be the greatest surprise to most people, since they have all the cleanness, crispness, and acidity of the northern wines plus unique and complex flavors, packaged up in a quite substantial body that feels only medium light on the palate because of its exquisite balance. Fiano especially, with its delicate hazelnut scents and tastes and its ability to improve and deepen in flavor with bottle age, is a longtime favorite of mine and the single wine I would most likely turn to as a peaceable and thoroughly pleasing companion to all these dishes.

Indulge me then and grant that of all the white wines we could have, we'll drink Fiano with our antipasti. What then shall we drink with our *primi*? They are, you remember, Pennette all'Arrabiata, Tortellini ai Quattro Formaggi, Linguine alle Vongole, and Risotto di frutti di mare, four dishes of very different character: short tubular pasta dressed with tomato sauce markedly accented by hot red pepper; small stuffed pasta rings topped with a mélange of Parmigiano, Gorgonzola, Fontina, and ricotta; long thin pasta dressed with a thin sauce of olive oil, clam juices, a bit of white wine, the clams themselves, parsley, and ample garlic; and sweet, meaty, short-grained rice, cooked in a light fish broth and studded with pieces of seafood. In terms of intensity of flavor, the first two dishes point to a red wine and the last two to a white, but the tomato acids of the Pennette all'Arrabiata at least theoretically call for a white wine, while the rich flavors and mouth-filling substantiality of the risotto at least theoretically make possible matching it with a red wine. (Both of the last two dishes are sometimes also prepared with tomato, which would simplify the problem here—paradoxically—by making both more amenable to red wine, not because of the color, but because the interaction of tomato and shellfish emphasizes the sweetness of both and minimizes the acidity of the tomato.)

So what shall we do? One solution, and not a bad one, is to continue drinking Fiano. It will certainly work well with three of the four dishes and will taste anything from okay to spectacular with the tortellini depending entirely on how aggressive their four cheeses are. Another possibility—still a bit of a pulling back from our original notion of having a different wine with each course, but practical nevertheless—is to have our two partners continue drinking the Fiano with their linguine and risotto while you and I start on a red wine we would all continue to drink with our *secondi*. A young Italian wine of middle range—middle range in heft and authority, not in quality—would work excellently in such a role: A top-quality Piedmont Barbera, for instance (the list offers us Giacomo Bologna's cru Bricco dell'Uccellone as well Pio Cesare's fine Barbera and two vintages of Gaja's cru Vignarey), or a simple, non-Riserva Chianti Classico from an excellent maker (Valentino's cellar abounds in them: for example, Antinori, Badia a Coltibuono, Fossi, Monte Vertine, Volpaia) would complement the hot-spiced pennette and the unctuously flavored tortellini equally well.

Italian Red Wines
Piedmont

	Vintage	Bottle	Magnum
Bricco Dell'Uccellone *Giacomo Bologna*	1984	33.00	65.00
Barbera d'Alba, *Pio Cesare*	1983	15.00	
Barbera d'Alba, *"Vignarey," A. Gaja*	1979	30.00	
Barbera d'Alba, *"Vignarey," A. Gaja*	1983	40.00	

In fact—as a reflective taste of either of these kinds of wine will tell you—they will partner perfectly happily with all four dishes, because they have that characteristically Italian combination of high acidity, rich fruit, and generous—but often soft—tannin that enables them to mesh with foods at many different points on the flavor spectrum. In this case I think Barbera would probably make the surer partner, because it is altogether a gentler wine than Chianti, lower in tannin—and therefore less abrasive on the palate—with acids of a kind and in a range more usually found in white wines and with a lovely, gentle black cherry tang that just plain tastes good with all sorts of food. For these same reasons, of the four nice choices the list affords us, I would suggest neither the Bricco dell'Uccellone—because, although it's a distinguished wine, its wood aging gives it precisely the kind of tannin we're not looking for here—nor the older Vignarey—because, although equally distinguished, its age will have minimized its fresh fruitiness in favor of other components less important to us in this context. The exact qualities that in most cases make these very desirable wines are what rule them out for these dishes. This leaves us to choose between a young Vignarey and a Pio Cesare Barbera of the same age. One could dither quite a while over this, but in this case I'll opt for the Pio Cesare because, for my palate, it's a little fruitier, a little softer than the Vignarey, and I think it will consequently interact better with all four dishes, neither overwhelming the seafood-flavored selections nor being overwhelmed by the others.

In another context we might well have chosen the Vignarey for its slightly greater austerity and elegance, but in another context we might just as well have considered "better" wines than either of

these, Barolos or Brunellos or Amarones. Context is almost everything in wine choices, and distinctions like these are precisely the
point of this book's emphasis on the necessity of a basic, dual
knowledge: knowing your own palate and weighing the circumstances in which the wine is to be served. The characteristics that
make a wine great may be the very traits that make it the wrong
wine to serve with the dinner you want to make or the dinner
you want to eat. They may make it bland or flavorless or even unpleasant with particular foods or overpoweringly strong or tannic
or acidic or alcoholic with others. We can destroy a lot of fine
wine by serving it with the wrong foods, and we can fall short of
getting maximum enjoyment out of even more wines by blindly
pursuing some abstract notion of the "best" wine despite all circumstances. (And then, ungrateful wretches that we are, blame
the critics who praised the wine for misleading us about it?) Wine
is a living thing. It alters with time and place, and like every other
living thing, each wine has its own excellences, its own moments
to excel. Anyone who has ever sat in a sun-dappled piazza in the
hills south of Rome on a hot summer day, munching a simple,
thin sandwich of *porchetta* and sipping a chilled glass of young,
fresh Frascati can tell you—with fervor—that there is, in the entire world, no better wine imaginable for that time and place.
Vice versa, does anyone doubt that a Barolo or a Brunello, from
no matter how splendid a vintage and accomplished a maker,
would be awful with these *primi*? That is precisely why we have
chosen, out of all the options Valentino's list affords, a "small"
wine like Barbera.

Our *secondi* are altogether easier to pick a wine for, since all
have marked flavors of a generous and wine-hospitable nature.
Even the seemingly delicate young chicken has been beefed up (I
can't help myself) by its *piccante* preparation, and, in the dish I've
chosen, the sometimes worrisome acidity of peppers is nicely compensated for by the succulence and sweetness of the pork chop they
accompany. In the other two dishes the rich-yet-gentle flavor of the
melted cheeses creates a perfect stage for a full-bodied, dry, and
distinctive red wine. The list provides many pages of wines that fit
that description—Barbarescos and Barolos, Brunello and Chianti
Classico Riserva, experimental Tuscan Cabernets and beautifully

aged Taurasi Riserva—but once again I suggest we stray from the beaten track and chose another insufficiently known and under-valued wine, an Amarone.

Veneto
Amarone

	Vintage	Bottle
Recioto Amarone della Valpolicella, Bolla	1974	29.00
Recioto Amarone della Valpolicella, Bolla	1975	26.00
Recioto Amarone della Valpolicella, Bertani	1968	47.00
Recioto Amarone della Valpolicella, Bertani	1965	40.00
Recioto Amarone della Valpolicella, Bertani	1969	43.00
Recioto Amarone della Valpolicella, Bertani	1973	30.00
Recioto Amarone della Valpolicella, "Le Ragose," Marta Galli	1979	27.00
Recioto Amarone della Valpolicella, Tommasi	1967	34.00
Recioto Amarone della Valpolicella, Tommasi	1971	36.00
Recioto Amarone, Masi	1977	27.00
Recioto Amarone, Masi, (demi-sec) Degli Angeli	1975	30.00
Recioto Amarone, Masi, (demi-sec) Degli Angeli	1977	29.00
Recioto Amarone, Negrar	1976	21.00
Recioto Amarone, Guerrieri-Rizzardi	1980	20.00
Amarone, Speri	1976	18.00
Amarone, Speri	1977	18.00
Amarone, Santa Sofia	1974	26.00
Amarone, Lamberti	1975	26.00
Amarone, Villa Girardi	1977	23.00
Amarone, Allegrini	1979	25.00

Amarone is a high-alcohol wine (normally around 15 percent), and for that reason it's not always the best dinner companion. It can easily seduce what the French so politely term *petites natures* into excess, and it can be too powerful for some foods. But we have been pretty temperate so far, and what Amarone characteristically possesses, in addition to power and elegance, that makes it a fine complement to our dinner is an extraordinarily rich and persistently fresh fruit, an invigorating, youthful flavor that continues to coexist within the wine in perfect harmony with the more evolved flavors of maturity. Valentino's list doesn't have some of my favorites—I particularly miss Quintarelli—but there is still ample here to choose from. With this wine and this list, we have recourse to a simple deciding factor: You want age on an Amarone. I think it's crazy to drink any of them before they're at least ten years old, and more years are usually preferable. The Amarones of the sixties, for instance, are drinking beautifully now: big and elegant and deep, amazingly complex and on top of that still startlingly fresh. Given that fact, my choice here would be the Bertani 1969, the oldest really distinguished Amarone vintage on the list ('65 was only so-so, '67 and '68 quite good, but for most producers in the Veneto less impressive than '69). Because it is a high-alcohol wine, and a palate-filling one, we will probably sip it slowly—if we're careful, slowly enough so that we'll have a bit left to drink with a nubbin of Parmigiano, which is a combination of flavors that defies comparison. *Buon appetito!*

IN SUM

You've come a long way, and you're no longer a baby as far as wine is concerned. In Valentino, you've dealt with the kind of wine list that is supposed to make sophisticated men faint and strong women tremble. We could have encountered a list like this sooner—The Four Seasons has one such—but you weren't ready for it then, because you didn't then appreciate how much you really know about matching food and wine. The fact is, there aren't many mysteries to it. All you need—as you now know very well—is the Decalogue-and-a-Half of principles we provided you with back at the beginning of this book and a minimal amount of information, at least a loose grasp of the relevant data about the foods and wines you're dealing with. After that, all it takes, as you've seen, is a few quick calculations and an artful nonchalance about your pronouncements.

But before you go off to hone your new-grown skills and to wow your friends and neighbors, let me underline the one caveat that wine lists like this last one so graphically illustrate: Don't always and automatically go for the "most." Sometimes, yes, certainly, when the circumstances warrant it. But whether it be the most famous wine or the most prestigious or the most bemedaled or the most costly or the most praised or the most uncommon or the most fine, it is not necessarily the most appropriate wine for the particular you of this moment, for your friends on this particular occasion, for your dinner in this particular restaurant—and most appropriate is the only "most" that counts, because it is the appropriateness of the wine to the moment, the palates, and the foods it accompanies that makes all the pleasure happen. Without that fit, that harmony, that—to use the old-fashioned word—decorum, the greatest wine tastes blah, the best dinner falls flat, the liveliest conversation flags. With it, a humble Barbera shines, a hamburger surpasses sweetbreads, and your wit soars.

This isn't a matter of once more dragging out the tired old paradox and insisting firmly that "less is more." Less isn't more and it never was, no matter what Robert Browning says, but we're not dealing here, in choosing wines, with "less" or "more," no more than we should be dealing with "most" or "least." We're dealing with "other," with "different," with "particular," with "special." Every well-made wine, from Beaujolais to Brunello, Rioja to Zinfandel, is all those things—other, different, particular, special—just as is every well-conceived meal and every well-chosen company, and all deserve and reward the same sort of respect and attention to their specialness that you accord to yours. And that is the final secret of matching wines and foods and people.

Utopia: Ideal Restaurant Wine Service

It's only fitting to close this section with a brief account of what constitutes ideal restaurant wine service. A great deal is involved here, both in the way of tangibles like the cellar and the stemware and intangibles like attitude. We've been looking at some of the tangibles in those four very different examples of admirable wine lists, so here we concentrate on the intangibles—like attitude.

Attitude starts with the way the restaurant conceives of its business, its relation to wine, and its relation to you. Every businessperson is entitled to a fair profit, and restaurateurs are no exception. But diners can't be treated as cattle in a chute, to be moved through the restaurant with the greatest possible expedition. The restaurant whose primary concern is to turn the tables frequently is not going to be very receptive to wine drinkers. Neither is the other extreme tolerable, the restaurant that allows diners to hold their table in perpetuity as they finish yet one more coffee or brandy, while there are other customers waiting for the table that in their innocence they thought they had reserved for an hour ago. The house that can't manage its seating and reservation system abuses its customers before they even get their coats off. Sadly, this particular form of customer-bashing seems to be growing more and more prevalent, even in smallish, chic houses that would, to innocent eyes, seem to want to pride themselves on service and attentiveness. There is only one way to deal with this sort of contempt for the customer: No matter how good you've heard the food is, no matter how fashionable the scene, walk out and do not come back, ever. And make sure you call the next day and tell the manager—better, the owner—what you have done, what you intend to do, and why. Otherwise, you are simply assuring the people-churner restaurateurs that they can get away with anything—in which case you deserve to have them dump on you.

The restaurateurs we all want to deal with, all the time, are the people who have chosen to make their mark and such fortune as they can by quality and attention. It would be nice if they were all wine aficionados—I can't help but harbor uneasy suspicions about people whose business is food who don't enjoy wine—but at least they must respect the place of wine in a meal and understand the importance for the diner of its ritual pace.

In practical terms that means, for starters, that the wine list should be readily available and produced without fuss as soon as asked for. Haven't you ever wondered why restaurants don't automatically present a wine list at every table along with the menu? Do they really think anyone will be offended by that? And why do so many restaurants have only one or two lists for the whole house? They'd never dream of making do with only one or two menus, yet they will make you wait your turn to find out what your wine options are. All such behaviors betray an unhealthy and unappreciative attitude toward wine and the wine drinker.

So our ideal restaurant will value the role of wine in the enhancement of its cuisine and of your enjoyment, and it will demonstrate that by making wine accessible and important from the moment you enter. In a really good establishment these days, this means at least a small Cruvinet at the bar so that half a dozen or so wines are available by the glass. The degree of pleasure that the invention of the Cruvinet has especially afforded solitary and dual restaurant diners can never be overstated. The Cruvinet has made possible the single glass of champagne as aperitif, the single glass of white wine with the hors d'oeuvre course of what is otherwise a red wine dinner, the extra glass of red that you need to finish your cheese, the little taste of dessert wine to finish everything off in style.

Needless to say, in our ideal restaurant the wines that repose in its Cruvinet and adorn its wine list need not be numerous, as long as they are of good quality and, most important, appropriate to the cooking of the house. A long list is truly a luxury only either when you have had the opportunity to become familiar with it in advance or when you are consciously searching for rarities—when, for instance, you choose to dine at a particular restaurant because you know it has the best collection of Zinfandel on the East Coast or because its cellar is strong in Barolo or Hermitage. But under most circumstances, a balanced short list will be more serviceable for the establishment and more comfortable for the diner (unless, as is rarely the case in the United States, the management does not plan to turn the table over at all; if it's yours for the duration, by all means enjoy a leisurely read through the longest wine list you can find).

Whatever the length of the list, our ideal establishment will:

- give you ample time to consider your choices
- have a waiter ready when you signal that you are ready
- have in stock the wines it lists as it lists them

Few things frustrate wine buffs more than mustering all their skill and thought to choose the right wine for their meal and then being told there isn't any more of it, or it's a different vintage, or it's in some other significant way—it's not estate bottled, not a reserve— different from the wine named in the list. That rankles just as much as false advertising and misleading sales claims, and unless both rare and much apologized for, it ought to stand as a black, black mark against the establishment.

Once we have ordered our wine, our ideal establishment will bring it promptly and show us the bottle before drawing the cork. This is usually unnecessary, but breakdowns in communication do happen, and it is always wise to check and make sure the wine brought is the wine ordered. If the wine is white, it will be well chilled, but not so numbingly cold that its flavor disappears. If red, it ought to be at a moderate cellar temperature (slightly cool by standard room temperature these days), and we should be asked if we wish it decanted if it is an older wine or simply opened right away to breathe or neither of these.

A pet peeve here: If you have any say in the matter at all, don't let your wine be placed in one of those silly baskets so that it takes up all the room of a toy cannon on the table. If a wine is old enough and has developed sediment enough to justify the use of an apparatus like one of those baskets, it is also old enough and sedimented enough to make careful decanting the preferable way of handling it.

Whatever the wine's color and whenever it is opened, you should be shown the cork, which is a little like trooping the colors. You can't escape it; you have to deal with that cork. Most of the time, just look at it. If it's sound, forget it. If it shows signs of crumbling, sniff it. It should smell only of wine. If it smells of anything else— must or mildew or even old cork—there is a chance that the wine may be off, so pay very careful attention when you taste. Of course, you ought to be doing that anyway, which renders this whole ritual superfluous. But that's the charm of trooping the colors.

You too have a role in this ideal wine restaurant, and that is to fulfill your part of the pact between you and the establishment. You have to act responsibly in choosing your wines. This means that if you don't know something, it's incumbent upon you to ask. You shouldn't try to send back the bottle of perfectly sound, still, sweet dessert Vouvray *moelleux* that you ordered thinking it was a dry, sparkling Vouvray *mousseux*. Pay attention to your wine. Pay attention to your food. Behave appropriately to both: Don't sniff and swirl and gargle a Beaujolais-Villages as if it were an antique vintage of Corton. Just as the wine waiter should not obtrude upon your conversation, so you shouldn't keep him standing there forever before noticing he's waiting for you to taste and approve the wine. None of this requires solemnity on your part or the staff's, just ordinary courtesy.

Ordinary courtesy is essentially what governs all the rest of wine protocol in this ideal restaurant of ours. Waiters don't hover over our shoulders but they do check our table regularly. They don't top up our glasses the second we put them down, like flies settling on fruit, but they do either leave the wine comfortably within our reach or watch carefully to see whose glass needs replenishing— the latter especially if our wine is not left at table with us. And in that case, or if our party is a large one, they discreetly tell us when the bottle is nearly done so we can decide whether we want more wine and if so what kind. And whether we have drunk a $20 Beaujolais or a $200 Vega Sicilia, they handle the wine and us with the same degree of courtesy. In the past, when that great gourmand Raymond Oliver was the chef-proprietor of Le Grand Véfour in the Palais Royal in Paris, that temple of fine dining practiced a wonderful piece of reverse snobbery. No wine bottle ever entered the dining room. Instead, after you had ordered from its wonderful list (very, very strong in mature Bordeaux), your wine was expertly decanted in the kitchen, and the decanter brought in on a silver tray. The wine's cork, which was shown only to the host, lay discreetly beside it. In that oddly democratic, patrician establishment, no one could swank anyone else with a label—or with prices. Only the host's menu had them. So no one was ever *bouleversé* by the reputation of a wine or browbeaten by the price of a dish, and such gratitude or admiration as anyone felt was for the genuine pleasures of the food and the wine. I don't know about your ideal restaurant, but mine would work that way too.

CHAPTER 8

Wines for the Cellar and for the Ages

KOKO: There is beauty in extreme old age—
Do you fancy you are elderly enough?
Information I'm requesting
On a subject interesting:
Is a maiden all the better when she's tough?

KATISHA: Throughout this wide dominion
It's the general opinion
That she'll last a good deal longer when she's tough.

KOKO: Are you old enough to marry, do you think?
Won't you wait till you are eighty in the shade?
There's a fascination frantic
In a ruin that's romantic;
Do you think you are sufficiently decayed?

KATISHA: To the matter that you mention
I have given some attention,
And I think I am sufficiently decayed.

—GILBERT AND SULLIVAN, *The Mikado*

AFTER ALL THE VARIANTS on "What is the right wine for locusts and honey?" the next most frequently asked question about wine has got to be some version of "Is this a good year?" The answer to that, whether it be "yes," "no," or "depends on what you want it for," usually doesn't tell the inquirer what he or she really wants to know. Whether the asker knows it or not, the real question being

311

asked is almost always about readiness: "Is this wine too old (or old enough) to drink? Will this wine last, or should I drink it now, or is it already over the hill? Should I buy more of it or use what I already have to dress my salad?" These aren't questions about vintage at all. They concern a wine's age and maturity, its progress toward completeness, and at this stage of our discussions they logically lead us to a consideration of the problem that wine buffs worry about almost as much as they do about matching food and wine: the whole phenomenon of buying wine young and laying it down to mature—in short, cellaring.

Like so much connected with wine, the simple prospect of cellaring a few bottles or a few cases seems for some people to tap into a deep pool of anxieties. Part of the problem may in fact just be the word *cellaring*. There seems to be a popular misconception that a wine cellar must be a baronial vault hewn from the living rock beneath the ancestral castle, where the sun never shines, the temperature never varies, and the tectonic plates are firm enough to withstand the gaping of the San Andreas Fault. Not accidentally, people who believe fairy tales like that also tend to take the truism "wine is a living thing" to mean that wine is a delicate and easily endangered species, a fragile flower likely to perish under the first rough breath.

The truth is very, very different. Wine is without doubt a living thing, and far from being a delicate blossom, it has all the tenacity and will to survive any other living thing possesses. It starts its life as a vine, and it happily inherits plenty of the vine's toughness. I have had wines so badly tossed about in shipment that they arrived at my door with some bottles broken—shattered glass and red goo inside all the boxes—and the rest so shaken up they looked like cherry pop. A few weeks of quiet, and they were drinking just fine. I've had white wines—they're the really fragile ones, right?— frozen in shipment from too long exposure on a loading dock or in an unheated truck, so that by the time they reached me small icebergs were visible in every bottle. That means water had separated from alcohol and the other components of the wine, and corks had pushed up through the foil caps and in some cases entirely out of the bottles—lemon slush in the boxes this time. As with the red wines, the only total losses were the bottles broken or from which the corks had been completely expelled. With the others I simply pushed the corks back in, wiped off the bottles, and let them rest for a month. They were perfectly fine drinking, tasting only a little older—say half a year more advanced—than I would have expected, and it's possible I wouldn't have noticed even that in a blind tasting.

Obviously, I'm not recommending that you freeze your wines or use them for a rousing game of soccer, but I am saying that you don't have to baby your wines. If you've been shying away from laying wines down because you thought you needed special conditions and elaborate precautions, forget it. Wine is a living thing, true, but don't forget that you are too, and where human beings can be comfortable, most wines can survive quite handily.

The Rock Bottom of Cellarage

So what do wines really need, and what do you absolutely have to provide if you want to lay away wines for future drinking? There are two answers to this. For optimal, maximal storage: cool, dark, and quiet. For practical, minimal keeping: relatively stable temperatures, absence of direct sunlight, and absence of vibrations. That's all. Anything else is window dressing. A dark corner of the cellar will serve perfectly well, as long as it's away from the furnace and the washer-dryer. So will an ordinary coat closet, as long as its temperature doesn't swing wildly up and down and as long as it doesn't abut an elevator shaft or a drill press. Think about it: You wouldn't much like being shaken about all day long either.

What I'm suggesting here runs counter to a lot of conventional wine wisdom. For that reason, it needs explanation and justification—at some length, unfortunately. So bear with me, and bear in mind that what I'm going to be explaining here is very much a contrarian—not to say maverick—opinion about cellaring wine.

Everything I've got to say about keeping wine is based on three distinct in theory, but in fact intertwined, considerations: first, the physical characteristics of a wine as they determine its potential for long-term development; second, the physical characteristics of the storage environment that affect a wine's longevity; and third—the least tangible but ultimately most important consideration of the three—the goals or desires of the person storing the wine.

CONSIDERATION NUMBER ONE: THE WINE

Alcohol, tannin, acid, the kinds of grapes, where the grapes were grown, and the methods of vinification are all elements that contribute to or subtract from a wine's potential for long life and bottle development. We've talked about a lot of these components in earlier sections of this book when we discussed varietal wines and national wines, so for now let's simply look at the typical life cycle of a typical wine under ideal storage conditions (what they are will be determined later).

Most wines with any potential for long-term storage are red, and the vast majority of them are wines vinified from a handful of favored grape varieties cultivated in a small number of blessed locations around the globe. The selection of the varieties for cultivation seems predominantly a human choice and is potentially expandable, but the blessing of the sites appears to be entirely nature's doing, a fact that puts a definite upward limit on the amount of potentially long-lived wine the world will ever produce. Here are the major grapes and locations at the moment:

- Cabernet Sauvignon in Bordeaux and California (and increasingly in Australia, Spain, and Italy)
- Pinot Noir in Burgundy and Oregon (and increasingly in California, Spain, and Italy)
- Syrah and Mourvèdre in the Rhône and Australia (and increasingly in California)
- Grenache in the Rhône and Spain
- Tempranillo in Spain
- Nebbiolo, Sangiovese, and Aglianico in Italy
- Zinfandel in California

You can add to these red wines an eclectic group of sweet dessert wines and an even more heterogeneous collection of dry white wines whose ability to age well seems much more tied to specific soils than it is related to grape variety. They are

- Riesling, Gewürztraminer, and Pinot Gris in Alsace
- Chardonnay in some years and some spots in Burgundy, Chablis, Tuscany, Friuli, and California
- the Viognier and a few lesser grapes in the Rhône
- Fiano, Greco, and Cortese in a few sites in Italy

That's it. That's all there is. Out of all the innumerable wines produced in the world, these few names include the vast majority of the wines that are even worth giving a thought to as wines to lay down. And of all these, it is an even smaller handful of red wines that most reward cellaring.

All really great red wines, from anywhere in the world, need—*need,* not "can stand"—bottle aging to develop their fullest character. I can't stress this enough. Most fine red wines are drunk far too young to give more than a hint of what they might become. The bane of winedom today is a depraved contemporary taste for infanticide. To most wine drinkers, fruit is all that seems to matter in a wine—perhaps because it's all that most people have learned to identify—so people drink their Médoc the same way they drink their Beaujolais: as young as possible, before it has lost its fruit. On this subject I speak as an unreconstructed old mossback. I like the flavors, plural—the multiple, complex, difficult-to-verbalize-because-they're-not-simple flavors—of mature wine. You don't get those flavors the moment the wine is released for sale, not even where the winemakers are altering their techniques of vinification to produce wines that are fruitier and fresher and ready to drink sooner to please contemporary mass-market taste. Great red wines pass through intricate and often protracted cycles of development, but their maturity is well worth waiting for.

Bordeaux reds are typical, in fact paradigmatic, in this regard. They go through at least four major changes, and the time it takes for each of them varies with every vintage. The newly fermented wine is usually raw and tannic beyond the casual wine drinker's belief. The aging and settling the wine receives before its market release usually—but not invariably—carry the wine past this stage. Very concentrated vintages (particularly in the normally fuller wines of Pauillac and the normally harder wines of St-Estèphe) will still be quite tannic when first released for sale, just as many Rhône wines and all Nebbiolo-based wines will be. As the tannin begins to subside somewhat, the fresh fruit flavors of the wines—in Médoc wines, those cedary, black currant flavors that seem to be all anyone ever talks about in them—come to the fore. This second stage may last, depending on the characteristics of the harvest, anywhere from a year to five years, and it is during this period that most of the world's claret and other red wines are consumed. *Tant pis.*

It's a truly moot point whether the attractiveness of the wine's fruit in its second stage or the sheer nothingness of its flavor in its third stage contributes most to its premature consumption. Certainly a lot of wine drinkers have been fooled by the nullity, the absolute void, of red wine's normal third phase into thinking their wine has died when it is merely resting. As its youthful fruit begins to subside, the wine goes dumb. Some people describe it as mute or muffled. It appears to have lost all its striking characteristics and become simply an inert liquid. Many wine drinkers panic at this point. They think their wine has somehow—probably because they didn't spend $30,000 on a temperature- and humidity-controlled cellar unit—gone over the hill, and they start drinking up what's left of it as fast as they can, before it dies completely. I know that's what I did the first time I experienced this phenomenon, and I bitterly regret right now all the wine I drank in its worst condition that, had I known more about what I was doing, I could now be enjoying at its best. Nobody ever told me a simple fact of vinous life: *All the great red wines evolve through this dumb phase, and all of them must endure this period of eclipse.* The wine has not gone bad or died. It is, in fact, intensely alive and passing through the most dramatic changes that it experiences after fermentation. Inside the cocoon of the bottle the whole flavor structure of the wine is metamorphosing: It is evolving from a simple, fruity entity into a complicated, many-layered phenomenon. What this requires of the wine drinker is patience—nothing more, nothing less, nothing else.

The exact length of time any particular wine's eclipse will last is unpredictable, but a good rule of thumb for Bordeaux wines is to figure two to three years for smaller châteaux and lesser vintages and upward from there for superior châteaux and finer vintages. For example, at the time I'm writing this—early 1989—most 1979 red Bordeaux have emerged from their eclipse. They now are drinking beautifully—some have been doing so for a few years already—and all give every sign that they will continue to do so for another two to five years at least. A very few harder wines—Cos d'Estournel, for instance—and most of the *premiers crus* of this year are not completely evolved yet. They need at least another year of benign neglect before they will show their best. I would not expect the 1981 clarets to reach this same level of maturity for another two to four years yet, and I wouldn't want to drink '83s or '85s, from no matter how modest a producer, anytime before 1995 at the earliest. St-Emilion and Pomerol wines of comparable vintages generally mature from one to five years earlier than Médocs, though the great ones can live as long, and there are always the few surprises, like the exceptionally hard 1961s, some of which are evolving yet. California Cabernets show more fruit at every stage than the Médoc wines do, and they seem always to be more forward. Barolo and Barbaresco present such massive tannin in their youth (except in truly unusual vintages like 1982) that they really begin to show their worth only after they've emerged from eclipse, which mellows their tannins and brings them into harmony.

This final stage—the wine's mature state—deserves all the patience you can give it because of what the wine at last gives you in return. With red Bordeaux, for instance, you get a heady aroma compounded of equal parts of ripe fruit (plums, black cherries) or fruit leather, tar, tobacco, and fresh earth, plus perhaps a few herbal or woody (especially cedar) scents; a taste of multilayered complexity, involving mature fruit (prunes, dried cherries), black pepper, hints of truffle, tar, and deeper and yet deeper flavors as the wine opens in the glass and on your palate. That's mature claret, and it's worth waiting for. Like most red wines (this is especially true of the Burgundies), clarets seem to have taken on bulk by this stage, as if they had somehow increased in weight and fullness in the bottle. However one accounts for it—I simply don't try—they definitely feel and taste like bigger wines than they did in their youth. These mature flavors and textures are the sort of thing all the handbooks really have in mind when they tell you that, for example, Médoc red wines ideally accompany red meats and game and strong cheeses.

CONSIDERATION NUMBER TWO: THE STORAGE CONDITIONS

These then are the growth phases of a wine under ideal storage conditions. Let me remind you what we said a little earlier those conditions are: "For optimal, maximal storage: cool, dark, and quiet. For practical, minimal keeping: relatively stable temperatures, absence of direct sunlight, and absence of vibrations." The last two conditions are almost self-explanatory. Too much motion can literally shake a wine apart. This is one of the reasons a wine tasted too soon after shipment almost always shows poorly. Most wines come back together after they've been allowed to rest for a few weeks, though some suffer more and longer than others (notably the Burgundies, as I theorized earlier). But if the place the wines are supposed to recover is itself subject to constant or even frequent vibration, then the wines get just about as much real rest as you or I would get in a narrow, economy-class seat on a bumpy transatlantic flight. If the torture is continued long enough, the wine never really recomposes itself and eventually it simply dies. This doesn't mean, however, that wines can't tolerate any motion at all. You don't have to go to the opposite extreme and reinforce your floor or mount the whole wine storage area on springs and gimbals with gyroscopic shock absorbers lest a stray footfall disturb them. And you emphatically can pick your bottles up and look them over without fearing that you're committing vinicide. Just use common sense and don't treat a bottle of wine as if it were a shakerful of daiquiris.

(A parenthetical note here on a related bit of commonsensical wine lore that is all too often ignored. Wines should always be stored on their side, so that the corks don't dry out and allow the wine to oxidize. Since they are lying on their side, the bottles should always be stored with their front label up so you can easily see what you've got without having to paw and pummel the wines unnecessarily. If you store them label up as you ought, such sediment as the wines deposit—and mature wines will throw sediment; it's perfectly natural—will always accumulate opposite the label. Ergo, it follows that you—or your host or your waiter—should always pour the wine with its label up in order to disturb the sediment as little as possible. This is true even if you are decanting the wine. Properly stored wine has been lying for a long time with its label up and should always be held so for pouring, no matter whether you are doing it by hand or from a cradle.)

The requirement of darkness for wine storage is equally commonsensical. Sunlight causes chemical reactions in wine (in beer too, by the way) that will eventually kill the wine. Dark bottles retard this but don't prevent it, so the only other sensible precaution is to store the wine out of the light. I have heard that some people get fanatical about this too and won't even use electric lights near their wines, preferring to grope with candles and flashlights for their treasures. This is obviously silly, but as much darkness as is conveniently possible remains the best practice.

Of darkness, stillness, and chill, the major factor affecting a wine's longevity is the temperature at which it is stored. Everybody agrees that wines should be kept cool and at as stable a temperature as possible—and this is where agreement stops. This is the requirement that people fuss about most and that I think inspires the greatest amount of nonsense and gimmickry. Stability doesn't mean invariability. It does mean that the wine develops best where the temperature range is not very wide nor its changes very abrupt. I am not aware of any extant scientific studies of this problem, so I'm speaking solely from my own experience here and what I know of the experience of other wine amateurs and professionals. On that basis, I'd say that a temperature swing of about twenty degrees in the course of the year does wines no harm at all. Sudden, sharp temperature fluctuations, whether up or down, seem to have about the same effect on wines as rough handling. The wines start to come apart and the flavors go dead, for at least an indeterminate while.

Even more problematic and far more troublesome is the matter of determining exactly which twenty degrees of the temperature range wines should inhabit. It's no easy matter for the conscientious wine lover to figure out what precisely is meant by "cool." Most people are aware that heat is the enemy of wine. Excessive heat during fermentation (and fermentation itself generates a great deal of heat), and the wine is dead before it ever lives. Excessive heat during vat storage or after bottling, and the wine's whole life cycle is accelerated, usually disastrously. Its metabolism, so to speak, is speeded up to such a degree that it rushes past maturity to a sort of feverish death. Very cool temperatures—as long as they stay above freezing—do the opposite. They slow down the whole developmental cycle through which wine passes so that each internal chemical change works itself out thoroughly and with infinite slowness, and the wine matures gradually and gracefully, with no awkward fits and starts. These of course are the very considerations that send people who've just invested in their first bottles of Château Pétrus scurrying out to buy what is in essence an overpriced, wood-paneled refrigerator to keep those bottles in for the next half-century, or at least until Saturday night.

In winespeak "cool" is conventionally interpreted to mean cellar temperature, not the actual temperature of any normal modern cellar, but in fact the temperature of some very old and unconventional cellars, the *caves*—some of them real caves—of Bordeaux and Chablis and Burgundy in which their respective wines have been vinified for centuries. That's where the rock-hewn-cavern notion of wine storage comes from, and as anyone who has visited any of those dark, damp *caves* can tell you, they're not cool, they're cold. Their temperatures hover in the forties, occasionally dipping into the high thirties or rising into the low fifties. And, of course, they are the paradigm of wine storage: literally rock solid, dark and damp, with a steady, unrelenting chill that grabs hold of your bone marrow and ices it. (Winemakers take a perverse delight in holding namby-pamby, too-lightly-clad wine writers at the very coldest spot in these cellars to deliver their longest diatribes about the perfidy of barrelmakers or bottle suppliers or rainmakers or insecticides, no one of which is a subject that generates much warmth in anyone other than a winemaker.)

In such cellars wines can sit for decades, unmoved, a mere hundred yards from where they were made, maturing with infinite slowness to whatever degree of perfection they are capable of— and that can be very impressive indeed. For example, I remember with constantly renewed pleasure a 1945 Château Lafon-Rochet— a *quatrième cru* not in very high esteem these days—that was poured on its fortieth birthday right at its birthplace, from whose cold cellars it had never stirred until it came to table that day. That wine tasted like the whole soul of St-Estèphe, deep and trufflelike and at the same time live and supple, a one-bottle argument for reclassifying every château in the commune. I suspect that many another equally low-ranked château throughout the Médoc— some I know for certain—could show just as impressively. And of course one may legitimately argue from lesser to greater: If a *quatrième cru* properly stored can develop so magnificently, what will a *premier cru* be like?

That, of course, is the lure that induces people to lay wine down in the first place. Sure, you save money (at least if you don't squander it on fancy storage units) by buying wines young and storing them yourself, but that isn't why you do it. It's because of what you know or hope those wines will taste like on that magical day when they are ready and you can at last start drinking them.

CONSIDERATION NUMBER THREE: THE PERSON

And there's the rub, the very thing that makes my final pole of consideration—"the goals or desires of the person storing the wine"—so very crucial. If a fourth-growth claret can take forty years to come round—and that Lafon-Rochet had by no means peaked yet, far from it—how long are you willing to wait for a first growth? How much time will you invest in a really slow-maturing wine like a Brunello di Montalcino? an Amarone? a Vega Sicilia? Just how old do you mean to be when you drink these wines?

Very few of us, I think, have sufficient confidence in our futures or our progeny—at least as far as their taste is concerned—to be thinking of laying down wine for our heirs and assigns, who may very well spurn our treasures in favor of diet soft drinks or "recreational" drugs. For most of us wine is a personal joy, to be shared with friends and family to be sure, but not to be assigned to or built into anyone else's future. We buy wines because we want to drink them, we want to taste them, we want to add that pleasure to our repertory, we want the fun of pouring them for someone else and seeing and hearing that someone's response.

If that is true for you, then it also follows that the storage conditions that are ideal for wine may not be at all ideal for you. You, of course, must decide for yourself. I can speak only personally and selfishly about this. As I think I've made clear many times so far in this book, I love older wines. I relish above everything else the complicated flavors and rich nuances of fully evolved claret and Barolo and all such big, powerful, slow-maturing wines, but I'm not much interested in wines I won't live long enough to drink. The eighties have given us some glorious vintages: 1981, '82, '83, '85, '86, and '88 in Bordeaux; 1985 and 1988 in Burgundy; 1982, '85, and '88 in Piedmont; 1983 and '85 in the Rhône; and more than I can figure out in the various viticultural areas of California and Oregon. Take Barolo, to which I am devoted (addicted is probably truer): If I were to "properly" cellar the '82s, '85s, and '88s—the last of which won't even be on the market for another few years—there's a better than even chance that I'd never live to taste a mature drop of them. And—lest you conclude that I'm already doddering—I am not what I consider old (is anybody?).

So where does all this leave us? Specifically, what does it mean for your laying down wines? As I see it, it means this: Heat may be the enemy of wine, but it can be a friend to the wine drinker. It accelerates the wine's maturation, remember? This means that the less-than-ideal storage conditions *for the wine* that most of us have to work with may very well be ideal *for what we want from the wine*. It will mature faster and be ready to drink sooner, and this, from our point of view, has to be a definite plus.

As you raise that twenty-degree temperature range within which your wines sleep from the 35-to-55-degree sector to 45 to 65 or 55 to 75 degrees (this last, I suspect, is the range of most people's cellars and closets, and just about as high as you want to go; above it I think you risk cooking the wine), you hasten the wine's development, bringing it more swiftly than is "normal" (and who has declared it normal?) from its first youthful fruit to and through its dumb stage and on to the various plateaus of its adulthood. It's as simple as that. The cycle remains the same. Colder storage conditions protract the process, and warmer accelerate it. Not by a large amount, mind you. If you accept temperatures in the low-to-middle fifties as "normal" or average, my guess would be that temperatures in the forties would retard the process by no more than 20 to 25 percent and those in the sixties or low seventies would advance it by no more than 20 to 25 percent. But this is entirely speculation. What is certainly true as a generalization, however, is that the greater the wine's potential, the longer the time it will need to evolve. The only way to be completely sure of the condition of your wines is to look in from time to time and see what the kids are doing. Open a bottle, taste, take a few notes, and relish the prospects you have before you.

A final caveat, because I don't want to fool you: Wines brought along at an accelerated pace will never achieve exactly the same degree of grandeur as wines that have been allowed to linger along the way. But they will still be magnificent wines, miles and miles ahead of their young selves in depth and complexity and grace, and you will have them for the drinking at your pleasure—and that, to my mind, is what cellaring wines is all about.

The Golden Years

This chapter began with a question about good years and bad. At that point, I spent a lot of time denying the validity and even the reality of that question because it was premature. Now we've reached the point where considerations of vintage become not merely relevant but the very heart of the matter, because—after all the other considerations of kind and locale and estate—it is primarily on the basis of vintage that you will choose wines to lay down for maturation and determine just how long that will take. With the same wine from the same estate—Château Chasse-Spleen or Chave Hermitage, Ridge's Montebello Cabernet or Bonny Doon's Cigare Volante, Pio Cesare's Barbaresco or Lungarotti's Rubesco, Muga's Prado Enea or López de Heredia's Viña Tondonia—the characteristics of each vintage dictate whether the wines will be drunk immediately or cellared briefly or put away for decades.

If the whole question of vintages confuses you, don't feel lonely. Misinformation about the importance of vintages abounds. Dogmatists will solemnly assure you that in buying wines from California, or Italy, or Spain, the vintage year makes no difference whatever, since the climate there is invariably sunny. Or they will tell you that older wine is always better, no matter what kind or color it is. Or the reverse, that all wine should be drunk as young as possible, no matter what kind it is. That every single one of those propositions is false doesn't prevent their being repeated, day in and day out, even by people who ought to know better.

Vintage need not be a great mystery. It's not even always a relevant concern. At the level of simple wines—what I think of as everyday, basic red and white, the kinds of wines we talked about in the early chapters of this book—a perfectly adequate rule of thumb is to drink your wines young, in fact the younger the better most of the time. There will certainly be variation from vintage to vintage, one year a little bit fruitier or fuller bodied, another a little more acidic or less alcoholic. But essentially, these small differences will occur within a broad range of pleasant drinkability.

Wines such as Beaujolais and Chinon or Bourgueil, Beaujolais-style Zinfandel and Gamay, simple Chianti or Barbera or Dolcetto, simple Rioja among the reds, the dry Vouvrays and Mâcon wines, all Chenin Blancs and most Sauvignons, Soave or Orvieto or Pinot Grigio or Verdicchio, new-style white Rioja or Penedès whites—all these are wines that, nine years out of ten, should be consumed young and fresh. This is especially true with white wines. Distrust most that are more than three years old, and be careful of the three-year-olds. With red wines, drinking them at five years of age or less (much less for Beaujolais) gives you a good margin of safety. Perhaps one year in a decade, wines like these will have a vintage so remarkably good or bad that it makes a substantial difference to the consumer. But most of the time their vintage variations are almost negligible. The only reason—and it's a good one—you would consider cellaring any of these is just to keep a ready supply on hand for immediate drinking, so you don't have to go dashing out to the store whenever you decide you'd like a glass of wine with your dinner. These are emphatically not wines that reward long-term storage.

It takes higher quality and greater complexity in the wine's essential nature to enable it to live longer and to benefit from extra aging. That higher quality and greater complexity cost much more to achieve in the first place, so such wines, white or red, will always cost more than simple, youthful ones. It's a fact of life: You pay more for a Chippendale chair than you do for a beach chair. With these better, more complex wines, the quality of a particular vintage plays a major role in the wine's potential for development and in your ultimate enjoyment.

No one thing determines the quality of a given vintage. A whole complex of factors comes into play—differences of weather from one harvest to another, the great diversity of vineyard geography and geology (soil kind and quality, vineyard altitude and exposure) and microclimate. Add to that the many different kinds of grapes grown around the world and the variability of vinification techniques, and you've got a situation in which any generalization about vintage quality has to be heavily qualified. Bear that in mind always: Even in the worst harvest some winemakers turn out good wine, and even in the best some winemakers foul up. The many popular so-called vintage guides that give general ratings of wine areas that, like Tuscany or Sonoma, embrace a wide range of microclimates and a large number of grape varieties under cultivation are at best optimistic averages, designed to reassure rather than inform.

As with cellar conditions, think very carefully about what you want to get out of laying wines away. The best vintage—the one that everybody unanimously rates 20 out of 20, off the top of the scale—may not be the best vintage for you to put away. It may cost much too much—I don't believe in drinking wines whose price makes my hand tremble when I lift the glass—and it may well take far too long to come around for your purposes. Many people—

wine drinkers rather than wine collectors—are better served by cellaring second-tier vintages, years like '67, '71, and '79 in Bordeaux and '76 and '79 in the Piedmont, simply because they mature sooner and are ready to drink in a much shorter space of time than the great years that overshadowed them: Bordeaux 1966, '70, and '78, Piedmont '74 and '78. Very great vintages like these are only for the longest-term storage—fifteen to twenty years and more—even under warmer, more accelerating conditions.

So, for instance, if you hope to drink some really great, fully mature claret to celebrate the now-fast-approaching new millennium, you should have put away some of the 1978s ten years ago when they came on the market. What few of them are still available at retail are very, very costly. The same holds true for many other great red wines: 1984 California Cabernet, 1977 Taurasi Riserva, 1982 Barolo and Barbaresco, 1983 Hermitage, Côte Rôtie and Cornas. This is not to say that there haven't been great vintages since these; there emphatically have been. Nature continues to be prodigal with her gifts, far beyond our deserving, but if we want to take maximum advantage of her bounty, we've got to plan ahead, to decide at least roughly when we want to drink our wines and to buy and store accordingly. If you've got the time and space and patience to wait twenty years and more, and sufficient disposable income to tie a good bit of it up in undrinkable wine for that period, seek out only the best wines in the best vintages, though don't forget that many so-called lesser wines can last as long and reward as greatly. If you lack either time, space, patience, or cash, then by all means look for those "lesser" wines in the "lesser" vintages, enjoy them sooner, and congratulate yourself on being a very canny shopper.

Cellar Selections

What follow are four lists of selected wines. The first constitutes a group of suggestions for an all-purpose, keep-on-hand cellar to satisfy the demands of everyday good dining plus the sudden windfalls, unanticipated pratfalls, and other emergent occasions of modern life. The next three lists suggest wines that reward short-, intermediate-, and long-term storage. Bear in mind that they are meant to be helpful guidelines, not exhaustive catalogs. There exist many other wines, even other kinds of wines, that could suit your individual palate and purposes.

One final note about storing wine, this time to do with the size bottles you store. Wine keeps and ages differently in bottles of differing size. Half-bottles, which can be very handy things on many occasions, mature much faster than the more common 75-centiliter bottles. By the same token, wine kept in magnums stays fresher and more youthful longer and matures more slowly than wine in ordinary-size bottles. This size differential becomes most obvious with dry white wines in half-bottles, which can go over the hill with what seems like lightning speed. So if you are cellaring or are planning to cellar any quantity of small bottles, keep a close eye on them for signs of deterioration.

AN EMERGENCY SIX-PACK: SELECTED WINES FOR A BASIC CELLAR-FOR-ALL-OCCASIONS

Here are suggestions for six types of wine to fit a variety of different circumstances. A few bottles of each class will make a complete wine cellar for a week or two in your mountain cabin or seashore cottage. Half a dozen bottles of the sparkling and sweet wines and a case of each category of still wine stored in the back of your closet will completely equip you to handle daily dinners, sudden guests, unanticipated celebrations, or quotidian changes of palate. An explanation for each of these choices follows the list.

THE SIX-PACK

Group 1

Basic brut nonvintage champagne (for example, Ayala, Bollinger, Charbaut, Heidsieck, Lanson, Moët & Chandon, Mumm, Perrier-Jouët, Pol Roger, Pommery & Greno, Taittinger, Veuve Clicquot)

or **California sparklers** (for example, Chateau St. Jean, Domaine Chandon, Domaine Mumm, Gloria Ferrer, Korbel Natural or Blanc de Blancs, Piper Sonoma)
or **top-of-the-line Spanish sparkling wine** (for example, Codorníu's Gran Codorníu or Non Plus Ultra, Freixenet's Cordon Negro or vintage bottlings)

Group 2

Alsace Pinot Blanc (for example, Aussay, Beyer, Dopff, Dopff & Irion, Hugel, Josmeyer, Lorentz, Muré, Schlumberger, Sparr, Trimbach, Willm, Zind-Humbrecht)
or **dry California Chenin Blanc** (for example, Alexander Valley, Almaden, Burgess, Callaway, Concannon, Dry Creek, Fetzer, Gallo, Guenoc, Hacienda, Martini, Mondavi, Monterey Vineyard, Parducci, Pedroncelli, Preston, Sebastiani, Simi, Souverain)
or **inexpensive Italian Chardonnay** (for example, Bollini, Cavit, Collavini, EnoFriulia, Favonio, Maso Poli, Tiefenbrunner)
or **good Mâcon** (for example, B & G, Bouchard Père & Fils, Drouhin, Jadot, Latour, Maufoux, Moreau, Pic, Rodet)
or **Beaujolais** (for example, B & G, Bouchard Père & Fils, Drouhin, Duboeuf, Jadot, Latour, Marquisat, Mommessin, Sarrau, Sylvain Fessy, Louis Tête)

Group 3

Barbera (for example, Bersano, Contratto, Dessilani, Einaudi, Fenocchio, Fontanafredda, Gaja, Giacosa, Granduca, Pio Cesare, Prunotto, Renato Ratti, Rinaldi, Vietti)
or **young Rioja** (for example, new-style makers such as Domecq, Marqués de Cáceres, Marqués de Riscal, Olarra, Paternina)
or **young Chianti** (for example, Antinori's Santa Cristina, Berardenga, Boscarelli, Brolio, Capezzana, Castello d'Albola, Castello di Ama, Castello di Nipozzano, Castello di San Polo in Rosso, Castello di Volpaia, Fossi, Il Poggiolo, Nozzole, Ruffino, Selvapiana, Villa Banfi, Villa Caffaggio, Villa Cusona)

Group 4

Claret-style Zinfandel (for example, Almaden, Benziger, Buena Vista, Fetzer, Gallo, Guenoc, Krug, Martini, Masson, Mirassou,

Montevina, Pedroncelli, Ridge, Santa Barbara, Sebastiani, Seghesio, Simi, Sutter Home, Wente)
or **Alsace Pinot Noir** (for example, Aussay, Beyer, Dopff, Dopff & Irion, Hugel, Josmeyer, Lorentz, Muré, Schlumberger, Sparr, Trimbach, Willm, Zind-Humbrecht)
or **Bourgueil** (for example, Audebert, Couly-Dutheil, Dutertre; also Chinon or Saumur-Champigny)
or **Dolcetto** (for example, Bersano, Ceretto, Cogno, Conterno, Fontanafredda, Gaja, Giacosa, Marchesi di Gresy, Mascarello, Oddero, Pio Cesare, Prunotto, Renato Ratti, Vietti)

Group 5

St-Emilion (for example, Château Cap de Mourlin, Château Cormeil Figeac, Château Couvent des Jacobins, Château Dassault, Château Fombrauge, Château La Fleur, Château Monbousquet, Château de Puisseguin, Château St-Georges)
or **moderately priced California Cabernet** (for example, Almaden, Beringer Napa Ridge, Charles Krug, Christian Brothers, Clos du Bois River Oaks, Fetzer, Gallo, Glen Ellen, Hawk Crest, Inglenook, J. Lohr, Martini, Wente)
or **Nebbiolo** (for example, Ceretto, Cogno, Conterno, Einaudi, Fontanafredda, Gaja, Giacosa, Marchesi di Gresy, Mascarello, Oddero, Pio Cesare, Prunotto, Renato Ratti, Vietti)
or **Penedès** (for example, the Cabernet of Jean Léon or the Torres's Coronas or Tres Torres or Gran Sangue de Toro)

Group 6

Asti Spumante (for example, Cinzano, Contratto, Fontanafredda, Gancia, Granduca, Martini & Rossi, Riccadonna, Villa Banfi Strevi)
or **oloroso sherry** (for example, Domecq's Celebration Cream, Gonzalez Byass's San Domingo Cream or Nectar Cream, Harvey's Bristol Cream, Sandeman's Armada Cream)
or **German Riesling Spätlese or Auslese from named villages or vineyards** (for example, Piesporter Goldtröpfchen or Wehlener Sonnenuhr, Hochheimer Domdechaney or Johannisberger Goldatzel) and from reliable importers like Deinhard or Sichel, Langenbach or Loeb

These six groups of wine represent differing types that fit varying niches.

- Group One, the dry sparkling wines, will serve either as aperitifs, cocktails, or celebratory wines.
- Group Two, light-bodied or medium-bodied white wines, will work well as dinner wines to accompany all but the richest dishes. They could also be used as aperitifs. Beaujolais appears in this list because its high acidity and light body make it substitutable for a medium-bodied white wine.
- Group Three is composed of relatively light-bodied, high-acid red wines. These are all-purpose food wines, good with all sorts of dishes from delicate to robust, plain to spicy.
- Group Four includes medium-bodied red wines with rather soft texture and an abundance of fruit. They will serve well with simply cooked steaks, chops, and roast meats.
- Group Five contains full-bodied red wines with a healthy presence of tannin. They accompany strong cheeses, the most assertive meats, intricately sauced meats and fowl, and game.
- Group Six suggests three versatile, readily available, and very reliable dessert wines.

All the wines named here provide thoroughly enjoyable drinking, and the final reasons for selecting one or another within any given category should depend upon variables like distribution and price as well as individual preference. For myself, if I were absolutely forced to select only one wine in each category, I would go with the first wine named in each case:

- Champagne from Champagne, because, after all is said and done, nothing quite matches the real thing
- Alsace Pinot Blanc, because its body and flavor make it as enjoyable as it is versatile
- Barbera, because it is probably the world's most happily adaptable "food wine," turning earthy or elegant according to what you serve it with

- Zinfandel, because of its unique flavor and idiosyncratic charm
- St-Emilion, for its comparative elegance paired with accessibility
- Asti Spumante, for its luscious Muscato flavor

There is a lot of concentrated quality in these six wines.

SELECTED WINES FOR SHORT-TERM CELLARING

The wines that appear on this list will benefit from receiving one to five years of aging in the bottle. Many of these can be drunk with pleasure at any point within those five years, but they will also show interesting development over that same span. Only a few of them will achieve greatness (some of the Chardonnays, for instance), but all will offer intense satisfaction. Remember also that lighter or off vintages of some wines that appear on the two subsequent lists will also reward a short period of cellaring.

WHITE WINES

Burgundy: The village wines, especially *premiers crus,* of reputable shippers (for example, Puligny-Montrachet or Meursault from Prosper Maufoux or Drouhin) in average or better vintages

Chablis: *Premiers crus* (for example, Fourchaume, Montée de Tonnerre, Vaillons) from reliable shippers (for example, Long-Depaquit, Pic) in average-to-good vintages

Chardonnay: California estate bottlings, especially Reserves, in all vintages from good makers (for example, Beaulieu, Beringer, Buena Vista, Callaway, Carneros Creek, Chalone, Chappellet, Chateau Montelena, Chateau St. Jean, Far Niente, Freemark Abbey, Hanzell, Heitz, La Crema, Martini, Mayacamas, Mondavi, Phelps, Roudon Smith, Simi, Sonoma-Cutrer, Sterling, Trefethen, Vichon)

Fiano di Avellino: All vintages from Mastroberardino

Gavi, Cortese di Gavi: Good to excellent vintages from the best producers (for example, Contratto, La Battistina, La Giustiniana, La Scolca, Pio Cesare)

Gewürztraminer: Alsace shippers (for example, Beyer, Dopff, Dopff & Irion, Hugel, Kuentz-Bas, Muré, Schlumberger, Sparr, Trimbach, Willm, Zind-Humbrecht) and estate bottlings, in all but the poorest vintages

Graves: Estate bottlings (for example, Château Carbonnieux, Château La Louvière, Château Olivier, Château Smith-Haut-Lafitte) in average-to-good vintages

Greco di Tufo: All vintages from Mastroberardino

Pinot Blanc: From Alsace (same growers and conditions as for Gewürztraminer); selected prime makers from California (for example, Chalone); selected bottlings from Italy (for example, Frescobaldi's Pomino from Tuscany, some varietal wines from Trentino–Alto Adige)

Pinot Gris: Sometimes called Tokay d'Alsace (the name is now being phased out). Same conditions and growers as for Gewürztraminer

Pouilly-Fumé: Good-to-excellent vintages from excellent makers such as Château de Tracy, de Ladoucette, Masson Blondelet, Michel Redde & Fils, Saget; also the related Sancerre (for Sancerre, some good makers are Archambault, Cordier, Prieur & Fils)

Riesling, dry: Alsace shippers and estate bottlings in all but the poorest vintages (same growers as for Gewürztraminer)

Riesling, dessert: German Spätlese or Auslese estate bottlings or individual vineyard wines in good vintages from top-rated areas (for example, Bernkastel, Deidesheim, Erden, Forst, Hattenheim, Hochheim, Johannisberg, Nierstein, Piesport, Rudesheim, Wehlen, Winkel)

Rioja: Average-to-good vintages from old-style producers (for example, Bodegas Muga, Marqués de Murrieta, Vina Tondonia)

Sancerre: See Pouilly-Fumé

Tocai: Good vintages from sound producers (for example, Abbazia di Rosazzo, Borgo Conventi, Jermann, Livio Felluga, Marco Felluga) in the Collio or Colli Orientali regions of Friuli–Venezia Giulia

RED WINES

Barbera: Average-to-excellent vintages from sound makers (for example, Contratto, Einaudi, Fenocchio, Fontanafredda, Gaja, Giacosa, Granduca, Pio Cesare, Prunotto, Ratti, Rinaldi, Vietti)

Beaujolais: The fullest-bodied cru wines (Chénas, Juliénas, Morgon, Moulin-à-Vent) in good-to-excellent vintages from makers such as Bouchard Père & Fils, Duboeuf, Jadot, Latour, Louis Tête, Marquisat, Sarrau, Sylvain Fessy

Bourgueil: Good vintages from sound makers (for example, Audebert, Couly-Dutheil, Dutertre; also the related Chinon and Saumur-Champigny)

Cahors: Average vintages from sound producers (for example, Baldès's Clos Triguedina, Vigouroux's Château Haute Serre)

Carmignano: Non-Riserva bottlings of average-to-good vintages from Villa Capezzana

Chianti Classico and Chianti: Non-Riservas of average-to-excellent vintages from good producers and estates (for example, Antinori, Badia a Coltibuono, Brolio, Cafaggio, Castellare, Castell'in Villa, Castello di Ama, Castello di Gabbiano, Castello di San Polo in Rosso, Cecchi, Fonterutoli, Fontodi, Fossi, La Querce, Lilliano, Melini, Monsanto, Monte Vertine, Ruffino). Also some fine makers outside the Classico zone (for example, Frescobaldi, Monte Antico, Spalletti, Villa Selvapiana)

Côte de Beaune: Good vintages from the best shippers (for example, Bouchard Père & Fils, Hospices de Beaune, Jadot, Latour), wines of the Côte de Beaune and Côte de Beaune-Villages as well as named communes or villages within the Côte (for example, Volnay, Pommard, Pernand-Vergelesses)

Côte de Nuits: In good vintages, the best shippers' wines (for example, Bouchard Père & Fils, Clair Dau, Dujac, Faiveley, Mugneret, Roumier) from named communes and villages (for example, Fixin, Gevrey-Chambertin, Morey St-Denis, Chambolle-Musigny, Vosne-Romanée, Nuits-St-Georges)

Crozes-Hermitage: Shippers' wines (for example, Chapoutier, Delas, Jaboulet) in average-to-excellent vintages

Dolcetto: Average-to-excellent vintages from reliable producers (for example, Ceretto, Cogno, Conterno, Fontanafredda, Gaja, Giacosa, Marchesi di Gresy, Mascarello, Oddero, Pio Cesare, Prunotto, Ratti, Vietti)

Gigondas: Good vintages from the best *négociants* and individual estates (for example, Chapoutier, Delas, Jaboulet, La Vieille Ferme). Also estate-bottled wines from other Rhône villages such as Rasteau, Sablet, Vacqueyras (for example, Roger Combe's Domaine Fourmone from Vacqueyras)

Merlot: Estate bottlings from good makers in Napa and Sonoma counties in average-to-good years (for example, Alexander Valley Vineyards, Buena Vista, Cain Cellars, Clos du Bois, Clos du Val, Duckhorn, Franciscan, Geyser Peak, Gundlach-Bundschu, Martini, Matanzas Creek, Robert Keenan, Sterling)

Nebbiolo: The best producers in average-to-good years (for example, Ceretto, Contratto, Gaja, Giacosa, Granduca, Marchesi di Gresy, Pio Cesare, Prunotto, Ratti, Vietti)

Pinot Noir: The best vintages of the best producers in California, Oregon, Washington (for example, Acacia, Adelsheim, Beaulieu Vineyard, Bouchaine, Buena Vista, Carneros Creek, Chalone, Clos du Bois, David Bruce, Eyrie, Knudsen Erath, Martini, Mondavi, Saintsbury, Sokol Blosser, Tualatin, Zaca Mesa)

Pomerol: Bottlings from the second- or third-tier estates (for example, Château Beauregard, Château Certan de May, Château

Nenin, Château de Sales, Clos L'Eglise, La Conseillante, La Fleur Gazin) in average-to-good years

Rioja: Non-Reserva wines of average-to-good years from reliable makers (for example, Bodegas Ollara, CVNE, Domecq, Gran Condal, Marqués de Cáceres, Marqués de Murrieta, Marqués de Riscal, Montecillo, Muga, Paternina, Viña Tondonia)

Rosso di Montalcino: The best vintages from the best makers (for example, Altesino, Barbi, Caparzo, Castelgiocondo, Col d'Orcia, Il Poggione, Villa Banfi)

St-Emilion: Bottlings from the second- or third-tier estates (for example, Château L'Angelus, Château L'Arrosée, Château Cap-de-Mourlin, Château Cormeil-Figeac, Château Couvent-des-Jacobins, Château Dassault, Château Fombrauge, Château La Fleur, Château Monbousquet, Château de Puisseguin, Château St-Georges, Château Fonplégade, Château Larmande, Château Latour-Figeac, Château Troplong-Mondot, Clos des Jacobins)

Taurasi: Non-Riserva bottles of average-to-excellent years from Mastroberardino

Teroldego Rotaliano: Estate bottlings of average-to-excellent years

Valtellina: Village or commune wines (for example, Grumello, Inferno, Sassella, Valgella) from sound shippers (for example, Nino Negri, Rainoldi) in good vintages

Zinfandel: Both single-vineyard and broader appellation bottlings from good makers all over California (for example, Amador, Buena Vista, Burgess, Chateau Montelena, Clos du Val, Conn Creek, Fetzer, Martini, Mondavi, Montevina, Pedroncelli, Phelps, Ridge, Simi, Sutter Home) in average-to-good vintages

SELECTED WINES FOR INTERMEDIATE-TERM CELLARING

The wines in this list will reward cellaring for from five to ten years. While many of the white wines listed here could be drunk pleasurably at any point within that span, most of the red wines will go through a "dormant" period during which they are best left alone. Remember also that lighter or off vintages of some wines on the next list as well as exceptionally fine vintages of some wines on the first list will also fall into this category.

WHITE WINES

Burgundy: Single-vineyard wines or *premier cru* wines from good *négociants* (for example, Bouchard Père & Fils, Drouhin, Dujac, Jadot, Lafon, Latour, Leflaive, Maufoux, Remoissenet) in good-to-excellent vintages

Chablis: *Grand cru* wines in good-to-excellent vintages. Some reliable makers are Auffray, Drouhin, Fèvre, Long-Depaquit, Pic

Châteauneuf-du-Pape: Estate-bottled wines (for example, Château Fortia, Château Mont-Redon, Château Rayas, Château de Vaudieu, Clos des Papes; also Delas, and Chapoutier's La Bernadine) in good vintages

Fiano di Avellino: Good-to-excellent vintages from Mastroberardino

Gewürztraminer: Alsace estate bottlings or individual-vineyard wines, especially *grands crus* or reserve wines, in good-to-excellent vintages. Good makers include Aussay, Beyer, Dopff, Dopff & Irion, Hugel, Josmeyer, Kuentz-Bas, Muré, Schlumberger, Sparr, Trimbach, Weinbach, Willm, Zind-Humbrecht

Graves: Estate bottlings in the best vintages (for example, Château Bouscaut, Château Carbonnieux, Château Chantegrive, Château de Cruzeau, Château La Louvière, Château Smith-Haut-Lafitte)

Greco di Tufo: Good-to-excellent vintages from Mastroberardino

Hermitage: Reliable *négociants* (for example, Chapoutier's Chante Alouette, Delas, Guigal, Jaboulet's Le Chevalier de Sterimbourg) and estate bottlings (for example, Chave, Grippat) from average-to-good vintages

Pinot Blanc: Alsace estate bottlings or individual-vineyard wines, especially *grands crus* or reserve wines, in good-to-excellent vintages (see suggestions under Gewürztraminer)

Pinot Gris: Also called Tokay d'Alsace. Choose Alsace estate bottlings or individual-vineyard wines, especially *grands crus* or reserve wines, in good-to-excellent vintages (see suggestions under Gewürztraminer)

Riesling: Alsace estate bottlings or individual-vineyard wines, especially *grands crus* or reserve wines, in good-to-excellent vintages (see suggestions under Gewürztraminer); German estate bottlings or individual vineyard wines from top-rated areas (for example, Bernkastel, Deidesheim, Erden, Forst, Hattenheim, Hochheim, Johannisberg, Nierstein, Piesport, Rudesheim, Wehlen, Winkel) of Auslese quality or better in excellent vintages

Rioja: The very best vintages from old-style producers (for example, Bodegas Muga, Marqués de Murrieta, Viña Tondonia)

RED WINES

Barolo and Barbaresco: Average-to-good vintages from sound producers (for example, Aldo Conterno, Borgogno, Bruno Giacosa, Castello di Neive, Ceretto, Cogno, Fontanafredda, Gaja, Giacomo Conterno, Granduca, Marchesi di Gresy, Mascarello, Moresco, Pio Cesare, Produttori di Barbaresco, Prunotto, Ratti, Roagna, Rocche di Manzoni, Valentino, Vietti)

Brunello di Montalcino: See Rosso di Montalcino

Burgundy: See Côte de Beaune and Côte de Nuits

Cabernet Sauvignon: Average-to-good vintages from the best California growers (for example, Beaulieu, Chappellet, Chateau Montelena, Clos du Bois, Clos du Val, Conn Creek, Freemark Abbey, Gundlach-Bundschu, Heitz, Jordan, Kenwood, Lyeth, Martini, Mondavi, Parducci, Phelps, Ridge, Sequoia Grove, Simi, Stag's Leap Wine Cellars, Sterling, Trefethen, Vichon)

Cahors: Good-to-excellent vintages from selected producers (for example, Château de Chambert, Château Haute Serre, Clos de Gamot, Prince Probus)

Carmignano: Riserva bottlings of good-to-excellent vintages from Capezzana

Châteauneuf-du-Pape: Average-to-excellent vintages from good producers (for example, Chapoutier's La Bernadine, Château de Beaucastel, Château Fortia, Château Mont-Redon, Château Rayas, Château de Vaudieu, Clos des Papes, Domaine de Beaurenard, Domaine Chante-Cigale, Domaine de la Nerthe, Jaboulet's Les Cèdres, Vieux Télégraphe)

Chianti Classico and Chianti: Riserva bottlings of good-to-excellent vintages from good estates (for example, Badia a Coltibuono, Cafaggio, Castellare, Castello di Ama, Castello di San Polo in Rosso, Fontodi, Monte Vertine, Poggio al Sole, Villa Antinori Riserva Marchese, Villa Banfi); also a few non-Classico growers (for example, Frescobaldi's Castello di Nipozzana and Montesodi, Monte Antico, Spalletti's Poggio Reale, Villa Selvapiana)

Côte de Beaune: Individual village wines or estate-bottled wines of *premier cru* quality in good-to-excellent vintages (for example, Aloxe-Corton Les Chaillots or Les Valozières, named vineyards from Beaune or Savigny-Les-Beaune, Pernand-Vergelesses or Pommard)

Côte de Nuits: Individual village wines or estate-bottled wines of *premier cru* quality in good-to-excellent vintages (for example, Gevrey-Chambertin Clos St-Jacques or Clos du Chapitre, Chambolle-Musigny Charmes, Vosne-Romanée or Nuits-St-Georges)

Côte Rôtie: Good vintages from fine shippers and growers (for example, Chapoutier, Delas, Grippat, Guigal, Jaboulet, Jasmin, Vidal-Fleury—the latter now owned by Guigal)

Gattinara: Good-to-excellent vintages from selected producers (for example, Antoniolo, Vallana)

Graves: Good-to-excellent vintages from sound châteaux below the *premier cru* level (for example, Carbonnieux, Haut Bailly, La Garde, La Louvière, La Mission-Haut-Brion, La-Tour Haut-Brion, Malartic-Lagravière, Olivier, Pape Clément, Smith-Haut-Lafitte)

Hermitage: Good vintages from sound makers (for example, Chapoutier, Chave, Delas, Guigal, Jaboulet's La Chapelle)

Médoc: Good vintages from sound châteaux below the *premier cru* level (for example, Batailley, Beychevelle, Brane-Cantenac, Calon-Ségur, Chasse Spleen, Cos d'Estournel, d'Angludet, de Pez, Ducru-Beaucaillou, Giscours, Gloria, Grand-Puy-Lacoste, Gruaud-Larose, Kirwan, Lafon-Rochet, Langoa-Barton, Lascombes, Léoville Barton, Les Ormes-de-Pez, Lynch-Bages, Montrose, Palmer, Phelan-Ségur, Pontet-Canet, Prieuré-Lichine, Rausan-Ségla, Ségur, Talbot)

Penedès: Jean Léon's Cabernet; Torres's Coronas, Gran Coronas Reserva and Tres Torres

Pomerol: Good vintages from sound châteaux below the top-most level (for example, Beauregard, Certan de May, Clos l'Eglise, Clos René, La Conseillante, Lafleur, La Fleur Pétrus, Latour à Pomerol, L'Enclos, L'Evangile)

Rioja: Reserva bottlings of good-to-excellent vintages from old-style makers (for example, Bodegas Lan, Faustino, Marqués de Murrieta, Muga, Viña Tondonia)

Rosso di Montalcino: Good-to-excellent vintages of selected makers and labels (for example, Altesino's Palazzo Altesi, Barbi's Brusco dei Barbi, Caparzo's Ca' del Pazzo, Vinattieri Rosso)

St-Emilion: Good vintages from sound châteaux below the top-most level (for example, Clos des Jacobins, Fonplégade, L'Angélus,

Larcis-Ducasse, Larmande, L'Arrosée, Latour-Figeac, Moulin du Cadet, Troplong-Mondot)

Taurasi: Riserva bottlings of good-to-excellent years from Mastroberardino

Zinfandel: Single-vineyard wines from good makers (for example, Amador, Burgess, Chateau Montelena, Clos du Val, Conn Creek, Martini, Mondavi, Montevina, Phelps, Ridge, Sutter Home) in good-to-excellent vintages

SELECTED WINES FOR LONG-TERM CELLARING

This list suggests some wines that will benefit greatly from more than ten years of cellaring. Just how fine they will become depends upon the variables of individual wine, individual vintage, and individual storage conditions, but all are wines that normally need long keeping to mature to the point of showing their real depth and complexity. Exceptional vintages of some wines on the preceding list will also reward longer cellaring (for example, Fiano or Greco, dry Alsace whites, white or red Rioja, Cahors, Gattinara).

WHITE WINES

Barsac: See Sauternes

Burgundy: The very best vintages of *grands crus* and single-vineyard *premiers crus* wines (for example, Bâtard-Montrachet, Beaune Clos des Mouches, Clos Blanc de Vougeot, Corton-Charlemagne, Meursault Perrières, Puligny Montrachet Les Pucelles)

Chablis: The very best vintages of *grands crus* wines (for example, Bougros, Grenouilles, La Moutonne, Vaudésir)

Châteauneuf-du-Pape: The best vintages of selected estate-bottled wines (for example, Château de Beaucastel, Château Fortia, Château Mont-Redon, Château Rayas, Clos des Papes)

Gewürztraminer: The best vintages of those Alsace estate bottlings or individual vineyard wines, especially *grands crus,* that bear the designations Vendange Tardive or Sélection de Grains Nobles

Hermitage: The best vintages from the best *négociants* and growers (for example, Chapoutier, Chave, Delas, Grippat, Guigal, Jaboulet)

Pinot Blanc: The best vintages of those Alsace estate bottlings or individual vineyard wines, especially *grands crus*, that bear the designations Vendange Tardive or Sélection de Grains Nobles

Riesling: The best vintages of those Alsace estate bottlings or individual vineyard wines, especially *grands crus,* that bear the designations Vendange Tardive or Sélection de Grains Nobles; also the best vintages of German estate-bottled or individual-vineyard wines bearing the designations Auslese, Beerenauslese, or Trockenbeerenauslese (for example, Bernkasteler Doctor from Dr. Thanisch, Hochheimer Königin Victoriaberg, Schloss Vollrads, the Staatsweinguter Eltville's Steinberger, Wehlener Sonnenuhr from J. J. Prum)

Sauternes: Good-to-best vintages from well-regarded estates (Chateau d'Yquem if you can afford it, but also châteaux Climens, Coutet, Doisy-Daëne, Doisy-Védrines, Gilette, Nairac, Raymond-Lafon, Rieussec, Suduiraut)

RED WINES

Amarone: Good-to-best vintages from the best producers (for example, Allegrini, Bertani, Le Ragose, Masi, Quintarelli, Tommasi)

Barolo and Barbaresco: The best vintages from sound producers (for example, Aldo Conterno, Borgogno, Bruno Giacosa, Castello di Neive, Ceretto, Cogno, Duca d'Asti, Fontanafredda, Gaja, Giacomo Conterno, Marchesi di Gresy, Pio Cesare, Produttori di Barbaresco, Prunotto, Renato Ratti, Roagna, Rocche di Manzoni, Vietti). Cru wines (for example, Martinenga, Montestefano, or Rabaja for Barbaresco, or Brunate, Cannubi, or Rocche for Barolo) are often—but not always—superior to the traditional multi-vineyard blends

Brunello di Montalcino: Good-to-excellent vintages from selected makers (for example, Altesino, Barbi, Biondi-Santi, Caparzo, Castelgiocondo, Col d'Orcia, Costanti, Il Poggione, Villa Banfi)

Burgundy: See Côte de Beaune and Côte de Nuits

Cabernet Sauvignon: The best vintages from the best California producers, especially their Reserve, single-vineyard, or special-label wines (for example, Beaulieu's Georges de Latour Reserve, Freemark Abbey's Cabernet Bosche, Heitz's Martha's Vineyard or Bella Oaks, Martini's Special Selection, Ridge's Montebello or York Creek)

Carmignano: Riserva bottlings of the very best vintages from Capezzana

Châteauneuf-du-Pape: The very best vintages from selected estates (for example, Chapoutier's La Bernadine, Château de Beaucastel, Château Fortia, Château Mont-Redon, Château Rayas, Clos des Papes, Domaine de Beaurenard, Domaine Chante-Cigale, Domaine de la Nerthe, Jaboulet's Les Cèdres, Vieux Télégraphe)

Chianti Classico: Riserva bottlings of the best vintages from selected makers (for example, Antinori [especially Tignanello], Badia a Coltibuono, Castellare's I Sodi di San Niccolo, Castello di Ama, Castello di Gabbiano, Castello di San Polo in Rosso, Fontodi, Fossi, La Querce, Lilliano, Monte Vertine, Villa Cafaggio); also some fine makers outside the Classico zone (for example, Frescobaldi's Castello di Nipozzana and Montesodi, Spalletti's Poggio Reale, Villa Selvapiana)

Cornas: The best vintages from the best makers (for example, Clape, De Barjac, Delas, Juge, Michel)

Côte de Beaune: *Grands crus* or individual-vineyard *premiers crus* wines of the best vintages (for example, Beaune Clos des Mouches or Fèves or Teurons, Le Corton or Corton Les Renardes or Latour's Château Grancey, Volnay Caillerets or Clos des Chênes)

Côte de Nuits: *Grands crus* or individual-vineyard *premiers crus* wines of the best vintages (for example, Chambertin or Chambertin Clos de Bèze, Chambolle Musigny Le Musigny or Bonnes Mares or Charmes, Clos de Vougeot, Morey St-Denis Clos St-Denis or Clos des Lambrays or Clos de la Roche, Nuits-St-Georges Boudots or Les St-Georges or Vaucrains, Vosne-Romanée Malconsorts or Suchots)

Côte Rôtie: The best vintages from fine shippers and growers (for example, Chapoutier, Delas, Grippat, Guigal, Jaboulet, Jasmin, Vidal-Fleury—the latter now owned by Guigal), especially wines designated as originating on single slopes (Côte Brune, Côte Blonde) or specific fields (for example, Guigal's La Landonne)

Graves: The best vintages from *premiers crus* and selected other châteaux (for example, Château Haut-Brion, Domaine de Chevalier, La Garde, La Louvière, La Mission Haut-Brion, La Tour-Haut-Brion, Malartic-Lagravière, Olivier, Pape Clément, Smith-Haut-Lafitte)

Hermitage: The best vintages from sound makers (for example, Chapoutier, Chave, Delas, Guigal, Jaboulet's La Chapelle)

Médoc: The best vintages from *premiers crus* and selected other châteaux (for example, Lafite, Latour, Margaux, and Mouton Rothschild; d'Angludet, Batailley, Beychevelle, Brane-Cantenac, Calon-Ségur, Chasse-Spleen, Cos d'Estournel, Ducru-Beaucaillou, Giscours, Gloria, Grand-Puy-Lacoste, Gruaud-Larose, Kirwan, Lafon-Rochet, Langoa-Barton, Lascombes, Léoville-Barton, Les Ormes-de-Pez, Lynch-Bages, Montrose, Palmer, de Pez, Phélan-Ségur, Pontet-Canet, Prieuré-Lichine, Rausan-Ségla, Ségur, Talbot)

Penedès: The best vintages of Torres's Gran Sangre de Toro and Gran Coronas Black Label

Pomerol: The best vintages from top-ranked châteaux and selected others (for example, Beauregard, Certan de May, Château Pétrus, Clos l'Eglise, Clos René, La Conseillante, Lafleur, La Fleur-Pétrus, Latour-à-Pomerol, L'Enclos, L'Evangile)

Rioja: Reserva bottlings of the best vintages, particularly the special labels of traditional makers (for example, Berberana's Viña Pomal, CVNE's Viña Real, Faustino Martinez's Faustino I, La Rioja Alta's Viña Ardanza and its numbered *Reservas,* Lopez de Heredia's Viña Tondonia, Marqués de Murrieta's Castillo Ygay, Muga's Prado Enea)

St-Emilion: The best vintages from top-ranked châteaux and selected others (for example, Ausone, Beausejour, Bélair, Canon, Cheval Blanc, Figeac, La Gaffelière, Magdelaine, Pavie, Clos Fourtet, Clos des Jacobins, Fonplégade, L'Angélus, Larcis-Ducasse, Larmande, L'Arrosée, Latour-Figeac, Moulin du Cadet, Troplong-Mondot)

Taurasi: Riserva bottlings of the finest vintages from Mastroberardino

Vega Sicilia: Good-to-excellent vintages of Valbuena and Unico

Zinfandel: The best vintages of single-vineyard wines (where available) from good makers (for example, Amador, Burgess, Chateau Montelena, Clos du Val, Conn Creek, Martini, Mondavi, Montevina, Phelps, Ridge, Sutter Home)

Index

345